DATE DUE

RIGHTLESSNESS IN AN AGE OF RIGHTS

AYTEN GÜNDOĞDU

RIGHTLESSNESS
IN AN AGE
OF RIGHTS

Hannah Arendt and
the Contemporary Struggles
of Migrants

OXFORD
UNIVERSITY PRESS

OXFORD
UNIVERSITY PRESS

Oxford University Press is a department of the University of Oxford.
It furthers the University's objective of excellence in research, scholarship,
and education by publishing worldwide.

Oxford   New York
Auckland   Cape Town   Dar es Salaam   Hong Kong   Karachi
Kuala Lumpur   Madrid   Melbourne   Mexico City   Nairobi
New Delhi   Shanghai   Taipei   Toronto

With offices in
Argentina   Austria   Brazil   Chile   Czech Republic   France   Greece
Guatemala   Hungary   Italy   Japan   Poland   Portugal   Singapore
South Korea   Switzerland   Thailand   Turkey   Ukraine   Vietnam

Oxford is a registered trade mark of Oxford University Press
in the UK and certain other countries.

Published in the United States of America by
Oxford University Press
198 Madison Avenue, New York, NY 10016

Cataloging-In-Publication data is on file with the Library of Congress

9780199370412 (hbk.)
9780199370429 (pbk.)

To my parents,

Selvinaz and Hasan Hüseyin Gündoğdu

Contents

Acknowledgments

THE RESEARCH for this book has lasted for more than 10 years. Over that time I have accumulated a long list of debts to friends, family members, colleagues, students, and institutions. Without their support and encouragement, this book could not have been written.

I started working on this project at the University of Minnesota, Twin Cities, as a graduate student. I was exceptionally fortunate to work with outstanding advisers and fellow graduate students in an environment that fostered critical thinking at the crossroads of political theory and international relations. I am deeply grateful to Mary Dietz and Bud Duvall, my dissertation co-advisers, for encouraging me to find my own voice, providing immensely helpful feedback, and motivating me at every stage of this project. Bud has helped me develop a critical understanding of the challenging problems of rightlessness in global politics. And without Mary, it is very likely that I would not have even considered becoming a student of political theory. Mary and Bud continue to inspire my work and life as exemplary scholars, teachers, and human beings. I am indebted to the other members of my dissertation committee, Bruce Braun, Bill Scheuerman, and Kathryn Sikkink, for supporting this project enthusiastically. I had the privilege to enjoy the personal and intellectual camaraderie of a remarkable group of fellow graduate students; I owe special thanks to Ashley Biser, Giunia Gatta, Ted Gimbel, Wanjiru Kamau, Robyn Linde, and Matt Weidenfeld.

Following graduation, I was fortunate to find a congenial academic home. Without the generous time afforded to me for research and financial support provided by Barnard College, the book could not have been completed on time. I am especially grateful to my colleagues in the Department of Political Science for their support and guidance. Séverine Autesserre deserves special mention; she read my book proposal carefully and provided extremely valuable advice at every stage of the publication process. Fred Neuhouser has been a very supportive mentor, helping me navigate the challenges of junior faculty life; I also owe him thanks for presenting an earlier version of the final chapter of this book at an international conference that I could not attend due to visa problems. I have had the good fortune to get to know an exceptional group of political theorists at Barnard and Columbia: Jean Cohen, Türküler Işıksel, David Johnston, Melissa Schwartzberg, Michelle Smith, and Nadia Urbinati. I would also like to give my thanks to the members of my junior faculty writing group, Abosede George, Maja Horn, Betsy Esch, and Molly Tambor, for providing much-needed interdisciplinary feedback on the early drafts of some chapters. Teaching has been one of the most rewarding experiences at Barnard, and I am indebted to the students enrolled in my courses on human rights and immigration for the stimulating classroom discussions that have helped me think about these issues in new ways. I was also very fortunate to have outstanding undergraduate students as research assistants; Raphaëlle Debenedetti, Skye Gao, Rachel Langlais, and Bo Yun Park contributed to this project by helping with bibliographic research and translations. I owe thanks to Nell Dillon-Ermers and Anne Wolff-Lawson for their administrative support, and I am especially grateful for Nell's friendship over the years.

In 2011–2012 I was awarded a post-doctoral fellowship by the Mahindra Humanities Center at Harvard University, and this fellowship introduced me to a vibrant intellectual community. I was fortunate to have the opportunity to present my research to this community; I would like to thank especially Homi Bhabha for his thoughtful comments. I am also grateful to Berit Hildebrant, who has supported this book with her friendship and good humor.

One of the most remarkable surprises in the last few years of my academic life has been the opportunity to meet Étienne Balibar, whose work has served as a source of inspiration for my thinking about rights, citizenship, and Arendt. It has been a pleasure to audit his seminars at Columbia, and I cannot thank him enough for inviting me to present my work in one of these seminars and for supporting this book wholeheartedly.

Writing a book would have been an impossible task without readers who are willing to take the time to provide critical feedback at different stages. I am indebted to Ayşe Dicle Ergin, James Ingram, Deme Kasimis, Justine Lacroix, Ella Myers, Serena Parekh, Andy Schaap, and Anna Yeatman for their helpful comments.

This project has traveled quite a bit over the years, and it has benefited from critical input in various academic settings. Earlier versions of some chapters were presented in the annual meetings of American Political Science Association, Association for Political Theory, International Studies Association, Northeastern Political Science Association, and Western Political Science Association. In addition to these conferences, I have had the opportunity to present different versions of this project in smaller academic settings: Political Theory Workshop at SUNY Albany (2014); research workshop on "The Public Authority in the Era of Globalization" at the University of Western Sydney (2013); Vassar Seminar on Politics (2013); workshop on "Global Justice and Ethics of Exclusion" at Northeastern University (2012); Conference on Philosophy and the Social Sciences organized by the Academy of Sciences of the Czech Republic and Charles University (2011); conference on "Old Europe, New Orders" at Indiana University, Bloomington (2009); and symposium on "Arendt after '68" at Columbia University (2009). I would like to thank all the participants who engaged with my work and provided helpful feedback in these academic forums, and I would like to specifically mention those who invited me to present my work: Shaunnagh Dorsett, Shaun McVeigh, Rosalind Morris, Himadeep Muppidi, Serena Parekh, Bill Rasch, Bill Scheuerman, Torrey Shanks, and Anna Yeatman.

I am grateful to Angela Chnapko, my editor at Oxford University Press, for her initial interest in, and continuing support for, this book. Her professionalism, promptness, and attentiveness to an author's concerns make her the ideal editor to work with. I would like to thank Peter Worger, Hemalackshmi Niranjan, and Manikandan Kuppan for their help during the production process. Jenna Leschuk deserves thanks for her assistance in proofreading. I have been fortunate to receive tremendously helpful readers' reports—three from Oxford University Press and three from another press. I owe a debt of gratitude to these readers who helped me clarify my argument with their insightful suggestions and constructive criticisms.

The research for this book has been generously funded by several institutions. I am deeply grateful for the grants and fellowships I received from the University of Minnesota, Twin Cities, at the early stages of this project: The Interdisciplinary Center for the Study of Global Change supported my research with a MacArthur Predissertation Grant (2005) and a MacArthur Research Stipend (2006), and the College of Liberal Arts granted me a Thomas F. Wallace Fellowship (2004–2005), a Doctoral Dissertation Fellowship (2006–2007), and a Graduate Research Partnership Award (with Bud Duvall, 2007). I also received a Sawyer Dissertation Fellowship (2007–2008), funded by the Andrew W. Mellon Foundation. My post-doctoral fellowship at the Mahindra Humanities Center at Harvard University (2011–2012) allowed me to take a yearlong research leave and prepare the manuscript for submission. Barnard College has supported my research with a Special Assistant Professor Leave Grant (2011–2012) and a Presidential Research Award (2013–2014).

I have been blessed with the wonderful friendship of Çiğdem Çıdam for 12 years now, and this book would not have been in its current shape without her input and encouragement at every stage. She has read numerous drafts of every single chapter (along with everything else I wrote) and dedicated countless hours to discussing this work with me. I will always be grateful for Çiğdem's invaluable feedback and enthusiastic support; it is a privilege to have her as my critical reader, intellectual companion, and devoted friend.

I would not have even dared to become an academic without the unwavering support of my family. I dedicate this book to my parents: Selvinaz and Hasan Hüseyin Gündoğdu. Neither had the opportunity to pursue higher education; it was their strong belief in the virtues of education and the independence of women that enabled me to enjoy long years of academic study. Without their unconditional love and trust, I would not be who I am. I am grateful to my loving sister, Aysun, and my marvelous niece, Defne, for not letting distance get in the way of our close relationship and for helping me put things in perspective.

I do not even know how I can begin to express my thanks to Pantelis Anastasakis. For more than 11 years now, we have shared many joys and sorrows. I am deeply indebted to him for his love, understanding, humor, and patience. Without his continuous encouragement, I would not have had the stamina to finish this book. Pantelis has helped me establish and maintain a place in the world that I am able to call "home." I can count on him (as well as our cats, Panos and Charlie) to make every day delightful.

RIGHTLESSNESS IN AN AGE OF RIGHTS

Introduction: Human Rights across Borders

I N AUGUST 2006, Nalini Ghuman, a British citizen and a music professor at Mills College, was barred from entering the United States at the San Francisco International Airport. Returning from a research trip to Britain, Ghuman was escorted by armed immigration officers to an interrogation room, where she was held incommunicado for hours. Since her visa was valid through May 2008, Ghuman could not understand why she could not enter the country. After conducting a body search and examining all her belongings, immigration officers questioned her for several hours, tore up her visa, and told her that she was ruled "inadmissible," without explaining why. She did not have much of an option: She could either fly back to London that night or be transferred to a detention center in Santa Clara, California. Not even knowing why her visa was revoked, Ghuman could not help but feel like a character in a Kafka story: "I don't know why it's happened, what I'm accused of . . . There's no opportunity to defend myself. One is just completely powerless . . . They told me I was nobody, I was nowhere and I had no rights."[1]

Ghuman's case was extensively publicized: The American Musicological Society mobilized a protest campaign; Leon Botstein, the President of Bard College where Ghuman was expected to participate in a music festival, wrote to then–Secretary of State Condoleezza Rice; there were several news stories and blog entries about her situation. Despite this publicity, it took Ghuman approximately a year and a half to resolve her visa problem; she could not return to her academic institution until January 2008.[2]

As Nina Bernstein of *The New York Times* puts it, Ghuman found herself in a "bureaucratic netherworld."[3]

Ghuman's case, while it is one of the few that received significant attention, is by no means exceptional; this Kafkaesque world has become home to millions of migrants in an age that is increasingly defined by extremely restrictive border policies. Deportation without any possibility of appeal and arbitrary detention have now become routine practices for states in managing the movement of people across borders. Ghuman's case is all the more striking because it demonstrates the possibility that even foreigners in relatively privileged positions can be denied fundamental rights. Immigration officers held Ghuman incommunicado, threatened her with detention, and in a move showing the obstacles set by racial and ethnic stratifications to migrants' exercise of rights, incorrectly recorded her ethnicity as "Hispanic" on their report. Ghuman's case is representative of the pervasive problems encountered by millions of migrants who become vulnerable to various forms of violence, discrimination, and abuse as they cross borders.

This book closely engages with the work of twentieth-century political theorist Hannah Arendt to understand these problems and the struggles they give rise to. Writing after World War II, Arendt looked into the challenges posed by the emergence of statelessness on a massive scale since the end of World War I. She used the term "stateless" to refer to not only those who formally lost their nationality but also those who could no longer benefit from their citizenship rights: refugees, asylum seekers, economic immigrants, even naturalized citizens who faced the threat of denaturalization in times of emergency.[4] What brought together these people, who otherwise held different kinds of juridical status, was that they were all ejected from "the old trinity of state-people-territory," and Arendt argued that this exclusion left them in a condition of rightlessness.[5] The stateless were rightless in the sense that they were deprived of legal personhood as well as the right to action and speech.[6] Expulsion from their political communities entailed an expulsion from humanity, as they lost not only their citizenship rights but also their human rights.

Particularly important for the purposes of this book is the intriguing move this diagnosis leads to in Arendt's analysis. Refusing to see the problem of rightlessness as an anomaly, Arendt embarks on a critique that aims at the ordering principles of the international system, including nationality, sovereignty, and most surprisingly, human rights. At the heart of this critique is the paradox revealed by the precarious condition of the stateless: Precisely when one appears as nothing but human, stripped of all social and political attributes, it proves very difficult to claim and exercise the rights that one is entitled to by virtue of being born human. Arendt's analysis of statelessness takes this paradox as a symptom of "the perplexities of the Rights of Man" and offers one of the most powerful criticisms of human rights. Questioning the idea that these are natural rights inherent in human dignity, her critique highlights how the effective guarantees of human rights rely on membership in an organized political community. Those who are deprived of such a community can hardly be recognized as human beings entitled to equal rights. They might be offered food and shelter as victims deserving compassion. Or worse, their alienness might be taken as a sign of barbarity that must be banished from the human community altogether.[7] The stateless find themselves in a condition of rightlessness, Arendt argues, as they are dispossessed of legal personhood, denied a political community that could render their actions and speech relevant, and driven away from the company of other human beings.

Arendt's attempt to read this paradox—*rightlessness of those who appear in their bare humanity*—as a sign manifesting the perplexities of human rights has become all the more pertinent given that the problem of rightlessness continues to haunt our present in many different ways. Unprecedented levels of migration have created what Alison Brysk and Gershon Shafir describe as the "citizenship gap," leaving millions of people without the protective mantle of citizenship rights.[8] According to estimates, there are currently approximately 232 million international migrants.[9] Intensified border controls around the world have criminalized various forms of international movement and impaired migrants' entitlement to rights. Ghuman's case, cited at the beginning, highlights that the paradox at the heart of Arendt's discussion of statelessness is far from being fully resolved in a globalizing age reconfiguring the relationship between sovereignty, citizenship, and rights.

Especially important in this regard are the challenging problems that asylum seekers, refugees, and undocumented immigrants face in claiming and exercising rights. Although these groups hold different juridical statuses that entail different sets of rights, what brings them together is their perilous condition in the current international order.[10] As I discuss in the next section, there have been important developments with regard to human rights since the time Arendt completed her analysis of statelessness. Despite these developments, "[t]he condition of undocumented aliens, as well as of refugees and asylum seekers, . . . remains in that murky domain between legality and illegality," as Seyla Benhabib notes.[11] These groups can be characterized as "stateless" in Arendt's revised sense of the term, as they find themselves outside the framework of state-people-territory with a precarious legal, political, and human standing. To avoid a possible confusion that might result from the prevalent juridical understanding of statelessness, however, I refer to them as "migrants" throughout the book if no categorization is warranted. The term "migrant" seems to be distant from the dispossession implied in Arendt's notion of "statelessness," perhaps because it conveys a misleading sense of easy, unimpeded mobility across borders. To resist this idea of free flow, it is worth remembering the long-forgotten associations of migration with expulsion, banishment, and excommunication, which urge us to attend to the de facto statelessness of many migrants.[12]

Contemporary manifestations of rightlessness demand an Arendtian critical inquiry that grapples with the perplexities of human rights. It is important to note that Arendt is not the only thinker to point to these perplexities. They have been quite well known for some time: As a universalistic framework premised on the idea that each human being is born with inalienable rights, human rights are taken to be moral entitlements that are derived from inherent human attributes such as reason, autonomy, and dignity. Understood in these terms, they are expected to transcend the contingencies of particular political contexts. Yet human rights must be politically enacted, recognized, and affirmed in particular institutions, orders, and communities if they are to find relatively stable guarantees.[13] Human rights discourse gives rise to perplexities precisely because it strives to articulate relations between terms that have conventionally been taken to be opposites (e.g., universal and particular, nature and history, human and citizen). To the extent that these terms are constitutive of this discourse in the sense that we could not have human rights without them, perplexities of these rights cannot be resolved or wished away.

What renders Arendt's critical inquiry of human rights distinctive and powerful is her attempt to understand these perplexities in political and historical terms. Hers is not an abstract, formalistic statement demonstrating the logical impossibility of human rights; instead, she offers a historically and politically informed analysis oriented by the challenging task of understanding the crisis of statelessness. Arendt's account points to the need for a critical inquiry that carefully examines the perplexities in existing human rights institutions, laws, norms, and practices to understand the contemporary problems and struggles of asylum seekers, refugees, and undocumented immigrants. The current international human rights framework turned away from the equivocal language of "man and citizen" in the 1789 Declaration, which was the focus of Arendt's critique, and introduced instead "human person" as an all-inclusive category. However, the formal guarantees of human rights at the national and international level continue to create divisions and stratifications within humanity, leaving various categories of migrants with quite insecure entitlements to a much narrower set of rights.

Does this mean that human rights are doomed to fail given their perplexities? The Arendtian framework that I propose in this book refuses to see these perplexities as dead ends leading nowhere other than rightlessness; instead, it takes them as challenging political and ethical dilemmas that can be navigated differently, including in ways that bring to view new understandings of the relationships between rights, citizenship, and humanity. The existing institutional framework of human rights represents one particular way of articulating the relationship between universal and particular, nature and history, human and citizen, and although it is the hegemonic one, it is by no means uncontested. The divisions that this framework introduces into the "human" of human rights—between citizens and non-citizens, asylum seekers and refugees, legal residents and undocumented immigrants, to give a few examples— are by no means settled, and they are now being challenged in various struggles that reinvent the meaning of human rights. These struggles represent in many ways contentious demands for "a right to have rights," to use the phrase that Arendt proposed in her efforts to rethink human rights in terms of a right *to* citizenship and humanity.[14] The critical analysis offered in this book draws attention to political struggles that introduce new understandings of human rights in response to challenging problems of rightlessness.

As I closely engage with Arendt's political theory for the purposes of understanding contemporary problems and struggles of migrants, my goal is not to dig out theoretical insights that can then be simply applied to our current problems. There are two reasons for refusing to engage in such an exercise: First, as I discuss below, there have been significant legal, political, and normative changes since the time Arendt offered her analysis of statelessness, and these developments must be taken into account in any critical inquiry drawing on her work. Especially important in this regard is the international institutionalization of human rights norms. How do we rethink Arendt's arguments about the rightlessness of the stateless, for example, given the international guarantees of legal personhood? Second, the task of understanding the contemporary struggles of migrants demands not only rethinking them with Arendt *but also reading Arendt against the grain*. We can draw crucial insights from Arendt's oeuvre only if we reinterpret and revise some of her key concepts and arguments in light of these struggles. This interpretive work involves creating encounters between Arendt's political theory and the contemporary situation, encounters that unsettle the oft-criticized distinctions that she draws between political and social issues, give unanticipated meanings to her well-known account of labor, work, and action, and take her proposition of a right to have rights in new directions. In fact, we can begin to read Arendt differently by closely engaging with the contemporary conditions of rightlessness and the struggles to which they give rise. What is at stake then is not a one-way process of applying theory to contemporary practice, but instead a critical task of reading back and forth, or an interpretive exercise that is constantly moving between Arendt's works on the one hand and "our newest experiences and our most recent fears" on the other.[15]

Global Transformations: A Postnational Constellation?

Arendt started writing *The Origins of Totalitarianism* in 1945 and finished it in 1949. The book paints quite a dismal portrayal of human rights advocacy at the time, arguing that the attempts to protect and institutionalize them "were sponsored by marginal figures—by a few international jurists without political experience or professional philanthropists supported by the uncertain sentiments of professional idealists."[16] She contends that "the concept of human rights was treated as a sort of stepchild by nineteenth-century political thought" and was not taken up by any major political party.[17] Alluding to the international efforts to draft a universal declaration, she suggests that these "best-intentioned humanitarian attempts" still remain within the confines of a state-centric international law and fail to provide guarantees for a right to have rights.[18] In an essay published in 1949, before the publication of *The Origins of Totalitarianism*, she refers to the declaration adopted by the United Nations (UN) and bemoans its "lack of reality."[19] In that same essay, she seems to catch a glimpse of hope in the emergence of humanity as a political reality, especially when she suggests that this new development "makes the new concept of 'crimes against humanity,' expressed by Justice Jackson at the Nuremberg Trials, the first and most important notion of international law."[20]

As these remarks highlight, Arendt wrote her analysis of statelessness on the cusp of major human rights developments at the international level. She witnessed the first phase of these developments, and these were mainly centered on the UN. In 1948, the organization adopted the Universal Declaration of Human Rights (UDHR). At the time, the declaration was mainly aspirational, as it aimed to raise awareness of human rights without providing any institutional mechanisms of enforcement—hence, Arendt's disapproving comment on its "lack of reality." However, it later served as the basis of two binding international covenants— the International Covenant on Civil and Political Rights and the International Covenant on Economic, Social and Cultural Rights—adopted by the UN in 1966 and put into effect in 1976.[21] These conventions, which constitute the pillars of the international human rights framework, are monitored by institutional mechanisms that have much stronger promotional and investigatory capacities compared to those few philanthropic societies of Arendt's time. But as many have noted, formal enforcement remains weak at the international level, with the exception of the regional framework in Europe where the European Court of Human Rights operates as a supranational enforcement mechanism.[22] The consequences of this enforcement problem have been somewhat mitigated as a result of developments in the mid-1970s. With the advent of détente in Cold War politics, human rights concerns started to occupy a prominent place in the agendas of non-governmental organizations. The transnational advocacy networks created by these organizations have been especially crucial in providing informal mechanisms of enforcement and putting pressure on governments to change those policies that are in violation of human rights.[23] In addition, in the mid-1970s, states also started to incorporate human rights into their foreign policy, which meant that they could use various forms of sanctions against those states that refuse to comply with human rights norms—a situation that is remarkably different from that of the "stepchild" that no major political party wanted to be affiliated with, if we remember Arendt's account.[24] Since the 1990s, with the end of the Cold War, the institutionalization of human rights has occurred at a much more rapid pace, and their normative power has significantly increased. As many scholars have noted, human rights have now become "matters of international concern," providing grounds for various forms of international action, including military humanitarian intervention, in the case of systematic violations.[25]

This brief historical overview underscores that there has been a sea change in our understanding of human rights since the time Arendt completed her analysis of statelessness; to use Louis Henkin's phrase, ours is "the age of rights."[26] As a result of the developments sketched above, human rights have arguably become "the major article of faith of a secular culture that fears it believes in nothing else," as Michael Ignatieff contends, and perhaps even "the lingua franca of global moral thought."[27] The perplexities arising from the fact that states continue to be the principal guarantors and violators of human rights are far from being resolved,[28] but what is noteworthy is the transformation that the concept of sovereignty has undergone as a result of these international developments. Sovereignty traditionally denoted the exclusive authority of a state over its citizens within its jurisdiction. As Louis Henkin notes, historically international law made only one exception to territorial sovereignty as it recognized that the treatment of a state's nationals in another state is its "proper concern." Within this framework, if the person subject to mistreatment was stateless, there was no remedy.[29] The institutional and normative framework of human rights has introduced a new notion of legitimate statehood based on the protection of individual rights; accordingly, how human beings are treated anywhere in the world has become a legitimate concern of the international community.[30]

Given these developments, it is quite tempting to think that the problems examined in Arendt's analysis of statelessness have been resolved by the institutionalization and global expansion of human rights norms since the end of World War II. One of the major transformations has been the codification of the right to asylum. Arendt describes this right as "the only right that had ever figured as a symbol of the Rights of Man in the sphere of international relationships."[31] She notes that a drastic consequence of the massive scales of statelessness in the twentieth century was the abolition of the right to asylum. States were able to abandon this right partly due to its lack of codification in either domestic constitutions or international law. Arendt saw in the historical destiny of the right to asylum the fate of the Rights of Man, which lacked legal protections and always had "a somewhat shadowy existence as an appeal in individual exceptional cases for which normal legal institutions did not suffice."[32]

International developments since the end of World War II have resulted in codifications of the right to asylum along with other human rights and have arguably removed them from this "shadowy existence." Article 14 of the UDHR recognizes a right to seek asylum, and the 1951 Geneva Convention Relating to the Status of Refugees and its 1967 Protocol enumerate several other rights for asylum seekers and refugees. The problem of mass denationalizations and denaturalizations that was at the center of Arendt's analysis of statelessness has been addressed by the Article 15 of the UDHR, which sets down a right to nationality and forbids states to arbitrarily deprive their citizens of nationality and deny them the right to change nationality. In addition, the International Covenant on Civil and Political Rights (ICCPR) requires states to grant all the individuals residing within their territory and subject to their jurisdiction a set of rights "without distinction of any kind, such as race, colour, sex, language, religion, political or other opinion, national or social origin, property, birth or other status."[33] Several commentators have come to interpret this formulation in terms of a principle of non-discrimination to suggest that distinctions between citizens and non-citizens are not justifiable within a human rights framework except in cases related to political rights and freedom of movement.[34] Most importantly, Article 26 of the ICCPR aims to address the problems arising from the legal dispossession of personhood, which were central to Arendt's analysis of rightlessness: "All persons are equal before the law and are entitled without any discrimination to the equal protection of the law." Codification of the rights to asylum, nationality, and legal personhood by no means exhausts the scope of post–World War II developments.[35] Yet, given Arendt's account of statelessness, they can be seen as the most significant ones.

Looking at these developments, several scholars have suggested that the institutional and normative ascendency of human rights framework reconfigures the relationship between citizenship, rights, and sovereignty, as it shifts the basis of entitlement to rights from nationality to universal personhood.[36] Citizenship has been known as "an instrument of closure, a prerequisite for the enjoyment of certain rights" since the French Revolution.[37] The global proliferation of human rights norms, these scholars argue, provides migrants with a universalistic vocabulary that can be invoked to contest the privileges attached to citizenship. As a result, migrants can make claims to many of the rights that were formerly associated with citizenship, including civil, social, economic, and cultural rights. Even those who are undocumented can stand before the courts as equal persons and demand rights such as access to public education—a development that is taken as a proof of the blurring distinctions between citizens and aliens.[38] This blurring is lamented by some as "the devaluation of citizenship" and welcomed by others as the harbinger of a "postnational membership."[39] These conclusions might sound somewhat inflated, but even scholars who take issue with them highlight that citizenship has been "denationalized" with the rise of a human rights framework, and its several components— citizenship understood as political membership, collective identity, basis of entitlement to rights—have been partially disaggregated.[40]

These contemporary reconfigurations of sovereignty, citizenship, and rights, however, have by no means resolved the pervasive problems encountered by different categories of migrants. As several international reports testify, the citizen/alien distinction has proved to be quite resilient, and migrants are still more likely to be subject to numerous forms of violence and abuse, including, among other things, arbitrary detention, illegal confinement, and inhuman and degrading treatment. In addition, various types of official and unofficial discrimination, as manifested in police profiling and racial segregation, can make it much more difficult for migrants to make use of the protections offered by human rights. These problems are further complicated by the fact that most migrants cannot access protective legal mechanisms to effectively challenge or remedy the multifarious forms of discrimination and abuse they face. In fact, they are often very hesitant to assert their rights in fear of retribution.[41]

These problems have been highlighted by several scholars, who warn against overstating the protections of the human rights framework and point to the discrepancy between formal guarantees of rights and the actually existing conditions of migrants—a gap that can be further widened depending on the legal status, race, ethnicity, gender, class, or age of the migrant in question.[42] This gap is recognized even by scholars who emphasize the possibilities of a postnational world order in the globalization of universal human rights. Yasemin Soysal, for example, points out that rights provided to migrants by the universal human rights framework can be "contested and undermined by various sets of political and economic factors," including various forms of discrimination targeting migrants. These problems, she argues, arise due to "an 'implementation deficit,' a discrepancy between formal rights and their praxis."[43]

Implementation deficit can explain the problems encountered by migrants, but only to some extent. Pervasive problems faced by asylum seekers, refugees, and undocumented immigrants cannot be simply understood in terms of the failure to enforce existing human rights norms due to some external factors; in fact, these problems bring to light the limits of these norms. These groups, to quote Benhabib again, "exist at the limits of all rights regimes and reveal the blind spot in the system of rights, where the rule of law flows into its opposite: the state of the exception and the ever-present danger of violence."[44] Precisely because of the global expansion of human rights, it has become all the more difficult to understand how certain subjects can be denied even the most taken-for-granted rights. The problem strikes us as a "blind spot in the system of rights," and as a blind spot, it denotes an area that escapes our understanding.

Arendt's work becomes particularly pertinent for the purposes of confronting this contemporary predicament and understanding *the perplexing persistence of rightlessness in an age of rights*. Although our political landscape has significantly changed, the reason why this paradox remains beyond comprehension might not be completely unlike the one Arendt pointed to when she wrote her analysis. At that time, it was the deceptive solidity of the nation-state system that rendered the plight of the stateless an anomaly: "It was precisely the seeming stability of the surrounding world that made each group forced out of its protective boundaries look like *an unfortunate exception to an otherwise sane and normal rule*."[45] The prevailing assumption then was that everyone had political membership in a territorially defined nation-state, and the plight of those who lacked this membership was cast as an unwelcome yet anomalous condition. As outliers, the stateless persons did not need to raise any questions about the ordering principles of the international system itself. Treating their cases as exceptional phenomena was "tempting because it left the system itself untouched."[46] Today it is the unprecedented ascendency of the human rights framework that risks turning the problems faced by asylum seekers, refugees, and undocumented immigrants into "unfortunate exceptions" to universal norms that are gradually detaching rights from citizenship status.

Arendt's analysis of statelessness urges a careful examination of these norms and poses the following question: To what extent do the ordering principles of the current international system, including existing human rights norms, contribute to the precarious condition of various categories of migrants? Taking its starting point from Arendt's argument that the predicament of the stateless should be treated not as an unfortunate exception but instead as a *symptom* manifesting the perplexities of the Rights of

Man, this book aims at understanding the contemporary problems faced by asylum seekers, refugees, and undocumented immigrants through a critical examination of the underlying assumptions, internal tensions, and paradoxical effects of human rights norms and practices.

Outlines of an Arendtian Critique of Human Rights

Human rights have been subjected to numerous criticisms since their early origins in the Rights of Man. One of the most memorable criticisms comes from Jeremy Bentham, who dismissed natural, imprescriptible rights as "nonsense upon stilts"—rhetorical confusions and illusions, lacking any specific meaning inscribed in existing laws. Another renowned criticism was offered by Edmund Burke, who denounced this abstract doctrine of equality and defended instead a notion of rights as an entailed inheritance handed down by our ancestors and meant to be passed into posterity. And there is, of course, Karl Marx's scandalous revelation that the abstract man, invoked as the subject of the Rights of Man, is the egoistic member of the bourgeois society prioritizing the right to property above anything else.[47]

As human rights discourse has achieved an unprecedented political and normative ascendency in the last two decades, these criticisms have intensified even further. If this transformation has been welcomed by some as the harbinger of an increasingly postnational or cosmopolitan era, several others have recognized in it an insidious development, giving rise to new forms of subjection, violence, and domination. Some critics see the discourse of human rights, especially as it is utilized in the new practice of international humanitarian intervention, as a distinct type of neo-imperialism.[48] Some others highlight more subtle forms of political power at work in this discourse and suggest that human rights subject us to the very state power from which they promise to protect us.[49] What is more troubling, they contend, is that this hegemonic discourse has such a strong hold on our political imagination that it has become almost impossible to invent alternative forms of politics that can bring to light different understandings of equality, freedom, justice, and emancipation.[50]

Since human rights can be, and have been, criticized from several different perspectives and for different purposes, it is crucial to outline the distinctive contours of Arendt's critique. To understand why the stateless find themselves in a condition of rightlessness, Arendt looks into the perplexities pervading the underlying assumptions of human rights. Unlike several classical and contemporary criticisms, her critique does not take us to a complete denunciation of these rights as hypocritical pretenses, ineffective illusions, or ruses of power. In fact, Arendt ends her critique with a proposal to rethink human rights as a right to have rights—a proposal that affirms the right of everyone to citizenship and humanity.

Chapter 1 aims to make sense of this double gesture in Arendt's analysis of human rights (i.e., a radical critique taking issue with their underlying assumptions and a call for their radical rethinking). I suggest that we can begin to make sense of this puzzling move only if we carefully examine *how* Arendt's critique proceeds. Especially important in this regard are her aporetic approach to "the perplexities of the Rights of Man," her attentiveness to the equivocal effects of modern rights declarations, and her effort to understand rightlessness of the stateless as a problem contingent on certain political and social conditions. Taking into consideration the distinctive orientations of Arendt's critique is crucial to understanding her conclusions about human rights and responding to some of the deeply embedded skepticisms about her approach, including those most recently raised by Jacques Rancière.[51]

To flesh out the aporetic dimensions of Arendt's critique of human rights in *The Origins of Totalitarianism*, I turn to her discussion of Socrates in her later writings and suggest that the Socratic example is crucial for clarifying her distinctive approach to the perplexities of the Rights of Man: First, as different from several other critics who see these perplexities as logical inconsistencies, hypocritical gestures, or deceptive ploys, Arendt takes them as genuine political and ethical dilemmas that characterize human rights as a discourse that establishes relations between man and citizen, nature and history, universal and particular. She highlights the need to grapple with these perplexities to understand both the challenging problems of rightlessness and the possibilities of rethinking human rights in response to these problems. Second, Arendt's critique is not an attempt to debunk widely shared assumptions about human rights. In a rather Socratic fashion, she carefully examines these assumptions in response to statelessness to see not only what has become untenable but also what has achieved a new meaning or relevance. What is perhaps most surprising is that Arendt finds a crucial insight even in the naturalistic position that she unwaveringly criticizes, as can be seen in her insistence that human rights cannot be reduced to the rights attached to citizenship status. Finally, Arendt follows the Socratic example when she concludes her inquiry aporetically and refuses to resolve the perplexities of human rights by grounding them in a new normative foundation or by putting forward a new institutional model. Her analysis suggests that the task of critical inquiry is not to offer such a resolution but instead to carefully examine how these perplexities become manifest in human rights norms, institutions, and policies as well as how political actors navigate and renegotiate them in response to challenging problems of rightlessness.

In addition to this aporetic dimension, it is equally important to take into account Arendt's distinctive approach to historical phenomena. Arendt was preoccupied with challenging historiographical questions as she wrote *The Origins of Totalitarianism*, and her reflections on these questions highlight her efforts to understand historical events by attending to their equivocal and contingent dimensions. Accordingly, she takes modern rights declarations as equivocal phenomena with multiple possibilities. Understood in these terms, the identification of "man" and "citizen" in the 1789 Declaration, for example, is not doomed to create problems of statelessness and rightlessness. In fact, that identification can give rise to democratic possibilities, as it can turn into a political site for demanding equal rights for all, regardless of race, ethnicity, or nationality. But certain political and social conditions can significantly undermine these possibilities, as is highlighted in particular in Arendt's analysis of nationalism and imperialism. Rightlessness of the stateless then is a contingent phenomenon arising from the crystallization of a set of elements, including the perplexities of human rights, the decline of the nation-state, the rise of racial categories, and the boomerang effects of overseas imperialism. Precisely because Arendt does not draw a necessary connection between the perplexities of modern rights declarations and the plight of statelessness, she can interweave a radical critique of human rights with their radical rethinking. This move differentiates her from several other critics of human rights; to make this point, I compare Arendt's arguments about human rights to those proposed by one of her most prominent contemporary readers, Giorgio Agamben.

To understand the multiple, contingent, and equivocal effects of human rights, chapter 2 clarifies the notion of "politics" that is at work in the critical inquiry developed in this book. It does that by rethinking Arendt's notorious concept of "the social." Many of Arendt's critics have argued that she subscribes to a problematical political/social distinction, which casts issues such as poverty, unemployment, or housing as "social" problems that should be addressed administratively; as such, these issues can never be the subject of our political deliberations and negotiations in the public space.[52] If this distinction were to be as categorical as Arendt's critics suggest, it would significantly undermine, and perhaps even invalidate, my attempt to use the resources of Arendt's political theory to rethink human rights by inquiring into the contemporary problems and rights struggles of migrants. For at the heart of these struggles is not simply a right to action and speech—crucial for an Arendtian politics—but also a demand for social and economic rights, including a right to work and a right to family.

I suggest that if we are going to rethink the politics of human rights along Arendtian lines, what is required is nothing less than reading Arendt *against* Arendt. This reading takes its starting point from the perplexities arising from her multiple, conflicting uses of the term "social." In the spirit of the aporetic inquiry proposed in chapter 1, I suggest that grappling with these perplexities is key to finding out what is untenable and what is worthy of affirmation in Arendt's account. A clear-cut political/social distinction cannot be upheld as a boundary-setting marker separating two domains and assigning each a distinct set of subjects and issues, given that most human rights problems cross that boundary. In fact, even Arendt's own remarks in different contexts blur the lines that are often associated with her analysis. But those remarks also underscore her crucial idea that no issue is inherently political. For an issue such as poverty to become *politicized*, there is a need to engage in practices of translation. Only with these practices can a once-private matter relegated to the realm of necessity become a public concern that relates to the ongoing constitution of freedom and equality in a political community. This revised reading of Arendtian politics endorses a different understanding of "social," one that alerts us to the conditions that might hinder such politicization.[53] Arendt's critical account in *The Human Condition* highlights, for example, the powerful tendency to yield to the dictates of an administrative rationality in efforts to tackle problems of social justice. This amended understanding of Arendt's political/social distinction suggests that we need to carefully examine the administrative, normative, and rhetorical frameworks that inform various types of human rights advocacy to see whether they enable or hinder the possibilities of politicizing challenging problems of rightlessness.

To develop this last point, I offer a new reading of one of Arendt's most controversial works, *On Revolution*. This reading centers on her critique of the Jacobin approach to "the social question" (i.e., poverty), which is often taken as an example of her opposition to the democratic politics enabled by the Rights of Man. Using the revised understanding of the political/social distinction, I argue that Arendt criticizes the Jacobins not because they politicized poverty but because they failed to do so. Arendt's critique suggests that the Jacobins took a profoundly anti-political approach to the Rights of Man, as they dispensed with the political practices of translation and resorted instead to violence in their attempts to resolve the problem of poverty. Turning the poor into an undifferentiated mass of suffering victims, they undermined any possibility of organizing a politics centered on solidarity and equality.

This reinterpretation guides my discussion of the anti-political orientations that can thwart the politicization of human rights in an Arendtian sense. I focus on three examples to draw attention to some of the worrisome trends that have emerged with the convergence of human rights and humanitarianism since the 1990s: the rise of a compassionate humanitarianism centered on suffering bodies, as can be seen in the various efforts to address refugee crises around the world; the tendency to treat challenging human rights questions as matters of humanitarian administration, as illustrated by the increasing turn to experts in making decisions related to asylum and residency; and the emergence of a military humanitarianism that reduces human rights to the rights of victims who have nothing else to fall back on. None of these tendencies is inevitable or irresistible, and they are being debated and criticized even by humanitarian actors and organizations; however, they point to some of the risks and problems requiring caution as we grapple with challenging human rights questions.

As different from several other critical approaches, an Arendtian framework does not conclude that human rights are necessarily anti-political, or even anti-democratic; nor does it lose sight of the political possibilities that these rights can engender. To explore how and when human rights can become political, chapter 2 turns to Arendt's account of the early labor movement in *The Human Condition*, which blurs the conceptual distinctions that she draws at other times. In this case, workers refused to be passive victims and inaugurated a new type of politics as they appeared in public space, translated their problems into common concerns, and reconfigured the political community in question by proposing new understandings of equality and freedom. What is perhaps most striking, and overlooked, in Arendt's account, is the crucial role that rights play in enabling the public appearance of workers as political actors. She ties their mobilization to their political emancipation, highlighting that modern rights introduce a political dynamic with indeterminable effects. This discussion of the labor movement suggests that an Arendtian politics of human rights centers on the political agency of those subjects whose rights are at stake and who venture to vindicate these rights and declare new ones.

As this overview highlights, the first two chapters of the book are intended to clarify the Arendtian critique of human rights by closely engaging with the various criticisms directed against it. The next three chapters turn to specific situations related to the contemporary problems and struggles of asylum seekers, refugees, and undocumented immigrants, but these situations are not to be understood as "case studies" applying Arendtian "theory": The first two chapters do not offer such a general theory applicable to a universe of cases, and such a rule-bound exercise would be incompatible with "thinking" in an Arendtian sense, which always involves attending to the unique and unprecedented challenges posed by events. I approach these problems and struggles instead as "incidents of living experience," which, as Arendt highlights, should always remain for thinking "the only guideposts by which to take its bearings."[54] Though such incidents are mentioned in the first two chapters occasionally, they still orient the questions asked and the interpretations proposed. They become much more prominent in the rest of the book, as I continue to revise and rethink Arendt's key concepts and arguments in their light.

Rightlessness: Precarious Legal, Political, and Human Standing

In her analysis of statelessness, Arendt repeatedly uses the term "rightless." The stateless found themselves in a fundamental condition of rightlessness, she argues, as subjects deprived of an equal standing before the law. Without any recognition of their legal personhood, the stateless were often subjected to lawlessness, arbitrary violence, and police rule. Rightlessness is not only a legal problem; Arendt highlights that the exclusion of the stateless from a political community in which their action and speech can be taken into account amounts to an expulsion from humanity.

The term "rightlessness" strikes us as anachronistic in an age of rights in which every human being, regardless of citizenship status, is assumed to be an equal person before the law. But as highlighted by the example of Ghuman, our world continues to be haunted by the spectral presence of Kafkaesque characters denied access to rights. Chapters 3 and 4 examine such cases by rethinking Arendt's notion of "rightlessness" in the specific contexts of immigration detention, deportation, and refugee camps.

Chapter 3 focuses on the legal dimensions of these problems and takes on the task of demonstrating how the recent developments in the field of human rights reconfigure, and yet do not fully resolve, the perplexities of the Rights of Man. It provides a much more equivocal assessment of the global transformations related to human rights. On the one hand, the importance of these developments, especially the institutionalization of a right to legal personhood, cannot be underestimated. From an Arendtian perspective that underscores the need for artificial guarantees for equalization among human beings, this institutionalization is significant because it allows migrants to stand before the courts and make rights claims. However, this crucial development must also be critically analyzed with particular attention paid to the fragility of the guarantees that international human rights law offers for the legal personhood of migrants.

This critical analysis centers on Arendt's phenomenological account of "personhood" as *persona*, or an artificial mask that not only allows public appearance by hiding one's countenance but also enables one's voice to sound through. Highlighting the idea that personhood is not an inherent essence but instead a legal artifact, Arendt's account draws attention to the need to carefully examine practices of making and unmaking personhood. Although personhood is no longer officially taken away when one is "ejected from the old trinity of state-people-territory," it can be significantly undermined and eroded in the context of asylum and immigration.[55] In particular, the normalization of deportation and immigration detention in the last two decades has rendered the legal personhood of asylum seekers and undocumented immigrants precarious. Within this environment, there is a need to inquire into the extent to which existing human rights norms provide migrants with robust guarantees for personhood, one that protects them from being subjected to arbitrary rule and allows their rights claims to be heard. With this question in mind, chapter 3 examines two cases concerning immigration detention and deportation at the European Court of Human Rights (ECtHR): *N v. UK* (2008) and *Saadi v. UK* (2008). These cases underscore that the legal standing of asylum seekers and undocumented immigrants remains quite insecure. They can be subjected to various forms of arbitrary treatment that would be unacceptable in the case of citizens; they can be detained, for example, simply for purposes of administrative expediency.

The Arendtian framework suggests that this problem brings to light the perplexities of international human rights law, especially those arising from its simultaneous affirmation of equal personhood and territorial sovereignty. The peculiar formulation of the right to asylum in the UDHR is a case in point. Article 14 of the Declaration guarantees "the right to seek and to enjoy in other countries asylum from persecution." This formulation aims to strike a balance between an individual right to asylum and the sovereign state's right to control its borders. During the drafting process, this was one of the most contested articles; several participants proposed the wording to be changed to "the right to seek and *to be granted* asylum" to place a positive duty on states, but that proposal was eventually rejected by the majority of state representatives due to concerns that it would put restrictions on sovereign power over immigration control.[56] Along these lines, detention and deportation are seen as legitimate measures in line with a sovereign state's right to control entry to and residence in its territory. International human rights law fails to provide robust guarantees of personhood to asylum seekers and undocumented immigrants who challenge their detention or deportation; as a result, their rights remain dependent on highly arbitrary political and legal decisions as well as unreliable sentiments such as compassion.

By providing a novel reading of Arendt's reflections on personhood as *persona*, this chapter aims to contribute to the growing literature on her understanding of law and puts her in a conversation with critical legal scholarship on personhood. My critical analysis of detention and deportation emphasizes that the "human person" at the heart of human rights law is subjected to various forms of stratification in the context of asylum and immigration; territorial borders end up creating borders within humanity—in effect assigning asylum seekers and undocumented immigrants a narrower set of rights with very uncertain and fragile guarantees. But this critical analysis does not lead to the problematic conclusion that personhood is a legal mechanism that necessarily engenders violent exclusion. From an Arendtian perspective, equality is in need of institutional guarantees to become relatively durable, and legal recognition of personhood is crucial because it allows one to appear in public without the pervasive fear of arbitrary violence and renders one's rights claims audible and intelligible.

As mentioned earlier, the plight of stateless persons cannot be understood in merely legal terms; their condition of rightlessness also denotes exclusion from a political community and expulsion from humanity.

Chapter 4 inquires into these fundamental dimensions of rightlessness by focusing on the protracted encampment of refugees, though the analysis also points to similar problems in the long-term detention of asylum seekers and undocumented immigrants. For the purposes of this inquiry, I offer an unconventional reading of *The Human Condition* by rethinking Arendt's arguments about action, work, and labor in her phenomenological account of *vita activa* (active life, or the life of activity). Arendt's analysis is often read as a hierarchical ordering of these activities, one that privileges action as the quintessentially human activity and denigrates labor as the least human, and perhaps even non-human, activity. Challenging this action-centric reading, I suggest that each activity makes a distinctive, irreplaceable contribution to living a life that can be recognized as human.

Especially important for this analysis is my reevaluation of labor in Arendt's account. For Arendt, labor is not only crucial for experiencing the elemental joy of being alive. It also cultivates a trust in the reality of life, endows human life with a sense of regularity and familiarity, and takes daily care of the world that human beings inhabit. Work is equally important, as it comprises activities of producing artifacts that provide the world with stability, durability, and objectivity. These artifacts anticipate and ease the discomfort of laboring bodies, and they establish a dwelling place that can enable action and speech. This reading allows us to rethink Arendt's arguments about statelessness in *The Origins of Totalitarianism*: I argue that the stateless are rightless because they are deprived of not only a right to action but also a right to work and a right to labor. Their plight does not merely consist of deprivation from a public space that allows them to appear, speak, and act before a community of actors. The predicament of the stateless also involves their forced dependence on compassionate humanitarians to meet even basic subsistence needs, loss of trust in the reality and regularity of life, disruption in the familiar routines of everyday life, and impediments to establishing relatively permanent dwelling places that can enable individual and collective life. Under these conditions, it becomes very difficult for the stateless to appear, and be recognized, as human beings entitled to equal rights. I discuss these conditions at length by examining the pervasive problems in the policy of long-term refugee encampment.

Following this interpretive work that recasts work and labor as crucial activities defining the human condition, I turn to action, which is crucial to Arendt's understanding of politics. But rethinking her concept of "action" for the purposes of understanding contemporary forms of rightlessness is not an easy task either. After all, Arendtian action is often seen as the lynchpin of a highly aestheticized vision of politics, lacking any meaningful content or purpose, and failing to address questions of injustice, power, and violence.[57] My reading of *The Human Condition* alongside Arendt's reflections on statelessness, however, offers a quite different assessment. Precisely by drawing attention away from questions of substantive content and specific purpose, I argue, Arendt brings into focus the *constitutive* effects of sharing words and deeds, or the crucial role of this activity in the ongoing constitution of political subjects, political community, and humanity. It is through action, especially action as speech, that we reciprocally recognize the "human" in each other, enact freedom and participate in our ongoing equalization, and transform the political community in question. On the basis of this reading, I suggest that one of the most fundamental forms of rightlessness manifests itself today in the speechlessness of migrants. This plight does not indicate the loss of the faculty of speech altogether; instead, it suggests that one's speech is rendered meaningless or not taken into account.[58] I examine this contemporary predicament by discussing the troubling use of lip-sewing by detained asylum seekers. This protest method, violently illustrating speechlessness, demonstrates how one's exclusion from a political community also marks one's expulsion from humanity, or from the common world of speaking beings.

A different picture of Arendt's account of *vita activa* emerges as we read *The Human Condition* alongside *The Origins of Totalitarianism* and rethink the arguments in both works in light of contemporary problems of rightlessness: What has often been criticized as an exclusionary framework centered on the public glories of the privileged few turns out to be a critical phenomenology providing a new grasp on the well-known problems in long-term encampment or detention.

A Right to Have Rights

These conditions of rightlessness can be, and have been, contested in various ways, as exemplified by the contemporary struggles of undocumented immigrants who demand "papers for all" and claim regularization as a human right. Chapter 5 demonstrates how an Arendtian framework can help us attend to the unique features and challenges of these struggles. Here I turn to Arendt's proposal to rethink human rights as "a right to have rights" toward the end of her reflections on statelessness in *The Origins of Totalitarianism*. Briefly, this proposal posits the right *to* citizenship as the condition of possibility for other rights.

Arendt's several clarifications also indicate that this new right demands a reconfiguration of citizenship beyond the nation-state framework. She argues that this right cannot be accommodated within the framework of international law that centers on agreements among sovereign states. More broadly understood, this formulation denotes a right to belong to a political community or to live in a framework where one's action, speech, and opinion count.[59]

Several scholars have turned to Arendt's notion of a right to have rights to address the question of how to establish a normative foundation that can provide a universal justification for this right.[60] Chapter 5 aims to reorient this debate by looking at Arendt's efforts to rethink political founding without engaging in a quest for foundations. I suggest that her call for a right to have rights points to the need to shift our focus from the question of what grounds human rights to the question of what generates, guarantees, and reinvents them—a shift that demands a close engagement with the *political practices of founding human rights*.

Arendt's proposal of a right to have rights provides a helpful starting point for thinking about the distinctive features of such practices: This right cannot derive its validity from existing legal frameworks, and she does not provide a normative foundation for it either; as a result, her account gives rise to perplexities about the source, status, and validity of this right. I suggest rethinking these perplexities, which are often taken as impasses of Arendtian political theory, as illuminating points of departure for grappling with the challenging political and ethical dilemmas attending struggles that articulate new rights or bring to view new subjects entitled to rights. These struggles introduce us to *declarations* of rights that cannot be authorized by existing legal and normative frameworks, and Arendt's call for a right to have rights draws attention to the vital importance of such inaugural practices, pervaded by perplexities, for the continuous reinvention of human rights in response to challenging problems of rightlessness.

I locate key resources for thinking about such political practices of founding human rights in Arendt's *On Revolution*. As her account of revolutionary beginnings highlights, modern rights declarations rupture the linear continuity of time and give rise to questions about their sources of origin and authority. It is quite tempting to resolve these questions by invoking an extra-political foundation that could justify these rights, as can be seen in the efforts of eighteenth-century revolutionaries to appeal to absolutes such as nature or God. But this foundationalist move works with a problematic understanding of politically instituted laws and rights, as it seeks to endow them with an absolute validity and render them incontrovertible. Drawing on the Roman tradition and turning to the work of Montesquieu, Arendt instead argues that laws and rights can have only "relative" validity, as they are dependent on the political practices of affirming and upholding them for their ongoing validation. Equally important is her suggestion that each new beginning carries within it a principle that saves it from complete arbitrariness; accordingly, what endows the beginning with its ongoing authorization is the re-activation and augmentation of this principle. It is important to note here that Arendt's Montesquieuan understanding of "principle" refers to neither a moral standard of action nor a foundational truth. It is instead what animates a new beginning such as a declaration of rights, inspires similar acts (e.g., invention of new rights), and orients judgments about these acts. Arendt highlights that a principle emerges in a specific historical context, but it can achieve a universal validity as it is taken up by different actors in different settings.[61]

In accordance with Arendt's account of revolutionary beginnings, I suggest that her proposition of a right to have rights is also animated by a principle—one that appears in the world with the modern declarations of rights. To capture this principle, I use the term "equaliberty." Étienne Balibar introduces this term as a translation of Greek *isonomia* to highlight the inextricably intertwined nature of equality and freedom in the Declaration of the Rights of Man and Citizen.[62] As different from ancient *isonomia*, which was tied to one's status as a citizen understood as a free man, equaliberty introduces "a politics of the universalization of rights," and it achieves a universal validity as it is reenacted time and again to make new rights claims.[63] Reconsidering these arguments in light of Arendt's discussion of revolution and civil disobedience, I suggest that human rights derive their validity not from extra-political sources of authority but instead from political practices augmenting the principle of equaliberty.

This point guides my analysis of a contemporary rights struggle waged by *sans-papiers* in France. Put in an irregular status due to restrictive immigration laws, *sans-papiers* articulate demands such as unconditional regularization, and as they do that, they bring to view new rights claims that cannot be easily accommodated within the existing legal and normative framework of human rights. Rethinking Arendt's call for a right to have rights by attending to the perplexities arising from its groundlessness alerts us to the challenging tasks that *sans-papiers* confront as they claim rights that they are not fully authorized to claim. To establish themselves as subjects entitled to rights and to validate their rights claims, *sans-papiers* have engaged in inventive political practices such as designating a name for themselves, occupying politically strategic sites, and perhaps most importantly, articulating their demands in a manifesto mimicking the eighteenth-century declarations of rights. Such practices are by no means sufficient to provide relatively durable guarantees of equality and freedom in the absence of institutions, but they are nonetheless indispensable to make sure that institutional mechanisms do not become blind to new problems of rightlessness and keep open the possibility of rethinking human rights in response to these problems.

This conclusion distinguishes the Arendtian critical inquiry offered in this book from those articulated by some contemporary thinkers who tie human rights inextricably to sovereign violence. Consider, for example, Giorgio Agamben's depiction of the present in terms of a catastrophe, especially his suggestion that we should no longer engage in "infinite negotiations" with a political discourse centered on citizenship and rights. In line with this conclusion, Agamben calls for a radical break in the name of "a *nonstatal and nonjuridical* politics and human life."[64] The Arendtian critique I propose, on the other hand, brings to light the possibilities of contesting rightlessness by navigating and reworking the perplexities of human rights. What Agamben dismisses as "infinite negotiations" with the sovereign state can give rise to new beginnings that radically transform existing legal and normative frameworks of rights. In fact, precisely by attending to rightlessness in its multiple dimensions, we can come to a different understanding of the contemporary struggles of migrants. The rights claims articulated in these struggles are not simply juridical appeals to the sovereign state; more importantly, they are political practices positioning migrants as subjects entitled to equal rights, manifesting a political community beyond the restrictions imposed by territorial borders, and ushering in new understandings of rights, citizenship, and humanity.

1.

Perplexities of Human Rights

FOLLOWING the catastrophes of World War II, just around the time when international actors were finalizing a universal declaration proclaiming the rights that all human beings have by virtue of their birth, Hannah Arendt, a stateless refugee, was drafting one of the most powerful criticisms of human rights to date. What motivated Arendt's critique was a frustration with the failure of these international efforts to fully confront the twentieth-century problem of statelessness, especially the fundamental condition of rightlessness endured by those who were deprived of citizenship in a nation-state. Taking her starting point from this problem, Arendt offered a provocative analysis of "the perplexities of the Rights of Man," highlighting the challenges posed by statelessness to the assumptions that have been commonly held about these rights since the eighteenth century: The Rights of Man were assumed to be natural; individuals were entitled to them by virtue of being born as human beings. As distinct from historically inherited rights that changed from one community to the other, these rights were derived from a universally shared human nature.[1] But the Rights of Man, which were supposed to be independent of political membership, turned out to be unenforceable in the case of the stateless. If these rights were inalienable in the sense that they could not be taken away from, or even renounced by, the subjects entitled to them, why did the stateless find themselves in a condition of rightlessness? If these rights were the source of all laws, and as such "irreducible to and undeducible from other rights or laws," why did they fail to offer effective protections to the stateless in the absence of such institutionalized rights and laws?[2] Arendt's critique brings to view the inextricable connections between human rights and citizenship, suggesting that it becomes very difficult for those deprived of membership in a political community to be recognized as human beings entitled to rights.

Arendt is not the first thinker to look into the perplexities of the Rights of Man. Similar inquiries have been undertaken since the eighteenth century. For those who hoped for a consistent, clear, and transparent language with unequivocal references, these perplexities illustrated the problems of vagueness and confusion, especially in political and legal discourse. Jeremy Bentham, for example, suggested that the contradictory statements were inevitable, as the language used in the Declaration of the Rights of Man and Citizen was "a perpetual vein of nonsense, flowing from a perpetual abuse of words, —words having a variety of meanings, where words with single meanings were equally at hand."[3] Bentham dismissed the idea of "natural, imprescriptible" rights as "nonsense upon stilts," insisting that the only real rights are legal ones that are established and upheld by a government.[4] For Edmund Burke, on the other hand, it was the revolutionary violence that clearly brought forth the inconsistencies of the Rights of Man; how could those who believed in inalienable rights engage in such unimaginable forms of violence?[5] Arguing against a metaphysics championing the "pretended" Rights of Man, Burke made a strong case for "the *real* rights of men," which were to be understood as "an *entailed inheritance* derived to us from our forefathers, and to be transmitted to our posterity."[6] The perplexities of the Rights of Man, understood mainly as contradictions and inconsistencies, were also at the heart of Marx's critique, though this time the abstractions of these rights were criticized not for the radical disruptions they introduced, as in Burke, but instead for their internal limits that prohibited them from fully achieving human emancipation. Marx argued that these limits were inevitable given the split between "man" and "citizen" introduced by this eighteenth-century vision of political emancipation, which guaranteed political equality for citizens without eliminating the inequalities embedded in civil society.[7]

Given the long history of the debates on the perplexities of the Rights of Man, what sets Arendt's critique apart? To answer this question, I suggest that it is necessary to attend to her distinctive approach to these "perplexities" or aporias—what we might call the "method" in her critical inquiry of human rights. Arendt understands this term in a non-technical sense to capture how we orient ourselves in thinking about a problem.[8] As she briefly notes in an essay on Hegel and Marx, "method" understood in this sense makes a difference, "for the way we approach any subject defines not only the *how* of our inquiry but also the *what* of our findings."[9] Attending to how Arendt approaches the perplexities of the Rights of Man (and even why she turns to these perplexities in the first place), I suggest, is important for understanding not only how her critical inquiry proceeds but also what kinds of conclusions it reaches.

Arendt's inquiry resonates with the classical criticisms of the Rights of Man in certain respects, as it reveals how the underlying assumptions of these rights (i.e., that they are abstract, natural, inalienable) are contradicted by challenging problems on the ground. However, her critique cannot be understood simply as an exercise in shaming human rights discourse by exposing its embarrassing limitations and exclusions. In fact, as different from the classical criticisms, the perplexities in her account are not verbal confusions, logical inconsistencies, or false appearances. They are genuine political and ethical dilemmas that define human rights as a modern discourse establishing inextricable relations between man and citizen, universal and particular, nature and history. The challenging task, from Arendt's perspective, is to face up to, and grapple with, these perplexities, in the face of pervasive problems of rightlessness. In addition, in a departure from many classical and contemporary criticisms, Arendt's critical inquiry is oriented toward the goal of rethinking human rights in the face of these problems. This goal is manifest in her proposition of "a right to have rights," which can be broadly understood as a right to citizenship and humanity.

Characterizing Arendt's critique of the Rights of Man in terms of this double gesture (i.e., a critique that reveals the limits of the human rights discourse and opens up the possibilities of rethinking its terms) can give rise to some objections. After all, Arendt's critique has elicited a wide range of responses, and if several of her readers find in her analysis an inspiration for rethinking human rights in the face of contemporary global problems, some suggest that what she offers is nothing less than a totalizing critique condemning these rights to inefficacy dating back to their early origins in the eighteenth century. For example, Hauke Brunkhorst argues that Arendt's analysis of statelessness reads into modern rights declarations an original failure that will lead them to an inevitable doom—rightlessness of the stateless at first and later the totalitarian catastrophe.[10] Similarly, Jacques Rancière claims that Arendt's critique paralyzes our political imagination with its perplexities and fails to see how the equivocalities of the Rights of Man—especially the simultaneous invocation of "man" and "citizen" as the subject of these rights—have given rise to several democratic struggles since the eighteenth century.[11] Read as a scathing attack on the Rights of Man, Arendt's critique seems to be unable to offer any insights into how we can rethink human rights today.

Given these criticisms, it is essential to attend to the distinctive method orienting Arendt's critique of the Rights of Man in order to develop a better understanding of its premises and conclusions. In what follows, I first propose reading Arendt's critique as an *aporetic* inquiry, and not simply because it centers on the "perplexities of the Rights of Man," or "die Aporien der Menschenrechte," as the German version puts it.[12] More importantly, Arendt's examination of these perplexities proceeds in an aporetic manner. To elaborate on this point, I turn to a figure who does not appear at all in Arendt's reflections on human rights: Socrates. In her later works, Arendt discussed Socrates to explore the possibilities of a type of thinking attuned to the distinctive challenges of politics. Taking my starting point from these discussions, my goal is to analyze how the example of Socrates can illuminate her thinking about human rights in *The Origins of Totalitarianism*. Similar to Socratic dialogues, Arendt's critical inquiry centers on the perplexities that pervade the commonly held opinions about a key concept of our everyday vocabulary. But her goal is not to debunk opinions such as those based on a naturalistic understanding of rights; instead, in a rather Socratic manner, she examines these opinions to find out not only what has become questionable but also what has achieved a new meaning and significance with the rise of statelessness. Arendt's inquiry is aporetic also because it does not offer a final resolution to the perplexities of the Rights of Man. In fact, it suggests that these perplexities cannot be resolved once and for all by grounding human rights in a new moral foundation or designing a new institutional model (even a postnational one). Arendt's inquiry resets the task of critical thinking; the task is neither to provide the discourse of human rights with a coherence that it originally lacked nor to call on alternative emancipatory languages that are presumably free of its illusions and disappointments. It is instead to come to grips with the perplexities of human rights for the purposes of rethinking these rights in response to challenging problems of rightlessness.

It is not simply the aporetic method that opens up possibilities for rethinking human rights in Arendt's critique. Equally important is her effort to understand historical events, including modern declarations of rights, in terms of equivocality and contingency in *The Origins of Totalitarianism*. For Arendt, historical events are equivocal phenomena that can give rise to multiple possibilities; as such, an inevitable destiny is not inscribed in them. As we analyze how a particular outcome arises from such equivocal phenomena, we need to think in terms of not logical necessity but contingency. Read in light of these historiographical orientations, Arendt's critique of the Rights of Man does not condemn these rights to failure and inefficacy since their early origins in the eighteenth century, as some of her critics have suggested. In a way that is different from more recent criticisms of human rights, especially the one offered by Giorgio Agamben, Arendt's analysis alerts us to the manifold, protean, and indeterminate trajectories of these rights. An Arendtian approach to human rights, with its attentiveness to their perplexities, equivocalities, and contingencies, allows us to bring together a radical critique of these rights with their radical rethinking. As such, it offers a promising framework for analyzing both the new forms of rightlessness encountered by migrants and the rights struggles that these problems give rise to.

Aporetic Thinking and the Socratic Example

It is impossible to know if Socrates was even in the back of Arendt's mind as she was writing *The Origins of Totalitarianism*. In this section, my goal is not to offer an exegesis that gets at her true intentions; instead, I hope to demonstrate that reading Arendt's analysis of the Rights of Man with her reflections on Socrates can shed light on the distinctive features of her critique of human rights. Most importantly, examining her arguments about Socrates can help us understand one of the puzzling moves of her analysis: its call for rethinking human rights in terms of a right to have rights at the end of a devastating critique. How is this rethinking possible given the critique? The brief response is that it is precisely *the critique that enables rethinking*: Only by attending to the *aporetic* dimensions of this critique can we understand how Arendt interweaves a radical scrutiny of human rights with an equally radical reformulation.

Arendt's interest in Socrates arises from her preoccupation with the challenging question of how to ward off the dangers of non-thinking, especially those that were illustrated by the troubling example of Adolf Eichmann.[13] She is particularly concerned that, if people stop critically examining commonly held beliefs, values, and standards, they will take shelter in the comforting possession of rules and follow them submissively. Non-thinking turns away from the worldly phenomena and refuses to recognize "the claim on our thinking attention that all events and facts make by virtue of their existence." We cannot be "responsive to this claim all the time," as that would be quite overwhelming. However, non-thinking, exemplified by Eichmann, is not even aware of this claim.[14]

Thinking—in its philosophical mode—is not up to the challenging task of responding to this claim either; it is intrinsically "unworldly," requiring a withdrawal from the realm of appearances to that of invisibles. For Arendt, Heidegger was perhaps the most exemplary figure illustrating the dangers of a type of thinking that is detached from, and even situated against, the world.[15] Thinking is also a potentially destructive activity, as it can undo any of our established ideas, beliefs, values, or criteria without offering anything else in their place.[16] It can leave us in a paralyzing state, not knowing how to act or judge. Arendt suggests that this seemingly negative dimension has salutary effects, as I discuss later, because it enables us to stop following rules obediently and take on the challenging task of forming judgments in the absence of such rules. But for now, it is important to highlight the most troubling possibility that she identifies with thinking: As an activity questioning commonly held assumptions about our key political and ethical concepts, it can leave us with nothing other than a deeply embedded cynicism about the possibility of any meaningful political or ethical life. There is a risk that thinking will turn against itself and give rise to an "unthinking" nihilism that destroys the possibilities of cultivating political and ethical practices that can sustain human plurality.[17]

If thinking is crucial for cultivating such practices, how can we ward off the dangers it poses against politics? It is this difficult question that takes Arendt to the example of Socrates, and she finds in Socratic dialogues resources for resisting the perils of both non-thinking and unworldly thinking. Given that these perils figure into Arendt's discussion of the twentieth-century crisis of statelessness, her later turn to the Socratic example offers an illuminating interpretive framework for rethinking her critique of human rights.

The response of the international community to the crisis of statelessness attests to the problems of non-thinking, or dogmatically applying existing rules without heeding the unprecedented challenges posed by this crisis. Following the dissolution of multiethnic empires and the creation of new nation-states at the end of World War I, the international community worked with the assumption of nationality, presuming that each national group needed to establish its own state. The unquestioning application of this principle turned all those who were "ejected from the old trinity of state-people-territory" into exceptions to the norm.[18] This position can be seen, for example, in the Minority Treaties that established "minority" as "a permanent institution" and recognized that these groups "needed an additional guarantee of their elementary rights from an outside body."[19] These treaties provided an international sanction for state policies denying non-nationals equal standing before the law.

This unthinking application of international rules and principles was blind to the failure of existing mechanisms, including repatriation, naturalization, or the right to asylum, to effectively respond to the novel phenomenon of statelessness created in the wake of World War I. Repatriation, which worked under the assumption that every person has a "homeland" (*patria*) to be returned to, failed precisely with the emergence of 'undeportable' people who had no country to which they could be returned.[20] The solution of naturalization, which was seen as an "appendage" to the organizing principle of nationality and reserved only for exceptional cases, also broke down with the emergence of statelessness on a massive scale.[21] The right to asylum, which Arendt describes as "the only right that had ever figured as a symbol of the Rights of Man in the sphere of international relationships,"[22] could not adequately cope with statelessness as a mass phenomenon either. Historically reserved for exceptional individual cases, this right also collapsed under the pressures of this crisis.

The problem, however, was not merely a dogmatic reassertion of already existing rules. There was also the related danger of a sinister cynicism in the face of statelessness on such a massive scale. In fact, a nihilistic attitude toward international principles and rules emerged in response to the failure of exceptional measures. As the stateless were confined in camps and subjected to lawlessness, many observers ended up with a skeptical conclusion that dangerously affirmed the "totalitarian movements' cynical claims that no such thing as inalienable human rights existed." As Arendt puts it, "[t]he very phrase 'human rights' became for all concerned—victims, persecutors, and onlookers alike—the evidence of hopeless idealism or fumbling feeble-minded hypocrisy."[23]

Arendt's analysis of the perplexities of the Rights of Man aims to respond to this new crisis without embracing either of these equally problematic positions: a dogmatic reassertion of existing international rules and a nihilistic thinking that resigns itself to a perpetual skepticism. Both of these positions fail to come to grips with the distinctive challenges posed by the plight of statelessness in the twentieth century. To understand how Arendt's critical inquiry of human rights resists both of these positions, it is worth carefully examining her later turn to Socrates as a figure who wards off the dangers of both dogmatism and nihilism.

For Arendt, Socrates represents a worldly mode of thinking that refuses to withdraw into a contemplative realm and is instead attuned to the unique challenges of politics. Arendt leaves aside the debates on the historical figure and invokes Socrates as "a model" or "an example" with "representative significance." Living as "a citizen among citizens" and thinking without ever becoming a professional philosopher, Socrates stands for a non-specialized form of thinking that could be exercised by anyone.[24] This thinking centers on "very simple, everyday concepts" that are "part and parcel of our everyday speech"; it carefully examines these concepts that we frequently invoke but rarely dwell on so that they do not turn into stock phrases or clichés.[25]

What strikes us about Socratic dialogues, Arendt highlights, is that they are aporetic; they are centered on the perplexities that our commonly held assumptions about these everyday concepts give rise to.[26] These perplexities are genuine dilemmas, confusions, and difficulties that Socrates and his interlocutors face as they examine these concepts, and not logical paradoxes that he invents in solitary contemplation. In addition, they are not riddles to which Socrates has ready-made answers; he is himself deeply puzzled by them and sincerely interested in seeing whether his interlocutors share his puzzlement.[27] This point is important for understanding what Arendt does in her critical inquiry of human rights. She does not survey the logical paradoxes or inconsistencies of these rights in the abstract; instead, she examines the widely shared assumptions about these rights and draws attention to the genuine political and ethical dilemmas that statelessness reveals about these assumptions.

Socratic dialogues are aporetic also because they offer no final closure; they do not present an incontrovertible or conclusive truth that could resolve, once and for all, the perplexities that a particular concept gives rise to.[28] This point is also important for understanding how Arendt's critique of human rights works; as we will see, her critique ends aporetically, without resolving the perplexities that it examines and at the same time giving rise to new ones with its puzzling formulation of a right to have rights. The lack of such final resolution might strike us as a negative outcome at first; in fact, at times, Arendt describes the way Socrates proceeds as circular, and this seems to indicate that aporetic thinking is futile because it leads to nothing other than the infinite regress of logical paradoxes. Yet, in Arendt's rendering, this movement from one perplexity to the other is valuable precisely because of its resistance to some kind of an absolute that would put an end to critical inquiry by restoring the comforting possession of a rule we could dogmatically follow. In fact, she sees the Socratic example as an appealing alternative to the predominant philosophical tradition that assumes thinking must necessarily result in certainty.[29]

Arendt highlights this last point to mark an important difference between the Platonic understanding of truth and the Socratic appreciation of opinion or *doxa*. For Socrates, "*doxa* was neither subjective illusion nor arbitrary distortion but, on the contrary, that to which truth invariably adhered."[30] *Doxa* contains truth as the expression of "*dokei moi*," or "what appears to me"; it arises from human plurality and suggests that "the world opens up differently to every man according to his position in it."[31] As a commonly held view representing such a distinctive perspective, *doxa* deserves to be examined carefully so that its *truthfulness* could be revealed. Arendt emphasizes that the Socratic method of *dialegesthai*, before its appropriation by Plato in the name of the philosophical truth, involves "talking something through," and it was this talk that would help the participants of a conversation inquire into the perplexities of their unexamined opinions and discover what might be truthful in these opinions.[32] This Socratic idea is crucial for understanding how Arendt approaches the perplexities of the Rights of Man. As discussed later, when she inquires into the conventional assumption that these are natural rights that all human beings have by virtue of their birth, her goal is not to discard it altogether but instead to find out its limits as well as its truthfulness.

All opinions, according to Arendt, are in need of such intersubjective affirmation, which involves critical assessment. Without such an examination, opinions risk turning into unexamined beliefs that can hinder our capacity to make judgments, especially in the face of novel phenomena that challenge our existing political and normative frameworks. To use the words of another thinker, John Stuart Mill, who was deeply influenced by the Socratic example, there is the danger that "however true it [an opinion] may be, if it is not fully, frequently, and fearlessly discussed, it will be held as a dead dogma, not a living truth."[33] Arendt alerts us to this problem, particularly in her discussion of "prejudices." Just like opinions, prejudices contain within themselves some truth; they are congealed expressions of our past judgments. But as they are "dragged through time" without any kind of reexamination, they can lose their "inherent legitimacy" and end up hindering judgment in the face of new reality.[34]

Aporetic thinking is of crucial importance for examining commonly held opinions and prejudices, and its critical role becomes clear particularly in the metaphors invoked in Plato's dialogues to describe Socrates. As a gadfly, Socrates demands that his interlocutors give an account of their taken-for-granted opinions, as he "stings" and provokes them into thinking.[35] But aporetic thinking is not merely provocation or prodding; it also entails midwifery, or the practice of delivering others of their "unexamined pre-judgments that would prevent them from thinking."[36] Just like the Athenian midwives, who are past the age of childbearing, Socrates is sterile; he is not in possession of a truth that he can pass to others.[37] For Arendt, this sterility highlights that only the concerted effort of talking something through with others can bring to view what is untenable and what might be worthy of reaffirmation. Probably the most interesting analogy is that of the electric ray, attributed to Socrates by Meno, one of his interlocutors. Socrates is quite apprehensive about this metaphor and is willing to accept it only if it is used in the sense that the electric ray paralyzes others because it is itself paralyzed. Arendt takes account of this amendment when she highlights that Socrates does not know the answers to the perplexities arising in the scope of a dialogue; he is himself puzzled by these perplexities.[38] Representing Socrates as the fish that can paralyze and benumb with its electric discharges evokes a negative image of aporetic inquiry—precisely the image that I am questioning in this chapter. However, as Arendt underscores, what looks paralyzing from outside is indeed a productive moment as it is "*felt* as the highest state of being active and alive."[39]

When these three metaphors—gadfly, midwife, electric ray—are taken together, aporetic inquiry assumes a much more critical function than what *aporia* conventionally indicates. The Greek term literally means "without passage," and is often taken to be an uncrossable path or an impasse.[40] But Arendt's discussion of Socrates suggests that aporetic inquiry would appear to be leading to nothing other than impasse only if we expect to arrive at an incontrovertible truth that could serve as the foundation of our thinking and judgment. Far from delivering such certainty, this kind of critical inquiry has a destructive effect on all those truths that seem to be self-evident. Yet, as a "truly discursive" exercise, moving from one perplexity to another and engaging with different views articulated from a multiplicity of standpoints, thinking (in its Socratic mode) becomes crucial for finding out what might be *truthful* in our commonly shared opinions.[41] To put it differently, and by using a distinction introduced by Sarah Kofman, aporetic inquiry does not lead to *odos* in the sense of a path or road on solid ground, but it does point to the possibility of navigating the uncertain world of perplexities to trace a passage, or *poros*, that was not available before—a critical practice that one takes on when there are "no fixed directions," familiar "landmarks" or "bearings" to rely on.[42]

This last point is key for Arendt, who attributes to thinking a crucial political and ethical import, particularly in times of emergencies or crises when we can no longer rely on existing norms to "tell right from wrong, beautiful from ugly"[43]—precisely when the truths that we took to be foundational are shaken to their core and we are faced with the challenging task of "thinking without a bannister" amid uncertainty.[44] Thinking, in its Socratic mode, and understood as an aporetic, dialogic activity, becomes pivotal in the face of emergencies or crises, as it allows a reexamination of key concepts, principles, and assumptions by attending to perplexing problems that defy easy resolutions. It can also have a "liberating effect" on the faculty of judgment, which orients us in the absence of general rules under which a particular case can be subsumed.[45] Arendt's reflections on Socrates suggest that aporia cannot be understood as "necessarily a failure or a simple paralysis, the sterile negativity of the impasse," to use Jacques Derrida's terms.[46] It can instead provoke thinking and encourage judgment in the face of political and normative crises that call into question existing norms, values, and criteria.

In the aftermath of World War II, Arendt proceeds in a Socratic manner, as she takes a crucial term of everyday vocabulary (i.e., human rights) and looks at the conventional accounts of what this term means. The very title of her article on human rights, published shortly before *The Origins of Totalitarianism*, resonates with the "*ti esti*" (i.e., what is it?) questions that instigate aporetic inquiry in Socratic dialogues: "'The Rights of Man': What Are They?"[47] Her analysis suggests that the crises of the twentieth century, including massive scales of statelessness, have shattered the façade of the international system, knocked political actors off their balance and forced upon them this deceptively simple but crucial question.[48] This question demands attention especially because the term "human rights" has been invoked frequently after World War II, but its meaning has become elusive just like the everyday concepts that Socrates inquires into: "[R]ecent attempts to frame a new bill of human rights have demonstrated that no one seems able to define with any assurance what these general human rights, as distinguished from the rights of citizens, really are."[49] More crucially, these international attempts failed to fully face up to the unprecedented challenges of the twentieth century, especially the crisis of statelessness that revealed the crucial importance of political membership for being recognized as a human being entitled to rights. The difficult task, according to Arendt, is to rethink human rights by responding to this crisis and render this concept "meaningful again."[50] She engages in this task as she inquires into the commonly held opinions about human rights, grapples with their perplexities, finds out what has become questionable in the wake of statelessness, identifies what has achieved a new urgency and meaning, and charts out a new possibility in her proposition of a right to have rights.

Arendt's writings on Socrates offer some responses to the criticism that her analysis of human rights leaves us at an impasse. Take, for example, Jacques Rancière's claim that Arendt's account of the perplexities of the Rights of Man leads to a dead end with two equally unappealing options: Either the Rights of Man are merely the rights of those who do not have any other rights and hence who have nothing else to turn to (i.e., poor, unpoliti-cized, or stateless persons who are deprived of the entitlements and privileges of a public life), or they are the rights of those who already have rights as members with full recognition in a political community (i.e., citizens). The first option reduces the Rights of Man to a "void," and the second renders them a "tautology:" "Either a void or a tautology, and, in both cases, a deceptive trick, such is the lock that she builds."[51] An analysis centered on perplexities, Rancière's criticism suggests, is debilitating since it locks thought to a binary logic, leads to nothing other than a "vicious circle," ensnares us in an "ontological trap," and blinds us to the political possibilities that release us from these conundrums—especially the possibilities of democratic contestation arising from the equivocalities of the 1789 Declaration, which invokes both "man" and "citizen" as the subject of rights.[52]

Turning to the Socratic example, however, allows us to see aporetic inquiry in a new light, as it recasts "tension and contradiction," as Jill Frank puts it in a different context, "not as stymying the possibilities for political action nor as making moot frameworks of falsity and truth, but rather as opening the way to less binary ways of thinking about age-old problems and dilemmas."[53] Arendt's reflections on Socrates suggest that, far from being paralyzing, aporetic thinking can offer crucial resources for critically assessing our key political and ethical concepts in times of crises. As I discuss below, in the face of massive scales of statelessness, Arendt's critical inquiry introduces possibilities for rethinking human rights beyond the binary formulations that prevail in the conventional understandings of these rights (e.g., man/citizen, universal/particular, nature/history).

Perplexities of the Rights of Man

Arendt's critical inquiry of human rights centers on the eighteenth-century discourse of the Rights of Man and its perplexities as manifested by the crisis of statelessness. Of particular importance for her analysis is the 1789 Declaration of the Rights of Man and Citizen. The problem of statelessness demands close attention to the title of the declaration, which invokes both "man" and "citizen" and leaves one uncertain about the subject of these rights. The scope of these rights, whether they are universal or particular, remains undecided as well; if they are the "rights of man," they are universal entitlements regardless of membership in a political community; if they are, however, "rights of citizen," then they are rights guaranteed by particular communities. The nature of these rights is also ambivalent; the declaration presents them as natural, pre-political rights, but it is proclaimed by a specific political community in a particular historical context.

Arendt's critique of the Rights of Man resembles those of Bentham and Burke in some respects, as she does emphasize the crucial importance of institutional guarantees of equality and freedom. But unlike Bentham, she does not suggest that the only valid rights are those codified in law and guaranteed by a sovereign; nor does she strive toward a logical coherence that will free us from the perplexities of the Rights of Man. And unlike Burke, she does not advocate a notion of rights understood as inherited entitlements, passed from one generation to another in a political community conceived as a family, even though she acknowledges how the plight of the stateless confirms some of his criticisms of natural rights. Perhaps the analysis that comes closest to hers among these classical criticisms is that of Marx. Both thinkers identify a politically important turning point in the declaration of these rights, and yet they also grapple with the internal tensions and limits of the Rights of Man—not to abandon these rights once and for all but to identify in their perplexities some possibilities for their rethinking. But they take on this challenging task quite differently: Marx's critique, at least as it is articulated in his essay "On the Jewish Question," operates with a novel reappropriation of Hegelian dialectics, whereas Arendt's aporetic inquiry proceeds in a quite Socratic mode. As she examines the commonly shared opinions about human rights, especially the conflicting claims privileging either "nature" or "history" as the ground of these rights, her goal is to identify not only what has been discredited by statelessness in these opinions but also what demands collective affirmation in the wake of this crisis.

If prejudices contain an element of truth as congealed expressions of past judgment, as suggested above, then the assumption that Rights of Man are natural rights is an opinion that arises from intersubjectively shared experiences. Arendt points to some of these experiences in *On Revolution*, when she highlights that the eighteenth-century revolutions confront us with an abyss: Whereas in the past a new body politic could legitimate its founding with reference to divine authority, secularization in the modern age leaves political actors with the problem of finding a new authority for the laws, rights, and institutions they establish.[54] This problem attending the founding of any body politic in the modern era becomes especially manifest in declarations of rights: "There is no period in history to which the Declaration of the Rights of Man could have harkened back. . . . [I]nalienable political rights of all men by virtue of birth would have appeared to all ages prior to our own as they appeared to Burke—a contradiction in terms."[55] Precisely because the past cannot authorize this new conception of rights, there is the urge to find a new foundation. Grounding rights in nature must be understood then in relation to revolutionary crises and emergencies that initiated the search for a new "transcendent source of authority" or "an absolute from which to derive authority for law and power."[56]

These experiences giving rise to the invocation of "nature" as a new source of validity for rights and laws suggest that the perplexities of the Rights of Man represent challenging political and ethical dilemmas in modern politics. However, the turn to nature does not fully resolve these dilemmas; in fact, it gives rise to new ones because it is not exactly clear what we mean by "nature." As Arendt examines human rights in response to the crises of the twentieth century, she underlines the concern that nature has come to be understood mainly in biological, singular, and pre-political terms in the context of late modernity; this problematic understanding of nature is at the heart of her critique of the urge to think of human rights as natural rights.

One of the problems with taking nature as the foundation of the Rights of Man comes to light with the modern tendency to understand this concept mostly in biological terms. The danger of equalization on the basis of a shared biological nature is that the Rights of Man will come to stand for the basic necessities of life. But the crisis of statelessness reveals the problems with this position: There might be cases where people may be provided basic necessities such as food and shelter but still lack the recognition as rights-bearing subjects.[57] Understanding human nature in terms of what is biologically given gets in the way of a political conception of human rights, centered on the right to have rights, or the right to citizenship and humanity, which Arendt describes as the condition for the effective exercise of all other rights.

The conventional opinion that the Rights of Man are natural rights also gives rise to problems because of the singularity that the notion of human nature implies and the plurality of human beings who are the subjects of these rights. After all, "not man but men inhabit the earth," and it is this condition of human plurality that risks being effaced if equality is understood in terms of a singular human nature, which emphasizes likeness or normality and represents any difference as anomalous.[58] As Arendt's analysis of imperialism highlights, the rise of racism in particular gave rise to a very exclusionary understanding of nature, casting those who are seen as naturally different as less-than-human and rendering them vulnerable to arbitrary violence—a problem that emerged first in the colonies and then in Europe.

The most crucial limit of taking nature as the basis of rights comes to view, according to Arendt, with the plight of the stateless who are "thrown back into a peculiar state of nature."[59] The Rights of Man are understood as "primary positive rights, inherent in man's nature, as distinguished from his political status."[60] The problems with this presupposition, implying that human rights can exist even in isolation or in the absence of a political community, become evident as soon as we encounter those who are stripped of all political qualifications and relationships:

The conception of human rights, based upon the assumed existence of a human being as such, broke down at the very moment when those who professed to believe in it were for the first time confronted with people who had indeed lost all other qualities and specific relationships—except that they were still human. The world found nothing sacred in the abstract nakedness of being human.[61]

Perhaps this is the most confounding perplexity that confronts us in thinking of human rights as natural rights: Those who appear in their mere givenness or naked humanity cannot be recognized as subjects entitled to equal rights. By grappling with this problem, Arendt aims to show that human rights do not precede and ground politics and citizenship; it is politics and citizenship that need to be prioritized for human rights to have any effective guarantees.[62]

This conclusion draws significantly on Burke's analysis; in fact, Arendt suggests that the plight of the stateless was "an ironical, bitter, and belated confirmation" of Burke's critique of the Rights of Man.[63] Burke, after all, criticizes the 1789 Declaration in a very similar way when he turns to the figure of the natural man, invoked as the subject of rights, only to find out that he is left rightless by those who advocate the Rights of Man. Burke makes this point in his discussion of the property qualifications introduced by the French Assembly; he argues that these qualifications, contradicting the "equalising principle" of the Rights of Man, end up excluding the very subjects that are most in need of these rights: "[I]t excludes from a vote, the man of all others whose natural equality stands the most in need of protection and defence; I mean the man who has nothing else but his natural equality to guard him."[64] This man who has nothing else but his natural equality resurfaces in Arendt's depiction of the stateless "who had indeed lost all other qualities and specific relationships—except that they were still human."[65] The plight of statelessness confirms Burke's criticisms targeting the naturalistic conception of rights, highlighting that one's bare humanity is not sufficient for being recognized as a subject entitled to equal rights.

Arendt's critical engagement with the assumption that nature is the ground of the Rights of Man suggests that human rights are in need of political practices and institutions that can provide relatively permanent guarantees: "We are not born equal; we become equal as members of a group on the strength of our decision to guarantee ourselves mutually equal rights."[66] Human rights are in need of artificial, conventional, man-made laws if they are to be effective, and Arendt underlines "the sad inefficacy of all declarations, proclamations, or enumerations of human rights that were not immediately incorporated into positive law, the law of the land."[67]

It is important to note here that the Declaration of the Rights of Man and Citizen, as its title indicates, does not overlook the importance of politics and citizenship for providing effective guarantees for these rights. Arendt's analysis highlights that the Declaration is equivocal on this score, positing nature as the foundation of the Rights of Man, and at one and the same time recognizing that these rights are in need of political institutions and practices. The Declaration announces that "men are born and remain free and equal in rights" (Article 1) and suggests that the goal of political community is "the preservation of the natural and imprescriptible rights of man" (Article 2). Hence, it establishes the Rights of Man as the basis of legitimacy, taking them as "the source of all political power" and "the foundation-stone of the body politic."[68] Yet, the Declaration simultaneously proclaims "the nation" to be sovereign (Article 3) and links these rights with membership in a nation-state. This move suggests that it is not man in his natural condition isolated from others that is the subject of these rights. It is man *as* citizen who is entitled to these rights as a member of a political community: "From the beginning the paradox involved in the declaration of inalienable human rights was that it reckoned with an 'abstract' human being who seemed to exist nowhere, for even savages lived in some kind of a social order."[69]

Arendt's critical remarks about the naturalistic conception of rights seem to validate Jacques Rancière's claim that her critique reformulates Burke's "polemical statement" against the Rights of Man.[70] This conclusion is quite hasty, however, as it overlooks the differences between Burke and Arendt on this score. Arendt does insist on the importance of membership in a political community to be recognized as a subject entitled to equal rights. But this community is by no means the one that Burke has in mind, which is a kinship-based polity conceived in "the image of a relation in blood," and she does not defend a notion of rights understood as hereditary entitlements "derived . . . from a more early race of ancestors" either.[71] In fact, it is precisely these kinds of statements that underlie her critique of Burke's notion of "entailed inheritance" for its "curious touch of race-feeling."[72] "History" understood as heredity, no less than "nature" understood in singular, biological, pre-political terms, would reproduce the problem of rightlessness. Leaving aside the racial overtones in Burke's understanding of rights, Arendt does not want to endorse his argument that takes political membership as a given. Burke's position, modeling community on kinship ties, would aggravate the problem of statelessness, as it presumes that everyone is a member of a nation, just as every child is born to a family.[73] If naturalistic understanding of human rights is problematic because it fails to recognize that rights ultimately depend on political guarantees of equality, the historicist understanding of rights is equally problematic because it cannot take into consideration the possibility of statelessness.

In light of Arendt's divergence from Burke, it is important to locate the Socratic moment in her critique of the tendency to take nature as the ground of rights: Just as Socrates engaged in aporetic inquiry not to debunk opinions but instead to find what might be truthful in them, Arendt's critical analysis does not aim to denounce the modern idea of "natural" rights as a mere hypocrisy or illusion. There is something truthful in this commonly held assumption, which after all arises from real political and ethical dilemmas in modern politics. It is worth remembering that, at the very beginning of the section on the Rights of Man in *The Origins of Totalitarianism*, Arendt presents the 1789 Declaration as "a turning point in history," a crucial event announcing that the source of laws and rights was no longer "God's command or the customs of history." The Declaration called into question all sorts of social privileges, including the hereditary ones, and indicated "man's emancipation from all tutelage."[74] The rights proclaimed were meant to provide "a much needed protection" in a modern society in which individuals could no longer rely on social estates or religious protections; these rights were particularly important given unprecedented forms of state and social power introduced by modern politics.[75] The declaration of these "natural" rights then corresponds to novel problems of modern life, and it is by no means the goal of Arendt's analysis to turn back the clock and reclaim the privileges of entailed inheritance, as Burke does. Her critique shows that the Rights of Man cannot be simply *natural* rights; but they cannot be simply *historical* rights either.

Burke's critique of natural rights, insisting on the importance of rights inherited in a political community, achieves a "pragmatic soundness" in light of the plight of the stateless who find themselves in a condition of rightlessness once they lose all their political and social relationships.[76] But from Arendt's perspective, this plight also reveals the problems with Burke's argument. Repudiating the Rights of Man and insisting instead on the historically grounded "rights of Englishman" would only exacerbate rightlessness in an international context in which millions were rendered stateless and could no longer make a claim to so-called "inherited" rights as nationals. The Burkean formula would in fact reproduce the problems of a world in which "man" becomes a "vanishing ground," to use Giorgio Agamben's phrase, of the citizen understood as a member of the nation-state.[77] Arendt's aporetic inquiry reveals the truthfulness of the historical understanding of rights only to the extent that it reaffirms the crucial role of political community for effectively exercising one's rights. However, it also reveals the inescapable problems and dangers of a Burkean position in a world where one can no longer take membership for granted.

Arendt's complex engagement with Burke brings out one of the persistent perplexities of human rights: Rights are in need of artificial inventions such as laws and other institutional structures to offer effective guarantees of equality and freedom. However, the institutions that we establish in order to have relatively permanent guarantees can end up destroying these rights. Refusing to resolve the "perplexities of the Rights of Man" by resorting to "history" as the ground of these rights, Arendt captures what Étienne Balibar aptly describes as the "antinomic" relationship between rights and institutions.[78] On the one hand, she insists that our humanness can only be recognized in a political community arising out of "common engagement in political action." Without the reciprocal guarantees of equality and freedom instituted in such a community, *there simply are no humans.*[79] On the other hand, she also recognizes that the relationship between institutions and rights is not simply one of compatibility or mutual reinforcement. In fact, she draws attention to the tense, uneasy, and at times conflictual relationship between rights and institutions.

The inescapable tension between rights and institutions can give rise to a conflict when institutions turn against rights either by failing to respond effectively to new demands of equality and freedom, or by undermining or violating the rights that they are supposed to uphold. Conversely, the antinomy also gives rise to a conflict when rights are turned against institutions and mobilized to contest the exclusionary formulations of equality and freedom.[80] The first possibility is at the heart of Arendt's analysis of the nation-state; and the second, as I explain in chapter 5, can be seen in her account of civil disobedience and her proposition of a right to have rights. By attending to the reciprocal but conflictual relationship between human rights and their institutionalized guarantees, Arendt insists on the need for both institutional structures and their sustained critique; as a result, her aporetic inquiry of human rights refuses to endorse the binary logic of institutionalism/anti-institutionalism.[81]

The antinomy between rights and institutions is palpable in Arendt's analysis of the nation-state. The institutional framework of the nation-state rests on a precarious balance between "nation" and "state": A state legitimizes itself as the "supreme legal institution" in charge of "the protection of all inhabitants in its territory," regardless of their nationality. A nation, however, represents an exclusive community composed of those who belong "by right of origin and fact of birth." The unstable balance that the nation-state strikes between these two was gradually undermined, especially with the rise of national consciousness, which turned the nation into a new absolute. Arendt describes this process as "the conquest of the state by the nation," highlighting how the state lost its representative function and became an instrument of the nation. Through this gradual conquest, nationalism identified citizens only with nationals.[82] As a result, the eighteenth-century equivocation between "man" and "citizen," which could have been politically navigated to guarantee equality and freedom for all the residents of a political community, was increasingly effaced in the name of the rights of nationals. As the egalitarian dimensions of the nation-state were further undermined with the rise of imperialism and emergence of tribal or ethnic nationalisms, it became even more difficult to invoke the Rights of Man to claim equal rights for those who were not nationals.

If the problem was merely with the nation-state, one could respond at this point: Wouldn't it be possible to resolve the tensions between human rights and the institutional orders established to protect them by moving beyond the nation-state? Very briefly put, Arendt's critical inquiry suggests that, although some institutional structures are more promising in terms of offering effective guarantees for equal rights, no institutional form, including an international, postnational, or even a cosmopolitan one, can be entirely free of these tensions. To illustrate this point, it is worth briefly discussing Arendt's arguments in favor of limited sovereignty and her reflections on world government and citizenship.

Arendt provides us with one of the most powerful criticisms of sovereignty, but in a puzzling section of *The Human Condition*, she also makes room for what she describes as "limited" sovereignty: "Sovereignty, which is always spurious if claimed by an isolated single entity, be it the individual entity of the person or the collective entity of a nation, assumes, in the case of many men mutually bound by promises, a certain limited reality."[83] Institutional structures based on limited sovereignty, one could argue, would provide more effective guarantees for human rights. In fact, Arendt draws a similar conclusion in her review of J. T. Delos's *La Nation*, when she argues that "[w]ithin federated structures, nationality would become a personal status rather than a territorial one."[84] Both in her reflections on the organization of post-war Europe and the establishment of a Jewish homeland in Palestine, she highlights that the nation-state form is no longer viable and advocates instead federative structures "made up of different peoples with equal rights."[85] Would a republican federation resolve the perplexities of human rights by detaching these rights from the framework of territorially defined nationality?

Arendt does not address this question explicitly, but given that mutual promises are not completely immune to the contingency and fragility that mark human action, they can provide guarantees that are only *relatively* stable. Hence, political actors still need to be attentive to how republican structures established to furnish guarantees of equality could give rise to disappointments on this score. First, as highlighted by Arendt's reflections on the failure of the American Revolution to establish lasting institutions that could maintain the revolutionary spirit, even republican arrangements with origins in mutual promises can end up petrifying rights in a set of institutional structures that leave no room for political practices of enacting, guaranteeing, and reinventing equality and freedom.[86] Second, even a republican federation can entail various forms of injustice, as highlighted by Arendt's references to slavery and poverty in the American context.[87] Finally, we can also add that a republican federation is still bound by territorial borders and can give rise to problematic distinctions between insiders and outsiders when it comes to the question of who is entitled to rights.

Could postnational, or even cosmopolitan, structures offer resolutions to the tensions intrinsic to the institutional forms centered on the principle of territorial sovereignty? Arendt's brief reflections on world government, world citizenship, and worldwide federation suggest that these perplexities would certainly be reconfigured in a cosmopolitan setting, but not always with the effect of providing more stable guarantees for human rights. For example, when she invokes the possibility of a world government at the very end of her analysis of human rights in *The Origins of Totalitarianism*, she immediately highlights the dangerous possibility that "a highly organized and mechanized humanity will conclude . . . that for humanity as a whole it would be better to liquidate certain parts thereof."[88] Even short of such liquidation, there is no guarantee that a world government would protect human rights and maintain human plurality. In fact, Arendt is concerned that, as this world government tries to achieve common bonds among different peoples, it can end up destroying differences, creating "a horridly shallow unity," and giving rise to "a forbidding nightmare of tyranny."[89] Similarly, a world citizenship does not necessarily resolve the tensions between rights and their institutional protections, especially given the possibility that it can end up eradicating differences between citizens of a diverse range of political communities.[90] Even more nuanced articulations of cosmopolitanism, according to Arendt, do not seem to be impervious to such risks arising from the antinomic relationship between human rights and the institutional structures established to guarantee them. A good example in this regard is Karl Jaspers's idea of "a world-wide federated political structure," which aims to sustain human plurality by advocating the ideal of 'limitless communication.' Although Arendt seems to be quite enthusiastic about this institutional proposal, she is still hesitant to fully endorse it. Pointing out that Jaspers's position might entail the abolition of war, she takes issue with this possibility and argues that a cosmopolitan federation "would harbor its own peculiar dangers," including the alarming prospect of "federated police forces."[91]

One can come up with highly sophisticated institutional proposals that can respond to some of these Arendtian concerns. Although these concerns do not pose necessary obstacles to non-national institutional solutions, they reveal one of the distinctive features of an Arendtian critique of human rights: a careful analysis of the necessary but also uneasy and at times conflictual relationship between human rights and their institutional guarantees. Even if these guarantees could be completely detached from the nation-state and assumed by other institutions, there is still a need to undertake critical inquiries into the tense and unpredictable relationship between human rights and the institutional orders established to protect them.[92]

Arendt's critique suggests that engaging with the perplexities of human rights is crucial for understanding contemporary forms of rightlessness. To understand how the deprivation of citizenship rights is accompanied by a loss of human rights in the case of the stateless, we need to carefully examine these perplexities pervading rights declarations, our commonly held assumptions, institutional frameworks, and political practices. Such an inquiry is necessary to understand how problems such as statelessness leave some people without any rights; it is also the condition of possibility for rethinking human rights in response to these problems, as exemplified by Arendt's own invocation of a right to have rights.

Equivocality and Contingency of Human Rights

To fully understand the distinctive features of Arendt's critique of human rights, we need to take into account not only her aporetic approach but also her attentiveness to *equivocality* and *contingency*. In calling attention to these features, I hope to respond to the claim that Arendt casts the rightlessness of the stateless as an inevitable outcome embedded in the Rights of Man. Take, for example, Jacques Rancière, who insists that Arendt's work provides the intellectual underpinnings of the more recent arguments that Giorgio Agamben makes about the inextricably intertwined histories of human rights, sovereignty, and totalitarian camps. Highlighting that Agamben's critique leaves us with *"an overwhelming historico-ontological destiny* from which only a God is likely to save us," Rancière ties this problematic conclusion to Agamben's endorsement of an Arendtian position on human rights.[93] In response to this criticism, I make two interrelated points: First, far from being a one-sided, deterministic account, Arendt's critique foregrounds the *equivocal* effects of human rights—their promising possibilities and risks—precisely because it is centered on their perplexities. Second, these perplexities are not ahistorical contradictions dooming human rights to an ontological destiny from the very beginning. Instead, they are political and ethical dilemmas that are shaped and transformed significantly by historically *contingent* events and conditions. Arendt's emphasis on equivocality and contingency distinguishes her critique of human rights from several others, including the one more recently offered by Agamben.

This argument draws on Arendt's own reflections on the challenging historiographical issues at stake in writing about unprecedented events such as the rise of totalitarianism.[94] These methodological reflections indicate that Arendt does not turn to the 1789 Declaration to locate a chain of causes that would inevitably lead to the massive scales of rightlessness for stateless persons and then to totalitarian domination. Rightlessness is neither historically inevitable nor completely accidental given the perplexities in the underlying assumptions of the Rights of Man. It owes its structure to a "crystallization" of a set of "elements," including the intrinsic tensions of the nation-state, dissolution of multi-ethnic empires, and international policies such as minority protection; but none of these elements in this particular configuration determines the outcome in advance.[95] In this reading, just as any other element in this configuration, the Rights of Man do not have a single, fixed trajectory but contain "an infinite number of abstract possibilities" and have an "equivocal past."[96]

Suggesting that Arendt attends to the multiple possibilities and equivocal effects of the Rights of Man is almost counterintuitive given her scathing criticism of the French Revolution and the 1789 Declaration, especially in *On Revolution*, which I discuss at length in chapter 2. But it is important to remember that Arendt interprets the French Revolution as an event exemplifying the "experience of man's faculty to begin something new" and representing the capacity to interrupt the linear progression of time and reclaim political freedom as a shared human possibility.[97] It is possible to understand the 1789 Declaration in similar terms. As new beginnings, both the French Revolution and the Rights of Man contain numerous possibilities and can be appropriated in different ways by political actors depending on historical circumstances. For example, Arendt's account of the Paris Commune reveals that the French Revolution can be, and has been, taken up in new and unanticipated ways by political actors. Arendt finds in the Commune, which she describes as an "unexpected and largely spontaneous outcome of the Revolution itself," the possibility of reclaiming this new beginning for a political organization that can actualize the republican promise of equality and freedom through self-governance.[98] Arendt also credits both the French and American revolutions for making "world politics" imaginable for the first time, heralding a new era in which politics would concern "all men *qua* men, no matter where they lived, what their circumstances were, or what nationality they possessed."[99] As one of the events inaugurating world politics in this particular sense, the 1789 Declaration holds the promise of equal rights for all regardless of nationality, ethnicity, or race. As I discuss at length in chapter 5, this promise has become manifest once again in the political demonstrations of undocumented immigrants who appropriate the equivocal legacies of the French Revolution and the Rights of Man in unanticipated ways.

Arendt's recognition of such political possibilities, despite her criticism of the transformation of the Rights of Man into the rights of nationals within the context of the nation-state, comes to light particularly in her analysis of the Dreyfus Affair. Arendt describes this case as one testing "the complete impartiality of the law", which was assumed to be the "greatest achievement" of the nineteenth century.[100] For the most part, she reads the case as one grimly affirming that there was no such impartiality, and that those who were cast as pariahs did not share in the promise of equal rights.[101] Yet, Arendt's description of the grounds on which Dreyfus should have been defended points to the possibility of turning human rights into a political site of contestation for claiming equal rights:

> There was only one basis on which Dreyfus could or should have been saved . . . the stern Jacobin concept of the nation based upon human rights—that republican view of communal life which asserts that (in the words of Clemenceau) by infringing on the rights of one you infringe on the rights of all.[102]

This statement is confusing given Arendt's criticism of the 1789 Declaration—particularly its Jacobin interpretation. Yet, if the declaration is understood as equivocal, in line with Arendt's historiographical orientations, it contains multiple possibilities, including not simply those that threaten equalization but also ones that hold the promise of fostering it. In particular, the tension between "man" and "citizen" carries within it a risk. Within the context of the nation-state, especially as a result of the rise of national consciousness, this tension was generally resolved in favor of the rights of citizens defined as nationals, making it difficult for those who were not recognized as full members of the political community to claim human rights. Yet, as an equivocal event, the Declaration contains other possibilities, including that of contesting these narrow interpretations and demanding equal rights regardless of race, ethnicity, or religion. According to Arendt, Clemenceau exemplifies this possibility as he defends Dreyfus by insisting on "the stern Jacobin concept of the nation based on human rights."[103] By defending Dreyfus in these terms, he demonstrates that the perplexities of the Rights of Man are not ironclad paradoxes resisting human agency; they are political and ethical dilemmas that can be politically navigated in ways that reconfigure the existing relationships between man and citizen, nature and history, universal and particular.

Arendt's critique of the Rights of Man, then, does not rule out the democratic possibilities arising from these abstract inscriptions of equality. In fact, as illustrated by her account of the Dreyfus Affair, it is attentive to these possibilities. But that account also highlights the need to carefully examine the historical conditions that can undermine or promote practices of guaranteeing equal rights, and this brings me to the second point about Arendt's approach (i.e., attentiveness to *contingency*).

Rights struggles do not take place in a historical vacuum; certain historical conditions can set obstacles to the political practices of claiming, enacting, and reinventing human rights. Arendt's analysis of imperialism highlights this point. As a "limitless pursuit of power after power," imperialism unmoors the sovereign nation-state from its modern anchors such as the rule of law, explodes the territorial boundaries that put at least some constraints on the detrimental effects of nationalism, solidifies racial categorizations that hollow out the notion of "humanity" that is central to human rights and international law, undermines the precarious balance between "nation" and "state," and paves the way for the decline of the constitutional state.[104] Once the practices and categories of imperialism are imported to Europe, we begin to see its "boomerang effects."[105] Especially troubling, for Arendt, is the emergence of a new form of state structure amidst the ruins of the modern constitutional state. This new structure, though "not yet fully totalitarian," does not recognize any legal and normative constraints in its exercise of power, aims to achieve total control by stratifying people on the basis of naturalized categories of race, ethnicity, and class, deploys mass denaturalizations in the management of its population, and gives rise to massive scales of rightlessness.[106]

Arendt's analysis of imperialism underscores the need to inquire into political and social conditions that can undermine the possibilities of invoking the Rights of Man for the purposes of claiming equality and freedom for all—regardless of race, ethnicity, and nationality. In his analysis of the 1789 Declaration, Étienne Balibar makes a similar point when he suggests that the indeterminacy of the document is both its strength and weakness, rendering its political effects "entirely dependent on 'power relations' and the evolution of the conjuncture in which it will always be necessary in practice to construct individual and collective referent for equaliberty."[107] Arendt's critical inquiry brings out this indeterminacy and urges us to examine the conditions that continuously shape the political possibilities of navigating and renegotiating the perplexities of human rights.

This attentiveness to equivocality and contingency is what differentiates Arendt's critique from several others that call for abandoning the discourse of human rights altogether. It is worth discussing Giorgio Agamben briefly at this point precisely because his critique draws on Arendt's, and as Rancière's charges against Arendt and Agamben illustrate, there is now a tendency to conflate the arguments of these two theorists.

Agamben takes his starting point from Arendt's efforts to resist the temptation to cast challenging problems of rightlessness as unfortunate exceptions to an otherwise well-functioning system. For both theorists, these pervasive problems are *symptoms* revealing the limits and exclusions of human rights in a nation-state system. This is the reason why any institutional solution working within the premises of that system cannot help but fail, especially when statelessness is no longer simply an exceptional case that can be addressed on an individual basis but instead has become a mass phenomenon.[108] Both Agamben and Arendt suggest that this problem cannot be understood without a careful analysis of the perplexities in the Declaration of the Rights of Man and Citizen, especially the simultaneous invocation of "man" and "citizen" as the subject of rights. Agamben draws on Arendt especially when he argues that, in the context of the nation-state, this equivocality carries within itself the risk that only nationals will be recognized as subjects entitled to rights.[109]

However, Agamben's approach to the perplexities of the Rights of Man departs significantly from that of Arendt. For Agamben, these perplexities represent nothing other than the impasses of biopolitical sovereignty understood as the power to make decisions over life—a power that has manifested itself in different forms in Western politics and metaphysics for more than 2,000 years. Accordingly, Agamben treats the tension between "man" and "citizen" as a reinscription of the centuries-old metaphysical divide between *bios* (politically qualified life) and *zoē* (natural life), which has held human life in the grip of sovereign power and subjected it to violence. Given this divide, he argues, it is inevitable that refugees find themselves in the dangerous threshold of *bios* and *zoē*, politics and nature, law and violence, as *homines sacri*, or sacred men who can be killed with impunity.[110] Agamben's analysis of human rights is based on sweeping statements speaking to the "24 centuries" of Western political history.[111] It is not surprising that he concludes with a call for a politics that renounces all concepts tied to sovereignty, including human rights and citizenship, since he offers a critique that ends up erasing the complex, ambivalent, and contingent histories of these concepts.[112]

Agamben's creative appropriation of Arendt has come to shape our contemporary interpretations of her position on human rights, but it is worth restating how Arendt's aporetic inquiry proceeds very differently, and as a result, arrives at different conclusions. For Arendt, the goal of critique is not to find out the logical or metaphysical contradictions that have determined the effects of human rights in some formalistic and atemporal sense. Her critique attempts "to untie aporia from logical determination."[113] Her critique does underscore the need to analyze the deep-rooted perplexities of the eighteenth-century declarations to understand the late modern phenomenon of statelessness. However, it does not suggest that these necessarily lead to the rightlessness of the stateless or the totalitarian catastrophe. The plight of the stateless is instead a contingent yet structured (hence, not accidental) constellation— one that arises from the crystallization of several elements, including the paradoxical assumptions of rights declarations, tensions intrinsic to the institutional structures established to guarantee these rights, and historical transformations that shape the perplexities of human rights. Precisely because of this attentiveness to equivocal and contingent effects of human rights, Arendt's concluding call is very different from that of Agamben: Instead of a politics beyond human rights, sovereignty, and citizenship, she calls for a right to have rights—a right that demands a radical rethinking of these key concepts, but not their total refusal or an exodus from the challenging political and ethical dilemmas of modern politics.

As discussed in this chapter, several critics suggest that Arendt's paralyzing quandary, stuck within binary conceptions of man/citizen, nature/history, universal/particular, dooms the Rights of Man to inefficacy from their early origins. Rancière's provocative call in his critique of Arendt exemplifies this assumption: "If we want to get out of this ontological trap, we have to reset the question of the Rights of Man."[114] In light of the reconstruction of Arendt's critique presented above, I argue that perplexities or aporias, understood usually in negative terms as paralyzing quandaries, can indeed be crucial resources in rethinking human rights beyond the conventional binaries, especially in times of crisis. In the face of the crisis triggered by massive scales of statelessness, Arendt shows how conventional accounts relying on these binaries can render human rights either "void" or "tautological," to recall Rancière's terms. Understood as natural rights grounded in some kind of a universally shared, abstract nature, human rights are assumed to exist independent of and prior to political community; yet, without intersubjective guarantees and mutual agreements that are possible only within a community of actors, human rights can be rendered meaningless and void, as the plight of the stateless reveals. Understood as historically grounded rights that we inherit as members of particularistic communities, however, the concept of human rights risks becoming tautological, as it indicates nothing more than the rights of citizens and leaves out those who are deprived of citizenship.

To use Rancière's terms again, for purposes counter to his, Arendt "resets" the question of human rights to think about them anew beyond these conventional binaries that fail to respond to the crisis of statelessness. This rethinking is exemplified by her effort to rearticulate human rights as a right to have rights, which Rancière fails to mention in his analysis. Arendt tries to clarify this perplexing phrase in several ways; it indicates a right "to live in a framework where one is judged by one's actions and opinions" and "belong to some kind of organized community"[115]—in short, "the right of men to citizenship" and "the right of every individual to belong to humanity."[116] This proposition resists reducing human rights to either the "rights of man" or "the rights of citizen" and insists on the importance of both citizenship *and* humanity for guaranteeing rights. This is by no means a happy medium that reconciles what was deemed to be irreconcilable and overcomes the gap between man and citizen, universal and particular, nature and history. Grappling with the perplexities of human rights in response to statelessness and traversing an unfamiliar terrain in the aftermath of World War II, Arendt traces a passage, or *poros*, with her proposition, to remember Sarah Kofman's formulation, but one that is not free of perplexities. In fact, her critics have argued that she does not settle the difficult questions related to the normative foundations and institutional protections of a right to have rights. As I discuss at length in chapter 5 in response to these criticisms, Arendt's proposition points to the impossibility of unequivocally determining the scope, subject, and ground of human rights in advance and suggests instead that these are always to be contested and redefined in political struggles that reconfigure the relations between rights, citizenship, and humanity.

For the purposes of this chapter, it is important to note that Arendt's attempt to rethink human rights along these lines manifests the distinctive orientations of her critical inquiry. Similar to the Socratic dialogues urging Athenian citizens to find the truthfulness of their own opinions by carefully examining them, Arendt's critique does not aim to abandon human rights but instead to render them meaningful again. Setting the task of critique as rethinking, Arendt's inquiry raises cautions against some of the more recent criticisms of human rights, such as the one offered by Agamben. Theoretically, a critique that assigns human rights a singular, uniform logic fails to attend to their multiple, equivocal, and contingent effects. Politically, a critique calling for an emancipatory politics completely severed from human rights risks overlooking the struggles that reclaim these rights in imaginative ways. An Arendtian critique is attentive to such political possibilities because its relentless scrutiny of the underlying assumptions and paradoxical effects of human rights takes heed of their equivocal and contingent histories.

If the goal is neither to find a new normative foundation for human rights nor to devise an institutional model for their protection, then what are the main tasks of critical inquiry according to this Arendtian framework? To put it very briefly, there are two crucial interrelated tasks. One involves understanding the new forms of rightlessness faced by asylum seekers, refugees, and undocumented immigrants, and it demands carefully examining the perplexities that these problems bring to view in the contemporary human rights institutions, norms, and policies. The other consists of understanding the political possibilities of contesting rightlessness, and this task requires closely examining how political actors, especially those who find themselves in a condition of rightlessness, navigate the perplexities of human rights and rearticulate the relations between man and citizen, universal and particular, nature and history.

I argued in this chapter that Arendt's critique of human rights provides crucial resources for both of these tasks, but one crucial question remains: What about her conception of politics? Doesn't her strict division between political and socioeconomic issues, embodied in her controversial concept of "the social" and criticized even by her sympathetic readers, get in the way of these tasks, especially since most human rights problems and struggles cut across such a divide? The next chapter turns to this difficult question to clarify the notion of politics that is orienting the Arendtian framework put forward in this book.

2.
Human Rights as Politics
and Anti-Politics

RENDT has often been criticized for drawing a strict conceptual distinction between political and social issues and for condemning all modern attempts to politicize questions of social justice. Her critical reflections on "the rise of the social" in *The Human Condition* and "the social question" in *On Revolution* are read as affirmations of this problematic divide. To what extent can Arendt's work inform a critical inquiry aimed at understanding contemporary struggles around human rights, especially given that most of these struggles cut across this divide? To give just a few examples from the issues that will be discussed in this book, how do we make sense of an asylum seeker's efforts to claim residency based on her HIV-positive status? What about the struggles over food rations and shelter conditions in refugee camps? Or the demands for the right to work and family unification articulated alongside the rallying cry of "papers for all" in the demonstrations of undocumented immigrants? If all of these issues are to be declared as "social," and hence not political, at the outset, then Arendt's political theory has hardly anything to offer to an understanding of contemporary problems of rightlessness and the struggles to which they give rise.[1]

This chapter works toward clarifying the notion of "politics" that orients the critical inquiry offered in this book, and it does that by rethinking and revising Arendt's controversial arguments about "the social." This is an important task, given that many critics have seen her critique of the Rights of Man as a perfect manifestation of her distaste for the politicization of social issues that are related to human needs. They highlight how modern democracy and the Rights of Man politicize problems such as poverty and blur the distinctions that Arendt draws between "public" and "private," "freedom" and "necessity," "political" and "social." Precisely because of this blurring, these scholars argue, Arendt criticizes the Rights of Man and holds on to a narrow understanding of politics that excludes many actors, issues, and problems from its scope.[2] These criticisms are very much at odds with the many contemporary accounts that draw on Arendt's work for the purpose of rethinking human rights in terms of a democratic politics centered on bottom-up practices of contesting existing forms of oppression, violence, and injustice.[3] However, these accounts have not fully responded to the deeply embedded skepticisms about some of the fundamental premises of Arendtian political theory, especially those regarding her conception of "the social."

In what follows, I suggest that, if we are going to rethink the politics of human rights along Arendtian lines, what is required is nothing less than a reading of Arendt *against* Arendt. Arendt's conceptual distinction between "political" and "social" reflects at times a desire to protect the public realm from the intrusion of actors and issues that are supposed to remain in the private realm. Yet several instances in her work defy this narrow and exclusionary understanding of politics. How do we explain, for example, her celebratory account of the early labor movement in *The Human Condition*? Or her critical remarks about the American revolutionaries' failure to address poverty? And perhaps even more strikingly, her positive statements about Marx as a theorist illuminating the violence of poverty? Grappling with such puzzling moves and attending to how they unsettle Arendt's political/social distinction can provide us with a new understanding of both terms.

According to this reading, "politics" does not denote a separate realm with its distinct set of issues and actors; instead, it encompasses practices of enacting freedom understood as the capacity to begin something new and interrupt processes that were taken to be automatic.[4] Hence, practices that contest the taken-for-granted meanings of "public" and "private," "freedom" and "necessity," or "political" and "social," and those that assert the possibility of intervening in processes that were assumed to be beyond the purview of human action are part and parcel of politics. Politics arises from such practices that enable "equalization" among human beings who are otherwise "different and unequal."[5] Equality does not exist prior to these practices as a characteristic inherent in human nature, in other words; it is these practices that institute a community of equals. Since any issue can be the subject of these practices, nothing can be categorically defined as "political" or "social" at the outset. What ultimately matters is *politicization*, which always involves inventive practices of translation that reconfigure the existing relations between "public" and "private," "freedom" and "necessity," "political" and "social."

If the lines between these categories are not fixed but politically contested, then "the social" denotes neither a separate realm with different issues or actors nor the undesirable intrusion of necessity into politics. It is instead a concept that alerts us to what might hinder our efforts to politicize challenging social issues related to human needs. Particularly troubling from an Arendtian standpoint is the tendency to handle these issues by subordinating politics to the dictates of administration and instrumental rationality. This tendency turns politics into a means to achieve specific ends and severs its connection with practices of enacting freedom and instituting equality. Just as problematic is the urge to approach social issues with a moralistic framework centered on compassion. As this framework aims to aid those who face injustice, it positions them as victims; as a result, it risks erasing their singularity and denying them equal standing. "The social," in its revised form, alerts us to how such antipolitical orientations can prevail in efforts to tackle problems of social injustice and undermine the possibilities of turning these problems into matters of common concern that affect equality and freedom.

This revised understanding of the relationship between "politics" and "the social" suggests that human rights do not simply represent the antithesis of politics from an Arendtian perspective. In fact, these rights can be crucial in practices of translation that are necessary to establish why problems such as shelter conditions in refugee camps, for example, can be addressed politically as matters concerning equality and freedom. However, in its new formulation, "the social" draws attention to what might thwart such politicization, and in response to this question, it invites a critical examination of the normative frameworks, administrative rationalities, and rhetorical moves that have come to shape certain forms of human rights advocacy. It urges us to inquire into, for example, the humanitarian tendency to mobilize a moral economy of compassion, which can end up undermining the political agency of subjects who are represented as suffering victims and get in the way of the very practices that are necessary for the continuous reinvention of human rights in response to new forms of injustice.

This chapter starts with Arendt's account of "the social" in *The Human Condition*, which delineates the modern processes that reduce politics to an administration of life's necessities. Highlighting the need to engage with the criticisms raised against this account, I then point to some of the perplexities that arise from Arendt's reflections on "the social" by turning to an interesting conversation that took place at a 1972 conference on her work. This conversation is quite important for my purposes, as it provides very concrete examples of the strong distinction that Arendt draws at times between "political" and "social" issues and then reveals how this distinction is constantly destabilized in her responses to the criticisms raised by her interlocutors. This dialogic encounter provides the starting point for my efforts to rearticulate the relationship between "politics" and "the social" along the lines suggested above. Arendt's account of "the rise of the social" in *The Human Condition*, I argue, needs to be read as a cautionary tale highlighting how a tendency to put politics in the service of administration and instrumental rationality can prevail in our efforts to attend to problems of social injustice. This tendency is neither inevitable nor irresistible, but it is a risk that we need to heed in such efforts.

The next section reexamines Arendt's account of the French Revolution and her treatment of "the social question" (e.g., poverty) in *On Revolution*. This account is taken by critics as the perfect example demonstrating her aversion to the politicization of socioeconomic issues, especially to the democratic struggles triggered by the discourse of the Rights of Man. Drawing attention to the conflicting claims and puzzling moves in the text, I offer a different interpretation. What is ultimately problematical for Arendt is not that the French revolutionaries politicized poverty but that they failed to do so. This failure arises from a profoundly anti-political approach to poverty: As the revolutionaries mobilized compassion, turned the poor into an undifferentiated mass of suffering victims, dispensed with politics as a laborious, uncertain, and inefficient process, and resorted to violence to immediately relieve suffering, they failed to institute conditions that could have enabled citizens to politically address poverty.

Rethinking Arendt's account of "the social" along these lines can shed light on some of the anti-political trajectories that human rights can take in the contemporary landscape. The third section turns to the recent convergence of human rights and humanitarianism to provide some examples: the rise of a compassionate humanitarianism that directs its gaze to suffering bodies and reduces human rights mainly to the basic necessities of life, the increasing tendency to treat challenging human rights problems as matters of humanitarian administration to be handled by experts in the management of populations, the emergence of a military humanitarianism that turns human rights into the rights of victims waiting to be saved from their abject misery. With these examples, I do not want to suggest that humanitarian mobilizations of human rights necessarily take anti-political trajectories. Contemporary humanitarianism is a complex, heterogeneous constellation incorporating a wide range of actors, organizations, practices, and policy frameworks, dedicated to the goal of alleviating suffering and saving human lives. Rethinking some elements of this constellation in light of the revised understanding of "the social" points to problematic tendencies that might end up reproducing conditions of rightlessness and get in the way of politicizing human rights in an Arendtian sense. This section provides concrete examples of the perplexities of human rights, especially those arising from the necessary but conflictual relationship between rights and the institutional orders established to guarantee them, without forgetting that these perplexities can be navigated differently, as discussed in the last chapter.

Finally, to explore how human rights can become political, I turn to Arendt's discussion of the early labor movement in *The Human Condition*. This discussion introduces us to subjects who refused to be passive victims, as they dared to vindicate their existing rights and demand new ones. The workers were able to inaugurate a new type of politics, Arendt's account suggests, as they appeared in public by taking political emancipation at its word, translated their problems into matters of common concern, forged new forms of solidarity, and reconfigured the distinctions between public and private, freedom and necessity, political and social. This example highlights that an Arendtian politics of human rights centers on the democratic agency of the very subjects who find themselves in a condition of rightlessness and yet take it upon themselves to contest that condition by bringing into view new understandings of equality and freedom. The chapter concludes that human rights cannot be simply reduced to anti-political and anti-democratic versions of humanitarianism, as some critics argue. The task of critical inquiry is to fully attend to the equivocal effects of human rights and carefully examine the wide range of discourses, practices, institutions, and norms that they are affiliated with to see if they empower or erode the possibilities of a politics that can turn challenging problems of injustice into common concerns that affect the active exercise of freedom and the ongoing institution of equality.

Unpacking and Unsettling "the Social"

Several readers of Arendt have drawn attention to her problematic conception of "the social," especially as developed in her most celebrated work of
political theory, *The Human Condition*. She provides in this work a detailed
account of "the rise of the social" as a modern development that introduces
the necessities of life into the public realm and reduces politics to an administration of these necessities. This modern condition is contrasted with the
ancient city-state and its clear distinctions between the public and private
realms, or the city (*polis*) and the household (*oikos*): In the city, Arendt
argues, the citizens were equals sharing the experience of freedom; there
was no domination in this public realm, since being free "meant neither to
rule nor to be ruled."[6] The household was the exact opposite of the city, as
it was meant to satisfy the "wants and needs" of human life and its "driving
force" was necessity.[7] Liberating oneself from necessity, which was the precondition for becoming a free citizen, entailed an exercise in mastery over
others, most notably slaves; force and violence, unacceptable in politics,
were justified in this private realm to achieve such pre-political liberation.[8]
Life in the city was the "good life," Arendt argues, drawing on Aristotle:

> It was "good" to the extent that by having mastered the necessities
> of sheer life, by being freed from labor and work, and by overcom-
> ing the innate urge of all living creatures for their own survival, it
> was no longer bound to the biological life process.[9]

Arendt sets this image of the ancient city-state in opposition to the
modern nation-state. The clear boundaries between the city and the household, public and private, freedom and necessity, political and biological
life—boundaries taken as "self-evident and axiomatic"—were gradually
blurred in this modern political form. Pre-political necessities of life
became subjects of nation-wide policies. The nation increasingly turned
into "one super-human family," as the modern state dedicated itself to
"collective house-keeping." Arendt invokes the term "political economy,"
which "would have been a contradiction in terms" for ancients, as a
paradigmatic example of this troubling development that collapsed the
distinctions between the household and the city.[10] "The rise of the social"
denotes the emergence of this "curiously hybrid realm where private
interests assume public significance."[11] Arendt takes this development

as a troubling one, as it "devour[s]" public, private, and even intimate life, turns politics into bureaucratic administration, and reinforces conformism in the name of equality. Political action is devalued in these "societies of laborers and jobholders," as it is no longer the "good life" of public glory that matters, to recall Arendt's invocation of Aristotle, but instead "the life process" with its concern for "sheer survival."[12]

For many readers, Arendt's idealization of the Athenian city-state leaves us with a problematic vision of politics that can maintain its purity only at the cost of violent exclusions. As Arendt holds on to the boundaries between the city and the household, her critics argue, she ends up defending the exclusion of slaves, women, resident aliens, and laborers as a necessary precondition for the public glories of free male citizens.[13] What is all the more problematic, for her critics and even for her more sympathetic readers, is her invocation of the ancient Greek city-state to disparage any modern attempt to politicize bodily issues, material concerns, and socioeconomic problems. Seeing politics as a realm endangered by the encroachments of social problems and demands, Arendt attempts to secure it as a "pristine" space for free citizens; yielding to the "impulse to purify" with her rigid, even "impermeable" distinctions, she ends up with a very narrow understanding of the public space as a realm emptied of any meaningful content.[14]

As I argue in chapter 4, reading *The Human Condition* as a glorification of the ancient city-state is problematic in many respects. But without going into how Arendt's phenomenological account of *vita activa* takes issue with the Greeks, it is important to address the concerns that critics raise about her problematic conception of "the social," which risks denouncing modern rights struggles. Arendt's statements that seem to portray the triumph of modern equality as another instance of conformism demanded by the society, for example, can be taken as a case in point: "[T]he victory of equality in the modern world is only the political and legal recognition of the fact that society has conquered the public realm."[15] When we add to this startling claim her very negative comments on the "admission of labor to public stature," or the "emancipation" of labor,[16] it is hard not to agree with several scholars who have argued that Arendt's critical remarks about the Rights of Man arise directly from her negative attitude toward the modern politicization of social issues. Jacques Rancière makes this argument quite powerfully when he suggests that Arendt criticizes the Rights of Man precisely because she associates them with modern democracy, which blurs the lines she wants to uphold between public and private, freedom and necessity, political and social.[17]

Criticisms targeting Arendt's political/social distinction have not been fully addressed by scholars who have drawn on her work to rethink human rights in terms of democratic, bottom-up practices of addressing challenging problems of injustice.[18] If Arendt's critics are right, her political theory would exclude from its scope most of these practices, especially if they invoke human rights in ways that dissolve the distinctions between public and private. We could include here, for example, rights struggles that politicize issues such as health, family, housing, or work. One possible solution to this problem, as Serena Parekh highlights, can be found in Arendt's essay, "Public Rights and Private Interests," which highlights that "public" and "private" rights are interdependent. But even this solution risks reintroducing the conceptual distinctions that critics want to challenge, when it affirms liberation from necessity, guaranteed by socioeconomic rights, as a pre-political condition for the public exercise of civil and political rights in spaces of freedom.[19] For critics such as Rancière, it is precisely the move to designate issues such as minimum wage as *prepolitical* that confines them to the realm of necessity in Arendtian political theory and hinders the recognition of many rights struggles as "political." Rancière's conclusion is shared by others who are drawn to Arendt's notion of a right to have rights, yet keep her account of "the social" at arm's length. Even if Arendt provides an insightful starting point for rethinking human rights, these scholars suggest, we need to turn to other thinkers to overcome the shortcomings of her political theory when it comes to politicization of issues and actors that she characterizes as "social."[20]

What is missing from this discussion, however, is the possibility of revisiting and revising "the social" in ways that can actually offer a much more nuanced understanding of how human rights relate to the democratic practices that many of these scholars affirm. Rethinking this concept and subjecting contemporary discourses of human rights to its critical gaze, as I discuss below, alerts us to the troubling possibility that not all mobilizations of these rights are political practices of founding freedom and equality; some of these might actually end up reinforcing rightlessness from an Arendtian perspective. In short, "the social," long reviled and repudiated, might have something important to contribute to our contemporary debates on how human rights can work not only as *politics* but also as *anti-politics*.[21]

This reading takes its starting point from scholarly accounts that draw attention to Arendt's multiple and not easily reconcilable uses of the term "social." Seyla Benhabib, for example, argues that Arendt uses the term in relation to capitalist economy, mass society, and sociability in civil society.[22] Hanna Pitkin's comprehensive analysis of Arendt's corpus adds more meanings to this list: conformism, modernization, markets and bureaucracies, generalization of laboring attitude, and poverty. "The social," Pitkin argues, is "a complex composite"; the concept is "internally incoherent, a conglomerate never brought to any satisfactory 'synthesis.'"[23] Richard Bernstein arrives at a similar conclusion when he alerts us to the "paradoxes and unstable tensions" in Arendt's thinking: "Indeed, the more we probe, the more we discover how her categorical distinction between the social and the political is unstable and reveals profound tensions."[24]

It is impossible to know which one of these is the definitive meaning that Arendt intended; but there may be something promising in the perplexities arising from these multiple, conflicting uses of the term. Perhaps it is possible to locate in these perplexities ways of *reading Arendt against Arendt*, using some invocations of "social" to contest others, destabilize her conceptual distinctions, and offer an Arendtian understanding of "politics" that can resist some of her most problematic moves and conclusions. I have in mind here a reading strategy that takes its starting point from the Socratic example discussed in the last chapter. To summarize briefly, Arendt's remarks on Socrates suggest that perplexities are not impasses or dead ends; as genuine dilemmas arising from the commonly held assumptions about everyday concepts, they can provoke critical inquiry, open up new ways of thinking, and enable judgment in the absence of yardsticks. Why not engage in such an aporetic inquiry to examine Arendt's concept of "the social"? If we were to treat Arendt's assumptions about "the rise of the social" and "the social question" as *doxai*, understood not as false illusions but instead as opinions "to which truth inevitably adhered," then inquiring into the perplexities of these assumptions can help us find out not only what is untenable but also what might be worth affirming.[25]

To begin to grapple with these perplexities, it is worth discussing at length an important exchange that Arendt had with the participants of a conference on her work in Toronto in November 1972. The exchange starts with a straightforward question that Mary McCarthy raises: What is left in politics once all the social issues are excluded? Arendt's response is quite interesting, as it reinscribes her private/public distinction in some respects, but not without unsettling it: "At all times people living together will have affairs that belong in the realm of the public—'are worthy to be talked about in public.' What these matters *are* at any historical *moment* is probably *utterly* different."[26] This seemingly straightforward response invokes "public" in two different senses of the term. First, Arendt uses the term to refer to a separate sphere or domain—"the realm of the public"— and that meaning risks reifying the public/private boundary as an ahistorical one. Yet, the second use of the term challenges the idea that the contents of that sphere are given at any time and suggests instead that any issue can become political if it is "talked about in public." This move opens up the possibility of resisting the idea that "the social" is a realm that should be kept separate from politics.

But Arendt's other responses at that conference seem to reaffirm her conceptual distinctions, with the effect of pushing certain issues outside the scope of politics. In response to Richard Bernstein, who suggests that it might no longer be possible to differentiate political issues from social ones, Arendt insists that there is still the possibility of making that distinction. Political issues, she suggests, are those that "we cannot figure out with certainty"; hence the need for public debate. Social issues, on the other hand, are those that "can really be figured out, in the sphere Engels called the administration of things."[27] This position is at odds with the refreshing possibility indicated by Arendt's response to McCarthy, as it risks endorsing a very ahistorical view that casts certain issues as necessarily administrative, hence "social." But when Albrecht Wellmer pushes the question further, challenging Arendt "to give one example in our time of a social problem which is not at the same time a political problem," pointing to specific examples such as education, health, urban problems, and living standards, Arendt offers another answer that blurs the lines and destabilizes the distinction. "With every one of these questions there is a double face," she argues; if we take the issue of housing, "whether this adequate housing means integration or not is *certainly* a political question," whereas "[t]here shouldn't be any debate about the question that everybody should have decent housing."[28]

This exchange with Wellmer is quite interesting for the purposes of clarifying what is untenable in Arendt's political/social distinction and what might be worthy of affirmation. On the one hand, the exchange seems to reassert the distinction in all its rigidity, dehistoricizing human needs and settling what is "political" in advance. That risk can be seen in Arendt's response to George Baird, who mentions the example of the British citizens refusing to move from the houses categorized as "inadequate" by the government and suggests that even issues that are administratively decided can be contested by the public:

> The political issue is that these people love their neighborhood and don't want to move, even if you give them one more bathroom. This is indeed entirely a debatable question, and a public issue, and should be decided publicly and not from above. But if it's a question of how many square feet every human being needs in order to be able to breathe and to live a decent life, this is something which we can really figure out.[29]

As rightly noted by several readers, Arendt's response does not resolve the problem satisfactorily because it takes human needs as self-evident and overlooks how our understanding of these needs can change over time.[30] There will always be administrative decisions about these needs, as can be seen, for example, in the international guidelines that stipulate the minimum floor space for a refugee shelter as 3.5 square meters (roughly 38 square feet) per person.[31] But as I discuss in chapter 4, these administrative decisions are constantly contested, and the response to the question of how many square feet a human being needs to live a decent life changes as a result of this *"politics of need interpretation."*[32] The exchange reveals that the political/social distinction, understood as a boundary designating separate spheres with different contents, is simply untenable, as each example Arendt gives to defend it reveals once more the arbitrariness of the line she draws and ends up destabilizing the distinction she wants to uphold.

However, Arendt's response to Wellmer can be read in a different way, especially by taking into account her response to McCarthy. The exchange makes clear that Arendt wants to resist Wellmer's position, which suggests that modern developments have rendered every social problem as necessarily political. In response to her interlocutors, she persistently reiterates the crucial importance of public debate for politics, and Wellmer's position, at least in the way it is formulated in that particular exchange, overlooks the importance of political practices that are required to transform any problem from a private issue into a public one. From an Arendtian perspective, nothing is immediately, inherently, or necessarily political; an issue can become political only as a result of mediatory practices that can represent it as a matter of common concern and foster its recognition as "a shared reality" that calls for concerted action.[33] Arendt's efforts to understand politics in terms of such practices can be used against her attempts to cast certain issues beyond the scope of public debate. Once we turn to her emphasis on the crucial importance of speech and action for establishing an issue as a public concern, the boundary between public and private, freedom and necessity, the city and the household becomes permeable and contestable.[34] Arendt's initial response to Mary McCarthy provides justification for this move; as that response indicates, the meaning of what is political changes over time, but not simply due to external factors. We can add, in an Arendtian vein, that equally important are the representative practices that take up issues formerly relegated to the private sphere and translate them into public concerns. Wellmer's position, as articulated in that brief exchange, is problematic not because it blurs the distinction between the public and private spheres—in fact, Arendt's own remarks unsettle that distinction throughout the exchange—but because it overlooks the importance of such representative practices that are necessary for the *politicization* of any issue.

Reading Arendt against Arendt, we can question her invocation of "the social" as an irreversible process of modernity bringing nothing but destruction or as a hybrid realm whose impurity endangers authentic politics. But such a reading also brings to view what is worth affirming in her critical account of "the social," as it highlights that the question is no longer what is political and what is not political but instead what *hinders politicization of an issue in any given context*. Once *The Human Condition* is reconsidered along these lines, it is no longer possible to uphold the distinctions that Arendt draws between public and private, freedom and necessity, the city and the household. But it is worth attending to her concerns about the rise of an administrative rationality that displaces political action and speech in favor of a bureaucratic rule unencumbered by accountability, perceives society as a uniform mass whose behavior can be studied in terms of statistical patterns and deviations, dedicates itself to the care of human life narrowly understood in terms of sheer survival, and turns politics into a means to be used in the management of populations.[35] This development makes it much more difficult to address problems such as poverty as matters of common concern demanding public deliberation and action; it turns them instead into matters of collective housekeeping to be handled by bureaucratic structures of governance. In its revised formulation, "the social" refers to "the absence of politics where politics belongs," to use Hanna Pitkin's terms; accordingly, it denotes a set of sensibilities, attitudes, orientations, and modes of conduct that are at odds with, and can even undermine, political practices of turning a specific issue into a common concern affecting freedom and equalization.[36] These sensibilities are not idiosyncratic choices of individuals or groups; as collectively shared orientations, they are significantly shaped by the institutions, norms, and discourses that generate and reinforce them.

This revised understanding of "the social" suggests that an Arendtian framework does not cast politics and human rights as necessarily antithetical (i.e., human rights as always anti-political); it is rather geared toward an analysis of what hinders us in understanding, and acting upon, these rights politically. Human rights can become *political* if and when they are invoked to create public spaces where those who are rendered rightless can appear and act in solidarity with others, translate their problems into common concerns, and participate in practices of founding and refounding equality and freedom. Human rights can become *anti-political* if and when they are invoked in ways that obliterate such possibilities and undermine "the capacity to form new relationships, new modes of relationship, [and] people's capacity to innovate institutional structures jointly."[37] Read in light of this interpretation, Arendt's account of the French Revolution and "the social question," as I discuss in the next section, provides insights into the anti-political trajectories that human rights can take.

The French Revolution and the Moral Economy of Compassion

If there is one work in Arendt's corpus that seems to reinforce the binary oppositions of political and social, freedom and necessity, public and private, it is *On Revolution*. This work appears to epitomize a narrow understanding of politics that insists on the need to protect the public space of freedom from the violent intrusions of the private realm of necessity. Arendt comes across as a staunch critic of the French Revolution, declaring that it could not help but end in terror given that the revolutionaries acted on the basis of a desire to solve "the social question" (i.e., poverty). This desire, she asserts, underlies the "transformation of the Rights of Man into the rights of Sans-Culottes,"[38] into the rights of those who are driven by their basic needs. Arendt seems to depict the problem of poverty, as well as the people suffering from it, as unfit for politics: Rage, vengeance, and violence characterize the entrance of the poor, with their urgent needs, in the public realm.[39] The lesson Arendt appears to draw from the violent trajectory of the French Revolution is that any attempt to politicize social problems is doomed to fail: "Nothing, we might say today, could be more obsolete than to attempt to liberate mankind from poverty by political means; nothing could be more futile and more dangerous."[40] She even suggests that it is better to leave social problems to expert administration since they defy political practices of persuasion and decision-making.[41] Among Arendt's works, *On Revolution* is probably the one that is most resistant to the alternative reading offered in the last section.

Yet, *On Revolution*, to use Hanna Pitkin's apt description, is "a profoundly incoherent book,"[42] and that incoherence is at times overlooked by Arendt's critics. Precisely because of this incoherence, it would be misleading to jump to a quick conclusion, "for what may initially seem straightforward and sharp," as Richard Bernstein reminds us, "is much more ambiguous, ambivalent, and even internally contradictory than is *prima facie* apparent."[43] In fact, it is the puzzling moves of the text that can guide us in rethinking Arendt's critique of the French Revolution and the Rights of Man.

One such puzzling move confronts us in Arendt's quite ambivalent discussion of Marx. On the one hand, she criticizes Marx as a theorist whose work embodies "the transformation of the Rights of Man into the rights of Sans-Culottes, the abdication of freedom before the dictate of necessity."[44] On the other hand, she also praises him for "interpret[ing] the compelling needs of mass poverty in political terms as an uprising, not for the sake of bread or wealth, but for the sake of freedom as well."[45] These statements represent two very different understandings of the relationship between politics and human needs. The first one suggests that problems such as poverty are bound to a law of necessity because of their origins in human needs, and it denounces attempts to politicize them as renunciations of freedom. The second statement, however, contests this view and suggests instead that human needs can be understood in political terms if their connection to freedom can be established.[46] In fact, Arendt applauds Marx as a theorist who shows that poverty is not a necessary and natural outcome due to a law of scarcity but a political phenomenon that results from "exploitation" or "expropriation by force."[47] Understood in these terms, poverty is a problem that violently denies freedom to the poor and demands to be confronted politically.

Arendt's positive remarks about Marx highlight once again that what is political and not political is not given in advance; a socioeconomic problem such as poverty can be politicized, though such politicization requires mediatory practices that can represent that problem as a shared concern demanding concerted action: "[I]t was necessary to translate economic conditions into political factors and to explain them in political terms."[48] It is important to note that Arendt describes Marx's representation of poverty as a practice of translation. Translation in this case does not indicate the mere transmission of content from one language to another; it instead entails the invention of a new language that depicts poverty in an entirely novel way, brings to view its origins in violence, and demonstrates that it is a problem that stands in the way of equalization and freedom.

A similar argument can be found in Arendt's critique of the American Revolution for failing to address poverty as a political problem. *On Revolution* is usually read as a historical account drawing a stark contrast between the French and American revolutions—a debunking critique of the former and a glorification of the latter.[49] Yet, if Arendt disapproves of the French for being driven by "the social question," or poverty, she also criticizes the Americans for their utter neglect of it. Far from justifying the exclusion of the poor from the political realm, she in fact insists that satisfaction of basic material needs and provision of negative liberties are not sufficient measures to tackle poverty.[50] The real challenge posed by poverty to any republican arrangement is that it relegates those who endure it into obscurity, invisibility, or darkness, as it denies them the possibility of actively participating in politics. Poverty then can be understood as a political problem, as an injustice that renders the lives of the poor "without consequence" and keeps them "excluded from the light of the public realm where excellence can shine."[51]

Recognizing the perplexities of *On Revolution* might be key to understanding not only the limits and problems of Arendt's account of "the social question" but also what might be "truthful" in it. What is worth attending to in this text, and what Arendt persistently and consistently defends (and not simply in *On Revolution*), is that, for any problem to become political, we need practices of translation that *represent* it as a common concern that is inseparably linked to the possibilities of founding freedom and equality in a political community. I develop this point by examining Arendt's critique of the French revolutionaries' approach to poverty and clarifying what kinds of orientations can undermine the politicization of issues and actors excluded from the public sphere.[52]

Arendt criticizes the French Revolution mainly because of the revolutionaries' anti-political approach to poverty as a problem that required swift, direct action, and if necessary, even violence. She targets the Jacobins, particularly Robespierre and Saint-Just, who mobilized a moral economy that invoked absolutes of "good" and "evil" and reduced politics to a means to end suffering. I use the term "moral economy," which is not in Arendt's text, to capture both the moralization of suffering by invoking absolutes and the instrumental calculations of expediency that such moralization utilizes in its assessment of politics.[53] Arendt's account reveals that both of these dimensions were at work in the French revolutionaries' approach to poverty. It was this moral economy that left no room for a political understanding of poverty and the Rights of Man, as it exclusively focused on the immediate need to reduce suffering, turned the poor into absolute victims and objects of compassion, and rendered political practices of deliberation and persuasion highly suspect and dispensable. In this sense, Arendt's account of "the social question" in *On Revolution* can be read not as a categorical rejection of the efforts to introduce challenging questions of human rights into politics but instead as a critical analysis of the anti-political approaches that can prevail in such efforts.

Arendt provides a detailed analysis of the moral economy at work in the Jacobin approach to poverty. Her analysis highlights how "virtue," understood as the capacity "to identify one's will with the will of the people," became the keystone of the policies enacted by revolutionaries.[54] When Robespierre seized power, he brought this passion for virtue to its culmination. He deified "the people," understood not as a multitude characterized by plurality but instead as an undifferentiated suffering mass, and elevated compassion for their suffering to "the rank of the supreme political passion and of the highest political virtue."[55] Poverty could have been approached politically as an injustice incompatible with the foundation of freedom, one that relegates those who endure it into obscurity and denies them the right to political participation, as highlighted earlier. Such a political approach, however, would require mediatory practices of translation, and French revolutionaries such as Robespierre and Saint-Just were suspicious of precisely these kinds of practices, according to Arendt. They turned instead to feelings and passions that were taken to be immediate and innate to unify the nation. Poverty seemed to indicate a gap between the objective conditions of the "people" on the one hand and their "representatives" on the other hand. Revolutionaries closed that gap by turning to compassion, or the capacity to feel the pain of those who are suffering.[56] In this reading, Arendt criticizes Robespierre and Saint-Just *not because they politicized poverty, but because they failed to do so.*

Arendt's account urges us to understand this failure in terms of a negative attitude toward practices associated with politics, or a refusal "to acknowledge the dignity of politics and to recognize an uncircumventable constitutive dimension in the plural existence of man," to use Miguel Abensour's words.[57] In the case of Saint-Just, for example, this refusal amounted to a desire for the revolution "to be accomplished without politics, even to be *opposed* to politics."[58] Political practices that rely on deliberation, persuasion, and contestation were displaced and denounced in the name of the moral goals of reforming conscience and eliminating self-interest. The moral economy of virtue eschewed a political approach, as it dedicated itself to the cause of immediately ending suffering by any means necessary. Once identification with the poor became the supreme virtue and eradication of suffering the absolute good, anything or anyone standing in the way was cast as the evil that needed to be obliterated. Politics, understood primarily in terms of violence, was seen as a means to be used in a war against the enemies of the nation.[59]

Read in this light, the lesson to be drawn from Arendt's account of "the social question" is not that the politicization of the Rights of Man necessarily ends in violence but instead that a moralistic approach to human suffering can easily turn into an instrumentalist understanding of politics as a means (if necessary, violent means) to achieve moral goals. This moral economy, *On Revolution* suggests, is neither inevitable nor irresistible in efforts to address human suffering; but such efforts need to be guarded against the danger of yielding to the demands of this moral economy, and as I discuss below, contemporary practices and institutions of human rights are not immune to this danger.

The problems of introducing a moralistic approach to politics are at the heart of Arendt's analysis of Melville's *Billy Budd* in her account of the French Revolution. As Melville puts it in his "Preface," and Arendt notes, the story strives to understand how a revolution aimed at the "rectification of the Old World's hereditary wrongs . . . became a wrongdoer, one more oppressive than the kings" and led to the Reign of Terror.[60] Melville's story particularly takes aim at the deification of the "natural" man as the representative of "absolute goodness" in the French revolutionary discourse. Billy Budd, who seems to represent this "natural" man— depicted in the story as unsophisticated, illiterate, uncivilized, almost like an animal, and yet remarkably beautiful and noble—ends up striking and killing Claggart, who falsely accused him of planning a mutiny on board. Billy Budd's violence, for Arendt, shows that "absolute goodness is hardly any less dangerous than absolute evil," because it resists being communicated by speech and is averse to political practices.[61] In fact, Billy Budd becomes speechless when Captain Vere asks him about Claggart's accusation; "goodness, because it is part of 'nature,' does not act meekly but asserts itself forcefully and, indeed, violently so that we are convinced."[62] Once Captain Vere intervenes in this conflict between "goodness beyond virtue" (Billy Budd) and "evil beyond vice" (Claggart), Arendt argues, the tragedy begins, as the law cannot simply side with "elemental goodness" and needs to punish its violence, even if it recognizes that "only the violence of this goodness is adequate to the depraved power of evil."[63] It is Captain Vere, after all, who tells the members of the court he summarily convenes to act practically and to "let not warm hearts betray heads that should be cool"; facts and laws, and not compassionate feelings or private conscience, should be the basis of a decision even in an exceptional case such as Billy Budd's.[64]

Arendt draws from the story the conclusion that introducing absolutes into politics "spells doom to everyone," as it paves the way for a cycle of violence by obliterating the possibilities of a politics centered on "predicative or argumentative speech," which is crucial for turning any issue into a common concern affecting freedom and equality among a community of actors.[65] She interprets the French revolutionaries' approach to the Rights of Man in line with that conclusion, and suggests that the Revolution gave way to the Reign of Terror because the revolutionaries invoked these rights as absolutes beyond politics and turned the subjects of these rights into suffering victims who needed to be defended by whatever means necessary.

Especially important in this regard are the destructive effects of compassion. According to Arendt, the French revolutionaries did exactly what Captain Vere forbids the officers in his court to do; they let "warm hearts," with their immediate passions, prevail. The revolutionaries reached out to the poor not on the basis of the political principle of solidarity, which could have created a community of equals among those coming from different classes of the society, but rather on the basis of pity, or a perverted form of compassion, marked by the capacity to feel the suffering of those who are not one's equals.[66] With its emphasis on affective identification, Arendt highlights, compassion works against political practices of articulating an issue as a common political concern. It demands immediacy and abolishes what she terms *inter-est*, or the "worldly space," "in-between," "interspace," which lies between people, simultaneously differentiating them from each other as distinct individuals and bringing them together around a common object, purpose, or interest.[67] Instead, compassionate selflessness achieves "a general human solidarization," which erases the differences among the actors involved and forges a homogenous community rooted in the innate capacity to suffer.[68]

Arendt argues that actions driven by compassion hardly ever attempt to change the conditions that produce and reproduce social injustice; they are mainly interested in the immediate relief of the suffering itself.[69] If compassion is ever mobilized in the service of such a radical transformation, however, it becomes an even more dangerous passion: Calling for "swift and direct action," it compels actors to dispense with political and legal processes and adopt violent means to achieve their goals.[70] Compassion appears in the public realm in its perverted form as pity. Because of its "vested interest" in misfortune and misery, pity revolves around the glorification of suffering, as can be seen in Robespierre's glorification of the poor.[71] Turning its gaze to "the boundless suffering of the multitude in their sheer overwhelming numbers," pity loses sight of the "singularity" of human beings, and as a result, it can easily become insensitive to the "specific suffering" of "particular persons" and even sacrifice them in the name of the cause it glorifies.[72]

Arendt's account of "the social question" highlights that such an anti-political approach to needs, suffering, and oppression does injustice to both those it aims to help and the rights it purports to defend. The rhetoric of compassion conjures a "spectacle" of suffering, which reduces "the people" to an undifferentiated mass waiting to be saved from their abject misery and erases the plurality arising from its divergent interests and voices.[73] What is lost is "the meaning of manyness, of the endless variety of a multitude whose majesty resided in its very plurality."[74] What is more, "the people" comes to be defined simply in terms of its suffering, misery, abjection, and misfortune—and not as the community of citizens capable of acting upon the problems that confront them: "[T]he men of the Revolution set out to emancipate the people not *qua* prospective citizens but *qua malheureux.*"[75] Arendt also emphasizes this point when she draws an analogy between Robespierre and Dostoevsky's Grand Inquisitor as two figures "attracted toward *les hommes faibles.*"[76] Both take compassion beyond its limits; if compassion is to be understood as "co-suffering," then it cannot be extended to the whole mankind. Grand Inquisitor embodies the problems of a compassion that has lost all singularity and become pity, for Arendt—a compassion that "had depersonalized the sufferers, lumped them together into an aggregate—the people *toujours malheureux*, the suffering masses, et cetera."[77]

This anti-political rhetoric also harms the rights it aims to protect. It conceives problems such as poverty very narrowly as suffering due to deprivation from basic necessities, and it aims at the immediate relief of suffering on the basis of that narrow understanding. Within this framework, rights lose their political import and come to be understood minimally. Arendt criticizes the French revolutionaries for adopting such an anti-political approach, which reduces the Rights of Man to the rights to "the necessities of life" or the rights to "food, dress, and the reproduction of the species."[78] This narrow understanding turns the Rights of Man into the rights of those who have nothing better to fall back upon in their abject misery. It dissociates rights from "the foundation of freedom" and limits their meaning to "the liberation of man from suffering."[79]

This reading casts Arendt's account of "the social question" in a new light and allows us to rethink the conception of "politics" at work in her critique of the Rights of Man. As mentioned earlier, readers who take Arendt's political/social distinction as a categorical one, demarcating two separate spheres with different contents, have suggested that her critique of the Rights of Man rests on her aversion to the politicization of social problems. According to this critique, Arendt fails to see the political efficacy of the Rights of Man. To remember Jacques Rancière's provocative formulation, discussed in the last chapter, she renders them "void," or reduces them to the rights of "the private, poor, unpoliticized individual."[80] Arendt's narrow understanding of the Rights of Man, which de-politicizes the problems, struggles, and actors that this modern discourse gives rise to, Rancière argues, is not unlike the more recent humanitarian understanding of human rights as "the rights of those who have no rights, the rights of bare human beings subjected to inhuman repression and inhuman conditions of existence."[81] The reading offered above, however, suggests that, far from de-politicizing the Rights of Man, Arendt's critique of "the social question" might actually alert us to what might hinder their politicization. In this reading, it is not Arendt who reduces the Rights of Man to "the rights of bare human beings," but instead the anti-political approach adopted by the revolutionaries who mobilized a moral economy that turned the poor into absolute victims; operated with a rhetoric of compassion that undermined the possibilities of politically deliberating questions of justice and focused instead on the immediate relief of narrowly construed suffering; and embraced an instrumentalist position that equated politics with means and justified violence in the name of a war between "elemental goodness" and "elemental evil." As several critics of contemporary humanitarianism, including Jacques Rancière, have pointed out, such an anti-political approach is at work in some contemporary invocations of human rights. The alternative reading of Arendt's account of "the social question" offered here can provide crucial insights into the problematic premises, moves, and effects of that anti-political approach.

Humanitarianism and the Risks of an Anti-Political Approach

To begin to inquire into some of the anti-political trajectories that human rights can take, it is worth reflecting briefly on a provocative statement that Arendt makes about the philanthropic organizations established to help the stateless: "The groups they formed, the declarations they issued, showed an uncanny similarity in language and composition to that of societies for the prevention of cruelty to animals."[82] Arendt does not say much about this "uncanny similarity," but what brings the two forms of advocacy together, from her perspective, is their focus on compassion, and this affect became a central part of our political and moral imagination beginning in the eighteenth century. Around this time, the scope of the moral community extended beyond the boundaries of insular communities, and one of the most important elements in this transformation was the growing recognition that others feel pain just as we do.[83] This recognition underlies the extension of moral community to all sentient beings, including animals. The assumption was that, although animals were not capable of reasoning or speaking, they shared with human beings the innate capacity to suffer.[84] This historical shift in our perception of animals needs to be situated within the context of the eighteenth-century rhetoric centered on compassion, which Arendt analyzes at length in *On Revolution*. Not surprisingly, advocacy organizations targeting animal cruelty emerged in the early nineteenth century, along with several other humanitarian efforts that mobilized compassion.[85]

The analogy that Arendt draws between organizations targeting animal cruelty and the early twentieth-century humanitarian efforts aimed at the protection of the stateless is illuminating when trying to understand the anti-political effects of this rhetoric of compassion. Driven by the goal of immediate relief of suffering, both types of efforts construed the problem at stake very narrowly and overlooked broader questions of justice. As with animals, human beings in need, including the stateless, were depicted as speechless victims who needed to be protected from cruelty and provided necessary sustenance. The stateless were not citizens; deprived of the political capacity to enact their rights, and perishing in abject misery, they were in need of our compassion. The language of philanthropic organizations working on human rights was troublesome for Arendt, precisely because it centered on compassionate obligation to reduce suffering, and, as such, undermined the political possibility of understanding human rights as a right to have rights, or a right to action and speech. "[T]he uncertain sentiments of professional idealists" turned rights into objects of charity and rendered the subjects of those rights extremely precarious, as always dependent on the generosity and goodwill of compassionate others.[86]

This kind of humanitarian approach to suffering also erases the possibility of constituting a community of equals between those who are relegated to a condition of rightlessness and those who see in their condition nothing but abject misery. It extends the boundaries of the moral community, yet it does that only by defining rights and needs in terms of a bare minimum. This anti-political attitude, Arendt's analysis suggests, does not leave any room for articulating the human rights of those who are stateless as *inter-est*, or as a common concern that brings together individuals without erasing their distinctiveness. Indeed, far from establishing human rights as a common political concern, the anti-political rhetoric of compassion transforms them into the rights of helpless victims, or into "a kind of additional law, a right of exception necessary for those who had nothing better to fall back upon."[87]

At the time Arendt wrote her analysis, humanitarianism did not have the power and legitimacy that it currently has, but her caution against compassion becomes all the more relevant given that we have seen an increasing convergence of human rights and humanitarianism since the 1990s. One of the most troubling effects of this convergence has been an increasing tendency to reframe challenging questions of injustice as problems of suffering based on a narrow understanding of human rights as "the minimum conditions for any kind of life at all."[88] In this rendering, human rights risk losing their democratic dimension as political claims articulated by those who are denied these rights to contest existing forms of injustice, including those that cannot be reduced to "minimum conditions" of life; instead, they come to be understood as the bare essentials of victims who need compassionate others to survive. In what follows, I briefly discuss three examples from contemporary humanitarianism in order to highlight some of the anti-political trajectories that human rights can take, especially when they are invoked within the bounds of a moral economy centered on suffering bodies, of an administrative rationality directed at the management of populations, and of an interventionist discourse justifying military force. These trajectories are not inescapable given the recent convergence of human rights and humanitarianism, but they are quite powerful tendencies that we need to be cautious about in view of this development.

The first example relates to the mobilization of compassion in various humanitarian efforts to respond to refugee crises around the world. As Liisa Malkki highlights, there is a humanitarian tendency to depict refugees as helpless, speechless victims who can be lumped together in an "imagined sea of humanity," which makes it impossible for the spectators of suffering to recognize the singularity of each refugee.[89] Even the pictures that represent refugees as individuals or in small groups have a tendency to render them anonymous and interchangeable as victims in need. To be able to stand as an individual with a name, the refugee has to have an exceptional achievement—a troubling fact that is highlighted by the United Nations High Commissioner for Refugees (UNHCR)'s list of "refugees who have made a difference," which includes Chinua Achebe, Béla Bartók, Albert Einstein, and Marlene Dietrich, among others.[90] This well-intentioned list aims at changing negative perceptions about refugees, but it inadvertently ends up reaffirming Arendt's sardonic statement that only the recognition of being a genius can rescue the stateless from anonymity: "[T]he chances of the famous refugee are improved just as a dog with a name has a better chance to survive than a stray dog who is just a dog in general."[91] Leaving aside these exceptional cases, compassionate humanitarianism often expects us to relate to the nameless refugees as sentient beings whose pain we can feel when we identify with them in terms of a bare humanity.

Arendt's account of compassion provides critical insights into how this kind of humanitarianism does injustice to both the people that it aims to protect and the rights that it supposedly upholds. Similar to the case in the Jacobin approach to poverty, this new moral economy of compassion erases the equality and singularity of the subjects it aims to help and turns them into suffering masses; they become the contemporary figures of *les hommes faibles.* In addition, Arendt's account draws our attention to how this humanitarian approach can end up with a very anti-political understanding of human rights. Narrowly focused on the immediate relief of suffering, it risks turning human rights into the rights to bare necessities of life, severing their connection to political freedom. In fact, as Guglielmo Verdirame and Barbara Harrell-Bond highlight in their account of refugee camps, this anti-political humanitarianism can even set aside rights altogether and embrace instead a "full-belly theory," which works with the assumption that "rights and legal protections are pointless for 'starving' refugees."[92] Such a compassionate humanitarianism can end up reproducing the very condition of rightlessness that it aims to redress, especially when it undermines refugees' efforts to create spaces where they can appear in their singularity and articulate their needs and demands.

If this first example highlights how compassion operates as a moral economy mobilized in response to humanitarian emergencies across the world, the second illustrates how this affect has come to play a crucial role in humanitarianism as a form of governmentality involved in the maintenance and management of persons and populations.[93] Humanitarianism has conventionally been understood as the desire to alleviate the suffering of distant others; in this sense, it has been involved in the administration of life in the global South since its early origins. One important development in recent years has been the introduction of a compassionate humanitarianism to deal with the challenging questions of injustice, including poverty, homelessness, and unemployment, in the global North; we might call this perhaps the "boomerang effect" of overseas humanitarianism in the spirit of Arendt's argument about imperialism, mentioned in the last chapter. This trend has also affected how asylum and immigration have been managed. There is now a "humanitarianization of asylum," to use Didier Fassin's phrase; since it has become increasingly difficult to claim asylum on the basis of political persecution due to restrictionist asylum policies, the suffering bodies of asylum seekers have turned into grounds for claiming rights.[94] Refugee status is now given mainly to those who can demonstrate that their suffering deserves exceptional consideration, and in many cases, that suffering has come to be understood primarily as life-endangering sickness—a development that puts asylum seekers in an extremely precarious situation, as I discuss at length in the next chapter.

It is worth remembering at this point some of the concerns that Arendt raises about the modern valorization of life as the "highest good" or "ultimate point of reference" in *The Human Condition*.[95] For Arendt, this modern attention to life comes at the expense of a narrow understanding of the human condition, one that overlooks the diverse range of human capacities, activities, needs, and interests and is concerned almost exclusively with the life process and sheer survival. The contemporary humanitarian focus on suffering bodies risks subscribing to a similar understanding of the human condition and severs the connections of human rights to a democratic politics that is centered on practices of actualizing equality and freedom and that demands the active involvement of subjects whose rights are at stake. This anti-political turn is not only due to the inclination to understand human rights as minimum conditions of life but also the movement toward handling challenging problems of injustice within the framework of an administrative rationality that turns politics into a means in the management of populations. These tendencies risk displacing democratic practices of debating, translating, and representing human needs, and as I discuss in the next chapter, they can even end up drowning the claims, reasons, and narratives of those who invoke human rights to contest their condition of rightlessness. A humanitarian framework that turns its gaze to suffering bodies is much more likely to privilege the experts who are ready to provide information about the suffering in question. Under these conditions, it is no longer the testimony of the asylum seeker that serves as the basis of a claim to rights, for example, but instead the statistics provided by the medical expert about the availability of HIV-medication in the asylum seeker's home country.

My final example of the contemporary convergence of humanitarianism and human rights brings to view the dangers of mobilizing compassion in more ambitious projects that "[set] out to change worldly conditions in order to ease human suffering."[96] These dangers have become especially visible in the past two decades with the emergence of an interventionist discourse that puts human rights in the service of a military humanitarianism. As many scholars highlight, this recent development marks an important turning point. For most of twentieth century, humanitarianism was mainly guided by a "medical ethic" centered on the immediate needs of the suffering body and the urgency of rescue.[97] The priority of the humanitarian workers was to create a space free of political conflict; advocating neutrality and impartiality, they were adamant about demonstrating their independence from states and political ideologies. To achieve these goals, early humanitarianism limited its framework to charity and stayed away from broader questions of justice that would necessitate an engagement with the underlying causes of suffering and conflict.[98] After the end of the Cold War, however, humanitarianism started to change and compassion came to be mobilized to justify more interventionist strategies that aimed at not simply alleviating and minimizing suffering but also preventing it.[99] Within this context, humanitarianism has increasingly resorted to the language of human rights to maintain its impartiality and to justify its new actions, including the use of violence.[100]

This turn to violence reaffirms Arendt's suspicion that compassion, put in the service of a moral economy working with absolutes, can actually end up obliterating the possibilities of politically addressing the conditions of suffering. If compassion "sets out to change" the conditions that create and aggravate suffering, Arendt notes, it will "shun the drawn-out wearisome processes of persuasion, negotiation, and compromise" and "claim for swift and direct action, that is, for action with the means of violence."[101] This problem surfaces in the humanitarian call for "political will" in response to human rights crises, which, as Bronwyn Leebaw argues, "often seems to reduce politics to a kind of force that would be needed to realize pre-existing norms without the limitations of conflict, deliberation, or compromise."[102] Compassionate humanitarianism risks turning human rights into these pre-existing norms, which are assumed to be self-evident and hence beyond debate as the minimum conditions of life; it demonstrates a propensity to treat politics as a means, if necessary violent means, to be used in the defense of these norms that are taken to be absolute.

Rethinking contemporary humanitarianism in light of the revised understanding of "social" in Arendt's works also reveals some striking similarities between her criticisms of the anti-political approach to human rights and the arguments made by one of her staunchest critics, Jacques Rancière. Of particular interest is Arendt's suggestion that compassion can turn out to be crueler than cruelty once it is put in the service of an absolute virtue and attempts to change the worldly conditions that sustain misery.[103] An absolute stands in the way of the political practices of argumentation because of its irresistible power to compel, and it creates assent forcefully when needed. If we remember Arendt's analysis of Melville's *Billy Budd*, "absolute goodness" does not leave any room for speech.[104] Similar concerns have been raised recently by Rancière in relation to the rise of a military humanitarianism that works with a dichotomous conception of good/evil and transforms human rights into "the rights of the *absolute* victim," or the rights of those who are the victims of "an absolute evil."[105] Rancière criticizes this particular humanitarianism for its obliteration of the "dis-sensual stage" or "the political space"—terms that recall Arendt's notion of "*inter-est*," or the worldly in-between—where the Rights of Man can give rise to democratic possibilities as they are claimed and exercised by the very subjects who are denied these rights.[106] Rancière argues that such pos-sibilities are undermined by an anti-democratic approach to the Rights of Man, which turns them into "the rights of others," or "humanitarian rights, the rights of those who cannot enact them, the victims of the abso-lute denial of right."[107] Arendt's critique of the international attempts that end up turning the Rights of Man into the rights of those who have noth-ing else to fall back upon does not suggest that she takes the Rights of Man to be simply "void"—one of the contentious claims in Rancière's critique. Instead, it indicates that these rights are bereft of their democratic possi-bilities when they are severed from and invoked against politics.[108]

Rethinking Arendt's notion of "the social" by wrestling with the per-plexities arising from its multiple meanings offers crucial insights into how human rights can take anti-political trajectories. This rethinking can also help us understand *politics* of human rights in a new light. In her analysis of the French Revolution, Arendt points to an alternative to the anti-political approach to the Rights of Man, as she sets solidarity against compassion and pity. Solidarity is neither a passion like compassion nor a sentiment like pity; it is instead a political principle that animates action.[109] It can be aroused by suffering, but it is not guided and consumed by it. Whereas compassion and pity demand immediacy and do not allow think-ing and acting in terms that are more general, solidarity can organize people around seemingly "cold and abstract" notions such as the "dignity of man."[110] Arendt's discussion of solidarity indicates that we can act upon human rights in ways that open possibilities of establishing a com-munity of equals who are bound by a common interest without losing their singularity. In what follows, I explore this political possibility by examining Arendt's discussion of the early labor movement in *The Human Condition*.

The Labor Movement and the Politics of Human Rights

Arendt's glorifying account of the labor movement in *The Human Condi-tion* is puzzling given her characterization of labor as a "somatic experi-ence" ruled by the biological needs and rhythm of the human metabo-lism.[111] In chapter 4, I question the conventional readings of this work, especially the tendency to cast labor as a not fully human activity, but for present purposes, it is important to note Arendt's negative attitude toward the "sociability" associated with the laboring activity. She insists that this collective dimension is not to be understood in political terms, as it turns laborers into an anonymous mass deprived of "all awareness of individuality and identity" and rests "not on equality but on sameness."[112] Arendt's negative characterization of labor becomes even more evident in her statement that "[t]he incapacity of *animal laborans* for distinction and hence for action and speech seems to be confirmed by the striking absence of serious slave rebellions in ancient and modern times."[113] But immediately after this scathing critique, we see a puzzling claim:

> From the revolutions of 1848 to the Hungarian revolution of 1956, the European working class, by virtue of being the only organized and hence the leading section of the people, has written one of the most glorious and probably the most promising chapter of recent history.[114]

The passage is puzzling mainly because of its contrast with Arendt's arguments about the laboring activity and *animal laborans*. Her account of the labor movement deserves attention also because it points to the possibility of politicizing issues of social justice as common concerns affecting freedom and equalization. Particularly striking in her account is the crucial importance she attributes to the dynamic introduced by modern equality, especially political emancipation, in creating possibilities of such politicization. Accordingly, Arendt's reflections on the labor movement call attention to how rights (including human rights), as inscriptions of equality, can enable, support, and engender politics in an Arendtian sense (i.e., as an activity that centers on freedom, or the capacity to initiate new beginnings, and involves the equalization of actors whose equality is not naturally given).

To understand how a social issue can be politicized as an *inter-est* that can "relate and bind" different actors, it is worth attending to the distinction that Arendt draws between the labor movement and the trade unions.[115] Some commentators see this distinction as another iteration of her efforts to exclude "social" issues from the public realm and criticize her for downplaying the importance of socioeconomic demands in the labor movement.[116] But given that both the labor movement and the trade unions made socioeconomic demands, the difference lies elsewhere: that is, in *how* they made these demands. If we remember Arendt's reflections on poverty, politicization of any social injustice involves a *translation* that can represent it as a shared problem that hinders equalization and freedom among a community of actors. In the case of the trade unions, there was no such translation: They remained interest groups approaching politics in instrumentalist terms as a means to achieve specific ends. In a way, the trade unions were representative of an anti-political approach to social questions, as they allowed the urgency of the problem to give rise to an expedient attitude that closed off the possibility of representing it as a matter of common concern. The labor movement was extraordinary, according to Arendt, precisely because it forged a political approach that inventively tied together questions of economic justice, social change, and democratic government. Its power arose from the fact that it defended its "economic interests" by fighting "a full-fledged political battle."[117] This is why Arendt claims that the difference between the trade unions and the labor movement was not "a matter of extreme social and economic demands but solely of the proposition of a new government."[118]

This last point is important for understanding the translation at work in the politicization of "social" demands. One possible way to understand that translation is a move from a more particularistic plane confined to narrow self-interest to a more universal one defined by general principles.[119] After all, Arendt highlights how the labor movement succeeded in appealing beyond the members of the working class to the political community at large by establishing connections between economic injustice and democratic government. But it is important to note that the translation that makes this broader appeal possible does not only indicate a move from a narrow, particularistic, private plane to a broad, general, public one; more importantly, it involves a radical transformation of what we take to be narrow, particular, and private and what we take to be broad, general, and public. That revolutionary dimension differentiates the labor movement, for Arendt, from the trade unions and political parties that claimed to represent the working class and their socioeconomic interests, but always within the confines of the existing social and political system, failing to make any attempt at "a transformation of society together with a transformation of the political institutions in which this society was represented."[120]

What kind of a political and social transformation is at stake here? In what sense is it revolutionary? And how was it possible for the workers to engage in such transformation given what Arendt tells us about the laboring activity? We can begin to address these questions only if we rethink *animal laborans* as a concept referring not to the working class or an individual worker,[121] but instead, in line with the analysis of "the social question" offered above, to a set of anti-political orientations instilled by a social order in which the worker is isolated from all others in the laboring activity—isolated even when that activity is undertaken with others, since even then the worker "meets others *qua* worker only."[122] In this social order, each laborer is assigned a particular task and absorbed in the laboring activity. This system, resting on the proper functioning of laboring bodies, does not allow "association and communication," in which the workers can recognize each other as equal and distinct beings.[123] The labor movement challenged the underlying presuppositions and organizing principles of such a social order that reduced workers to laboring metabolisms. And it did that not only by proposing a new form of democratic government in which equalization in politics was unimaginable without social justice but also by turning workers into political actors. In other words, what is at stake is politicization of not only issues but also actors.

But given that the laboring activity is so isolating and makes any association or communication impossible, how was it possible for workers to become political? In a departure from various possible explanations that could have referred to the crises of capitalism or the role of working-class culture, Arendt's account draws attention to a modern political development and its unforeseeable effects: The "apparently flagrant discrepancy" between the isolated, repetitive, homogenizing, and anti-political aspects of the laboring activity and the political innovations of the labor movement, she argues, "is likely to disappear" once we take into account the unpredictable effects of the political emancipation of workers.[124] Arendt's positive assessment of modern equality in a brief, and often overlooked, discussion warrants a close reading since it highlights that modern rights introduce a political dynamic with indeterminable effects.

To point out the importance of political emancipation, Arendt underscores the difference between slave labor and modern, free labor. The difference is not simply that the slave lacks "personal freedom," she argues, but that the modern worker "is admitted to the political realm and fully emancipated as a citizen."[125] This modern development, starting with "the abolition of property qualifications for the right to vote," is crucial, as it sets the modern worker apart from even the emancipated slave, whose status is similar to that of resident aliens, not citizens.[126] In contrast with a conventional Marxian analysis that would have highlighted the illusory nature of this political emancipation by pointing to the socioeconomic inequalities it disguises, Arendt draws attention to its "important side effects."[127] Her argument about political emancipation suggests that rights are not simply paper claims or deceptive traps; their recognition can set in motion a dynamic that cannot be completely controlled by the constitutional order that recognizes and grants them.

One of the unpredictable effects of political emancipation is that "a whole new segment of the population was more or less suddenly admitted to the public realm, that is, *appeared* in public."[128] More than anything else, it is this public appearance that is crucial to the politicization of modern workers. What makes that appearance even more striking and potent is that it involves the taking of the public stage by subjects that are not assimilated into the society.[129] This disruptive, radically transformative power of public appearance by those who are seen as outcasts is at the forefront of Arendt's two other examples in this section. In a footnote, Arendt reflects on "an anecdote, reported by Seneca from imperial Rome" to "illustrate how dangerous mere appearance in public was thought to be."[130] The anecdote relates to a proposal to establish a uniform dress code for slaves to distinguish them more easily from citizens; the senate rejected the proposal, Arendt argues, precisely because of the power of public appearance: "The proposition was turned down as too dangerous, since the slaves would now be able to recognize each other and become aware of their potential power."[131] Arendt's other example also highlights the crucial role of public appearance for politicization of subjects who are seen as social outcasts:

> "[L]aborers, when they entered the scene of history, felt it necessary to adopt a costume of their own, the *sans-culotte*, from which, during the French Revolution, they even derived their name. By this costume they won a distinction of their own, and the distinction was directed against all others."[132]

It is striking that Rancière does not even mention Arendt's account of the labor movement, which anticipates some of his arguments about politics. For Rancière, politics denotes the disruption of the "police" order that allocates individuals and groups to particular functions corresponding to their "nature" and assigns them to places according to these functions.[133] As discussed earlier, Arendt seems to be reproducing the kind of "policing" that Rancière's politics takes issue with when she uses the conceptual distinctions between public and private, freedom and necessity, political and social almost as ontological, unchanging truths about the human condition. However, we have also seen that this ontologization is at odds with, and constantly undermined by, Arendt's understanding of politics. Her discussion of the labor movement is a perfect example of the untenability of these distinctions as binary oppositions. In this case, we are confronted with a social order that attempts to turn workers into laboring bodies, defining them exclusively in terms of their functions in the workplace and "level[ing] them down to the mere instinct for survival and subsistence," to use Rancière's words.[134] Refusing to be reduced to *animal laborans*, Arendt's account highlights, these workers create spaces of appearance, become visible in public with their actions, and propose a new form of government. These activities involve "political subjectification," in Rancière's sense, as they require questioning and disowning previously naturalized identities, functions, positions, and roles.[135] In addition, they entail practices of translation that can transform what was taken to be a private matter into a common concern. In this regard, Rancière, not unlike Arendt, highlights the crucial importance of building connections between things that are not seen as logically related (e.g., juxtaposing inscriptions of equality in rights declarations with the injustice of long work hours).[136]

An even more interesting comparison with Rancière's notion of subjectification is Arendt's argument that this public appearance was one of the "important side effects" of the political emancipation of workers. Departing from Marxian theorists who criticized the declarations of rights as mere formalism, Rancière has persistently emphasized the political efficacy of these seemingly "idealistic and fleeting inscriptions," which can be put into use by subjects to demonstrate a common world established on the basis of the equality of speaking beings.[137] Similarly, Arendt's account of the labor movement draws attention to the political efficacy of emancipation and citizenship rights, which created the possibility of occupying the public space for workers.

Finally, from the perspectives of both Arendt and Rancière, the labor movement deserves praise for its refusal to accept the position of a special interest group seeking the resolution of its problems within the existing configuration of the system. For Arendt, the labor movement was "the only organization in which men acted and spoke *qua* men—and not *qua* members of society."[138] This remark, which is often taken to be another example of Arendt's political/social distinction, achieves a new meaning when we read it alongside Rancière's understanding of "police" as a social order that assigns specific functions, places, and ways of being to individuals and groups. The labor movement refused to speak on the basis of the identity, position, or role allocated to it; instead, it "had the audacity to identify itself with the whole of the community."[139] It was able to do that precisely by engaging in speech acts that established a common stage, forging connections between things that were seen as unrelated, and demonstrating that the injustice inflicted on wokers required nothing less than a reconfiguration of the existing order.

Drawing attention to how modern rights can give rise to such possibilities of transformation, Arendt's political theory urges us to resist the problematic conclusion that these seemingly abstract and formalistic formulations of equality are simply null and void. Instead, it invites a careful examination of how these rights can turn democratic politics into "the theatre of a contestation," to use Claude Lefort's terms, allowing individuals and groups to articulate new demands.[140] In chapter 5, as I turn to the struggles of *sans-papiers*, migrants who found themselves in irregular status due to French immigration laws that became increasingly restrictionist since the 1990s, I provide an in-depth discussion of an Arendtian politics of human rights. Similar to workers, *sans-papiers* translated their plight of rightlessness into an *inter-est* that relates and binds a community of actors, and they did that by engaging in inventive practices such as coining a name that evokes the memories of *sans-culottes*. Appropriating the French revolutionary discourse of the Rights of Man and insisting on that discourse as an inscription of equality, they strived to vindicate their rights and demand new ones. Their struggles, proposing new understandings of equality and freedom, highlight how human rights can be crucial to the politicization of issues and actors relegated to invisibility.

Human rights have been at the center of a heated debate, particularly due to their normative and institutional ascendency, since the 1990s, and an Arendtian perspective can make a crucial intervention in this ongoing debate on the political effects of human rights. For some, the rise of human rights is a welcome development inaugurating a new form of *politics* that places normative setbacks on sovereign power and gives voice to victims of oppression.[141] Several scholars have argued that human rights understood as "principled ideas," or normative beliefs about right and wrong, present a new understanding of legitimate statehood that centers on the protection of individual rights.[142] According to these accounts, human rights discourse introduces the idea that a state does not have exclusive authority when it comes to the fundamental rights of its residents. In this new landscape, it is no longer simply material state interests and military might that matter; new forms of transnational activism establish a "global civil society" that is increasingly shaped by practices of deliberation and persuasion.[143]

For many others, however, human rights discourse introduces new forms of power, hegemony, domination, and violence, and it amounts to nothing less than an *anti-politics* undermining democratic practices and institutions. Drawing attention to how rights discourse reconfigures freedom as a relationship between the individual rights holder and the state, several critics argue that human rights do not constrain sovereign power but instead reinforce it. To the extent that expanding the scope of rights also ends up expanding the scope of state power by allowing it to have control over every minute detail of our lives, global proliferation of human rights should be seen as an alarming development, according to these critics.[144] Equally troubling for many are the ways in which human rights discourse, despite its claims to be above and beyond politics, works as a new form of power. Critics highlight, for example, the new subject positions created by this discourse, which establishes hierarchical relations between different individuals, groups, and states, positioning some as passive victims in need and others as heroic saviors.[145] The non-governmental actors, celebrated for their transnational activism, these critics argue, are culpable in sustaining this new world order that prepares the ground for military interventions justified by states invoking the discourse of human rights.[146] Emphasizing that human rights discourse has been tainted as a result of its mobilization in the service of various forms of power, some critics call for devoting our energies to inventing new languages of emancipatory politics and supporting different international justice projects.[147]

Rethinking Arendt's conceptualization of "the social" suggests that both of these positions are problematic to the extent that they fail to fully come to terms with the *multiple, contingent, and equivocal* effects of human rights as a discourse pervaded by perplexities. This reading urges us to think more carefully about what we mean by politics and anti-politics (or politicization and de-politicization) as we invoke these terms in debates on human rights. "The social," in its revised form, draws attention to the anti-political trajectories that human rights can take when they are deployed in conjunction with a moral economy centered on compassion, an administrative rationality directed at the management of populations, and an interventionist discourse relying on military force. These anti-political trajectories have proliferated as a result of the contemporary convergence of human rights and humanitarianism, as I highlighted in this chapter, but they are neither inevitable nor irresistible given this convergence, and there are sincere efforts to counter them even within humanitarian circles. To conclude from this contemporary conjuncture that human rights discourse is irredeemably tainted by its associations with various forms of power would be problematic, however, not simply because it would neglect these ongoing efforts. That move would also overlook how human rights can become political in various struggles that turn challenging problems of injustice into matters of common concern, expose the violent exclusions of existing institutional orders (including those established to protect rights), and propose new understandings of equality and freedom. From an Arendtian perspective, instead of seeking some kind of "oppositional purity" in human rights, or any other emancipatory project, there is a need to come to terms with the equivocal effects of human rights as a "scandalously impure" discourse.[148] Understood in these terms, it is by no means certain that a particular mobilization of human rights will enable or hinder the political practices that are necessary to guarantee and reinvent equality and freedom, and it is precisely this uncertainty that demands a critical inquiry of existing human rights practices, institutions, and norms.[149]

This argument follows from the last chapter, which highlighted how a critical inquiry, developed along Arendtian lines, grapples with the perplexities of human rights in ways attending to their *multiple, contingent, and equivocal* effects in modern political history. In line with that conclusion, this chapter cautions against celebrating human rights as a new form of emancipatory politics as well as condemning these rights merely as anti-political tools of violence and oppression. Instead, it underscores the need to carefully examine how and when human rights can take political or anti-political trajectories. As I demonstrate in the next three chapters, this Arendtian understanding of human rights can provide us with a more informed understanding of the rightlessness and rights struggles of asylum seekers, refugees, and undocumented immigrants.

3.
Borders of Personhood

They live in camps surrounded by razor barbed wire. They tie plastic garbage bags to the sides of the building to keep the rain out. They sleep on cots and hang sheets to create some semblance of privacy. They are guarded by the military and are not permitted to leave the camp, except under military escort. The Haitian detainees have been subjected to predawn military sweeps as they sleep by as many as 400 soldiers dressed in full riot gear. They are confined like prisoners and are subject to detention in the brig without a hearing for camp rule infractions.[1]

THESE were the words used by the US District Court Judge Sterling Johnson Jr. to describe the living conditions of migrants in Guantánamo Bay in his 1993 ruling declaring their detention in camps unconstitutional—a ruling vacated by the Supreme Court's later review of the case. Long before Guantánamo made the headlines with the US government's indefinite detention of "enemy combatants," it was used as a "safe haven" or "shelter" for migrants from Haiti and Cuba. The US Coast Guard would capture these migrants on the high seas before they could reach the United States and send them to the US Naval Base in Guantánamo Bay to determine whether they had a credible fear of persecution and qualified for asylum.[2] Those who had a credible fear and tested negative for HIV would be sent as refugees to the United States. Those who qualified for refugee status but were HIV-positive were kept on the island as a threat to public health, isolated from others in a detention center called "Camp Bulkeley."[3] And those who could not establish a credible claim were forcefully returned to their countries of origin. Camp X-Ray, which became one of the most infamous symbols of the War on Terror following the publication of photos of detainees in orange jumpsuits, was first established in 1994 for Cuban refugees who "posed serious and documented threats"; these refugees were "held indefinitely in open air cages in order to 'avoid a breakdown or disruption of law, order and discipline in the camps.'"[4]

The story of the migrants held in Guantánamo Bay highlights how the legal standing of certain subjects can be unmade to the effect of putting them "outside the pale of the law," to use Arendt's terms:[5] Whereas the asylum seekers processed in the United States did have a right to independent review of their primary refugee determination, the asylum seekers held in Guantánamo Bay enjoyed no such right. In addition, the asylum seekers processed in the United States had a right to a lawyer present during their interviews; it was much more difficult for asylum seekers in Guantánamo Bay to enjoy this right to legal representation, as their lawyers were at times denied entry to the naval base.[6] When a group of human rights lawyers and law students brought a case challenging the legality of the US policy of interdicting migrants on the high seas and detaining them in Guantánamo without access to legal counsel, the US government responded in ways that foreshadowed the arguments it presented later in defense of the indefinite detention of "enemy combatants." The Justice Department argued that, since the naval base was not within the territorial jurisdiction of the United States, the due process clause did not apply to the plaintiffs.[7]

The Guantánamo example is by no means exceptional. In fact, Judge Johnson's description of the conditions of detention at this US naval base provides an accurate representation of many sites where asylum seekers and undocumented immigrants can be confined with very limited, if any, access to law.[8] We can think of, for example, the detention centers on thousands of Pacific islands excised from Australian sovereignty for the purposes of "offshore processing" of asylum claims,[9] "waiting zones" and administrative retention centers established in France to evade the rights and protections under the rule of law,[10] or various detention centers located in North Africa to hold the migrants intercepted in international waters by European countries such as Spain and Italy.[11]

Multiplication of these sites within the context of contemporary immigration controls reveals the challenging problems that various categories of migrants encounter as they claim and exercise human rights. In this chapter and the next one, I analyze these problems by turning to one of the key arguments in Hannah Arendt's reflections on statelessness in the first half of the twentieth century: The stateless found themselves in a "fundamental situation of rightlessness," Arendt claims, as they lost not only their citizenship rights but also their human rights.[12] In the absence of a political community that could recognize and guarantee their rights, the stateless were deprived of legal personhood as well as a right to action, opinion, and speech.

In an age characterized by unprecedented developments in the field of human rights, the term "rightlessness" is likely to strike us as an anachronism. As discussed in the Introduction to this book, one of the most crucial transformations since the time Arendt wrote her analysis of statelessness has been the shift from citizenship to legal personhood as the basis of an entitlement to rights. This shift is manifest, for example, in the Preamble of the International Covenant on Civil and Political Rights (ICCPR), which announces that human rights "derive from the inherent dignity of the human person." Many scholars have interpreted this development as a dissociation of legal personhood from the status of citizenship and argued that it has allowed migrants to stand before the law and demand education, health care, family unification, and even political participation as fundamental human rights.[13]

This chapter aims to offer a critical assessment of this historic development by rethinking Arendt's arguments about the rightlessness of the stateless. It suggests that the gap between "man" and "citizen," which was characteristic of the eighteenth-century idea of rights, has not been overcome by moving to the more universalistic concept of "human person." International human rights law reinscribes that gap in many respects and often leaves migrants without effective guarantees against the violent practices of border control. Although this critique insists on the need to examine how the existing inscriptions of personhood in human rights law can give rise to new divisions and stratifications within humanity, it diverges from some of the entirely negative assessments of personhood or legal standing as a mechanism that necessarily engenders violent exclusion.[14] From an Arendtian perspective, personhood, or the artificial mask provided by law, is important, as it allows public appearance without the pervasive fear of arbitrary violence and enables rights claims to be articulated. Without this mask, one is relegated to a certain form of civil and social death.

But given that legal personhood is an artifact and not an inherent essence, it is also necessary to attend to how it can be effectively unmade or undermined in certain conditions. And because legal personhood is seen as "more fundamental, natural, essential, less of a construct, less subject to manipulation," and hence taken to be much more secure than citizenship as the basis of rights, there is the danger of overlooking how it can be "subject to various forms of qualification and evasion."[15] Such possibilities of qualifying and evading personhood are nowhere more visible than in the cases of asylum and immigration, due to the centrality of the principle of territorial sovereignty to the ordering of the international system. Given these possibilities, "rightlessness" must be reconsidered as a critical concept that can alert us to various practices that undermine the legal personhood of migrants.

Once we attend to the nuances in Arendt's account of statelessness and rethink her arguments by taking into consideration the more recent changes in the field of human rights, we come to understand "rightlessness" not as the absolute loss of rights but instead as a fundamental condition denoting the *precarious* legal, political, and human standing of migrants. The term "precarious," with its Latin etymology, denotes "lives that are not guaranteed but bestowed in answer to prayer," as Didier Fassin notes, and I use it to highlight the vulnerability of lives that are dependent on the favors, privileges, or discretions of compassionate others.[16] I focus on the legal dimensions of this predicament in this chapter and address issues related to political and human standing in the next, though these different aspects, as the discussion will reveal, are closely interrelated.

Human rights law can be seen as an attempt to address the problem of precarious legal standing, as it endows every individual with personhood and attaches to this status a set of universal, inalienable rights. These rights are not privileges granted to a "passive beneficiary" at the discretion of others; they are instead "entitlements" that authorize the rights-holder to press claims in cases where these rights are denied, and these claims should normally prevail over political and moral considerations such as utility, social welfare, national security, or public order.[17] But as I highlight in this chapter, human rights law leaves various categories of migrants with quite insecure legal standing because it affirms the principle of territorial sovereignty. Border controls, justified as legitimate acts of sovereign statehood, end up creating divisions within humanity itself, thereby rendering the rights of migrants (asylum seekers and undocumented immigrants in particular) vulnerable to discretionary decisions and uncertain sentiments such as compassion.

Following a reconsideration of Arendt's arguments about the rightlessness of the stateless, this chapter turns to her phenomenological reflections on personhood to grasp why she attributes such a crucial importance to equal standing before the law. This section aims to contribute to the growing literature on Arendt's understanding of law by rethinking her conception of personhood and situating it in relation to some of the arguments in the critical legal scholarship on this topic. I then offer a close analysis of the limits and exclusions of the existing inscriptions of personhood in human rights law by examining two recent cases concerning immigration detention and deportation at the European Court of Human Rights (ECtHR or "the Court"). These cases underscore how rightlessness, understood as a precarious legal standing, persists despite the significant legal and normative changes in our conceptions of human rights. My choice of the ECtHR is intentional. Enforcement is often taken to be the greatest weakness of the existing human rights system, but as a supranational court with the capacity to issue judgments that are binding for the members of the Council of Europe, the ECtHR is often taken to be one of the most promising institutions for detaching personhood from citizenship status.[18] By examining the problems with regard to the personhood of migrants within the European context, I hope to make a stronger case for the argument that the perplexities of the Rights of Man, examined by Arendt, have not been fully resolved by moving to a universal discourse of human rights.

Statelessness and the Condition of Rightlessness

Arendt's account of statelessness repetitively invokes the term "rightless" to describe how the loss of citizenship was accompanied by the loss of human rights, but what she means by this term is far from obvious.[19] In Arendt's rendering, the term aims to capture not specific violations of rights but rather a condition that can render void even the rights that one formally has. The stateless might be granted certain rights such as the rights to life, freedom of opinion or movement, she argues, but they are in a fundamental condition of rightlessness to the extent that they are dependent on the charity or goodwill of others who grant these rights.[20] On the other hand, not every denial of rights amounts to rightlessness: Citizens can be deprived of certain rights, including the right to life (e.g., soldiers during a war), but they are not rightless as long as they have legal and political standing.[21] Arendt explains this seemingly paradoxical situation by defining rightlessness as a condition arising from the "loss of polity," which entails not only "the loss of government protection" and legal personhood but also the loss of home, or "a distinct place in the world" where one is judged by one's actions and opinions.[22]

Arendt's understanding of rightlessness as a *condition* challenges conventional understandings of the plight of migrants in terms of the loss of specific rights. When we attempt to address the problem in these terms, we identify a specific violation for which we can hold an identifiable entity accountable, and the right that is violated can be restored even if the person who is denied this right continues to remain in the condition that systematically gives rise to such violations in the first place. Those advocating the rights of migrants often adopt this approach because it would be practically impossible to redress violations of rights if the plight of migrants were to be understood as a fundamental condition arising from their de jure or de facto statelessness. As scholars working on human rights advocacy underscore, in order to be effective, human rights campaigns are compelled to present problems in "intentionalist frames" that assign causes to "the deliberate (intentional) actions of identifiable individuals."[23] Such framing is much more feasible if there is an identifiable rights violation and more difficult when it comes to structural problems such as poverty or patriarchy, which cannot be easily recounted in "a short and clear causal chain (or story) assigning responsibility."[24] This difficulty does not necessarily force activists to give up campaigning on these structural problems; in fact, they often try to reframe them in a more intentionalist, causal way, focusing on specific rights violations. For example, instead of tackling patriarchy as a structural problem, activists for women's rights focus on violence against women and highlight bodily harm in order to be able to assign responsibility for identifiable violations. In the case of migrants, this conventional frame centers on problems such as the violation of a right to be free from indefinite and arbitrary detention, and as I discuss below, to make that argument, it can end up reasserting the legitimacy of the structure (i.e., territorial sovereignty) that systematically produces the problems faced by migrants. Arendt's notion of "rightlessness," highlighting a fundamental condition that can undermine the very possibility of claiming and exercising even the rights that one formally has, draws attention to what gets lost in this conventional frame and renders statelessness more comparable to structural problems such as poverty, racial inequality, and patriarchy.

Arendt's account of statelessness draws attention to the multiple, interrelated dimensions of rightlessness. Legally speaking, the term denotes the loss of legal personhood that guarantees equal standing before the law. Politically, it captures the loss of an organized community where one's actions, opinions, and speech are taken into account. In addition, the term also indicates the precarious human standing of the stateless, highlighting their expulsion from the human world established and maintained through the activities of labor, work, and action.[25] Protracted confinement in refugee camps, examined at length in the next chapter, is a concrete manifestation of this expulsion.

Arendt's analysis of the legal dimension of rightlessness draws attention to the tight connection that the nation-state established between citizenship and legal personhood; within this institutional framework, those who were rendered stateless found themselves without any formal recognition of their rights and legal standing: "Their plight is not that they are not equal before the law, but that no law exists for them."[26] Incapable of being incorporated into the legal community of the receiving nation-states and deprived of rights in international law, the stateless were subjected to "a form of lawlessness, organized by the police."[27]

To explain what the loss of personhood entails, Arendt draws a very striking comparison between the stateless person and the criminal: Whereas the criminal has a legal standing in a political community, the stateless person is deprived of any recognition in the legal domain. The crime committed by the criminal will be punished according to "the normal juridical procedure in which a definite crime entails a predictable penalty."[28] Loss of personhood, Arendt argues, subjects the stateless to an arbitrary rule that imposes utterly unpredictable penalties in the absence of any definite crime; under these conditions, what the stateless endure has no relation to "what they do, did, or may do."[29] The punishment of the criminal results from "a deliberate act," whereas the actions of the stateless have no impact on what they will endure.[30] Without a right to residence or a right to work, the stateless constantly face the threat of internment or deportation for their mere presence or for attempting to make a living for themselves, and they have no right to appeal and challenge their internment or deportation.[31] In the absence of these rights, they become completely dependent on compassion to merely meet their basic needs such as habitation or food, whereas the criminal has "jail and food . . . not out of charity but out of right."[32] In a quite interesting move, Arendt argues that committing a crime becomes the only way for the stateless person to acquire a legal standing:

> Only as an offender against the law can he gain protection from it. As long as his trial and his sentence last, he will be safe from that arbitrary police rule against which there are no lawyers and no appeals. . . . He is no longer the scum of the earth but important enough to be informed of all the details of the law under which he will be tried. He has become a respectable person.[33]

Deprived of the artificial mask provided by legal personhood, the stateless fall "outside the pale of the law" and appear to others in their naked humanness or as "unqualified, mere existence."[54]

Arendt's theatrical understanding of personhood as an artificial mask created by law and her distrust of the quest for a real essence hiding behind the mask are very much in accord with her phenomenological approach to politics, which calls into question the metaphysical tradition that privileges "being" and is suspect of "appearances." This peculiar understanding of personhood also has much to share with "the Renaissance and eighteenth-century tradition of *theatrum mundi*," as highlighted by Dana Villa, to the extent that it represents the world as a stage on which actors appear with their public masks.[55] Arendt's theatrical conception of personhood revitalizes this tradition, which comes under attack with the rise of Romanticism and its expressivist model of the self. This Romanticist notion of the self, best represented by Rousseau, looks for a true inner self from which our words and deeds spring and is distrustful of a politics centered on "the ideas of playacting, maskwearing, and a distinct public self."[56]

In her account of the French Revolution, Arendt highlights the lethal dangers of this metaphysical quest for a real, true, and essential being that is hidden behind the mask, that precedes it, and that is entitled to rights by virtue of its nature. She is especially critical of the revolutionaries who equated masks with hypocrisy and ended up "[tearing] away the mask of the *persona* as well" with their "passion for unmasking society." These revolutionaries, Arendt insists, had "no respect" for the idea that we become equals through artificial inventions such as *persona*, or the idea that "everybody should be equally entitled to his legal personality, to be protected by it and, at the same time, to act almost literally 'through' it."[57]

Arendt highlights this danger again in her analysis of statelessness, as she underscores how those who are stripped of legal personhood are exposed to arbitrary forms of violence under police rule. The plight of the stateless epitomizes the collapse of a metaphysical vision that locates the ultimate source of rights in the sanctity of the being that comes prior to, and is hidden behind, the mask:

> The conception of human rights, based upon the assumed existence of a human being as such, broke down at the very moment when those who professed to believe in it were for the first time confronted with people who had indeed lost all other qualities and

specific relationships—except that they were still human. The world found nothing sacred in the abstract nakedness of being human.[58]

Confronted with this problem, Arendt rejects the assumption that those who appear to others in their "mere givenness" or bare humanity, stripped of all political and social qualifications, will be recognized as equals. The plight of the stateless reveals that equality is not a given or natural condition but instead the result of legal and political efforts to achieve equalization among a community of actors: "We are not born equal; we become equal as members of a group on the strength of our decision to guarantee ourselves mutually equal rights."[59]

If equality is not inherently given, it cannot be taken for granted and it needs to be established by, and continuously reinforced with, relatively stable institutional guarantees. Legal personhood is perhaps the most important of such guarantees to the extent that it allows equalization without obliterating the distinctiveness of each individual. The artificial mask of legal personhood is important, for Arendt, because it covers one's face (or one's "mere givenness," understood as bare humanness) not to erase the differences among human beings but instead to make sure that they do not become justifications for naturalized stratifications and inequalities within a political community.[60] According to this perspective, "man," invoked as the subject of rights, does not precede these rights but instead arises out of them: "*Man*, as philosophy and theology know him, exists— or is realized—in politics only in the equal rights that those who are most different guarantee for each other."[61]

Arendt's peculiar etymology, stressing the Roman origins of legal personhood, deserves attention not simply because of its critique of the metaphysical ideas that attach rights to a pre-existing subject ("man") and ground them in the sanctity of human life. It is also important for drawing attention to the practices that go into the making and unmaking of personhood, and this brings me to my second point about the relevance of Arendt's discussion of *persona* as mask to her analysis of the problem of statelessness. If personhood is an artifact, and not an inherently given essence—if there is no intrinsic overlap between humanness and personhood, in other words—then it is quite possible that not every human being is automatically recognized as a person. And even when one has the formal recognition, it is conceivable that personhood can be taken away, and if not completely taken away, it can be undermined so much so that some human beings might be effectively rendered semi-persons or non-persons.

Roman law is helpful for understanding this second point. Although Arendt does not make explicit reference to it, her discussion of statelessness in terms of the loss of legal standing evokes the Roman practice of depersonalization, or *capitis diminutio*.[62] There were three elements of *caput*, or legal standing, in Roman law: freedom, Roman citizenship, and membership in a Roman family. Correspondingly, there were three degrees of depersonalization. In its minimal form (*capitis diminutio minima*), the practice involved the loss of family rights; this occurred, for example, when a father gave his son up for adoption. In a certain sense, the stateless in Arendt's account face this form of depersonalization as they leave behind or lose family members.[63] A more comprehensive form of depersonalization (*capitis diminutio media*) involved the loss of citizenship. In the case of criminals facing banishment for life (*deportatio*), this loss entailed a life in isolation on an island near the Italian shore or an oasis in the Libyan desert.[64] In either case, the criminal was banned from the possibility of sharing a common life with fellow citizens; if he were to return without permission, he was stripped of legal protection, and as an outlaw, he could be killed by anybody with impunity.[65] This kind of civil death is at the heart of Arendt's analysis of statelessness, which highlights the loss of membership in a political community. Finally, the most comprehensive form of depersonalization (*capitis diminutio maxima*) indicated a change from a condition of freedom to that of slavery and entailed the loss of liberty, citizenship, and family rights. Arendt's comparison of statelessness to slavery, which I discuss in the next chapter, suggests that rightlessness involves this most comprehensive form of depersonalization in a certain sense; both the slaves and the stateless, she argues, are denied even "the possibility of fighting for freedom."[66]

In light of *capitis diminutio*, Arendt's Roman understanding of personhood exposes the fragility of this legal artifact. Refusing to treat personhood as an inherent attribute that cannot be stripped away, her analysis highlights the need to inquire into how legal standing can be unmade.[67] It is quite tempting to think of the history of personhood as one of gradual expansion and to treat depersonalization as an archaic practice of a bygone era. But the history of personhood is also "one of persistent and shameful stereotyping and exclusions in which . . . the legal community of actors extended only grudgingly," as Ngaire Naffine puts it.[68] That history underscores the need to attend to the ways in which personhood can be curtailed even today; if personhood can no longer be officially taken away, as Linda Bosniak highlights, it may still be "diminished in its effect, evaded, effaced, diluted, displaced."[69] That danger is especially palpable in the case of asylum seekers and undocumented immigrants facing detention and deportation, as I discuss below.[70]

This attentiveness to the fragility of personhood brings Arendt closer to some critical scholars who maintain that formal recognition of equality before the law can disguise, perpetuate, and justify various forms of inequality. However, Arendt's phenomenological account sets her apart from many other critics of law, and this brings me to my third and final point about the implications of her analysis of personhood for rethinking the problems of rightlessness today. Arendt's unique position is encapsulated in her peculiar dissection of *persona* as *per-sonare*, or as a mask allowing the voice to sound through, and her insistence on this highly improbable etymology is quite noteworthy. For Arendt, personhood is an artificial mask that not only disguises the countenance of its wearer but also allows the possibility of speaking and being heard. Those who are stripped of the protections of this mask appear to others in their "mere givenness" and become much more vulnerable to arbitrary forms of violence. In addition, they lack the means to make their speech "sound through"; without the mask equalizing them with other actors, their speech either does not count or is rendered inaudible and unintelligible. By insisting on this peculiar etymology, tracing personhood to *per-sonare*, Arendt urges us to understand the legal recognition of personhood not merely as a juridical issue but also as a political one that is directly linked to the question of whose action and speech are taken into account in a given community; understood in these terms, personhood has significant implications for one's political and human standing.

This phenomenological analysis of personhood, highlighting how legal fictions can enable public appearance, is quite different from critical accounts that see the law's artifacts mainly in negative terms as mechanisms disguising, suppressing, and dividing humanity. Legal scholar and jurist John T. Noonan Jr. presents such a view when he describes masks as legal devices "classifying individual human beings so that their humanity is hidden and disavowed."[71] For Noonan, masks are dangerous "monsters," showing how the "fiction-making capacity [of law] can run amok," as they conceal real persons, or "ontological realities," and displace them from the legal process.[72] For Arendt, on the other hand, there is no person without the mask, and masks are the only ways in which persons can appear as equals before the law.

More recently, Giorgio Agamben has offered a scathing critique of human rights as biopolitical mechanisms that render human life vulnerable to sovereign violence, as I discussed in chapter 1. In his analysis of habeas corpus, for example, Agamben casts this writ, which is often taken as one of the most fundamental legal safeguards against arbitrary state action, as another reinscription of sovereign power on the human body. He highlights how modern democracy turns *corpus*, or the body, into the subject of rights with this writ: Compelling the physical presence of a human body before a court of law not only endows the political subject with rights but also renders it vulnerable to the violence of sovereign decision.[73]

An Arendtian account of personhood also suggests that existing norms of human rights cannot be understood simply as protections against sovereign violence; in fact, as I discuss below, to the extent that these norms cast some forms of sovereign violence as legitimate, they can partake in the reproduction of rightlessness. However, in Agamben's biopolitical account, personhood, as inscribed in legal inventions such as habeas corpus, is inextricably intertwined with the logic of sovereignty. Arendt's phenomenological account, on the other hand, underscores that personhood is not merely a juridical tie between an individual and a state. More importantly, it is an artificial convention that institutes relationships among different individuals—in ways similar to the mask that establishes relationships between different actors on stage—and is a necessary, though by no means sufficient, condition for their equalization as distinct individuals. Underlying Arendt's insistence on the importance of personhood is her Roman conception of law as *lex*, which takes legislation as a political activity that establishes relationships, connections, and ties between different entities.[74]

As this discussion highlights, personhood is not simply a juridical matter for Arendt; it has significant consequences for one's political and human standing; it is that "which makes his [a human being's] actions and part of his destiny a consistent whole," to revisit the quote at the beginning of this section.[75] What Arendt offers is nothing less than "a hermeneutic phenomenology of the person," to use Paul Ricoeur's terms, tying together how the person appears in language, action, narrative, and ethical life.[76] The artificial mask of personhood is crucial for human beings to appear as speaking subjects and be recognized as such by their interlocutors, to become actors capable of designating themselves as the agents of their own actions, to establish themselves as the narrators of their own life stories that endow their identities with some cohesion throughout time, and finally, to situate themselves as participants in institutional frameworks enabling and guaranteeing reciprocity, equality, and justice.[77]

This phenomenological attention to the multiple dimensions of personhood refuses to sign on to a critique that sees legal artifacts simply as cunning devices producing injustice, oppression, and violence, although this is not to say that Arendt's account has no critical insight to offer. In fact, her distinctive understanding of personhood as a mask that covers the face but also allows the individual voice to "sound through" and be perceived as intelligible speech can be mobilized as a critical framework in examining the existing institutional frameworks guaranteeing personhood: To what extent do the current formulations of personhood in international human rights law, for example, provide the asylum seekers and undocumented immigrants with artificial masks that can allow them to appear in public without the pervasive fear of being subjected to arbitrary violence? To what extent do these legal mechanisms cover their "face" and ward off the threat of being perceived as bare lives exposed in their "mere givenness"? And finally, to what extent do these artificial conventions allow these migrants to appear as equals before the law and let their rights claims "sound through"?

These questions are crucial starting points for understanding how rightlessness continues to haunt our present. Given the significant transformations in international human rights and humanitarian law, it has become very difficult to imagine how one can be deprived of legal standing. Arendt's analysis of statelessness and her phenomenological understanding of personhood, however, raise caveats against the hasty conclusion that rightlessness becomes extinct in an era in which every human being is recognized as a person before the law. From an Arendtian perspective, a careful examination into the diverse and unpredictable effects of this recent institutionalization of human rights is needed to assess the extent to which this development enables the equalization of human beings regardless of citizenship status.

In the following section, I undertake such a critical inquiry as I examine different ways of diminishing personhood in the context of deportation and detention. This analysis rests on a slightly revised definition of "rightlessness." At the time Arendt wrote her analysis, the term denoted the absence of any international legal recognition, especially for those who were de facto stateless. In my reformulation, which draws on Arendt's emphasis on the fragility of the artificial mask provided by personhood, I take into account the post–World War II international legal developments and suggest that "rightlessness" denotes the fragility of these formal guarantees, which can be unmade in ways dispossessing various categories of migrants of their legal standing. Within this new context, the term alerts us to the *precarious* legal, political, and human standing of those who are juridically or effectively deprived of the protections of citizenship status. It draws attention to contemporary practices and processes that give rise to divisions, stratifications, and thresholds within the concept of universal personhood and render the rights of various categories of migrants dependent on quite unreliable sentiments and highly arbitrary decisions.

Rightlessness and Deportation

Only citizens have the unconditional right to enter and remain in the territory of a state, and those who are not citizens (including permanent residents) can be deported.[78] Deportation, or the physical expulsion of an alien, has always been one of the mechanisms used by nation-states to exclude those deemed undesirable from the political community. It has been recognized as a practice in accordance with the sovereign state's right to control entry to and residence in its territory, and conventionally its legitimacy has been judged within a legal framework centered on the international obligations that states have to each other.[79] As Arendt reminds us, "sovereignty is nowhere more absolute than in matters of 'emigration, naturalization, nationality, and expulsion,'" but the formal and informal agreements between states established some guarantees against mass denationalizations and deportations for most of modern history.[80] Normalization of mass denationalizations and collective expulsions with the rise of totalitarianism revealed the fragility of these guarantees.

This state-centric picture has changed to some extent with the rise of human rights norms after World War II, and the discretionary power of sovereign states in making deportation decisions has been curtailed in certain respects. Collective or mass expulsion of aliens, for example, is now prohibited, and there are procedural safeguards in place to protect migrants from arbitrary deportations and to ensure their right to individual assessment of their cases.[81] There are also several norms, including those upholding the rights to life, bodily integrity, and freedom from cruel, inhuman, or degrading treatment, which can be invoked to challenge the conditions under which a deportation order is executed.[82] In addition, the principle of *non-refoulement*, which prohibits refugees from being returned to places where their lives and freedoms could be threatened, has become one of the strongest norms in place to constrain the sovereign right of states to control their borders.[83] It has even been suggested that this norm has achieved the status of *jus cogens*—i.e., it has become a peremptory norm of international law from which no derogation is permissible.[84] The institutionalization of these norms in international human rights law marks an important development in establishing the legal personhood of migrants, as it enables them to challenge the legitimacy of deportation decisions that were once deemed to be beyond the reach of the rule of law.

Yet, it is also important to understand the various ways in which these norms continue to reinstate the precarious legal standing of various categories of migrants, especially in the context of deportation. Even the principle of *non-refoulement* affirms sovereign power of states to control their borders, as it allows for exceptions on very ambiguous grounds that leave room for arbitrariness: According to the Refugee Convention, *non-refoulement* may not be applicable when there are "reasonable grounds" that the refugee in question constitutes "a danger to the security of the country" or "a danger to the community of that country."[85] These exceptions urge us to understand human rights norms not simply as instruments constraining the sovereign power of states but also as mechanisms legitimating that power in many respects. They also underscore that the perplexities of the Rights of Man analyzed by Arendt are not resolved but instead reconfigured in international human rights and humanitarian law. Especially important in this regard are the ways in which a desire to reassert "the old trinity of state-people-territory," to remember Arendt's characterization of the nation-state framework, pervades existing international norms, as highlighted by their exception clauses.[86] This trinity, which Arendt concluded to be untenable in the face of the crisis of statelessness in the twentieth century, continues to have a strong hold on the universalistic political and moral frameworks that attribute rights to the human person.

From an Arendtian perspective, there is a need to attend to the specific conditions that can enable or undermine the political possibilities of navigating the perplexities of human rights for the purposes of guaranteeing equalization regardless of nationality. Accordingly, it is important to take note of some of the worrisome developments that make it more and more difficult to invoke human rights norms to contest deportation decisions. Notable among these is the normalization of deportation within a new security discourse that depicts asylum and immigration in terms of a permanent crisis or state of emergency.[87] Within this new context, deportation has come to be used as a symbolic tactic to produce an effect of sovereign power at a time when the authority of states seems to be undermined by various global processes and structures.[88] The exception clause of *non-refoulement*, which was reserved for states of emergency (e.g., wartime) in the past, has been increasingly invoked by states to deport those deemed to be posing a threat to national security or public order. As a result, "a palpable sense of deportability," to use Nicholas De Genova's terms, has rendered the personhood of an ever-growing number of migrants increasingly precarious.[89]

In what follows, I turn to a 2008 case from the European Court of Human Rights (ECtHR or "the Court"), N. v. UK, to discuss how the existing inscriptions of personhood in international human rights law fail to provide effective guarantees against this condition of rightlessness, especially in the case of migrants without a regular status, including rejected asylum seekers and undocumented immigrants.[90] My reading highlights the need to understand this condition in relation to the deeply embedded tensions between the principles of equal personhood and territorial sovereignty in human rights law. It also points to how these tensions can be navigated in different ways, some leaving migrants with a more precarious personhood, and some others giving rise to possibilities of equalization regardless of citizenship status. By analyzing this case closely, I hope to underscore that human rights law has both "jurisgenerative" and "jurispathic" dimensions, to use Robert Cover's terms.[91] We become aware of the "jurisgenerative" dimension of law when existing rights are "reposited, resignified, and reappropriated by new and excluded groups," as Seyla Benhabib notes.[92] But it is equally important to look at how human rights law gives rise to "jurispathic" processes when its norms are invoked to affirm the sovereign right to detain or deport rejected asylum seekers and undocumented immigrants. At those moments, as Cover notes, we realize that legal interpretation is different from other fields of interpretation; it "takes place in a field of pain and death," providing "justifications for violence which has already occurred or which is about to occur."[93]

N. v. UK deserves attention as a case that underscores the equivocal effects of human rights law, which extends personhood to migrants with its universal scope but also holds on to the principle of territorial sovereignty that can give rise to practices of unmaking that personhood. N., an asylum seeker from Uganda, applied for asylum in the UK in March 1998, claiming that her life was in danger if she returned to Uganda; because of her association with the Lord's Resistance Army, she had been persecuted and raped by the government soldiers. N. was seriously ill when she arrived in the UK, and later she was diagnosed as HIV-positive. After treatment with antiretroviral drugs, her condition significantly improved, and in March 2001 a consultant physician prepared an expert report in support of her asylum application, suggesting that her life expectancy would be less than one year if the treatment were discontinued. Despite the report, the UK Secretary of State refused N.'s asylum application and decided that her deportation would not amount to "inhuman or degrading treatment," according to Article 3 of the European Convention of Human Rights (ECHR). The government justified its position by arguing that the applicant could access AIDS treatment in Uganda. After exhausting all domestic remedies, N. submitted an application to the ECtHR to challenge the deportation decision on the grounds that her return to Uganda would amount to a violation of not only Article 3 but also Article 8, which guarantees a right to private life. In May 2008, the Grand Chamber of the ECtHR ruled that there would be no violation of Articles 3 and 8 in case of N.'s return to Uganda.

N. v. UK reveals the continuing relevance of Arendt's argument about the perplexities of human rights: N. has "a right to seek and enjoy asylum," according to the Universal Declaration of Human Rights (UDHR), but she does not have a "right to be granted asylum," as I mentioned in the Introduction. As a result, she is vulnerable to the highly unpredictable, even arbitrary, consequences of an asylum adjudication process. This vulnerability is further reinforced by the relatively subjective nature of decisions as to what constitutes a "well-founded fear" or what can be characterized as "persecution."[94] In addition, the claims made by asylum seekers have come to be seen as increasingly dubious in a climate that has criminalized asylum and immigration by representing them as security threats. Their asylum applications can now be easily rejected for minor flaws or incoherence in the narrative of persecution, even though such problems are common in post-traumatic situations.[95] Unlike the stateless of the Arendtian world, today's asylum seekers do have formal recognition of their legal standing; but their personhood is unlike that of any other subject standing before the law, as they are considered to be "guilty until proven innocent" and the whole process centers on the question of whether they are really the person they say they are.[96]

As narratives of persecution have become suspect, the human body has become a crucial site for claiming rights, giving rise to what Didier Fassin aptly calls "biolegitimacy."[97] States, courts, and refugee advocates have increasingly turned to the suffering bodies of asylum seekers and other migrants to locate more irrefutable truths. This contemporary context is important for understanding why the appeal in *N. v. UK* is based not on N.'s political biography as a member of a resistance group but on her biological condition as an HIV-positive patient. The case exemplifies the recent trend to turn to Article 3 of ECHR, which places an absolute prohibition on inhuman or degrading treatment, in an attempt to overcome the limits of asylum and *non-refoulement*.[98] Read along with the principle of *non-refoulement*, this non-derogable right has been invoked to stop states from returning asylum seekers and refugees to places where they can be subjected to the kind of treatment prohibited by the ECHR. More recently, this argument has been extended to cases in which the person in question has a medical condition that cannot be treated in the country she or he is returned to. In a landmark case, *D. v. UK* (1997), ECtHR ruled that the deportation of a drug courier dying of AIDS to St. Kitts would violate Article 3, as having no family support and adequate medical treatment would hasten his death.

In some respects, these recent interpretations of human rights law are "jurisgenerative" processes, broadening the scope of the prohibition on inhuman and degrading treatment, resignifying the meaning of *non-refoulement,* and augmenting the personhood of migrants. But a closer analysis of *N. v. UK* reveals that these interpretations also end up exposing migrants to "jurispathic" processes that render their personhood extremely precarious. It shows that the turn to the prohibition on inhuman and degrading treatment as the basis of asylum claims does not put an end to the interpretive controversies arising from the perplexities of human rights but instead gives rise to new ones that demand decisions over life and death. The case also poses challenging questions in light of Arendt's account of personhood, as it alerts us to the vulnerability of those who are forced to assume the guise of a bare humanity to make rights claims.

The Court's judgment in *N. v. UK* highlights how the turn to the suffering body gives rise to highly volatile decisions about life and death, subjecting migrants to a new form of arbitrary rule. The majority of the judges agreed with the government's position that the probability of significantly reduced life expectancy could not be invoked to challenge an expulsion order.[99] The humanitarian exception could not be granted in this case, the Court argued, since the applicant was not critically or terminally ill. In addition, she had family in Uganda, even though N. insisted that they would not be willing or able to take care of her. Finally, the antiretroviral medication was available in Uganda, the Court pointed out, ignoring the fact that only half of those who needed this medication could access it.[100] In a very problematic move, the majority of the judges characterized the ECHR as a convention that is "essentially directed at the protection of civil and political rights," agreeing in effect with the UK government's claim that extending Article 3 in this case would amount to provision of social and economic rights that should be seen as aspirational. More strikingly, they represented their judgment as an attempt to balance individual rights with "the demands of the general interest of the community," risking with this move to relativize the absolute prohibition against inhuman and degrading treatment in Article 3.[101] They went so far as to portray the UK government as a generous but overburdened host that "provided the applicant with medical and social assistance at public expense." But this generosity, they concluded, should not be seen as "entail[ing] a duty on the part of the respondent State to continue to provide for her."[102]

To understand how this ruling risks eroding the personhood of migrants, it is important to attend to the arbitrary distinctions it sets up in an attempt to adjudicate rights claims based on suffering bodies. Take, for example, the distinction between "ensuring a dignified death" and "prolonging life," introduced by the UK government and affirmed by the majority of judges. Whereas the former was seen as the irrefutable basis of an absolute prohibition against deportation, the latter was cast as an unwarranted demand putting strains on the socioeconomic resources of a government. But the distinction was not clear-cut; even the descriptions used by those invoking this distinction reveal the arbitrariness of the line drawn. During the examination of N.'s appeal at the House of Lords, Lord Nicholls of Birkenhead compared N.'s situation in the case of a deportation to "having a life-support machine turned off."[103] The judges at the ECtHR took note of this characterization in addition to the overwhelming evidence that if N. were to be deported to Uganda, she would have difficulty accessing medical treatment and "her condition would rapidly deteriorate and she would suffer ill health, discomfort, pain and death within a few years."[104] Yet, despite all this evidence, N.'s case was not seen as one that is so extreme as to warrant a humanitarian exception to the sovereign right to control borders. Though her case was seen as worthy of "one's sympathy on pressing grounds," its "humanitarian appeal" was not "so powerful that it could not in reason be resisted by the authorities of a civilised State."[105]

N. v. UK points to a new form of arbitrary rule faced by migrants. Unlike the "form of lawlessness, organized by the police,"[106] which is at the heart of Arendt's analysis, this new arbitrariness is highly regulated by laws. Nevertheless, we can still describe it as arbitrary to the extent that it renders migrants' rights vulnerable to the quite erratic decisions based on ambiguous terms and distinctions. This new arbitrary rule is directly related to the compassionate humanitarianism discussed in the last chapter. As states, courts, and rights advocates turn to compassion to make decisions about suffering, they risk unmaking the equal personhood of migrants, rendering their rights dependent on a capricious moral sentiment. As a result, we are not too far away from Arendt's argument that the stateless find themselves in a fundamental condition of rightlessness because of their dependence on the goodwill or generosity of others: "The prolongation of their lives is due to charity and not to right, for no law exists which could force the nations to feed them."[107] In fact, the Court's ruling suggested that there was no violation of N.'s rights under Articles 3 and 8 precisely because what she was demanding was "prolongation of her life"; it was the generosity of the British government that prolonged her life so far "at public expense," but that in itself could not be taken as the basis of rights imposing positive duties on the UK.

The perplexities at the heart of the eighteenth-century discourse of rights, especially those arising from the simultaneous invocation of "man" and "citizen" as the subject entitled to rights, have not been resolved with the move to the inclusive notion of humanity. As the ECtHR ruling in *N. v. UK* demonstrates, these perplexities are reinscribed in human rights norms; what cannot be denied as a fundamental right to citizens can be seen as dependent on the compassion of the "host" states in the case of migrants, which diminishes their personhood.

These perplexities can be navigated in different ways, however, and some of these can be more promising than others to establish migrants as

equal persons before the law, as can be seen in the dissenting opinion of
Judges Tulkens, Bonello, and Spielmann in *N. v. UK*. Criticizing the problematic hierarchy drawn between civil rights and socioeconomic rights,
the dissenting judges argued instead that "there is no water-tight division
separating that sphere [of social and economic rights] from the field covered by the Convention."[108] They were equally concerned about the utilitarian calculus that the Court set to weigh rights against their costs, warn-
ing that this reasoning makes the enjoyment of even non-derogable rights
dependent on policy considerations.[109] The dissenting opinion also questioned the Court's quick dismissal of N.'s complaint under Article 8, which
guarantees a right to respect for private and family life and has been interpreted to indicate "a person's right to physical and social integrity." Given
that N. was being "sent to certain death," the dissenting judges insisted,
the Court's refusal to examine the complaint under Article 8 was simply
unjustifiable.[110]

Despite all these important points, the dissenting opinion could not
break away from the logic of humanitarian exception altogether. In fact,
as the dissenting judges defended that N. should have a right to stay in the
UK, they were affirming, not questioning, the logic that undermines the
personhood of migrants by rendering their rights dependent on quite arbitrary decisions about suffering bodies. If the majority decided that N.'s
case was significantly different from D.'s case as one concerning prolonging life, and not death with dignity, the dissenting judges insisted on the
similarities of these two cases: Just like D., N. was a "very exceptional"
case, they argued, given that she would not be able to survive more than a
year or two if she were to be returned to Uganda.[111] It is possible to see this
attempt to depict N.'s case as a very exceptional one deserving protections
under Article 3 as a strategic move—one that is easier to justify, for example, than a broader interpretation that could have described deprivation
from adequate access to health care as "inhuman or degrading treatment."[112] Such an interpretation would have involved representative practices that could have established connections between things seen as unrelated (to recall the "political" approach to human rights discussed in
chapter 2) and would have reframed what was perceived to be a social
issue—health care—as a political problem that is inextricably linked to
N.'s equal personhood. By challenging the deportation order on the
grounds of a humanitarian exception reserved for those who are critically
ill, the dissenting judges tried to avoid the controversies entailed by such an
interpretation that would have effectively dismantled the distinction

between civil-political rights and socioeconomic rights; instead, they turned to the seemingly self-evident truth of a suffering body. But with that move, placing their dissent at the intersection of a moral economy centered on compassion and an administrative rationality directed at the management of vulnerable populations, they ended up subjecting the rights of asylum seekers to highly arbitrary decisions about the conditions under which a human life can be deemed to be worthy of special protections.

The rise of a humanitarian logic centered on the suffering body, as illustrated by the case of *N. v. UK*, poses significant challenges to establishing migrants as equal persons before the law. Arendt's phenomenological account of personhood sheds critical light on these challenges. For Arendt, we become rights-and-duty-bearing subjects with the artificial mask of *persona*. As highlighted earlier, one of the crucial functions of this mask is that it covers the countenance of the human being so as to shield her "mere givenness" from an arbitrary violence to which she would otherwise be more likely to be exposed. The logic of humanitarian exception, on the other hand, risks unmaking the personhood of migrants precisely by forcing them to stand bare naked before the court, to become nothing but human, so as to make claims to human rights. But as Arendt reminds us, the stateless become most vulnerable to arbitrary forms of rule and violence when they appear to others in their bare humanity, especially because their fate becomes dependent on the unpredictable sentiments of others.[113] In very exceptional circumstances, that exposure can invoke a response extending them a set of rights; but in the majority of cases, it leads to the commonplace reaction that their plight is worthy of compassion but does not entitle them to the rights enjoyed by citizens. Compassion turns out to be a quite tenuous basis for human rights, as it does not imply any positive duties—even the officials in the UK government admitted that N.'s case demanded "sympathy," without recognizing any obligations arising from her plight.[114]

In addition, compassion, as the analysis in chapter 2 highlighted, is also a quite unreliable feeling, as it can end up sacrificing those who are cast as the most misfortunate in the name of the cause it glorifies. In fact, among the cases that both the UK and the ECtHR cited to support their position, we see a long list of such sacrificed lives for the purposes of upholding a humanitarian morality that makes exceptions only for those in extreme situations.[115] If "death and pain are at the center of legal interpretation," as Robert Cover argues, they are even more prominent in decisions related to humanitarian exception.[116] To qualify for this exception,

migrants must meet the "high threshold" set by the ECtHR in the interpretation of Article 3, but as the differing opinions in N.'s case reveal, it is
not always clear where that "threshold" is, and it must be located in each
case by making a new decision in response to challenging questions about
life and death.[117] These decisions "concerning the *threshold* beyond which
life ceases to be politically relevant," to use Giorgio Agamben's terms,
have quite troubling effects:[118] When the majority of the judges represented N.'s suffering as a problem related to social and economic rights,
and not civil and political rights, her life "cease[d] to be politically relevant" in their eyes. Such discretionary decisions over life and death effectively turn migrants with physical and mental illness into *homines sacri*,
to use Agamben's terms again, as subjects who could be subjected to sovereign violence (e.g., deportation) and left to die.[119]

Approaching human rights on the basis of a humanitarian framework
centered on suffering bodies is problematic not simply because it renders
the personhood of migrants very precarious but also because it reinscribes
their rightlessness as speechless subjects—a problem that I discuss at
length in the next chapter. If the artificial mask of *persona* has an opening
to allow the voice of the individual to "sound through," as in Arendt's
characterization, an exclusive focus on suffering bodies in the adjudication of rights claims ends up depriving migrants of such a mask, as it ends
up drowning their voices amidst the more authoritative statements made
by medical, humanitarian, and legal experts. In an international environment that makes their narratives highly suspect, the bodies of migrants
become material sites bearing witness to truths that seem to be beyond
any dispute. As a result of this shift, it is no longer the migrants' accounts
of their suffering that count; it is experts who are "called on to speak the
truth in their place."[120] From an Arendtian perspective, which urges us to
ask the extent to which existing inscriptions of personhood in international human rights law allow migrants to speak and be heard, the shift
from migrants' narratives to expert testimony is troubling, as it ends up
rendering migrants' speech irrelevant.

Rightlessness and Immigration Detention

Similar to deportation, detention was mainly used as an exceptional measure in times of emergency (e.g., war), especially to confine those who were
categorized as "terrorists" or "enemy aliens." Since the 1990s, however,
detention has been normalized as a legitimate tool used by states in

immigration control, especially due to the increasing securitization and criminalization of asylum and immigration—a process that has intensified in the wake of 9/11.[121] It has now become a routine administrative procedure to detain asylum seekers whose claims are being processed, unaccompanied minors who are waiting for their status to be regularized, undocumented immigrants and rejected asylum seekers, and non-citizens who have completed their criminal sentences and are awaiting deportation.

A brief look at the numbers in Europe confirms this troubling normalization of detention in the immigration context: From 2000 to 2012, the number of "camps" used for immigration detention in Europe and in the Mediterranean countries has increased from 324 to 473, according to the estimates of *Migreurop*, a European network of non-governmental foundations working on immigration detention. This estimate is quite conservative because it includes only permanent structures that can hold five or more people and excludes a plethora of other sites that can be temporarily utilized for immigration detention (e.g., waiting zones in airports).[122] In France, for example, in addition to the 24 *centres de rétention administrative* (administrative detention centers) where detainees can be held up to 45 days in cases where immediate deportation is not possible, there are 150 *locaux de rétention administrative* (administrative detention facilities) where detention is limited to 48 hours and 85 *zones d'attentes* (waiting zones) that are located at various ports of entry and can be used to detain individuals up to 20 days by a court order. The number of people detained by the French government in these sites rose from 28,220 in 2003 to 35,008 in 2007.[123]

In many respects, we are confronted with a situation that is quite similar to the one that Arendt described in her account of statelessness, as what was once exceptional has been normalized as "the routine solution" and internment camp, in its several guises, has become "the only practical substitute for a nonexistent homeland."[124] Those who can be characterized as de facto stateless, including asylum seekers and undocumented immigrants, are now again "liable to jail sentences without ever committing a crime," and confined to these sites, they can rarely access the protections guaranteed to other detainees under the rule of law.[125]

Many of these detention sites bear an eerie resemblance to the structure of internment camps used to contain the stateless in a space of lawlessness, always subject to an arbitrary rule of discretionary decrees. Although these sites serve administrative purposes and are supposed to be non-penitentiary, they are regulated by a very disciplinary regime reminiscent of ordinary prisons. There are fixed eating times, designated hours for recreation, and mandatory curfews. If detainees violate the rules that regulate their daily routine, they can be subject to various forms of punishment, including solitary confinement.[126] In addition to the formal rules in place, detainees' lives are regulated by a set of informal rules that create an environment of arbitrariness, uncertainty, and vulnerability.[127] The arbitrariness of the system has become even more worrisome with the more recent move to privatize immigration detention in many countries. As states are increasingly transferring responsibility to private prison management companies, it has become more difficult to ensure accountability in cases of human rights violations.[128]

Despite the important similarities, the picture is also different from the one Arendt painted in certain respects as a result of developments in the field of international human rights and humanitarian law. Article 31 of the Refugee Convention forbids states from imposing any penalties on asylum seekers and refugees on account of their unauthorized entry or presence, "provided they present themselves without delay to the authorities and show good cause for their illegal entry or presence," and it limits restrictions on their freedom of movement to only "those which are necessary." The United Nations High Commissioner for Refugees (UNHCR) stipulates that asylum seekers and refugees should not be detained unless there are exceptional grounds such as verifying identity, conducting a preliminary assessment of asylum claim, dealing with cases involving fraudulent documents, and protecting national security and public order.[129] In addition, Article 9 of International Covenant on Civil and Political Rights (ICCPR) guarantees "the right to liberty and security of person," regardless of citizenship status, and forbids arbitrary arrest and detention; it demands states to inform those who are arrested of the reasons for their arrest. It also prohibits mandatory and indefinite detention and guarantees access to courts for those who are detained to determine the lawfulness of their detention.

In what ways do these human rights norms protect migrants against the lawlessness that Arendt criticized and allow migrants to make claims to rights as equal persons before the law? To what extent do these norms ensure the personhood of migrants in the context of detention and provide them with an artificial mask that can protect them against arbitrary forms of rule and violence? In what respects do these human rights norms reconfigure the perplexities that Arendt pointed to in her account of statelessness? And how do different actors, including states, migrants, lawyers, and rights advocacy groups, navigate these perplexities when it comes to detention? *Saadi v. UK*, a 2008 case from the ECtHR in which an asylum seeker challenged his detention, offers crucial insights into these questions.[130]

Shayan Baram Saadi fled the Kurdish Autonomous Region of Iraq in December 2000; as a hospital doctor, he treated three fellow members of the Iraqi Workers' Communist Party who had been injured in an attack and then facilitated their escape. Upon his arrival at Heathrow Airport on December 30, 2000, Saadi immediately claimed asylum and was given "temporary admission." Although he reported to the airport as required in the next three days, he was arrested on January 2, 2001, and transferred to Oakington Reception Center for detention. On January 8, Saadi's asylum claim was rejected, but the next day he was released from Oakington and granted temporary admission pending the determination of his appeal. On January 14, 2003, Saadi's appeal was allowed and he was granted asylum. Saadi and his lawyers challenged his detention at the ECtHR. They claimed that his detention was in violation of Article 5 (1) of ECHR, which guarantees "the right to liberty and security of person" and prohibits the deprivation from liberty except in cases of arrest or detention on permissible grounds.

Saadi v. UK was a landmark case because it was the first time the ECtHR was called upon to make a decision on the permissibility of detention in cases of unauthorized entry.[131] The UK government argued that the detention of Saadi was lawful, as it aimed at the prevention of unauthorized entry in accordance with the Article 5 (1) of the ECtHR.[132] It also challenged the claim that the detention was arbitrary by highlighting that Saadi was detained in order to enable the speedy examination of his asylum claim and that he was held in a "relaxed regime" with access to legal advice and other facilities for only seven days.[133] Saadi's lawyers contested the lawfulness of the detention by underscoring that there was no unauthorized entry since his temporary admission would make his presence in the UK lawful. In addition, in the absence of any risk of absconding, they argued, Saadi was detained purely for the purposes of administrative convenience and expediency.[134] The Court found no violation of Article 5 (1) and endorsed the short-term detention of asylum seekers for the purposes of processing their claims speedily.

The reasoning adopted by the majority of judges in *Saadi v. UK* highlights that "personhood operates . . . in the shadow of the border" in the context of asylum and immigration and "has often found itself stunted as a result."[135] Precarious personhood of migrants in international human rights law can be seen in the Court's argument that states enjoy an "undeniable sovereign right to control aliens' entry into and residence in their territory." On the basis of this strong endorsement of the principle of territorial sovereignty, the majority of judges declared any entry not explicitly authorized by the state in question to be "unauthorized," even in cases where the individual claims asylum upon arrival.[136] They argued that Saadi's detention was not arbitrary, since it was carried out in good faith to quickly assess his asylum application and he was detained for only seven days under conditions that were specifically adapted to the needs of asylum seekers.[137] In a move justifying detention undertaken simply for administrative expediency, the Court concluded that Saadi's detention was not in violation of the right to liberty given the "administrative problems" faced by the UK in the face of "increasingly high numbers of asylum-seekers."[138] The Court found only a violation of Article 5 (2), which requires the authorities to promptly inform those who are detained of the reasons for their arrest and charges against them.

Saadi v. UK provides a justification for detention as a routine administrative procedure to be used against those who have entered states without prior authorization. In addition, the judgment risks endowing detention with a humanitarian aura when it presents it as a legitimate measure benefiting the interests of the asylum seekers.[139] It also confers this aura on detention centers such as Oakington. Highlighting how this center meets the specific needs of asylum seekers, including "recreation, religious observance, medical care and, importantly, legal assistance," the judgment ends up obscuring the surveillance functions of facilities such as Oakington:[140] Oakington is located in the former army barracks, and just like the refugee camps located on Guantánamo mentioned at the beginning of this chapter, it is a highly securitized space used for the confinement of those who are cast as undesirables: "It has high perimeter fences, locked gates and twenty-four hour security guards." Detainees have no privacy and they need to comply with strict rules: "Detainees must open their correspondence in front of the security guards and produce identification if requested, comply with roll-calls and other orders." There are rules stipulating fixed times for eating and returning to rooms.[141] In many respects, Oakington resembles the internment camps in Arendt's analysis, revealing the precarious legal, political, and human standing of its inhabitants as subjects who can be interned without committing a crime and become dependent on the benevolence of their captors. Sites such as Oakington, where even the most basic human activities (e.g., eating, walking, sleeping) are always undertaken in the shadow of a perpetual threat of punishment, confirm Arendt's argument that a fundamental condition of rightlessness can persist even when there is no explicit violation of specific human rights.

Normalization of detention in the context of asylum and immigration demonstrates that the perplexities of human rights have not been fully resolved with their codification in law. To the extent that international human rights law affirms not only equal personhood but also territorial sovereignty, it reinscribes these perplexities in new ways. I have already mentioned the peculiar formulation of the right to asylum as "a right to seek and enjoy asylum," as opposed to "a right to be granted asylum," to highlight this point. In addition, the exception clauses of various human rights norms, including the right to liberty and security of person, render the personhood of migrants precarious, as they allow for detention to prevent unauthorized entry. Finally, although there are human rights norms regulating the conditions of detention and prohibiting arbitrary and indefinite detention, there is still an ongoing legal debate on the maximum duration of detention and what constitutes arbitrariness in the context of immigration-related detention. As highlighted in the *Saadi* judgment, the ECtHR has not "formulated a global definition as to what types of conduct on the part of the authorities might constitute 'arbitrariness,'" and the UN Human Rights Treaty monitoring bodies have yet to establish clearly articulated, globally recognized guidelines.[142] In the absence of such guidelines, an EU Directive adopted in 2008 has stipulated that the initial detention period can be as long as six months, and that period can be extended further up to 12 months.[143] Saadi's detention was much shorter, but his case is important for understanding the indeterminate nature of the line that is drawn in decisions related to arbitrary detention: The Court ruled that the seven-day period "cannot be said to have exceeded that reasonably required for the purpose pursued,"[144] but there are no explicitly stated and generally recognized rules defining what would be a "reasonably required" detention period for the purposes of assessing the validity of an asylum claim.

Saadi v. UK was a very controversial case, and several international and non-governmental actors have taken issue with the judgment. The criticisms raised by the dissenting judges in particular deserve attention, as they highlight how the perplexities of human rights could have been navigated differently to ensure more robust guarantees for the personhood of asylum seekers. The partly dissenting opinion called into question the Court's characterization of the detention regime in Oakington as a humanitarian one when it instead highlighted the administrative functions of the site (i.e., "speedy resolution" of asylum claims), and took issue with the dangerous claim that "detention is in the interests of the person concerned."[145] This instrumentalist logic, the dissenting judges argued, amounted to a blanket justification of detention as a legitimate means toward the humanitarian end of asylum—a small price to be paid for the rights to be gained.[146] In addition, they were particularly worried that justification of detention on the grounds of administrative expediency would subject asylum seekers to an arbitrary rule and undermine their personhood:

> [S]uch a situation creates great *legal uncertainty* for asylum seekers, stemming from the fact that they could be detained at any time during examination of their application without their being able to take the necessary action to avoid detention. Hence, the asylum seeker becomes an object rather than a subject of law.[147]

This possibility of being relegated to an "object" of law explains why the legal personhood of various categories of migrants remains precarious despite significant transformations in the field of human rights since the time Arendt completed her analysis of statelessness. Asylum seekers still find themselves in a fundamental condition of rightlessness to the extent that they can be subjected to detention given the monopoly that states continue to have on the legitimate means of movement.[148] As different from the case in Arendt's time, they can challenge their detention conditions if there are specific human rights violations. But as the *Saadi* ruling suggests, in the absence of any such violation, they cannot contest the detention itself, or take action to avoid detention during their asylum determination process. Without the possibility of such action, however, it is difficult to speak of equal personhood of migrants before the law. To recall Arendt's words, "[p]rivileges in some cases, injustices in most, blessings and doom are meted out to them according to accident and without any relation whatsoever to what they do, did, or may do."[149]

If the *Saadi* judgment highlights the continuing relevance of Arendt's argument about the rightlessness of the stateless, the dissenting opinion points to the promising possibilities of interpreting human rights in ways that question rightlessness. These possibilities become manifest, for example, in the concluding remarks of the dissenting judges who questioned the privileges attached to citizenship as they refused to accept the idea that asylum seekers have a necessarily diminished personhood given their status as foreigners:

Ultimately, are we now also to accept that Article 5 of the Convention, which has played a major role in ensuring controls of arbitrary detention, should afford a lower level of protection as regards asylum and immigration which, in social and human terms, are the most crucial issues facing us in the years to come? Is it a crime to be a foreigner? We do not think so.[150]

Although the dissenting opinion was important for contesting the condition of rightlessness created by the *Saadi* judgment to a certain extent, it had some crucial limits. In fact, the criticisms raised by both the dissenting judges and the third-party interveners also reveal the normative, institutional, and discursive constraints that can hinder or undermine the possibilities of interpreting human rights in ways ensuring equal personhood for everyone regardless of citizenship status. These criticisms failed to fully attend to the underlying conditions perpetuating contemporary forms of rightlessness faced by migrants, and in certain instances, they risked reproducing these conditions by reinforcing problematic categories and creating hierarchies within "personhood."

As they articulated their criticisms of the *Saadi v. UK* decision, the dissenting judges, the UNHCR, and several human rights organizations refrained from taking issue with detention as a legitimate practice of territorial sovereignty in migration control. They attacked the decision mainly for blurring the distinctions between asylum seekers and other migrants:

[T]he judgment does not hesitate to treat completely without distinction all categories of non-nationals in all situations—illegal immigrants, persons liable to be deported and those who have committed offences—including them without qualification under the general heading of immigration control, which falls within the scope of States' *unlimited sovereignty.*[151]

This position fails to confront how these distinctions themselves are at the root of the problem, as they allow the states to legitimize detention as a necessary and effective measure taken to determine which migrants are entitled to asylum and which ones are not. By insisting on distinguishing asylum seekers from other migrants, the dissenting opinion ends up justifying the problematic categories that cast some as undeserving intruders who can be treated differently in accordance with the "unlimited sovereignty" of states in the field of immigration control. Appeals to human rights on the basis of such categorical distinctions risk turning asylum into a "filtering process" that "keeps migration exclusion morally defensible while protecting the global gatekeeping operation as a whole," as Jacqueline Bhabha highlights.[152] These distinctions turn personhood into a stratified category, as they draw hierarchical divisions within humanity. They end up relegating the majority of migrants to a fundamental condition of rightlessness as subjects who can be rendered vulnerable to various forms of violence that can be justified as legitimate in accordance with the state's sovereign prerogative to control its borders. The predicament of these migrants, who find themselves stranded in "the indefinite space that opens like a kind [of] a trap door below the person," to use Roberto Esposito's terms, brings to light the haunting presence of semi-persons, and even non-persons, in an age of rights.[153]

The universal discourse of human rights introduces personhood as the basis of entitlement to equal rights. With this move, it aims to "fill in the chasm between man and citizen left gaping since 1789."[154] It is quite tempting to think that the shift from citizenship to personhood resolves the fundamental problem of rightlessness that Arendt examined in her discussion of statelessness. After all, one of the defining features of this condition, according to Arendt's account, was the loss of legal personhood. In a nation-state framework tying legal standing to citizenship, those who were rendered stateless effectively became non-persons relegated to lawlessness. That problem can no longer exist, one might conclude, once personhood is ascribed to every human being regardless of citizenship status.

What arises out of this chapter is an equivocal picture of this novel development, highlighting not only its political and normative significance but also its limits and problems. The rise of a universal discourse of human rights, centered on legal personhood, is a welcome development to the extent that it allows migrants to have a standing before the law and make claims to rights. As Arendt's phenomenological account of personhood highlights, such formal recognition is not simply a juridical matter. As an artificial mask that enables equalization of different actors, legal personhood is inextricably tied to one's political and human standing. However, Arendt's account also brings to light the fragility of personhood and urges us to look into the various practices and conditions that can end up undermining and diminishing it. As the discussion of deportation and immigration detention underscores, human rights norms do not provide robust guarantees against this troubling possibility. To the extent that they affirm not only the principle of equal personhood but also that of territorial sovereignty, these norms are not completely free from "the perplexities of the Rights of Man" analyzed by Arendt.

"Rightlessness" becomes a crucial critical concept in examining the contemporary practices and conditions that can render the legal standing of migrants precarious. This precarity cannot be understood as a condition that is created simply by external factors, though such factors do need to be taken into account, as the discussion of the contemporary normalization of detention and deportation points out. Rightlessness needs to be understood also as a condition symptomatic of the perplexities of human rights. As the detention and deportation cases from the ECtHR underscore, some of the clauses in international human rights law can give rise to the possibilities of eroding the personhood of migrants and rendering their rights dependent on discretionary decisions. These cases indicate the need to conduct critical inquiries into international human rights law to see how "it leaves open the possibility of its own retraction" in certain circumstances.[155]

This argument does not suggest that rightlessness, understood as de-personalization, is inevitable given the tensions between equal person-hood and territorial sovereignty. In fact, as highlighted by both of the ECtHR cases, there are different ways of navigating the perplexities of human rights, and some of these ways are more promising than others for the purposes of establishing migrants as equal persons before the law. At-tending carefully to these different possibilities, an Arendtian framework refrains from the conclusion that human rights norms are doomed to per-petuate problems of depersonalization or that depersonalization is intrin-sic to the concept of personhood.[156]

One of the crucial reasons for rethinking "rightlessness" as a critical concept in an age of rights, then, is the fragility of the guarantees offered by existing inscriptions of legal personhood in international human rights norms. As Arendt's analysis of statelessness highlights, however, what is at stake in rightlessness is not merely an unmaking of one's legal status. Rightlessness also denotes a precarious political and human standing. The next chapter aims to make the case for rethinking "rightlessness" as a critical concept for understanding the plight of asylum seekers and refu-gees who are confined in camps that deny them the possibilities of partici-pating in the ongoing constitution of a political and human community through their labor, work, and action.

4.

Expulsion from Politics and Humanity

ON NOVEMBER 1, 2007, Italy put into effect an emergency decree that allowed citizens of other EU states to be summarily expelled on the order of local prefects if they were judged to be a threat to "public safety." The expulsion order had to be approved by a local justice of the peace, but the immigrants to be expelled had neither the right to trial nor the right to appeal. The decree resulted from the public outrage following the rape and murder of an Italian woman allegedly by a Roma immigrant. Drafted by the Italian government in an emergency session on October 31, it came into force overnight, and the next day bulldozers started to level the shantytowns where Roma immigrants lived. According to many Italian politicians and administrators, the severe measures were justified. For instance, Carlo Mosca, the prefect of Rome at the time, defended the decree by referring to the "bestial" nature of the crime: "A hard line is needed because, faced with animals, the only way to react is with maximum severity."[1]

The stipulations of the Italian decree effectively denied legal standing to a group of immigrants who were already criminalized within an anti-immigrant discourse that stratified populations along ethnic and racial lines. The decree deprived these immigrants of any possibility of appearing before the courts and appealing their expulsion orders. What was denied, however, was not merely access to law. The Italian case exemplifies how the unmaking of legal personhood often goes hand in hand with the destruction of political and human standing. The deportation order and the leveling of homes endeavored to remove the Roma immigrants from the political and social fabric of Italy. In addition, the statement of the prefect shows that such extreme measures cannot be taken without some kind of "de-subjectivation," to use Judith Butler's term, as the immigrants in question were rendered non-subjects, constituted "as the less than human without entitlement to rights, as the humanly unrecognizable."[2]

The last chapter addressed the pervasive problems that migrants face, especially in the context of detention and deportation, by examining the limits of existing human rights norms in providing robust guarantees for migrants' recognition as equal persons before the law. But rightlessness is not merely a juridical problem in Arendt's account of statelessness. In fact, bearing in mind her phenomenological account of *persona*, even the unmaking of legal personhood points to the need to inquire into the nonjuridical dimensions of this condition. Arendt highlights that the stateless lost "the entire social texture into which they were born and in which they established for themselves a distinct place in the world."[3] What results from this loss is dispossession from a political community that could render one's actions, speech, and opinions relevant and meaningful. Since it becomes very difficult, if not altogether impossible, for the stateless to be recognized as subjects participating in the ongoing constitution of the human world with their own activities, this loss also amounts to an "expulsion from humanity."[4]

This chapter aims to examine how rightlessness becomes manifest in the precarious political and human standing of asylum seekers, refugees, and undocumented immigrants confined in camps and detention centers for extended periods of time. To do this, the chapter offers a close engagement with the main concepts of Arendt's political theory, especially with her analysis, in *The Human Condition*, of the fundamental human activities of action, work, and labor. Reading Arendt's account of rightlessness with her account of *vita activa* (active life, or life of activity) suggests that rightlessness comprises the loss of not only the right to action but also the right to work and the right to labor. Asylum seekers, refugees, and undocumented immigrants, subjected to long-term confinement, are rightless not simply because they are excluded from a public space that allows them to appear, act, and speak before a community of actors. They are rightless also because they are forced to live under conditions that make it very difficult for them to engage in the everyday laboring activities that instill confidence in the reality, regularity, and familiarity of life. In addition, they are rightless as they are denied the possibilities of establishing a relatively durable, inhabitable world with their own work. This reading brings to light less visible forms of violence that can hinder the efforts of asylum seekers, refugees, and undocumented immigrants to claim and exercise human rights.

Rethinking rightlessness in light of Arendt's famous conceptual triad of action/work/labor also provides a new understanding of her key concepts and arguments. Many readers of Arendt take action to be the quintessentially human activity in her political theory. On the basis of this assumption, they either applaud Arendt for revealing what is properly human or criticize her for offering a truncated understanding of what it means to be human. Questioning this action-centric reading, which overlooks or downplays the crucial contributions of work and labor to the human condition, I suggest that Arendt's phenomenological account presents action, work, and labor as different yet interrelated ways of being in the world with others and highlights how each activity is crucial to living a life that can be recognized as "human."[5]

The chapter begins with a reinterpretation of Arendt's arguments about the fundamental human activities of action, work, and labor. Especially important in this reinterpretation is the restoration of the full dignity of labor, which is often taken to be an activity that is not properly human. The conclusion that Arendt's analysis displays contempt for labor fails to take into account her argument that this activity is indispensable not only for enjoying the sheer bliss of being alive but also for cultivating a trust in the reality of life and establishing some degree of regularity and familiarity. If work is important for transforming earth into a habitable world with relatively permanent structures, labor aids work in the daily care and maintenance of this world. Distinctive contributions of labor and work to the human condition, as well as the connections between these two activities, can be seen, for example, in the lives of refugees who are confined to camps. The conditions of these camps render their inhabitants almost completely dependent on the compassion of others to meet the necessities of life and rarely allow for the possibility of turning the earth into a world that provides a dwelling place for human beings.

Following this interpretation that recasts "labor" and "work" as crucial activities defining the human condition, I turn to "action," or "the political activity par excellence."[6] Arendt's conceptualization of action is often seen as the linchpin of a politics defined by aestheticism and lacking any meaningful content or purpose.[7] Arendtian action, which is inextricably linked to speech, seems inadequate for addressing questions of injustice, power, and violence. My reading of "action" in the context of Arendt's reflections on statelessness arrives at a different conclusion. Precisely by drawing attention away from questions of substantive content and specific purpose, I argue, Arendt's account of action and speech brings to view the *constitutive* effects of these activities, or their vital role in the ongoing constitution of political subjects, political community, and humanity. What emerges out of this reading is a different picture of Arendt— not an elitist celebrating the public glories of the privileged few who are entitled to engage in action but a critical theorist bringing to light the predicament of those who are deprived of the possibility of acting, and especially speaking, in public. Read along these lines, rightlessness in its most fundamental form consists of being denied the possibility of enacting a right to action and speech. This denial amounts to an expulsion from political community and humanity, as I highlight in my discussion of asylum seekers who stitch their lips to protest the conditions that relegate them to speechlessness.

A Critical Phenomenology of the Human Condition

Arendt provides a distinctive account of the human condition by examining *vita activa* in terms of three activities: labor, work, and action. In *The Human Condition*, she defines all three as "fundamental human activities" and adds: "They are fundamental because each corresponds to one of the basic conditions under which life on earth has been given to man."[8] Labor corresponds to life, work to worldliness, and action to plurality; all of these activities and their corresponding conditions are connected to the basic conditions of human existence: natality and mortality.[9] "Human condition" is the term that Arendt proposes to capture these basic conditions of human existence as well as the conditions that human activities create and change. As different from "human nature," which denotes a static essence, "human condition" indicates a dynamic interaction between what is given and what human beings create with their own activities; if that which is given shapes these activities to some extent, it cannot completely determine them and continuously changes as a result of them.[10] Precisely because of this dynamic interaction,

labor, work, and action are not static categories or "a-historical structures of the mind," to use Paul Ricoeur's terms, but instead "historical
structures" that undergo "manifold permutations."[11]

In broad strokes, the distinctive features of these activities can be
summed up as follows: *Labor* encompasses several activities that attend
to "the vital necessities" of human life.[12] There is no end to laboring
activity as long as one is alive; this bodily "toil and trouble" needs to be
monotonously and repetitively performed in a cyclical routine.[13] *Work*
denotes the fabrication of durable objects and comprises all of the activities that human beings engage in to establish "a dwelling place more
permanent and more stable than themselves."[14] Although human beings
make these artifacts, the finished products achieve a "relative independence" and endow the world with an "objectivity" that it would otherwise lack.[15] *Action*, or "the political activity par excellence," arises
from natality, or the human capacity to begin something new and take
initiative.[16] Its distinctive feature is its reliance on the condition of
human plurality: Whereas the activities of laboring and fabrication can
be undertaken in isolation from others, action requires the presence of
others.[17]

For many readers, Arendt's conceptual triad represents a hierarchical
ordering of *vita activa* since it seems to elevate action above all other activities in an attempt to break with the Western philosophical tradition
that harbors contempt for politics. Because of her strong assumption that
"only the political life is human,"[18] these readers argue, Arendt endows
action with an "existential supremacy" as the only activity that creates
public spaces, allows the exercise of freedom, and renders us "properly
human."[19] This action-centric reading acknowledges the crucial importance Arendt attributes to work, even though it also suggests that she
accords a lower esteem to this activity. Enabling human beings to transform earth into an inhabitable world, work contributes to the cultivation
of "a *specifically human* life, a life removed from the ceaseless motion of
nature," as Dana Villa puts it.[20] According to the action-centric reading,
labor occupies the lowest rung of the hierarchy. Comprising the activities
that human beings share with animals, labor is not seen as "distinctively
human."[21] In fact, for many readers, Arendtian labor is a "pre-human"
activity, or "the most animal of human activities,"[22] embodying a "solip-
sistic, herdlike level of consciousness."[23] As "the least 'human' of human
activities," Jennifer Ring argues, labor can be easily dispensed with and
"given over to machines most readily."[24]

This action-centric reading gives rise to different reactions. Some embrace Arendt as a theorist recovering what is genuinely political and properly human. Her political theory, they argue, provides resources for an agonistic politics in which citizens, freed from the demands imposed by the necessities of life, actualize their freedom by taking initiative and disclosing their authentic selves in a public realm.[25] Others draw attention to the inevitable exclusions of this agonistic freedom. They highlight that Arendt's "action metaphysics,"[26] harboring an elitist disdain for the laboring activity, equates bodily needs with animality and posits liberation from these needs as the precondition of a truly human and political life. Excluded from the scope of Arendtian politics, according to this criticism, are all those who are bound by the necessities of labor (e.g., women, laborers) and relegated to a less-than-human status.[27] Finally, for others, although Arendt's conceptual distinctions are not "empirical or sociological generalizations" that identify each activity with a particular group, class, or gender,[28] they are problematic to the extent that that they overlook multitudinous connections between action, work, and labor.[29]

This brief overview does not do full justice to the wide range of positions on Arendt's conceptualization of labor, work, and action, but it provides a helpful backdrop for my argument: Challenging the action-centric reading, I suggest that The Human Condition is an attempt to illuminate vita activa (and not simply action) in its full dignity. Arendt's phenomenological account brings out the distinctive contribution of each activity to the human condition and establishes crucial connections between them, preventing her analysis from being construed in hierarchical terms. Arendt does characterize action as "the political activity par excellence,"[30] but it is important to note that human life is not simply centered on action in her account; it includes a variety of other activities, including labor and work but also thinking and judgment, which are not covered in The Human Condition.[31] More importantly, though action is the activity that is most closely affiliated with politics, it includes a wide range of interactions in which human beings take initiative; to put it simply, action is not simply political activity.[32] Arendt's account of vita activa provides us with a richer conception of what it means to live a life that can be recognized as "human," and that recognition depends not only on action understood simply as political activity but also on labor and work, among other things. As a related point, although Arendt insists on drawing distinctions between these activities, her account also brings to view multifarious connections between them. Such connections arise partly because all three activities are "rooted in natality" and "conditioned by the fact that men live together"; in other words, labor and work partake of the two characteristics associated with Arendtian action: natality and plurality.[33] In addition, no single activity is sufficient in itself; each is in need of the other activities to be a meaningful part human life. To make this argument, I turn to labor in this section and offer a new interpretation that reclaims its distinctively human elements and brings to view its connections to work and action.

We can begin to loosen the hold of the action-centric view on our readings of *The Human Condition* by remembering the goal that Arendt sets for her analysis at the beginning of the book: to understand *vita activa* in its full complexity and dignity. This task involves calling into question a philosophical tradition that has elevated *vita contemplativa* to "the only truly free way of life" and conferred on *vita activa* only a "very restricted dignity" for its provision of bodily needs.[34] This hierarchical ordering ends up not only devaluing *vita activa* but also erasing the distinctions among the different human activities.[35] Challenging this philosophical tradition, Arendt's analysis represents *vita activa*, or "human life in so far as it is actively engaged in doing something," in a new light, capturing what renders it delightful and worthy of respect; without the activities of labor, work, and action, she reminds us, we would not even have "the world into which we are born."[36]

Arendt's representation of *vita activa* is also different from the modern attempts to break with the philosophical tradition privileging *vita contemplativa*. These attempts, including most notably the "re-evaluation of all values" that Marx and Nietzsche undertake, turn the hierarchy upside down and glorify active life. But such modern reversals, according to Arendt, leave "the conceptual framework . . . intact," as they also work with the assumption that all the different activities within *vita activa* are governed by "one comprehensive principle" and fail to clarify the distinctions among these activities.[37] Arendt's critique of these modern attempts suggests that what she undertakes in *The Human Condition* is not simply a reversal placing action at the top of the hierarchy. Equally important in this critique is her refusal to define human life with "one comprehensive principle," which underscores that the human condition cannot be reduced to simply one activity.[38]

Most readers of Arendt would agree with these points, but what remains a challenging task is to establish that her account values labor as an activity that makes an irreplaceable contribution to living a recognizably human life. At first look, it is hard not to join those who see nothing properly human in labor, which comprises all the activities that we need to engage in to meet our biological needs. The repetitive, cyclical nature of these activities seems to be completely at odds with the emphasis Arendt puts on the human capacity to initiate new beginnings and break away from the routines of ordinary life. In addition, these activities undertaken for the maintenance of life bring human beings closer to the rest of the animal species. Arendt seems to share the disdainful attitude of Greek antiquity toward labor, when she declares that, "the use of the word 'animal' in the concept of *animal laborans*, as distinguished from the very questionable use of the same word in the term *animal rationale*, is fully justified."[39] Looking at this statement, it is hard not to conclude that Arendt denigrates labor as an activity reducing human beings to the level of animals.

This conclusion, however, overlooks how Arendt breaks with the beliefs of Greek antiquity, as I discuss below, to recognize the crucial importance of labor. Equating labor with life, necessity, and animality also fails to take into consideration that each of the concepts in Arendt's account, including labor, consists of "a multiplicity of interconnected elements that defy attribution in terms of a settled meaning or unified synoptic picture," as Mary Dietz argues.[40] Life, necessity, and animality are definitely part of Arendt's account of labor, but they do not by any means exhaust the meaning of labor.

For the purpose of understanding labor in its multiple dimensions, it is important to remember that Arendt identifies the repetitive, cyclical activities that human beings engage in to sustain their lives with a sense of joy that cannot be found in any other activity.[41] Only by engaging in labor, Arendt reminds us again and again in *The Human Condition*, can human beings enjoy "the sheer bliss of being alive,"[42] "[t]he blessing of life as a whole," "felicity with which earthly life has always been blessed,"[43] "vitality and liveliness."[44] When the "cycle of painful exhaustion and pleasurable regeneration" is "throw[n] out of balance," according to Arendt, we lose "the elemental happiness that comes from being alive."[45]

Arendt does emphasize how this happiness is shared by "all living creatures,"[46] but this does not mean that labor is an inferior form of activity that is not properly human. That problematic reasoning would exclude from the realm of what is properly human, for example, the urge to appear—something that many of Arendt's readers would agree to be crucial to living a life that can be recognized as human by others. After all,

Arendt takes appearance, which she relates to the urge to be seen by spectators, as a characteristic shared by both human beings and animals.[47] Hence, the fact that we share the sheer bliss of being alive with animals does not make labor a less-than-human activity.

What is at stake in this feeling of happiness and vitality is not simply something biologically shared with the rest of the living creatures, however. If labor were to be completely eliminated, Arendt claims, it "would not only rob biological life of its most natural pleasures but deprive the *specifically human* life of its very liveliness and vitality."[48] Far from being non-human, then, there is something that is all too human about labor in Arendt's framework. This distinctively human element is manifest in the happiness that we derive from labor and without which "real grief and sorrow could hardly be borne."[49] Neither the sense of achievement attained in work nor the rare joy experienced in action, Arendt argues, can be a substitute for the happiness and contentment obtained from labor.[50] A life without labor would be defined by "boredom,"[51] and as we will see in the case of refugees confined in camps, without these everyday activities that we take for granted, human lives are resigned to a profound sense of void and futility. This is not to suggest that Arendt attributes to labor simply joy and happiness; there is, of course, the "toil and trouble" that she repetitively refers to. But the key point is that, as long as this "painful exhaustion" is accompanied by a sense of "pleasurable regeneration," human beings experience a bliss that they can find in no other activity.

Labor is important for Arendt because it instills in human beings not only this elemental happiness but also a trust in the reality of life. Arendt's concerns about the modern processes that give rise to a sense of being alienated from the world are well known, but it is equally important to attend to her concerns about the possibility that human beings might also be alienated from life.[52] *The Human Condition* opens with the launch of Sputnik; Arendt identifies in the commentary on this event a "wish to escape the human condition" and "a rebellion against human existence as it has been given."[53] Labor is crucial for instilling in human beings a sense of being "earth-bound creatures" connected to other living organisms.[54] As Arendt puts it, the danger of life-alienation can be kept at bay only if human beings are "willing to take the burden, the toil and trouble of life, upon themselves."[55] Far from proposing to eliminate labor, she insists that human beings need to engage in labor to sustain their "[t]rust in the reality of life" and argues that this trust "depends almost exclusively on the intensity with which life is felt, on the impact with which it makes itself felt."[56] The pain and pleasure that accompany labor are crucial for sustaining this trust, as they place human beings in the cycle of nature and allow them to directly experience life in its vitality. More importantly, labor instills this trust by endowing human lives with a sense of posterity and even immortality. It provides human beings with "the quiet confidence that he who in 'toil and trouble' has done his part, remains a part of nature in the future of his children and his children's children."[57] If all of the human activities in Arendt's *vita activa* "are, in their own ways, attempts to confer *immortality* upon perishing things," as Paul Ricoeur suggests, then labor helps us "endure our mortal condition" by cultivating this trust in the reality of life and providing us with the confidence that there will be life once we pass away.[58]

Repetitive activities of labor are also important for endowing life with a sense of regularity, familiarity, and reliability. Arendt is often taken to be a theorist fascinated by extraordinary beginnings that have the capacity to unsettle the familiar routines of everyday world.[59] But this fascination does not entail a dismissive attitude toward all that is ordinary. The crucial importance of such routines becomes visible especially when we are confronted with human beings who are thrown out of the habitual fabric of everyday life. Arendt points to this possibility in her discussion of Kafka's *The Castle*, in which K. tries to lead an ordinary life but fails to settle in "as a normal member of human society." Her discussion of K.'s struggle highlights that "[m]en's lives must be normal, not exceptional."[60] In her essay "We Refugees," she makes a similar point when she highlights that one important loss that characterizes the lives of refugees is the loss of home, which entails the loss of "the familiarity of daily life" as well as "the rupture of [their] private lives."[61] As we will see in the case of various categories of migrants living in confinement, an extraordinary life in which even the most basic human activities become political—e.g., eating, sleeping, moving—has its tolls. When Arendt describes labor in terms of "the same happy and purposeless regularity with which day and night and life and death follow each other," then, she is not necessarily denigrating its repetitiveness, as it is often thought.[62] Implicit in that statement is a subtle recognition of the confidence that arises out of the settled, recurrent, and familiar habits of ordinary life.

Deprived of labor, Arendt's analysis underscores, human beings would have neither the joyful sensation of being alive nor a confidence in the reality and regularity of life. So then, why have we come to see Arendt as a theorist

looking down upon labor with disdain? The answer to this question probably lies in the tendency to read her as a nostalgic thinker sharing the ancient Greek contempt for labor. But *The Human Condition* is far from a
celebration of the Athenian way of life; in fact, Arendt criticizes the Greeks
for the institution of slavery and draws our attention to "[t]he price for the
elimination of life's burden from the shoulders of all citizens."[63] It is especially important to note that she takes issue with slavery not simply for "the
violent injustice of forcing one part of humanity into the darkness of pain
and necessity" but also for its negative impact on the lives of citizens. By
eliminating labor from their lives, she argues, citizens ended up with a more
impoverished experience of human life because "the price for absolute freedom from necessity is, in a sense, life itself, or rather the substitution of vicarious life for real life."[64] Without labor, the Athenian citizens experienced
life only "vicariously"; they did not even have a direct experience of their
senses, as they "could 'see and hear through their slaves.'"[65] Arendt diverges
from the ancient Greek assumptions about labor by pointing out how this
activity connects human beings with what is sensorily given in their earthly
environment and endows them with the immediate sensation of being alive.
She sees this embodied experience, which places human beings in the cycle
of nature, as indispensable for cultivating a trust in the reality of life.

The presumption that Arendt is a philhellene affirming the Greek contempt for labor also overlooks the fact that she draws on a different tradition in an effort to capture the distinctive contribution of labor to the
human condition. For Greeks, labor in itself, and not just harsh labor, was
a curse; as can be seen in Hesiod, it was a punishment that Zeus gave to
human beings for Prometheus's deception.[66] Turning to the Old Testament, Arendt uncovers a different understanding of labor as an activity
undertaken to preserve the world. In this alternative tradition, she argues,
the punishment is not labor and birth, which are conceived as blessings,
but instead "harsh" labor and "birth full of sorrow." Arendt even suggests
that we have come to see labor as a curse "due to an unconscious interpretation of the Old Testament in the light of Greek thinking."[67] According
to Genesis, she highlights, labor is an activity that human beings need to
engage in to care for the world and protect it against destruction from
natural forces. To make this point, Arendt follows the lead of Martin
Buber and Franz Rosenzweig, who, in their German translation of the
Old Testament, use the words *Adam* and *Adama* to establish a connection
between man and soil. In her English rendering of the Buber-Rosenzweig
translation of Genesis, Arendt repeats their use of "[p]aronomasia—the

sound-alike quality of words indicating a mutual relation of ideas"[68]—to recover the crucial importance of labor for human life: "and He, God, created Adam of the dust of *adamah*. . . . He, God, took Adam and put him into the garden of Eden to till and to watch it." According to this alternative tradition, "man (*adam*) had been created to take care and watch over soil (*adamah*)."[69]

Arendt's turn to the Buber-Rosenzweig translation of the Old Testament emphasizes the crucial connections she establishes between labor and work. She insists that labor has two tasks: the fulfillment of bodily needs and the fight against natural growth and decay. If the first task is characterized by activities that have no long-lasting effect because they take place in that endless cycle of production and consumption, the second task is closely related to work because it involves "[t]he protection and preservation of the world against natural processes."[70] What human beings build and create with their work needs to be maintained regularly with the recurrent practices of labor. Engaging in labor ties human beings to not only the biological life cycle, then, but also the human world; without it, human beings risk both an alienation from life and the dissolution of the permanent structures they establish in the world.

These connections are often overlooked, however, because of the tendency to read *The Human Condition* as "a phenomenological topography of the *vita activa*," to use Dana Villa's terms, assigning each activity a proper place.[71] Such a reading seems justified given that Arendt underscores how "each human activity points to its proper location in the world."[72] But given the connections between these activities, there is a need to rethink what it means for each activity to have "its proper location." Patchen Markell offers a helpful suggestion in this regard, when he proposes that the walls that Arendt erects between these activities and their locations might not be as "impenetrable" as many of her readers suggest, and their function might not be to simply separate but also to connect.[73] After all, the goal that Arendt sets for her analysis of the human condition is to attend to the "distinctions and articulations within the *vita activa*."[74] Arendt's recurring references to "articulations" in addition to "distinctions" indicates that her analysis aims to capture not only how the activities of labor, work, and action are distinguished from each other but also how they are interconnected or conjoined. In addition, Arendt's phenomenological orientation entails a different approach to the work of conceptual distinctions in thinking. It is worth remembering a point that she makes when she introduces her quite controversial distinction between "power" and "violence" in her essay "On Violence": Noting that such distinctions "hardly ever correspond to watertight compartments in the real world," she adds that "[p]ower and violence, though they are distinct phenomena, usually appear together."[75] This remark cautions against seeing the distinctions between labor, work, and action as hermetically sealed boundaries and invites a reading that attends to how these activities appear together in the world.

Once we attend to the distinctive contribution of each activity to the human condition as well as the connections between them, the idea that there is a hierarchical ranking of activities in Arendt's account of *vita activa* becomes highly suspect, especially if the conclusion to be drawn is that her positive assessment of action can come only at the expense of a denigrating account of the other activities in the *vita activa*. As several scholars have noted, this conclusion overlooks the crucial connections between work and action, especially the reliance of action on the work to become memorable and achieve immortality.[76] But it is not only work that calls into question the hierarchical reading of *vita activa*. As the discussion in this section highlights, labor does not simply sustain the needs of biological life. As an activity that instills in human beings the sheer bliss of being alive, cultivates their trust in the reality of life, endows their lives with regularity and familiarity, and takes care of the daily maintenance of the world, labor is fundamental to living a life that can be recognized as "human." These features not only distinguish labor from work and action but also connect it to these two other activities: It is labor that takes care of the durable works built by *homo faber*. That connection also hints at why labor is important for action. Without the repetitive, mundane activities that sustain a trust in life, it becomes very difficult, if not impossible, for human beings to create a space in which they can act and speak in the presence of others.[77]

Once we recognize the irreplaceable contribution of each activity to the human condition and recover the strong connections between them, Arendt's account of *vita activa* appears in a new light—not an exclusionary schema or a rigid taxonomy but instead a critical phenomenology that can shed new light on less visible forms of violence endured by asylum seekers, refugees, and undocumented immigrants. Among these forms of violence, we can cite formidable obstacles to deriving a sense of joy and vitality from daily activities of life, cultivating a confidence in the reality and regularity of life, establishing a relatively stable world that one can inhabit with others, and creating spaces of appearance by acting and speaking in the company of others. These problems suggest that the fundamental condition of rightlessness that Arendt examines in her account of statelessness can continue to exist even in cases where there is no outright violation of the rights listed in existing conventions of human rights.

Between Life and Death: Rightlessness and Labor

Arendt's reflections on labor bring to light two extremes that can make it very difficult to live a life that can be recognized as human: One extreme points to a life that is deprived of the possibilities of engaging in many of the laboring activities that can instill a trust in the reality and regularity of life. It would be a mistake to assume that this loss affects only the privileged, who have the means to impose labor on others, as was the case for slave owners in Greek antiquity. In some cases, life without labor can be a burden instead of a privilege, as I discuss below. The second extreme highlights the possibility that human beings can be imprisoned in their biological metabolisms, constantly preoccupied with survival needs. This possibility comes to light particularly in Arendt's characterization of late modern societies in terms of "the victory of the *animal laborans*."[78] There, Arendt criticizes not only the assimilation of all human activities to labor but also the elimination of any individuality in the name of the "survival of the animal species man."[79] She is even hesitant to use the term "laboring" for the activities human beings engage in under these circumstances. When the activity in question is reduced to simply "a sheer automatic functioning," Arendt suggests, "laboring " becomes "too lofty, too ambitious a word for what we are doing."[80]

In what follows, I examine how these possibilities manifest themselves in the lives of refugees confined in camps for extended periods of time. For the purposes of this discussion, it is worth briefly looking at Arendt's own reflections on camps. Unlike some contemporary thinkers who generalize about contemporary problems of refugees on the basis of Nazi extermination camps (e.g., Giorgio Agamben),[81] Arendt's analysis is attentive to the differences in the structures and functioning of different types of camps. She identifies three types of camps, calling them Hades, Purgatory, and Hell, and she argues that each corresponds to distinct Western conceptions of life after death. Among these, Purgatory and Hell refer to the camps that specifically emerged within the context of totalitarianism—Purgatory exemplified by the Soviet labor camps and Hell the Nazi concentration camps. As different from these totalitarian camps in which everything is permitted with no consideration of rights, interests, or utility, Hades refers to "relatively mild forms" of camps that are more commonly seen. Invented within the context of late nineteenth-century imperialism, Arendt argues, these camps have been used to deal with "undesirable elements," including "refugees, the stateless persons, the asocial and the unemployed."[82] Although there are significant differences between these different types of camps, they also share something in common:

> [T]he human masses sealed off in them are treated as if they no longer existed, as if what happened to them were no longer of any interest to anybody, as if they were already dead and some evil spirit gone mad were amusing himself by stopping them for a while between life and death before admitting them to eternal peace.[83]

Camps as spaces for excluding the undesirable from the rest of the human world, derealizing their human status, and suspending them between life and death, Arendt contends, precede and survive totalitarianism understood as a specific historical constellation. In fact, in an international system organized into tightly knit national communities, camps become "the only practical substitute for nonexistent homeland" in the case of those who are stateless.[84]

The contemporary proliferation of refugee camps shows that the situation of refugees as undesirables is not drastically different today, despite the significant developments in the field of international human rights. Camps remain the primary domicile for refugees on the basis of the assumption that their condition is temporary. The international community continues to approach refugees as unfortunate exceptions to the norm of nationality.[85] Accordingly, it promotes the ideal solution as one of repatriation to the country of origin at the expense of other solutions, such as resettlement. This false assumption of temporariness justifies camps as "intermediate holding grounds."[86] What is presented as an interim solution, however, often turns into "a long-standing and intractable state of limbo."[87] In fact, the majority of refugees find themselves in what is referred to as "protracted" situations, and the average duration of these protracted situations is now close to 20 years.[88] Most refugees and internally displaced persons in the global South live in camps and become dependent on humanitarian aid.[89]

Critics have highlighted the problems with these camps, which restrict the freedom of movement and threaten several rights of refugees, including the right to employment and education.[90] More importantly, camps easily turn into spaces beyond the rule of law, rendering refugees vulnerable to an arbitrary exercise of power. As anomalous sites located within the territories of host countries but effectively put under the de facto sovereignty of humanitarian organizations, they are plagued by problems of violence, abuse, and corruption.[91]

In addition to these well-documented human rights violations, long-term encampment engenders less visible forms of violence that can be illuminated by an Arendtian analysis. As spaces of confinement for those who are rendered undesirables, camps give rise to a fundamental condition of rightlessness, as they undermine the possibilities of engaging in the familiar routines of life (labor), establishing a reliable and durable dwelling place (work), and creating public spaces where one can act and speak in the presence of others (action). In what follows, I discuss how Arendt's notion of "labor" can become a critical concept for understanding some of these less visible forms of violence in a new light.[92]

Camps are characterized by a disruption of the basic activities, rhythms, and cycles of life that we take for granted. Refugees can be woken up at night, for example, simply for "head counts" to verify their numbers.[93] In addition, it becomes very difficult for refugees to perform even the most basic activities of fulfilling their bodily needs. From an Arendtian perspective, such quotidian activities are crucial for "remain[ing] and swing[ing] contentedly in nature's prescribed cycle" and experiencing life in its full vitality, as discussed earlier.[94] In the case of refugees, it is very difficult to speak of this kind of contentment, as they become almost completely dependent on the compassion of others to meet their needs. They lack control over even their own nourishment, which is regulated by the food rations that provide them with a bare minimum necessary for subsistence.[95]

Not being able to engage in the laboring activities to fulfill bodily needs makes it very difficult to live a life that is recognizably human. This predicament is manifest in various forms of dehumanization that refugees face in camps, and what is even more striking is that such dehumanization can be discerned even in humanitarian practices that are intended to help refugees. One such practice is "fixing," or the initial counting of refugees, which involves identifying them with tamper-proof plastic wristbands or marking their fingers, hands, or toes with visible or invisible ink.[96] The "head count," mentioned earlier, is another practice prone to dehumanization. In this exercise, refugees can be placed in fenced enclosures that are sometimes referred to as "corrals" as if they were livestock;[97] to make sure that their movement is orderly, they can be put under the control of "ushers" who are also called "shepherds."[98] Encampment necessarily involves such practices of "care and maintenance," to use a phrase frequently invoked in humanitarian circles, which risk rendering refugees "humanly unrecognizable" by reducing them to "worldless specimens of the species mankind."[99]

It is not simply biological activities that are thwarted in the context of long-term encampment; more importantly, it becomes very difficult for refugees to engage in occupational activities that could free them from complete dependence on humanitarian aid. Many refugees cannot find official employment inside or outside of camps; deprived of work permits, they are forced to resort to illegal means of sustaining their lives.[100] Those who become dependent on humanitarian aid to meet their basic needs express feelings of impotence and loss of self-esteem. In fact, even the term "refugee" comes to stand for weakness, poverty, and dependency, as can be seen in the following statement by a Somali refugee located in the Dadaab camps in Kenya:

> The word refugee, in my opinion, in our heads, it means a weak individual; that is how we see ourselves. We ourselves don't like it when we are called "refugees"; we are not happy with it. But what can you do? It is a weak person, a person whose country was destroyed; it means a poor person, who has nothing, who is begging food that is handed down. That is what it means to me.[101]

This statement resonates strongly with Arendt's observations of the daily struggles of refugees in their host countries. In "We Refugees," Arendt highlights the feeling of humiliation that arises out of dependence on the charity of others for survival:

> If we are saved we feel humiliated, and if we are helped we feel degraded. We fight like madmen for private existences with individual destinies, since we are afraid of becoming part of that miserable lot of *schnorrers* whom we, many of us former philanthropists, remember only too well.[102]

Being able to meet one's own needs by engaging in the activities of labor is crucial for establishing a private existence with an individual destiny.

Without that possibility, there is the risk that refugees will be seen merely as an undifferentiated mass of destitute victims.

But labor is not simply about the fulfillment of subsistence needs, for Arendt. It is also crucial for cultivating a trust in the reality and regularity of life. Repetitive activities that we engage in on a daily basis endow our lives with a sense of familiarity or ordinariness that is the only guarantee against the threat of alienation from life. In an analysis of Sudanese women in a refugee camp in Kakuma, Kenya, Ruth Russell and Frances Stage highlight how refugee camps are characterized by a "deadening experience of unlimited and aimless time."[103] The authors compare the stillness of the camp with the hustle and bustle of the neighboring village, where the villagers are busy with everyday activities such as preparing food or gathering fuel. In the absence of these activities, for refugees in the camp, "time seemed to drag on" or "felt elongated."[104]

It is worth remembering here Arendt's criticism of the Greek institution of slavery not simply for its imposition of an unbearable injustice on the slaves but also for its relegation of the free male citizens to a life lived vicariously. Arendt characterizes the lives of these citizens in terms of a loss despite the fact that they were able to engage in politics in the leisurely time created by freedom from labor. In the case of refugees in camps, the loss is much more devastating precisely because leisure is experienced as a "burden" or as "an abundance of meaningless free time," and not as an opportunity for "self-fulfillment and creative action."[105] In the absence of the quotidian activities that Arendt associates with labor, refugees often find themselves trapped in "long periods of unstructured time" and experience a profound sense of boredom, impotence, and superfluity.[106] Suspended in the deadly stillness of "an endless present," to use Michel Agier's terms, many refugees often feel "physically and mentally imprisoned" and even consider committing suicide.[107] From an Arendtian perspective, this contemplation of suicides can be seen as the most troubling sign of life-alienation—a problem that arises from the loss of happiness, vitality, and trust generated by the everyday activities of labor. In fact, in her essay "We Refugees," Arendt also notes the high rate of suicide among the refugees.[108] As subjects thrown out of the habitual fabric of everyday life, it becomes more likely for refugees to lose the confidence associated with participation in the ongoing generation of life. Without that confidence, it becomes very difficult to endure the sense of futility that can be instilled by the human condition of mortality, as highlighted in Arendt's account of labor, and there is the danger that human life itself will lose its meaning.

The experience of camps as spaces of the "living dead" is one of the extreme conditions brought to light by Arendt's reflections on labor; the other extreme condition of worldlessness is equally important for understanding the plight of refugees. Because concerns about subsistence are so central to life in camps, it becomes very difficult for refugees to establish a social life that is enriched by a variety of activities. Given the extreme conditions of poverty and hunger, survival often takes over every other consideration, as can be seen in the statement of a Somali refugee:

> Refugee is poverty and hunger. A loser standing around, that is a refugee. I think of poverty, praying to Allah: "Allah, take us out of this misery," this suffering and hardship, carrying water on your bare back, searching for wood in the bushes, lack of milk for your children, unemployment, that is it.[109]

To the extent that this anxious struggle for basic survival creates an experience of "being imprisoned in [one's] metabolism," it risks resigning refugees to what Arendt calls "worldlessness."[110] Any laboring body, preoccupied with biological needs, would have this experience, according to Arendt; but under normal conditions, worldlessness is countered by the elemental joy of being alive as well as a cultivated trust in life. In the case of refugee camps, where there is an extreme uncertainty of survival, there is neither that felicity nor that confidence. In the absence of these, what is left is a laboring body that experiences "painful exhaustion" with no possibility of "pleasurable regeneration." In such cases "where the mills of necessity, of consumption and digestion, grind an impotent human body mercilessly and barrenly to death," worldlessness is much more profound.[111]

Needless to say, refugees do not simply accept the conditions in camps as passive victims, and many do struggle to overcome them. For example, despite the restrictions on their right to work, they engage in various commercial activities; they also barter or sell their food rations to protest its inadequate quantity or bad quality.[112] These activities affirm Arendt's claim that natality and action are present in every activity, including labor. By taking the initiative to engage in such activities, refugees refuse to be relegated to bare lives dependent on charity, and instead try to establish themselves as participants in the generation of life as well as the constitution of a human world. Everyday activities of production and consumption, including cooking and eating food, are also important for establishing a sense of regular and habitual life. These routinized activities, which "enable a consoling bodily repetition of physical actions familiar from the past,"[113] help refugees reconstruct the habitual fabric of their lives, and fight the burden of empty, prolonged time. Arendt's account of labor, illuminating its irreplaceable contribution to living a life that can be recognized as human, assumes critical significance in understanding the importance of such quotidian activities for instilling a trust in the reality and regularity of life—a point that would have been overlooked in action-centric readings of her political theory.

Taking initiative, however, is quite risky given the restrictions in refugee camps. If humanitarian organizations are willing to encourage certain forms of self-sufficiency (e.g., basket-weaving), they strongly discourage initiatives that challenge the administration of life in camps. When refugees barter or trade food, for example, they risk confiscation of that food or even arrest by local police.[114] Their attempts to lead ordinary lives can be stunted in various ways due to the structural conditions of camps. As a result, they are forced to lead rather extraordinary lives in which even buying food becomes quite political. In her account of refugees, Arendt draws attention to the heavy burdens of such extraordinary lives:

> We have become a little hysterical since newspapermen started detecting us and telling us publicly to stop being disagreeable when shopping for milk and bread. . . . We try the best we can to fit into a world where you have to be sort of politically minded when you buy your food.[115]

As this mordant comment highlights, Arendt, often hailed as the theorist of the extraordinary, is quite attentive to the devastating effects of the disruption of ordinary life. Her account of labor, read along with her work on refugees, provides critical insights into the less visible forms of rightlessness that define the lives of those who are deprived of the sheer bliss of being alive as well as a trust in the reality and regularity of life.

Loss of a Durable World: Rightlessness and Work

In Arendt's conceptual triad, "work" consists of the activities of making, which range from building a house to writing a poem. These activities of fabrication differ from those of laboring, for Arendt, and she tries to capture the distinction by invoking the Lockean formula of "the labor of our bodies" and "the work of our hands."[116] Whereas labor takes on a cyclical, repetitive rhythm, material artifacts produced by work have the function of stabilizing human beings amidst this movement, though the connections between the two, discussed earlier, highlight how labor can also participate in this stabilization with its daily care of human artifacts.[117] Work also has a different relationship with nature, as it destroys nature with the purpose of turning it into a habitable world for human beings.[118] For Arendt, instrumentalism involved in work distinguishes it from action. *Homo faber* produces according to the categories of means and ends; whereas the end of action lies in the activity itself and is not dictated from outside, the end of fabrication precedes the activity and guides the fabricator toward the final product.[119] Arendt does not take a negative attitude toward the reification, violence, and instrumentality involved in work, however, as long as "the fabrication experience" is not generalized so as to impose "usefulness and utility" as "the ultimate standards for life and the world of men."[120] In fact, her account highlights the distinctive contribution of work to the human condition as an activity endowing the world with stability, durability, and objectivity.

Given this role, work has significant connections to both labor and action. If labor is necessary to take care of the world built by the activities of working, objects made by *homo faber* are necessary to relieve the pain of laboring.[121] Arendt does not fully develop this last point, but Elaine Scarry's reflections on everyday artifacts can be helpful in understanding the relationship of work to labor and action:

> [A] bodily attribute is projected into the artifact (a fiction, a made thing), which essentially takes over the work of the body, thereby freeing the embodied person of discomfort and thus enabling him to enter a larger realm of self-extension. The chair, for example, mimes the spine, takes over its work, freeing the person of the constant distress of moving through many small body postures, empties his mind of absorption with the pain in his back, enabling him instead to attend to the clay bowl he is making or to listen to the conversation of a friend.[122]

Scarry's illuminating account highlights that a chair is not simply a utilitarian object providing seating. As a projection of human imagination, it anticipates, and responds to, the discomfort of the human body. In easing the pain of the laboring body, everyday objects also allow human

beings to extend themselves beyond the confines of their biological metabolisms and engage in activities such as making other artifacts or having
a conversation. They allow human beings, in the words of Scarry, to "share
endless other concerns, work to eliminate other pains, so that increasingly
the pleasure of world-building rather than pain is the occasion of their
union."[123] To this point, which calls attention to the connections between
the activities of work, labor, and action, one should add Arendt's insight
that work is also important for preserving a memory of what would otherwise be forgotten. Without "the help of the artist, of poets and historiog-
raphers, of monument-builders or writers," Arendt argues, the words and
deeds of human beings would be consigned to oblivion.[124] Finally, in addition to its distinctive contributions to the lives of those who labor and act,
work enables human beings as mortals to establish a "dwelling place more
permanent and more stable than themselves."[125]

Unlike labor, the importance of work in Arendt's political theory
has been widely recognized. But scholars have focused almost exclusively on lawmaking as a form of fabrication, which risks not only
overlooking Arendt's Roman understanding of legislation as a political
activity but also missing the presence of work in the multitude of
"worldly artifacts that are relevant to action."[126] Especially important
in this regard are everyday objects such as tables, chairs, tools, cloth-
ing, photographs, books, and all sorts of items that continuously interact with human beings and enable human interaction in a variety of
ways. Such artifacts are important for endowing the self with a sense of
continuity, as they establish connections between past, present, and
future "by providing foci of involvement in the present, mementos and
souvenirs of the past, and signposts to future goals."[127] In addition to
the stabilization of human life, such artifacts make non-utilitarian contributions to the human condition, as they engage in a dynamic relationship with human beings. They have "phenomenality," to use
Patchen Markell's term, as they appear in public and become objects
cared for and judged by human beings.[128] Moreover, these artifacts
turn the earth into an inhabitable world that we share with others.
They allow human beings to appear, and to be seen by others, in a
common world established by multifarious activities of making. Accordingly, Arendt insists that such artifacts make the human world "a
place fit for action and speech."[129]

Arendt's analysis of statelessness calls for an interpretation attending
to her distinctive understanding of work. The plight of the stateless

consists of the loss of a relatively durable dwelling place, or "the entire social texture into which they were born and in which they established for themselves a distinct place in the world."[130] To illustrate what it means to be deprived of such a place, Arendt presents a very controversial analogy: "If the tragedy of savage tribes is that . . . they live and die without leaving any trace, without having contributed anything to a common world, then these rightless people are indeed thrown back into a peculiar state of nature."[131] One way to read this analogy is to treat it as a sign of Arendt's Eurocentric, even racist, worldview. Accordingly, the analogy indicates that Arendt privileges activities of making, especially cultural fabrication and artistic production, as the measure of civilizational superiority and the standard of humanity. Her use of the term "savage tribes," without any hesitation, lends credence to such a reading.[132] Another possibility arises, however, when we recall that none of the fundamental human activities examined in *The Human Condition*—not even action and speech—are "essential characteristics of human existence."[133] A life without labor, work, and action does not simply cease to be human, but it becomes much more difficult for that life to be recognized as human by others. Read in this way, Arendt's controversial analogy between the stateless and the "savages" alerts us to the conditions that can stand in the way of such recognition:

> The more highly developed a civilization, the more accomplished the world it has produced, the more at home men feel within the human artifice—the more they will resent everything they have not produced, everything that is merely and mysteriously given them.[134]

Arendt does not endorse this "deep-rooted suspicion" of givenness that has characterized Western thinking since the Greeks but instead draws attention to how this resentment reaches an unprecedented level within a modern context in which everyone is assumed to inhabit a world created and sustained by the human activities of fabrication.[135] Those who are seen as beings deprived of this human artifice are cast as less-than-human because of this modern resentment. These subjects might be perceived as suffering victims deserving compassion from those who are more privileged. A more dangerous possibility is that their reliance on compassionate others to meet their basic needs will turn them into subjects whose spectral humanity, bordering on the inhuman, needs to be kept at bay if human artifice is to be preserved.[136] Being denied the possibilities of establishing a relatively stable, inhabitable world of artifacts, then, the stateless find it extremely difficult to be recognized as human beings entitled to equal rights.

Arendt's distinctive understanding of work can shed crucial light on the contemporary problems of rightlessness defining the lives of refugees confined in camps for extended periods of time. As mentioned earlier, these camps operate on the basis of the assumption that being a refugee is a temporary condition. Even the material construction of camps reflects this assumption. It is helpful to remember here Judge Sterling Johnson Jr.'s description of refugee camps on Guantánamo, quoted at length at the beginning of chapter 3: refugees sheltered in makeshift buildings covered with plastic bags to keep the rain out and surrounded with sheets to create some privacy. This description accurately represents many refugee camps, which are "ephemeral buildings that are increasingly constructed out of lightweight materials, taken down as quickly as they are put up, and moved elsewhere," to use Michel Agier's words.[137] These camps hardly fulfill the function of providing a relatively durable dwelling place for refugees. In fact, with their tents or huts built out of mud, camps might not even properly protect refugees from the elements of nature.[138]

These problems are powerfully present in the contemporary artist Ives Maes's "Recyclable Refugee Camp" project. For this project, Maes built a refugee shelter following the guidelines of the United Nations High Commissioner for Refugees (UNHCR), which stipulate the minimum floor space as 3.5 square meters (roughly 38 square feet) per person. Adding a twist to these guidelines, Maes built the shelter out of an ostensibly recyclable material.[139] The result is a quite small, cardboard-like cover, not even spacious enough to fit a human body underneath.[140] Apart from the shelter, the most noticeable artifacts in this camp are the latrine and refuse pit, which are listed by the UNHCR among the other basic structures that must be established in a refugee camp in times of emergency. In Maes's "recyclable refugee camp," the latrine is an enlarged children's potty, and the refuse pit is composed of blown-up Lego blocks—highlighting that what might seem fit for human needs at first look can in fact turn out to be practically useless. The cheap "recyclable" material, which Maes sarcastically describes as an "ecological" solution that will "never run the risk of overburdening any eco-system," draws attention to the problematic assumption of temporariness that humanitarian agencies work with in responding to refugee crises.[141] Each of the objects in the camp, including the shelter, is marked by an expiration date, ranging from one to four years; after that date, the camp will disintegrate, with the assumption that the refugees will either go back to their home country or move to another camp. The "Recyclable Refugee Camp" project brings to view the spartan structure of refugee camps established during emergencies, comprising only those objects that are deemed to be vital and often providing things that do not properly respond to human needs.

The scarcity of artifacts that could turn unfamiliar, even hostile, spaces into dwelling places renders refugees extremely dependent on the generosity of their hosts and humanitarian agencies. To revisit Scarry's argument, a chair is not simply a use-object but also the concrete manifestation of a human desire to alleviate pain. Understood in these terms, artifacts are durable forms incorporating "a certain *minimum* level of objectified human compassion," and they are important for allowing the possibility of living a life without constantly counting on the highly unpredictable sentiments of other human beings.[142] To put it differently, their objectification of compassion takes away the capriciousness of this human emotion. Scarry draws attention to the indispensability of artifacts for mitigating the reliance of human beings on unreliable acts of benevolence with a startling observation: "This is why, as the films of Ingmar Bergman so frequently suggest, the first act of tyrants and other egoists is often to replace a materially bountiful world . . . with a starkly empty one in which each nuance of comfort depends on the vagaries of the egoist's own disposition."[143] There is no need to imagine what egoists or tyrants would do under such conditions; even well-intentioned humanitarian actors can come to exercise an arbitrary form of power over the lives of refugees in the structure of a camp that is barely fit for dwelling.

Scarry's observation, along with Maes's "Recyclable Refugee Camp" project, highlights one of the less visible forms of rightlessness in refugee camps: deprivation from a relatively durable world populated by artifacts that effectively meet refugees' needs and release them from dependence on compassionate others. Many refugee camps are established on the basis of an emergency logic, which presumes that refugees will live in these spaces only temporarily. From an Arendtian standpoint, this logic resists the transformation of camps into dwelling places that can house human beings and surround them with a wide range of everyday objects that anticipate, and respond to, the discomfort of the human body, turn the earth into an inhabitable world, and transform space into a place fit for action and speech.[144]

Over time, refugees try to turn uninhabitable spaces into dwelling places by engaging in various activities of making and gradually reestablishing the social texture that they lost with their displacement. Growing their own food, improving the appearance of their shelters, setting up stalls in a marketplace, they begin to turn camps into homes that are relatively durable and familiar. Camps can even become places fit for action and speech, as refugees share tales of the past, make plans for the future, and organize demonstrations to claim rights. Engaging in such activities, organizing space in inventive ways, and establishing new political and social relations, refugees can reject the victim identity assigned to them.[145] These possibilities show the importance of activities that Arendt associated with work for staking out a relatively stable world in a refugee camp; they also highlight the crucial connections of work to labor and action. It is important not to lose sight of these possibilities in refugee camps since there are many other sites, including those used for detention, that are not at all conducive to establishing even the semblance of an ordinary life.[146]

But in the case of refugee camps, it is equally important to attend to the conditions that make it very difficult for such possibilities to arise as well as the conditions that can undermine or destroy such possibilities once they arise. In their comprehensive study of refugee camps, Guglielmo Verdirame and Barbara Harrell-Bond examine the obstacles faced by refugees who try to establish a relatively stable home. These obstacles become especially visible in the policy of "uprooting" employed by the UNHCR. One troubling example of this policy was the destruction of the Ogujebe transit center in northern Uganda in February 1998. Many of the refugees located in Ogujebe had been living there for years; during that time, they had established social relations and built a relatively large market. But citing the costs of keeping the transit center as the main reason, the UNHCR pushed for resettling these refugees in agricultural settlements across the Nile. To evacuate the center, the agency employed the help of NGOs; in addition, the army was brought in, and refugees who resisted were moved at gunpoint.[147] In total, 24,000 refugees were uprooted; their businesses and homes were bulldozed. From the perspective of the UNHCR, the eviction was necessary to settle refugees in agricultural lands where they could establish self-sufficiency. The uprooted refugees were given plastic tarpaulins and poor-quality tools to start from scratch and rebuild the homes they lost.[148]

The Ogujebe incident is very similar to the Roma case mentioned at the beginning of this chapter. There are egregious forms of human rights violations in both cases, but an exclusive focus on these violations might occlude from view more subtle forms of rightlessness confronted by refugees and the stateless. In addition to a violation of rights such as the right to housing, both cases reveal that those who are uprooted are forcefully deprived of their entire social texture, including the everyday objects that are crucial for turning the earth into a common world shared with others. Furthermore, in the case of Ogujebe, it becomes clear that an anti-political form of humanitarianism, mobilizing a moral calculus centered on a narrow understanding of suffering and dispensing with political practices of deliberation (especially with those in whose name it acts), can end up aggravating the rightlessness that it aims to redress, as discussed in chapter 2. Arendt's conceptualization of work sheds light on these less perceptible forms of violence by bringing to view the loss of these artifacts that aid human beings as laboring and acting beings. Reconsidered alongside her analysis of statelessness, Arendt's concept of work assumes a critical force, drawing attention to the conditions that expel refugees from a world that they can inhabit with others.

Vanishing Freedom and Equality: Rightlessness and Action

For Arendt, action denotes the capacity to take initiative and begin something new. Drawing on Augustine, she suggests that this capacity springs from natality, or "the fact that human beings, new men, again and again appear in the world by virtue of birth."[149] The most distinctive aspect of action lies in its reliance on the condition of human plurality: Whereas the activities associated with labor and work can be undertaken in isolation from others, action requires the presence of others.[150] Action, especially political action, is crucially linked to speech; in fact, Arendt describes these two activities as "coeval and coequal." Action is speech in the sense that most political action is "transacted in words"; speech is action in the sense that "finding the right words at the right moment" is itself action. Furthermore, action is in need of words to become meaningful and relevant to others.[151]

Arendt's theorization of action and speech is often taken to be representative of an aesthetic understanding of politics, which brackets off questions of substance and purpose. This aestheticization is generally attributed to her non-instrumentalist understanding of action in Aristotelian terms as *energeia*, or as an activity in which "the end (*telos*) is not pursued but lies in the activity itself."[152] For some, this aesthetic vision is appealing because it refuses to subject action and speech to the dictates of material interests and moral ends and brings to view an agonistic politics centered on self-revelation.[153] Many critics, however, suggest that Arendt's aesthetic vision ends up turning action and speech into futile, purposeless, and contentless activities valued for sheer performance. Understood in these terms, Arendt's political theory fails to address challenging questions of injustice, power, and violence.[154]

In what follows, I reconsider Arendt's conceptualization of action and speech in the context of the long-term confinement of asylum seekers, refugees, and undocumented immigrants in camps and detention centers, and offer a reading that draws attention to the *constitutive* effects of these activities. Although action and speech are not driven by considerations of utility and defy representation in terms of ends-means categories, they are not without effects. In fact, drawing our attention away from questions of substantive content and specific purpose, Arendt's conceptualization of action and speech illuminates their crucial role in the *ongoing constitution of political subjects, political community, and humanity*.

First, action and speech are crucial for the constitution of political subjects as distinct individuals with unique life stories. Here it is important to note Arendt's distinction between "who" and "what" a person is: Whereas "what" a person is relates to her "qualities, gifts, talents, and shortcomings," the disclosure of "who" pertains to "unique personal identities" that can only become manifest in one's words and deeds.[155] One of the crucial aspects of rightlessness in refugee camps, as I discuss below, is anonymity resulting from the difficulties of acting, speaking, and appearing as distinct individuals. Second, action and speech are also central to the ongoing constitution of a political community, which has objective and subjective dimensions, according to Arendt. Far from being contentless, these activities are often about "specific, objective, worldly interests." In addition, sharing words and deeds is not futile given that only action and speech can turn an issue into an "*inter-est*," or a common concern that relates people to each other, as discussed in chapter 2.[156] There is also a "subjective" dimension to this ongoing constitution of political community. Action and speech are crucial for establishing a "web of human relationships."[157] Arendt's conceptualization of action and speech can shed light on the devastating effects of excluding human beings from this ongoing constitution of political community. Finally, action and speech are fundamental to participation in the ongoing constitution of humanity. Arendt highlights that the stateless find themselves in a condition of rightlessness to the extent that their action and speech are rendered meaningless or irrelevant. Excluded from a political community that can take into account their action and speech, it becomes very difficult for them to be recognized as human beings entitled to equal rights.[158] Rethinking these arguments in the context of contemporary practices of encampment and detention brings to view the critical resources offered by Arendt's conceptualization of action and speech.

For the purposes of this discussion, it is crucial to understand what Arendt means when she suggests that the stateless find themselves in a condition of rightlessness as they are deprived of "the right to action."[159] If action is rooted in the human condition of natality, how can anyone lose a right to action? To answer this question, it is necessary to remember Arendt's argument that, although action is a capacity that each human being has, it is always in need of a political space and "the constant presence of others" to become meaningful and relevant.[160] The stateless are deprived of a right to action in the sense that they do not have a political space in which they can enact their capacity to begin something new in the company of other actors. This point also comes across in Arendt's attempts to contest conventional understandings of freedom as "an inner human disposition" and redefine it as "a character of human existence in the world."[161] Freedom, inextricably linked to the capacity to act or begin something new, cannot become "a demonstrable fact" in the absence of "a politically guaranteed public realm" or a "worldly space to make its appearance."[162] This impossibility is brought to light by Arendt's account of statelessness, which introduces us to human beings sealed off from political life. The loss of a right to action in such a context denotes a deprivation from the possibility of turning the human capacity for freedom, this "hidden source" of creativity, into "a worldly, tangible reality."[163]

Arendt's understanding of political freedom in spatial terms underscores that the loss of a political community entails the loss of the very space in which one can actualize the capacity for freedom: "Whoever leaves his polis or is banished from it loses not just his hometown or his fatherland; he also loses the only space in which he can be free—and he loses the society of his equals."[164] Some of Arendt's readers take this loss of political community as an exclusion from a state, or even a nation-state.[165]

But this reading fails to capture the distinctive predicament faced by the stateless persons of Arendt's time and various categories of migrants today. What is at stake in rightlessness cannot be adequately represented by the loss of formal membership; in fact, such a loss does not occur except in cases of de jure statelessness. Rightlessness denotes a much more fundamental deprivation from "a right to belong to some kind of organized community," remembering Arendt's formulation, and this community might not necessarily take the institutional form of a state.[166] Rightlessness understood as the loss of a right to action indicates that one is deprived of the possibility of becoming part of a polis, which Arendt considers to be a space that "arises out of acting and speaking together" and "can find its proper location almost any time and anywhere."[167] The stateless are rightless if and when they live under conditions that eradicate the possibility of establishing such a "portable" polis in which their actions and speech can become meaningful in the presence of others.[168]

Moving from the stateless in Arendt's account to the contemporary landscape, in what ways can asylum seekers, undocumented immigrants, and refugees be denied the possibility of constituting a polis through their action and speech? What are some of the specific conditions that make it very difficult for various categories of migrants to participate in the ongoing constitution of political community and humanity?

Perhaps the most extreme cases of rightlessness in this particular sense can be seen in detention centers that hold asylum seekers and undocumented immigrants for extended periods of time. These spaces risk bordering on internment camps that shut off their inhabitants from "the world of the living."[169] With the recent normalization of detention, discussed in the last chapter, there has been a troubling resurgence of such spaces in the context of immigration controls. There are now many detention centers where asylum seekers and undocumented immigrants can be banished from the outside world. These camp-like spaces instill in detainees the sense of "disappear[ing] into a black hole."[170] It becomes very difficult for those confined in these spaces to act in concert to contest the conditions of detention and make claims to equal rights. In fact, such action can be grounds for various forms of punishment, including solitary confinement and restrictions on visitors.[171] In the face of systematic obstacles to political action, asylum seekers and undocumented immigrants detained in these spaces have increasingly resorted to protests such as self-mutilation, hunger strikes, and suicide attempts.[172]

Such spaces risk expelling their inhabitants from humanity, as they attempt to rid not only life but also death of any meaning. Living in isolation from the world in these spaces, asylum seekers and undocumented immigrants are often deprived of human solidarity and testimony. Even if they commit suicide—a self-destructive act that can be interpreted as a desperate attempt to protest rightlessness and assert one's capacity for freedom by taking initiative—they are at times denied a commemorated death. To remember Arendt's account of camps, even martyrdom becomes impossible without the presence of witnesses who could endow death with a meaning by their testimony.[173] Such spaces can "[rob] death of its meaning as the end of a fulfilled life" and render it "anonymous."[174] Rightlessness in its most extreme form indicates then not only a total exclusion from the political community but also a disappearance or nonexistence in ontological terms: "In a sense they took away the individual's own death, proving that henceforth nothing belonged to him and he belonged to no one. His death merely set a seal on the fact that he had never really existed."[175] The problem of anonymous and unaccounted deaths has resurfaced in the detention centers used for the confinement of asylum seekers and undocumented immigrants.[176] Due to lack of transparency and accountability, immigration detention makes it very difficult to keep an accurate record of these deaths. For example, in August 2009, the US government acknowledged that "[m]ore than one in 10 deaths in immigration detention in the last six years have been overlooked."[177] These deaths can be "swept under the rug while potential witnesses are transferred or deported," erasing the traces of an individual's existence.[178] Anonymous and unrecorded deaths in immigration detention are the most troubling signs of rightlessness understood as an expulsion from the human world.

Confinement of asylum seekers and undocumented immigrants in lawless spaces hardly allows for the possibility of engaging in action with others to make political demands or claim rights. It is extremely difficult, and at times altogether impossible (in the case of solitary confinement, for example), for the inhabitants of such spaces to constitute a polis that "arises out of acting and speaking together." After all, Arendt suggests that polis understood in these terms can arise "almost," and not always, "any time and anywhere";[179] that qualification becomes all-important in the case of immigration detention.

It is much more likely to constitute such a polis in the case of refugee camps, although it is important not to underestimate the systematic obstacles to fundamental human activities posed by encampment, which were discussed earlier. Refugees are often represented as passive victims in a humanitarian framework that centers on the provision of their basic needs, and these representations can hinder political agency. But refugee camps provide more possibilities, compared to detention centers, for engaging in action that can establish a "web of human relationships" and transform a specific problem into an *"inter-est,"* or a shared concern that can bring individuals together.[180]

In his account of refugee camps, Michel Agier draws attention to such possibilities when he discusses the case of 50 Sierra Leonean women who mobilized at the Boreah camp to demand plastic sheeting to protect their shelters from rain damage. Following the UNHCR's refusal to meet this demand, the women engaged in a demonstration and stopped the vehicles of humanitarian organizations, asking from them a "written commitment to obtaining plastic sheeting" and urging them "to receive a delegation from the demonstrators."[181] By turning their vulnerability into a political claim, positioning themselves as political subjects with the capacity to appoint their own representatives, and demanding plastic sheeting as a right and not as a gift to be bestowed by compassionate others, these women were able to mobilize a politics of human rights, along the lines discussed in chapter 2. Such cases show that Arendtian action does not need a space purged of basic needs or material interests. Life's necessities can become "interests" when they are articulated as common concerns that bind and relate a diverse set of actors. Such politicization is crucial for contesting the conditions that cast refugees as anonymous victims and that make it very difficult for them to become political subjects, speak in their own name, and establish a political community.

Detention centers and refugee camps underscore why we need to understand action, or the capacity to take initiative, always in relation to the human condition of plurality. As Arendt puts it, "plurality is specifically *the* condition—not only the *conditio sine qua non*, but the *conditio per quam*—of all political life."[182] Plurality is not merely a necessary condition, in other words, but the one and only condition of politics. For Arendt, plurality has "the twofold character of equality and distinction," and it needs to be sustained with practices that allow human beings to establish themselves as equal in their "unique distinctness."[183] Neither of these characteristics is inherent in some kind of shared human nature, and speech plays a crucial role in their ongoing constitution.

Drawing on Aristotle, Arendt contends that political community is "not made out of equals, but on the contrary of people who are different and unequal."[184] Political community comes into being by "equalizing" those who are otherwise unequal—a task that Arendt captures with the Greek term *isasthēnai*.[185] The central role of speech in such equalization can be best seen in her reflections on the ancient Greek institution of *isonomia*. Although this term is often taken to be the equivalent of modern equality before the law, Arendt underscores, it denotes "merely that all have the same claim to political activity, and in the polis this activity primarily took the form of speaking with one another. *Isonomia* is therefore essentially the equal right to speak."[186] To highlight the inextricable connection between speech and equalization, Arendt also calls attention to terms such as *isēgoria* and *isologia*, which are etymologically linked to speech and were used interchangeably with *isonomia* in the ancient context. Both of these terms indicate equality in speech, especially the equal right to speak in political assemblies.[187]

Arendt's insistence on *isonomia*, as distinct from the modern conception of freedom of speech, could be seen simply as another example of her Hellenic nostalgia. But read in light of her account of statelessness, her turn to this seemingly antiquated notion has critical purchase. The stateless might have a right to freedom of speech, especially if this right is understood in "negative" terms as a right to express oneself without interference. But lacking an equal share in the political community they reside in, they find it very difficult to be recognized as subjects whose speech is meaningful. Their rightlessness then consists more fundamentally of "the loss of the relevance of speech."[188]

This last point follows from Arendt's distinctive take on the famous Aristotelian definition of "man" as "a being commanding the power of speech and thought."[189] When Aristotle defines man as "*zōon politikon*" and "*zōon logon ekhon* ('a living being capable of speech')," Arendt argues, his goal is not to state an unchanging truth about man's essence.[190] Instead, these formulations reflect "the current opinion of the *polis*," according to which "everybody outside the *polis*—slaves and barbarians—was *aneu logou*."[191] These subjects were considered to be *aneu logou*, or "without words," not because they lacked the faculty of speech but because they were excluded from political membership understood as an equal claim to political activity.[192] Given this fundamental exclusion, even when they used their faculty of speech, their utterances were not recognized as meaningful, relevant, or even intelligible.

This point bears close resemblance to the argument that Jacques Rancière makes about speech by critically engaging with Aristotle:

> Politics exists because the logos is never simply speech, because it is always indissolubly the *account* that is made of this speech: the account by which a sonorous emission is understood as speech, capable of enunciating what is just, whereas some other emission is merely perceived as a noise signaling pleasure or pain, consent or revolt.[193]

When Arendt describes the rightlessness of the stateless as the loss of a right to speech, then, that loss must be understood in terms of the loss of a political community where their speech is not dismissed as an incomprehensible noise but instead taken into account as a meaningful human utterance. Rightlessness denotes the loss of an equal share in a political community—understood mainly in terms of "the reciprocity of actions" or "a common engagement in political action," to use Étienne Balibar's apt formulation—that is necessary to endow one's speech with meaning and relevance.[194]

Arendt's understanding of speech sheds critical light on contemporary forms of speechlessness confronted by asylum seekers, refugees, and undocumented immigrants. Several scholars have highlighted how certain forms of contemporary humanitarianism, aiming to alleviate the suffering of asylum seekers and refugees, can paradoxically end up aggravating their condition of rightlessness by rendering their speech mute, unintelligible, or inconsequential. Especially problematic in this regard are the humanitarian representations of refugees, which portray them as anonymous figures lost in an "utter human uniformity," as Liisa Malkki puts it, and obscure "that each of the persons in the photograph has a name, opinions, relatives, and histories."[195] These representations, depicting the "abstract nakedness of being human," make it very difficult to recognize not only "who" but "what" these refugees are—to recall Arendt's distinction. Particularly predominant in these representations are the images of women and children; mobilizing stereotypical assumptions about their innocence, these images end up construing refugees as victims who cannot act or speak on their own and are in need of the help of compassionate others.[196]

Apart from these images, the denial of a right to speech can be particularly detected in the skepticism toward the narratives of asylum seekers, refugees, and undocumented immigrants, discussed in the last chapter. The recent shift from these narratives to suffering bodies in the adjudication of rights claims draws attention to "the question of voice— the ability to establish narrative authority over one's own circumstances and future, and also, the ability to claim an audience," to use Malkki's terms again.[197] An exclusive focus on the suffering bodies transfers that narrative authority to experts such as doctors and area specialists. In doing that, it risks rendering migrants *aneu logou* and undermines the relevance of their speech for their rights claims. This new form of right-lessness highlights how and why those who do not have an equal claim to political activity find it very difficult to be recognized as equal and distinct human beings.

To contest the conditions that give rise to speechlessness, migrants have increasingly resorted to various forms of self-inflicted harm in recent years. In one of the most troubling examples of this contemporary problem, nearly 60 detainees in Australia's Woomera camp sewed their lips together in 2002 to protest immigration authorities.[198] What prompted this protest was the impossibility of making rights claims heard in a camp that was isolated from the outside world. In fact, in their written statement, the detainees who sewed their lips together explicitly stated that the protest was not simply about delays in processing visas but instead about "a barbaric immigration policy, which locks refugee men, women and children behind razor wires for months and even years at a time."[199]

Woomera was closed in April 2003 after public pressure, though Australia continues its policy of mandatory detention of asylum seekers in camps. Lip-sewing has become globalized as a protest method adopted by migrants around the world. It is tempting to see lip-sewing as a new form of political agency showing the possibility of resisting sovereignty even in dire circumstances. But there is a need to caution against putting lip-sewing side by side with other forms of protest such as street demonstrations as "creative ways of provoking sovereign power and embroiling it into a political or power relation."[200] In an international environment that is extremely hostile to migration, lip-sewing has become one of the few means of inserting oneself in the public realm, and it is a symptom of the ascendency of a humanitarian discourse that centers on "biolegitimacy" and assigns rights to suffering bodies.[201] To the extent that such insertion takes place without words, it cannot reveal "who" the actor is, remembering Arendt's insistence on the crucial connection between action and speech. In fact, the Woomera incident affirmed action's need for speech, when the detainees who sewed their lips circulated three letters to render their actions meaningful in the eyes of others.[202] Before hailing lip-sewing as a new form of political agency, then, it is important to attend to the conditions that eradicate the possibilities of political participation and obstruct other means of making rights claims.

Lip-sewing protests demonstrate that the human faculty of speech is no guarantee against being rendered *aneu logou*. For those who are confined in spaces that deter the constitution of a political community, understood in the sense of a polis that can arise out of common engagement in action and speech, it becomes impossible to get their utterances recognized as meaningful and relevant speech. A Woomera detainee provides us with a striking demonstration of this predicament when he says, "[w]e want to go back to Iran because at least there we will be tortured and imprisoned by people who speak our own language."[203] This statement could be read simply as a reaffirmation of political belonging in a nation-state for equal rights. But given that it nurtures no nostalgic illusions about "homeland" as the original site of rights and citizenship, it can be better understood as an affirmation of the need for a "home," organized community, or a polis, which can be constituted anywhere as long as there is the possibility of sharing words and deeds in the presence of others.[204] Camps such as Woomera deny the possibility of constituting such a political association to their inhabitants.

Lip-sewing attests to a fundamental condition of rightlessness that Arendt tries to capture by comparing the plight of the stateless to that of slaves. Instead of seeing slavery simply as a loss of liberty, Arendt describes it in terms of an expulsion from political and human community, which consists of the exclusion of "a certain category of people even from the possibility of fighting for freedom." She suggests that slavery's "crime against humanity" begins with this expulsion that casts a specific group of people as less-than-human on the basis of an assumption of natural inequality.[205] Arendt's analogy suggests that the stateless share with the slaves a condition of rightlessness defined by the loss of a share in the common world constituted in and through action and speech. The rise of lip-sewing and other forms of self-inflicted harm must be understood within the context of violent conditions that deny asylum seekers, refugees, and undocumented immigrants "even the possibility of fighting for freedom," to use Arendt's terms, by placing them in detention centers and camps isolated from the political and human world.

Arendt's comparison of slavery and statelessness also underscores that the stateless find themselves in a worse condition in some respects:

> [Even] slaves still belonged to some sort of human community; their labor was needed, used, and exploited, and this kept them within the pale of humanity. To be a slave was after all to have a distinctive character, a place in society—more than the abstract nakedness of being human and nothing but human.[206]

As I have noted, in discussing Arendt's distinction between the criminal and the stateless in the last chapter, these analogies should not be read as pitting one group against another, trivializing the injustice and violence encountered by one so as to draw attention to the predicament of the other. The slavery analogy aims to make the plight of statelessness imaginable to modern readers who are more likely to renounce slavery and yet might not be able to immediately see how and why the exclusion of the stateless from politics is troubling. Both the slaves and the stateless endure social death, albeit in very different forms. But the reliance of slaveholders on slave labor results in what Orlando Patterson calls "liminal incorporation" of slaves within society.[207] For Arendt, the stateless do not even have such a liminal place, as they are confined in camps that risk rendering them utterly superfluous by expelling them from the common world constituted through the activities of *vita activa*.

Arendt's conceptualization of *vita activa* can illuminate the distinctive plight of many migrants who can no longer meet their basic needs on their own, cultivate a trust in the reality and regularity of life, establish a relatively permanent dwelling place, and render their action and speech meaningful in the presence of others. This conclusion is quite surprising given that Arendt's account of action/work/labor has often been criticized as an exclusionary framework limiting politics to the privileged few. For even those who do not necessarily agree with this characterization, she offers a rich understanding of freedom that is conspicuously inattentive to questions of justice. But as this chapter highlights, once Arendt's conceptualization of *vita activa* is read alongside her account of statelessness, it begins to appear in a new light as a critical phenomenology providing crucial resources for understanding the conditions that can make it very difficult for some lives to be recognized as human. In addition, rethinking *vita activa* in these terms allows us to have a new grasp on the well-known problems associated with the long-term encampment of refugees or the use of solitary confinement in the context of immigration detention. It allows us to see these problems in a different way by accentuating the less visible forms of violence (e.g., loss of the regular rhythms of life, deprivation from worldly artifacts, inability to share one's life-story) and urging us to think carefully about how they contribute to a fundamental condition of rightlessness.

Arendt's political theory can help us understand rightlessness as a fundamental condition that makes it very difficult for migrants to claim and exercise even the rights that they have according to international conventions. But as I highlighted at several points, policies and processes that undermine the legal, political, and human standing of migrants can be and have been contested. The next chapter turns to a striking example of this contestation and examines the contemporary struggles of *sans-papiers* by engaging with Arendt's proposal to rethink human rights as a right to have rights.

5.

Declarations of a Right to Have Rights

"PAPERS FOR ALL" has been one of the rallying cries of political struggles waged by undocumented immigrants today. It is quite tempting to understand this demand as a call arising from, and justified by, the human rights framework that has been used to address various forms of injustice in the past few decades. Many of the demands made in these struggles refer to already existing rights such as equal personhood before the law or non-discrimination in the workplace. But "papers for all" is also indicative of how these struggles take human rights in new directions by proposing reconfigurations of sovereignty, citizenship, and rights. Terms such as "regularization," "legalization," and "amnesty" hardly do justice to the political and normative implications of the call for "papers for all," as they fail to capture the radical dimension of this demand. What we are confronted with is a deceptively simple formula that calls into question the denial of rights such as freedom of movement, participation in public affairs, and family unity to those who find themselves in an irregular status. To the extent that the current human rights framework allows the states to deny these rights to migrants who are not authorized to stay in their territories, "papers for all" is a call that brings to view the limits and exclusions of that framework.

To examine the unique characteristics and challenges of the new rights claims made by undocumented immigrants, this chapter turns to Arendt's proposal to rethink human rights as "a right to have rights" toward the end of her analysis of statelessness. Arendt only briefly invokes this "tantalizing" and "teasing" phrase, to use Frank Michelman's description, without elucidating what she means by it in full detail.[1] As mentioned in chapter 1, a right to have rights indicates a right "to live in a framework where one is judged by one's actions and opinions" and "to belong to some kind of organized community"[2]—in short, "the right of men to citizenship" and "the right of every individual to belong to humanity."[3] This right, Arendt suggests, is not a right that is codified in any international document, but rather a right that one becomes aware of in the face of "the new global political situation" defined by large-scale statelessness.[4] Confronted with this global problem, a right to have rights emerges as "the one right without which no other can materialize."[5]

Arendt's brief invocation of a right to have rights continues to puzzle her readers, and scholarly debates have particularly centered on the questions related to the status and source of this right that is not legally codified: If this new right cannot derive its validity from any existing legal framework (domestic or international), what is its foundation? And can Arendt's political theory offer a normative framework that can justify this new right? Seyla Benhabib, for example, argues that Arendt's political theory provides no such foundation: "[B]y leaving ungrounded her own ingenious formulation of the 'right to have rights,' Arendt also leaves us with a disquiet about the normative foundations of her own political philosophy."[6] Scholars such as Peg Birmingham and Serena Parekh respond to this criticism by locating foundations for human rights in Arendt's political theory. Far from being a theorist opposed to the philosophical projects of normative justification, they argue, one of Arendt's "primary concerns" is "the working out of a theoretical foundation for a reformulation of the modern notion of human rights."[7]

It is not surprising to see that the question of normative foundations has taken center stage in the scholarly debates on Arendt's notion of a right to have rights. After all, this question has been at the heart of the broader debates on human rights.[8] As I turn to Arendt's puzzling phrase for the purposes of rethinking the new rights claims articulated in the contemporary struggles of undocumented immigrants, I propose a different approach to human rights—one that takes its starting point not from a foundation derived through justificatory procedures but instead from *political practices of founding human rights*. Arendt's inventive formulation, I argue, draws attention to historical and contemporary struggles that propose new rights, take existing rights in unanticipated directions, and introduce us to new subjects of rights. A right to have rights, in its striking groundlessness, urges us to understand new rights claims such as the ones raised by undocumented immigrants as *declarations* that do not have prior authorization for the new propositions of equality and freedom that they introduce. Human rights owe their origins and continuous reinvention to such inaugural acts that involve the invention and disclosure of a new political and normative world—a point that I make by rethinking Arendt's argument in light of Claude Lefort's and Étienne Balibar's reflections on human rights.

The chapter first introduces Arendt's invocation of a right to have rights and proposes to read this puzzling formulation as an invitation to rethink human rights in terms of political practices of founding. I suggest that this reading is much more in line with Arendt's disinclination to engage in "the very project of philosophical foundation-giving"[9]—an aversion that follows from her efforts to understand freedom as the capacity to initiate new beginnings. Arendt argues that such new beginnings expose us to the "abyss of freedom," as they rupture the linear continuity of time; because they "cannot be accounted for by a reliable chain of cause and effect," they give rise to perplexities related to their sources of origin and authority.[10] Revolutions and rights declarations confront us with such an abyss. Accordingly, I propose taking the perplexities arising from Arendt's call for a right to have rights as helpful starting points for attending to the political and ethical dilemmas that pervade new beginnings. Grappling with these perplexities can help us understand the distinctive features and challenges of new rights claims that cannot derive their validity from existing legal and normative frameworks.

To examine how to approach these new beginnings, I then turn, in the second section, to Arendt's account of modern revolutions. Because the revolutionaries who founded a new polity with new laws and rights did not have prior authorization for their acts, as Arendt recognizes, they were tempted to invoke an extra-political absolute that could serve as the source of authority. Resorting to such foundations in an attempt to escape the radical contingency of founding, however, risks subordinating politics to external standards and forfeiting the notion of freedom understood as the capacity to begin something new. Arendt's account of revolutions takes issue with various forms of foundationalism, but it does that without embracing an anti-foundationalist position. Her discussion of principles that become manifest in new beginnings offers an alternative to these two positions that have prevailed in the debates on human rights. Insisting that a new beginning carries within itself a principle that saves it from its own arbitrariness, Arendt suggests that political founding derives its ongoing authorization from deeds that are inspired by this principle. Following Montesquieu, she urges us to understand "principle" not as a transcendental norm regulating politics but instead as an animating spirit that can become manifest only in the political practices that it sets into motion. Arendt also highlights that a principle can achieve universal validity by being repeated time and again. This point urges us to rethink the universal validity of human rights as inextricably intertwined with practices of founding and refounding them.

Arendt's Montesquieuan insight introduces us to a new question: What is the principle that inspires, and becomes manifest in, her call for a right to have rights in particular and new rights claims in general? The third section of this chapter locates the answer to this question in the principle that emerges with the eighteenth-century rights declarations. Drawing on Étienne Balibar's work, I suggest that this principle can be best captured with the term "equaliberty," which foregrounds the inextricable connection between equality and freedom in modern democracy, affirms a universal access to politics, and animates struggles that contest exclusions from rights and citizenship.[11] As this principle resonates outside its original context and is taken up in new rights claims that strive to elicit our assent, it achieves a universal validity. Arendt's work on revolution and civil disobedience calls for rethinking these claims as practices of augmentation that involve conservation and amendment of the principle of equaliberty. Human rights owe their ongoing authorization and universalization to such practices that reconfigure existing relations between rights, citizenship, and humanity by proposing new understandings of the reciprocity between equality and freedom.

Rethinking a right to have rights in terms of political practices of founding human rights is promising not simply because it is more in line with the fundamental premises of Arendt's political theory. As I argue in the final section of the chapter, this new reading is helpful also for attending to the distinctive features and challenges of struggles proposing new rights or taking existing rights in new directions. To make this case, I examine some of the rights claims articulated in the struggles waged by *sans-papiers*. These struggles, originating in France and then spreading to the rest of Europe, illustrate the difficult tasks confronted by subjects who paradoxically claim and exercise the rights that they are not fully authorized to claim and exercise. In the absence of prior authorization, *sans-papiers* have engaged in inventive practices to render their speech audible and intelligible, position themselves as political subjects capable of making rights claims, and establish the validity of these claims by wooing the consent of their interlocutors. As these ongoing struggles testify, political practices of founding human rights are characterized by contingency and fragility; it is by no means certain that these inaugural practices will result in the political and legal recognition of these new rights claims. But the Arendtian framework suggests that human rights can neither be universally validated nor politically guaranteed without such practices.

Perplexities of a Right to Have Rights

Arendt's very brief discussion of a right to have rights toward the end of her analysis of statelessness in *The Origins of Totalitarianism* continues to baffle her readers. Particularly confounding is the fact that she underscores the impossibility of grounding this new right in the eighteenth-century notions of "nature" and "history" without clearly articulating what, if anything, might take their place. She briefly hints at a possible answer when she turns to the notion of "humanity," though the implications of her peculiar use of this term are by no means straightforward:

> [H]umanity, which for the eighteenth century, in Kantian terminology, was no more than a regulative idea, has today become an inescapable fact. This new situation, in which "humanity" has in fact assumed the role formerly ascribed to nature or history, would mean in this context that the right to have rights, or the right of every individual to belong to humanity, should be *guaranteed* by humanity itself. It is by no means certain whether this is possible.[12]

Perhaps the most striking aspect of this formulation is that Arendt invokes the incipient sense of humanity not as a foundation but as a guarantee. Instead of asking how we can philosophically establish a new foundation for human rights, she invites an engagement with the challenging problem of how these rights can be politically founded, recognized, and affirmed through mutual promises that find some relative stability in laws and institutions.[13]

It is also important to note Arendt's claim that humanity is no longer a Kantian "regulative idea" that serves the heuristic function of guiding our thinking and action without necessarily corresponding to any factual reality.[14] Arendt draws attention to various forms of global interdependence that have turned humanity into "an inescapable fact," though she is far from hopeful about the prospects for the recognition of a right to have rights under these new conditions. She mentions especially the institutional challenges of guaranteeing this right within the state-centric framework of international law.[15] In her later writings, primarily in her essays on Karl Jaspers, Arendt reiterates the argument that "mankind" has become "an urgent reality" and refers to technological developments such as the production of atomic weapons.[16] She expresses her concern that this newly emerging notion can easily take the form of "negative solidarity, based on the fear of global destruction."[17] Only if this sense of a shared present and future can be accompanied by "political responsibility," Arendt argues, can we then speak of a positive solidarity attending the emergence of humanity as a fact.[18] Yet she is far from sanguine about the prospects of cultivating solidarity and responsibility at the global level, as can be seen in her fear that this new notion of humanity might also engender the sense of "an unbearable burden" and even lead to "political apathy, isolationist nationalism, or desperate rebellion against all powers that be."[19]

A right to have rights can only be guaranteed by humanity, then, but that guarantee turns out to be fraught with tension, ambiguity, and uncertainty. Arendt's brief discussion of this right discloses what Frank Michelman calls "an irreparable groundlessness of rights, affirming our own precarious, existential, collective self-care when it comes to creating and maintaining in this world the conditions of civility and humanity for any and for all."[20] Several scholars have attempted to repair this groundlessness by introducing a normative foundation, as noted earlier. Michelman considers this possibility when he offers an analytical dissection of a right to have rights and locates two different notions of "right" at work in it; the first denoting "a universal abstract human moral right," and the second referring to "empirical rights."[21] This dissection would suggest that the first "right" should be understood in Kantian terms as a universal moral claim to membership, which needs to be grounded in a post-metaphysical foundation.[22] But as Michelman notes, this interpretation is at odds with Arendt's political theory that questions the conventional subordination of "is" to "ought" and demands rethinking the "ideality, or criticality, or oughtness" of human rights as "arising out of practice and action."[23]

In agreement with Michelman's argument, I suggest that, if we are to understand a right to have rights from an Arendtian perspective, it might be more promising to adopt an interpretation that does not shy away from its "irreparable groundlessness" but instead recognizes it as the distinctive feature of a demand that breaks away from, and is not fully authorized by, existing legal and normative frameworks. Accordingly, a right to have rights gives rise to perplexities that are not unlike the ones we confront in new beginnings that disrupt the linear continuity of time and leave political actors and spectators with "nothing whatsoever to hold on to."[24]

In making this interpretive move, I take my starting point from the puzzling statement that Arendt makes at the very end of *The Burden of Our Time*, the British edition of *Origins*:

> The Rights of Man can be implemented only if they become the *prepolitical* foundation of a new *polity*, the *prelegal* basis of a new *legal* structure, the, so to speak, *prehistorical* fundament from which the *history* of mankind will derive its essential meaning in much the same way Western civilization did from its own fundamental origin myths.[25]

It is tempting to read this statement as an invitation to understand human rights as pre-political, pre-legal, and pre-historical rights, but that reading would go against not only the main premises of Arendt's political theory but also the main arguments in her critique of human rights.[26] We can begin to make sense of Arendt's statement, especially her quite confusing reference to "fundamental origin myths," only if we read her call for a right to have rights as a new beginning that provokes perplexities similar to the ones that pervaded modern revolutions and rights declarations. In her early efforts to grapple with this new right, Arendt ponders solutions resembling the ones that the revolutionaries of the eighteenth century came up with to escape these perplexities. In fact, resorting to "foundation legends" was one of the strategies that the revolutionaries used "to solve the problem of the beginning, of an unconnected, new event breaking into the continuous sequence of historical time."[27] Arendt makes no reference to such a solution in the later edition of *The Origins of Totalitarianism*, but since the discussion in that work leaves many questions unanswered about a right to have rights, it might be much more helpful to turn to her extensive discussion of modern revolutions, as I do in the next section, to find out the most promising way to grapple with the perplexities of new beginnings.

For the purposes of developing this alternative interpretive strategy, Judith Butler's brief but evocative suggestion to read Arendt's call for a right to have rights as a declaration provides important insights. Butler argues that Arendt's analysis of statelessness, characterized mostly by disillusionment about human rights, enters into "a declarative mode" as she introduces this new right—a shift that urges us to understand declaring rights as a political practice of freedom:

> "Declaring" becomes an important rhetorical movement, since it is the very freedom of expression for which it calls or, rather, it is the very call of freedom. Freedom cannot pre-exist this call . . . but can only exist in its exercise.[28]

Butler's suggestion is very much in line with Arendt's efforts to understand freedom not as an inner disposition or a given status but instead as a political practice. Freedom in its political manifestation denotes the capacity "to call something into being which did not exist before, which was not given, not even as an object of cognition or imagination," and declaration, understood as an inaugural speech act, is exemplary practice of freedom.[29] Accordingly, Arendt's call for a right to have rights can be taken as a new beginning, which brings forth a right that was not known or given in the existing configuration of rights and citizenship in an international order organized around the principle of nationality. Understood in these terms, it invites us to rethink human rights in terms of practices of political founding and draws attention to the vital importance of declaring rights in this regard.

To highlight what is politically and normatively at stake in this alternative reading, it is worth reflecting on the meaning of "declaration" especially by taking into account how this political genre, popularized by the eighteenth-century revolutions, radically changes our understanding of rights. The unconventionality of proclaiming rights in a declaration becomes clear especially when we compare it to other ways of demanding and instituting rights. A bill or a petition, for example, appeals to a higher authority and attempts to demarcate the boundaries of its power.[30] As recognized by Abbé Sieyès, one of the prominent political figures of the French Revolution, such a pact indicates "the *implicit recognition* of a seigneur, a suzerain, or a master to whom one is naturally obligated."[31] This is not to say that bills and petitions are not important for our contemporary understanding of rights; they manifest in certain respects what Rainer Forst refers to as "a right to justification" to the extent that they recognize the subject of rights "as an agent who can demand acceptable reasons . . . for any social or political structure or law that claims to be binding upon him or her."[32] But the declaration goes beyond the logic of justification that is at work in a bill or petition, as it no longer appeals to an external power that holds the authority to grant rights. It is instead a public utterance through which human beings reciprocally recognize each other as subjects entitled to equal rights. With the eighteenth-century revolutionary events, what we are confronted with is a new form of articulating and instituting rights, or in Claude Lefort's terms:

> a declaration by which human beings, speaking through their representatives, revealed themselves to be both the subject and the object of the utterance in which they named the human elements in one another, 'spoke to' one another, appeared before one another, and therefore erected themselves into their own judges, their own witnesses.[33]

Declaration is a revolutionary speech act that transforms the organization of political community as well as the terms of human co-existence by constituting human beings as the subjects with the capacity to declare rights and the objects to which the declared rights are addressed. Once we understand declaration as a practice of political founding and attend to its inaugural effects (i.e., constitution of rights, subjects, political community, humanity), we realize that what is at stake is not only justification or reason-giving but instead the *political invention and disclosure of a new world.*[34]

Reading Arendt's call for a right to have rights as an invitation to rethink human rights in terms of political practices of founding (especially declaratory practices) has three main implications. First and foremost, this reading draws attention to the crucial role of action, especially speech, in the continuous reinvention of human rights. The eighteenth-century declarations of rights introduce us to the extraordinary idea that it is the essence of rights to be declared, and as a result, the source of human rights becomes nothing more than "the human utterance of right," as Lefort puts it.[35] To look for a source that antedates the declaration in an attempt to provide human rights with a foundation freed from the contingencies of speech would precisely miss the revolutionary discovery that human beings appear as subjects entitled to rights only by sharing words and deeds that testify to their equality and freedom. As discussed below, Arendt's account, not unlike Lefort's, highlights that human rights have their origins not in pre-political or extra-political sources of authority but in public declarations and mutual recognition of equality and freedom.[36]

Second, this reading highlights that a right to have rights marks a new beginning radically interrupting the existing regime of human rights and introducing "a hiatus between the end of the old order and the beginning of the new," or "between a no-longer and a not-yet."[37] This ruptural dimension is crucial for understanding the distinctive features of historical and contemporary struggles that expose the limits of existing rights regimes *and* point to the possibilities of reinventing human rights. Such struggles reveal that human rights are not simply normative constraints regulating an existing political and legal order but also political inventions that can constitute a new order, bring to view new subjects and objects of rights, and reconfigure existing relations between rights, citizenship, and humanity. Understood in these terms, human rights have an "insurrectional" dimension, to use Étienne Balibar's term, because they can turn against the constituted political and normative order for the purposes of founding a new one.[38]

Finally, this reading allows a different understanding of the perplexities arising from Arendt's call for a right to have rights; instead of seeing them as representative of the normative deficiencies of her political thought, it takes them as illuminating starting points for wrestling with the perplexities of new beginnings that break with the existing order. There is always the temptation to cover over the abyss of freedom that confronts us in such new beginnings by resorting to a foundation; even Arendt's early reflections on this new right demonstrate the appeal of such foundationalist moves. But this solution might not be the only option, as Arendt's account of modern revolutions highlights.

Revolutionary Beginnings: Human Rights and Political Founding

Arendt is one of the key political theorists attuned to the perplexities of new beginnings, as highlighted by her account of modern revolutions. These revolutions expose actors and spectators to the abyss of freedom, as they reveal the possibility of initiating something that cannot be traced to a prior cause or reduced to the actualization of an already existing potentiality. Arendt underscores how tempting it is to cover up this abyss in her reflections on the eighteenth-century revolutionaries who tried to validate the new laws and rights they introduced either by depicting their actions as the restoration of a previous order or by invoking an absolute that can serve as a transcendent source of authority. In certain respects, these attempts confirm that it is not simply "[p]rofessional thinkers" who have historically displayed a strong inclination to turn away from the radical contingency of action; "men of action" also share this unwillingness "to pay the price of contingency for the questionable gift of spontaneity."[39] Nevertheless, in her close engagement with the words and deeds of the eighteenth-century revolutionaries, Arendt also discovers crucial resources for a different approach to the perplexities of new beginnings—one that suggests that we do not need to turn anywhere other than political founding itself to find out what saves the new beginning from its inherent arbitrariness as well as what might authorize new laws and rights.

Perplexities of modern revolutions need to be understood in light of the novel conception of temporality they introduce. As a term originating in astronomy and "designating the regular, lawfully revolving motion of the stars," revolution in the premodern era came to stand for the "eternal recurrence" of a few forms of government in the realm of politics.[40] Arendt underlines that modern revolutions depart from this cyclical understanding of time, as they introduce the possibility of rupturing the historical continuum and inaugurating an entirely new order. They instill in us the sense "that the course of history suddenly begins anew, that an entirely new story, a story never known or told before is about to unfold."[41] Arendt's contrast of moderns and Romans is important in this regard. For Romans, political founding was not "an absolutely new beginning" but instead a "restoration and re-establishment."[42] This Roman understanding of founding was revitalized in the modern era, as American revolutionaries described their own actions as a restoration of Rome. Although Arendt embraces the Roman understanding of political founding as the source of authority in the body politic, as I discuss below, she takes issue with this attempt to cover up the "abyss of spontaneity" by "understanding the *new* as an improved re-statement of the old."[43] In the end, even American revolutionaries had to admit that what they were involved in was not merely founding "Rome anew" but instead "the entirely unexpected and very different task of constituting something entirely new—founding a 'new Rome.'"[44] This realization is manifested, according to Arendt, in the Americans' decision "to vary Virgil's line from *magnus ordo saeclorum* to *novus ordo saeclorum*," or from "the great order of the ages" to "the *new order*" of the ages.[45] That change captures the modern revolutionary possibility of instituting an entirely new order that cannot be understood as a restoration of a historical antecedent.

Precisely because of their spontaneity and radical novelty, modern revolutions pose the challenging question of what authorizes the actions of the revolutionaries who set out to establish a new order: "[T]hose who get together to constitute a new government are themselves unconstitutional, that is, they have no authority to do what they have set out to achieve."[46] Whereas in the past a new political and legal order could be legitimated with reference to divine authority, secularization in the modern age leaves political actors with the problem of finding a new authority for the laws, rights, and institutions they establish.[47] As Arendt examines how the eighteenth-century revolutionaries grappled with the perplexities arising from the lack of prior authorization for their actions, she draws attention to the appeal and risks of an absolute. By invoking an absolute, the revolutionaries tried to resolve, once and for all, two types of perplexities attending these founding events:

> [The absolute] was needed to break two vicious circles, the one apparently inherent in human law-making, and the other inherent in the *petitio principii* which attends every new beginning, that is, politically speaking, in the very task of foundation.[48]

In a revolutionary context, the absolute has a powerful appeal precisely because it seems to resolve both of these perplexities: It sanctions the man-made laws by introducing a transcendent and "higher law."[49] It also allows the revolutionaries to turn away from the abyss of their founding act, as it offers an origin or source "from which it [the new beginning] springs and by which it is 'explained.'"[50]

Arendt argues that revolutionary actors on both sides of the Atlantic invoked absolutes in an attempt to resolve these dilemmas. Such an attempt can be seen, for example, in Sieyès's turn to the nation as the source of both laws and constituent power, or Robespierre's invocation of an "Immortal Legislator."[51] The appeal of the absolute could not be simply explained by the hold of the absolutist tradition in the Old World.

To the extent that absolutes were also invoked in the American context, the problem was a common predicament that arose from the difficulty of providing authorization for the new order established by a revolution in a modern secular era. Arendt reminds us here of John Adams's reference to 'the great Legislator of the Universe' and Thomas Jefferson's appeal, in the Declaration of Independence, to 'the laws of nature and nature's God' to underscore that the quest "for a divine principle, for some transcendent sanction in the political realm" was present in the American case as well.[52]

Arendt's discussion of modern revolutions highlights that the revolutionary appeals to absolutes were attempts to escape from the perplexities of new beginnings. In certain respects, this point brings her closer to other thinkers of revolutionary founding. For example, in his reading of the 1789 Declaration of the Rights of Man and Citizen, Jean-François Lyotard highlights "the aporia of sovereignty" and argues that those who spoke in the name of the "people" lacked the authorization to do what they did prior to their declaratory act.[53] Jacques Derrida makes a similar point in his reading of the American Declaration of Independence: The Declaration is signed in the name of a "people" that does not exist prior to the act of signing. To overcome this circularity and to authorize their acts, the signatories of the declaration invoked absolutes such as "nature" and "God" to serve as a foundation for the new laws and rights. For Derrida, it is impossible to determine whether the declaration is a performative utterance bringing forth new rights or a constative utterance stating the rights that the "people" are already entitled to by laws of nature and God, and this undecidability is ultimately necessary to authorize the act of founding.[54]

Although Arendt's focus on the perplexities of founding brings her closer to these thinkers, the conclusions that she draws point in a quite different direction. From Derrida's perspective, for example, the invocation of absolutes demonstrates that law cannot establish its authority without a "'mystical' limit;" it is in need of "a violence without ground."[55] Lyotard's verdict about the perplexities of the 1789 Declaration is that "[a]ttempts at legitimating authority lead to vicious circles . . . to infinite regressions."[56] Arendt, on the other hand, does not stop at locating the abyss and arbitrariness of revolutionary beginnings, and she refrains from the conclusion that law ultimately derives its authority from an originary violence that it conceals. She differs from these two thinkers in that she points to the possibilities of politically navigating the two types of perplexities inherent in lawmaking and new beginnings.[57] She suggests that these perplexities are not vicious circles from which only an absolute can save us, and for alternatives, she turns to the resources of Montesquieu's political theory and offers a quite peculiar reading of the American Revolution.

As discussed earlier, the first set of perplexities that Arendt addresses in her account of revolutionary beginnings arises from the fact that the revolutionaries lacked prior authorization for their undertaking; they tried to resolve these perplexities by invoking an absolute. The search for a transcendent sanction for man-made laws, Arendt argues, results from a conventional tendency to think of law as a commandment or imperative in line with the Hebrew-Christian tradition.[58] Understood in these terms, the law instills a sense of absoluteness, as if it were independent of "consent and mutual agreements" and in need of "a transcendent source of authority for its validity."[59] To counter this anti-political framework, Arendt turns to the Roman understanding of law as *lex*, which means "intimate connection," "relationship," or "lasting tie," and suggests that legislation should be understood as a political activity that links different entities through mutual agreements.[60] This Roman understanding is later revived in the work of Montesquieu, who takes law to be "*rapport*, the relation subsisting between different entities."[61] According to this view, laws do not need "absolute validity," since they are by definition "relative" or dependent on political practices of consenting, agreeing, and upholding them; as such, they do not derive their validity from a transcendent authority beyond human power.[62]

In addition to the Romans and Montesquieu, Arendt turns to the example of the American Revolution to call attention to the possibilities of navigating the first set of perplexities related to the authority of laws in a revolutionary context. Her discussion of the Declaration of Independence is important in this regard. In many respects, the Declaration manifests the powerful appeal of absolutes, as it makes reference to "the Laws of Nature and of Nature's God" to authorize the equal rights that it invokes. Yet, in this declaration, Arendt also locates the possibility of countering this appeal, as she reminds us of Jefferson's famous statement: "*We hold* these truths to be self-evident." The statement is puzzling, as it holds on to the idea of an absolute that is beyond human power and independent of human agreement, while simultaneously acknowledging that the "truths" proclaimed in the declaration are in need of our assent.[63] Arendt's analysis of this statement identifies the crucial role of speech, especially the practice of giving assent, in validating man-made laws. Modern rights declarations "install the radical contingency of linguistic proclamation into the heart of constitutional arrangements," to use Costas Douzinas's words.[64] There is always the temptation to seek shelter from this radical contingency in an absolute. For example, characterizing rights as "self-evident truth[s]" suggests that they do not need any "argumentative demonstration or political persuasion" and that they are as absolute as "the revealed truths of religion or the axiomatic verities of mathematics."[65] But as Arendt's emphasis on "we hold" underscores, politically instituted laws are not in the same category as mathematical laws; the political statement "all men are created equal" is not analogous to the mathematical truth of "two times two make four."[66] Laws and rights, understood along the lines of Roman *lex* and Montesquieu's *rapport*, do not have an incontestable and irresistible authority; they are in need of political practices of argumentation, demonstration, and agreement.[67] Even when political actors invoke rights as self-evident or natural, Arendt's analysis suggests, it is important not to forget that they are engaging in political practices that aim at persuading others to give their assent.

Arendt's account also points to the possibilities of navigating the second set of perplexities that arise in the context of modern revolutions, which relates to the *petitio principii* inherent in every new beginning. In response to the challenging question of where the new beginning originates from, Arendt offers an answer that draws on her reflections on Augustine's notion of natality and contends that each new beginning arises from the human capacity to begin anew.[68] The fact that these new beginnings can neither be accounted for with a historical precedent nor validated by a transcendent source of authority, she argues, does not mean that they are completely arbitrary: "What saves the act of beginning from its own arbitrariness is that it carries its own principle within itself, or, to be more precise, that beginning and principle, *principium* and principle, are not only related to each other, but are coeval."[69] Precisely because a new political and legal order can derive its authority from the ongoing augmentation of the principle that becomes manifest in its origin or beginning, it does not need the sanction of an external source of authority.

To understand this point, there is a need to examine Arendt's distinctive understanding of "principle," which challenges the conventional meanings of this term; she has in mind neither a moral standard regulating action nor a fundamental truth serving as the foundation of a system.[70] Arendt's unique understanding of the term significantly draws on Montesquieu's distinction between "principle" and "nature" of a government. For Montesquieu, whereas the latter denotes the "particular structure" of each government, the former refers to what "makes it act" or "the human passions that set it in motion." For example, the nature of democracy consists of the sovereignty of the people, whereas its principle is virtue understood as "love of equality."[71] Democratic government can only be preserved if this love of equality continues to motivate the everyday practices of citizens. And that love can only be maintained if it is continuously practiced by citizens and instituted in laws that allow for equalization of inequalities.[72] Montesquieu lists three principles, each inspiring a specific form of government: honor in monarchy, virtue in republic, and fear in despotism. Arendt takes this Montesquieuan idea and even adds to his list some other possible candidates for principles, including fame, freedom, justice, and equality. She argues that such principles "move human beings to act" and provide "constant nourishment for their actions."[73] They also serve as some kind of "guiding criteria," as they orient judgments about the actions in the public realm.[74]

Three crucial points need to be highlighted here. First, diverging from conventional understandings of principle as a regulative norm, Arendt uses the term to understand what inspires, animates, or energizes action. In turning to Montesquieu, Arendt's goal is not to regulate, contain, and tame freedom but instead to develop a conceptual framework that can come to terms with the spontaneity of action.[75] She highlights that, if action merely followed "the guidance of the intellect" or "the dictate of the will," it would not be free, as it would be subject to and constrained by an external force.[76] Springing from principles that can become "fully manifest only in the performing act itself," action can maintain its spontaneity.[77] Arendt's distinctive understanding of principle shifts the terms of the debates on human rights, including those on her proposal of a right to have rights. The task is not philosophically grounding human rights in normative and ontological foundations. It is instead understanding the political practices of founding and refounding human rights by taking into account the principle that becomes manifest in them.[78]

Second, Arendt's Montesquieuan notion of principle offers a unique understanding of universal validity—one that is achieved through execution or performance: "In distinction from its goal, the principle of an action can be repeated time and again, it is inexhaustible, and in distinction from its motive, the validity of a principle is universal, it is not bound to any particular person or to any particular group."[79] In other words, it is the inexhaustible iterability of a principle in different spatio-temporal contexts that endows it with a universal validity. This argument suggests that the universality of the principle animating new human rights claims cannot be separated from the political practices of repeating and enacting that principle time and again.

Third, by adopting a Montesquieuan understanding of "principle," Arendt avoids the pitfalls of both foundationalism and anti-foundationalism.[80] As her account of modern revolutions highlights, she refuses to shy away from the radical spontaneity and contingency of new beginnings by turning to extra-political or pre-political foundations that can validate man-made rights, laws, and institutions. She also refuses to endorse an anti-foundationalist position that would brush aside any effort to examine what kind of universal validity human rights claims might hold. Rejecting both foundationalism and anti-foundationalism, Arendt instead turns to principles as "guiding criteria" that can orient our judgment about political practices.[81]

Following Arendt's reflections on Kant, the judgment that we exercise in light of these inspiring or energizing principles can be best characterized as "reflective judgment." Unlike a "determinant judgment," which would "subsume the particular under a general rule," "reflective judgment" is confronted with the challenging task of judging a particular "for which the general has to be found."[82] When we are judging a painting, for example, we cannot evaluate it according to a given standard of beauty because that painting expands what we understand of beauty in unpredictable ways. Reflective judgment is necessary when we can no longer appeal to past experience or an already existing standard.

Arendt insists on the need to exercise this faculty not simply for aesthetic objects; more important for her purposes are the new beginnings that strike us with their spontaneity and contingency. Here we can think of new rights claims that inaugurate radically novel understandings of equality and freedom. Any such claim works like an "example" in a Kantian sense; it "is and remains a particular that in its very particularity reveals the generality that otherwise could not be defined."[83] Just as we can experience and understand the universal predicate of beauty only in our encounter with a particular work of art, we become aware of the *universality* of human rights whenever we are confronted with *particular* rights claims that anticipate general assent for the new meanings of equality and freedom they introduce. As different from a merely relativistic, subjective statement, a new rights claim strives for universal agreement and appeals to our common sense (or *sensus communis*).[84] Particularly important in this regard are the imaginative practices that re-present, or "make present what is absent," and invite new ways of seeing by forging new connections between seemingly disparate issues.[85] Such representative practices are crucial for ushering in novel ways of understanding rightlessness and rights. Arendt's own proposal of a right to have rights relies on similar practices that allow us to see statelessness in a new light as an unacceptable form of injustice—take, for example, the analogy that she draws between slavery and statelessness, discussed in the last chapter. Unlike the objective validity of a scientific truth that can compel us without any persuasion, a new rights claim can achieve its intersubjective validity by striving to "'woo' or 'court' the agreement of everyone else."[86] As I explain below, the principle that manifests itself in the world with the eighteenth-century declarations achieves an "exemplary validity," when it "set[s] the imagination in motion" and resonates outside its original context with new rights claims that strive for universal assent.[87]

With its insistence on the coeval existence of new beginnings and principles, Arendt's account of revolutionary founding points to the political possibilities of navigating the perplexities of modern rights declarations. It suggests that these perplexities are not vicious circles that need to be resolved by way of an absolute that will serve as the foundation of authority and source of validity. They are political and ethical dilemmas that confront us at every new beginning. New beginnings do contain within themselves the resources that can help us grapple with and respond to these dilemmas. More importantly, they carry within themselves the very principles that save them from arbitrariness. If Arendt's proposal of a right to have rights signifies such a new beginning, "what is the foundation or ground of this new right?" might not be the right question. Following Arendt, we might instead ask, "what principle inspires, and becomes manifest in, the articulation of this new right?"

A Right to Have Rights and the Principle of Equaliberty

To answer this question, I suggest adopting an approach similar to the one we see in Arendt's analysis of the American Revolution and her discussion of civil disobedience. In each case, Arendt embraces the Roman idea of turning to the political founding to locate the principle that illuminates the distinctive characteristics of a polity and serves as the source for the ongoing authorization of its laws. Taking this idea as my starting point, I read Arendt's proposal of a right to have rights as an invitation to rethink new rights claims as political practices that reactivate and augment the principle at work in the eighteenth-century declarations of rights. Drawing on the work of Étienne Balibar, I use the term "equaliberty" to name the principle that appears in the eighteenth-century declarations of rights and that animates Arendt's call for a right to have rights.

Arendt's discussion of modern revolutions suggests that we should look nowhere other than political founding itself to locate the source of authority for the new laws and rights introduced by revolutionaries. In the case of the American Revolution, she argues, the political founding is animated by "the interconnected principle of mutual promise and common deliberation," and it is this principle that serves as the fountain of authority for the American polity.[88] Arendt's argument about the American Revolution draws attention to her unique understanding of authority. Insisting on the etymological connection between authority (*auctoritas*) and augmentation (*augere*), Arendt renders authority dependent on the ongoing practices of augmentation, which involve not simply conservation but also strengthening and amendment. Accordingly, laws and rights do not have an irresistible and incontrovertible authority derived from an extra-political source; they are in need of an ongoing authorization in and through political practices that reenact and augment the principle manifested in the founding.[89]

Arendt's essay "Civil Disobedience" further clarifies her Montesquieuan notion of principle and dispels the doubt that her understanding of authority in terms of practices of augmentation entails "a unitary and consensual" picture overlooking the conflicts, disagreements, and exclusions that characterize political acts of founding.[90] In many ways, acts of civil disobedience also confront us with the perplexities of founding. After all, as Arendt reminds us, quoting Carl Cohen, "the law cannot justify the breaking of the law."[91] Similar to revolutionaries, civil disobedients are not legally authorized to do what they set out to do. In the face of these perplexities, it is appealing to turn to an absolute and justify civil disobedience as a moral obligation arising from a "higher law." But Arendt rejects this foundationalist move in her account of the acts of civil disobedience in the late 1960s. She instead reinterprets these acts as augmentations of the principle of consent that became manifest in the American founding.[92] To make this point, she declares in a Montesquieuan vein that civil disobedience is an action that departs from the letter of the law but does that in accordance with its "*spirit.*"[93] In addition, Arendt also provides a unique understanding of the principle of consent that she attributes to the

American founding. For consent to be different from passive acquiescence, she argues, there must be the possibility of dissent; when confronted with acts of civil disobedience, it is this principle that should orient our judgments about the legitimacy of these acts.[94] By insisting that consent presupposes dissent, Arendt challenges the view of a consensual political community and brings to view the violent exclusions from the *consensus universalis* that is taken to be the authorizing ground of the constitution. Referring specifically to African Americans and Native Americans, she highlights that "these people had never been included in the original *consensus universalis* of the American republic."[95] Without civil disobedience, which could allow the possibility of challenging the constitutionality of existing laws, these violent exclusions would taint the legitimacy of the constitution and undermine its authority and stability.

On the basis of Arendt's reflections on American founding and civil disobedience, it is possible to read her articulation of a right to have rights as a statement manifesting and augmenting the principle at work in the eighteenth-century declarations. Arendt's statement brings to view, and takes issue with, the exclusions of the equation of "man and citizen," and yet, paradoxically, it also reaffirms that formula and takes it in a new direction as it insists on rethinking human rights in terms of a right to citizenship. In ways similar to the civil disobedients' reiteration of the principle of consent implied in dissent, a right to have rights both conserves and amends the principle it reenacts.

Arendt never explicitly names the principle that animates the modern declarations of rights, but this principle can be best captured by Étienne Balibar's notion of "equaliberty," which is a translation of Greek *isonomia* via its Latin formulation ("*aequum ius* or *aequa libertas*").[96] This term is also appropriate given Arendt's reflections on *isonomia* in different contexts, including her argument that the eighteenth-century revolutionaries turned to the ancient examples of Greek *isonomia* and Roman *civitas* as they constituted new forms of government in which laws took their validation from the consent of the citizenry.[97] Balibar highlights that the Declaration of the Rights of Man and Citizen marks a radical transformation because it introduces us to "the proposition of equaliberty" and affirms a universal access to politics and rights. Similar to ancient *isonomia*, equaliberty denotes an equal claim to political activity, and it highlights the inextricably intertwined nature of equality and freedom. Writing against the liberal tendency to prioritize freedom over equality and the socialist tendency to prioritize equality over freedom,

Balibar insists that it is impossible to deny freedom without also denying equality (and vice versa).[98] However, if modern equaliberty shares this connection with ancient *isonomia,* it also diverges from the latter with its "politics of the universalization of rights"—a politics centered on the struggles of those who are denied rights and yet nevertheless venture to claim rights.[99] This universalization is by no means a linear process guaranteeing progressive extension of rights to an ever-growing number of subjects. To the extent that the proposition of equaliberty can achieve a "truth-effect" only in the rights struggles that reenact and verify it, Balibar underscores, politics of universalization can always face setbacks from existing power relations and institutions.[100] Arendt's notion of a right to have rights, challenging the instituted limits on the equal claim to political activity within the framework of the nation-state, gestures toward this politics of universalization that has no guaranteed end.

Rethinking Arendt's call for a right to have rights as a proposal that is animated by equaliberty offers us a new perspective on the scholarly debates on the normative foundations of human rights. First, this reading embraces a historically informed understanding of human rights and their validity. Arendt's emphasis on the founding acts that interrupt linear schemes of temporality urges us to understand equaliberty as a principle that emerges within a specific historical context. To the extent that this principle marks "a hiatus between the end of the old order and the beginning of the new," it is at odds with scholarly accounts that establish the universality of human rights by tracing them back to values embedded in Greek Stoicism, the code of Hamurabi, natural law, or the Bible.[101] Instead, the Arendtian framework calls attention to the political invention and disclosure of a new political and normative world in the eighteenth-century declarations. These declarations represent a historic breakthrough since they introduce us to the idea that rights have their origins in public utterances that involve mutual recognition of equality, and with this revolutionary move, they set the stage for new declarations of rights.

Recognizing the ineluctable historicity of the principle of equaliberty and turning attention to the revolutionary acts with which this principle manifests itself in the world, however, does not mean adopting a historicist perspective. As discussed earlier, Arendt's Montesquieuan framework offers a unique understanding of universal validity as arising from the reenactment of a principle time and again. In relation to the eighteenth-century declarations of rights, the Arendtian perspective endorses a position similar to the one proposed by Claude Lefort, who maintains that the principle that emerges with these declarations "cannot be annexed by historicism:" "[I]t is more than something which appears within time and which is destined to disappear into time. A principle arises, and henceforth we cannot understand the individual, society or history unless we go back to it."[102] Lefort's remark, read alongside Arendt's Montesquieuan insight, suggests that the principle of equaliberty, introduced by modern rights declarations, is not confined to the original context in which it appears. This principle can inspire rights struggles in different contexts, and it owes its ongoing universal validation to such struggles that reiterate and augment it time and again.[103]

Here, we can think of, for example, how the Haitian Revolution appropriated the terms of the 1789 Declaration, which had carefully side-stepped the issue of slavery, in unpredictable and imaginative ways to question slavery. As Laurent Dubois highlights, our understanding of the universality of rights has been profoundly transformed as a result of the actions of slave insurgents in the Caribbean. When these slaves did what was considered to be unthinkable and acted *as if* they were citizens, their action "outran the political imagination of the metropole, transforming the possibilities embodied in the idea of citizenship."[104] The universal validity of the principle of equaliberty is to be understood as an ongoing achievement that relies on such reenactments that are not fully authorized by the instituted configurations of rights, citizenship, and humanity. Such iterative practices change the boundaries of our political and normative universe, as they introduce us to new subjects who were formerly not recognized as human beings entitled to rights. These radical practices of reinventing equality and freedom augment (i.e., conserve and amend) human rights, and this augmentation is what provides these rights with a relatively permanent political foundation.

This last point shares similarities with Seyla Benhabib's proposal to understand human rights in terms of "democratic iterations" that involve practices of contesting and redefining existing inscriptions of rights. Drawing on and reinterpreting Jacques Derrida's work, Benhabib suggests that such iterations do not simply reproduce what they repeat; each iteration "transforms meaning, adds to it, enriches it in ever-so-subtle ways."[105] This conclusion is quite in line with the Arendtian understanding of augmentation as a practice involving preservation, strengthening, and amendment. In addition, Benhabib's account of democratic iterations places the emphasis on the practices of groups who "claim that they belong within the circles of addressees of a right from which they have been excluded in its initial articulation,"[106] and this emphasis is similar to the one that Arendt puts on groups excluded from *consensus universalis* in her account of civil disobedience. Despite these similarities, it is important to note that, for Benhabib, *"the validity of cosmopolitan norms"* rests not on democratic iterations but instead on "independent normative grounds."[107] According to this framework, a right to have rights derives its validity from context-transcendent norms that are taken to be the underlying presuppositions of communication.[108] The reading offered here works with a different understanding of universal validity, as it is no longer centered on the immanent presuppositions of speech but instead the revolutionary propositions of modern rights declarations as well as the political struggles that these propositions set in motion. It is these declarations that introduce us to a novel speech situation by putting forward the radical idea that rights have their origins in public utterances that involve reciprocal recognition of equality and freedom. Arendt's proposal of a right to have rights is situated within the political and normative horizon represented by this historic breakthrough; it reactivates and augments the principle of equaliberty that appears in the world with the eighteenth-century declarations. The universal validity of this principle cannot be detached from the political struggles that enact it in different contexts, expand what we understand from equality and freedom in unpredictable ways, and strive for universal assent for the novel conceptions of rights that they propose.

So far I have shown that rethinking a right to have rights along these lines is more in line with the premises of Arendt's political theory, which turns our attention away from philosophical foundations to political acts of founding. But as the example of the Haitian Revolution highlights, this reading might also be more promising for understanding historical and contemporary struggles for rights. Particularly important in this regard are the perplexities of authorization that I discussed in relation to revolution and civil disobedience; we are confronted with similar perplexities in struggles that introduce us to new conceptions of rights, as can be seen, for example, in the eighteenth-century efforts of women to appropriate the terms of the Rights of Man. Take the case of Olympe de Gouges, who "act[ed] as a self-appointed legislator" when she proclaimed the Declaration of the Rights of Woman and the Female Citizen, as Joan Scott highlights, and challenged the "definition of women as passive citizens."[109] Like the revolutionaries and civil disobedients in Arendt's account, de Gouges set out to do what she was not authorized to do: Exercising the very rights that she did not yet have, especially the most politically salient right of self-legislation, she acted as if she were an active citizen and participated in the ongoing reformulation of rights with her own declaration. Women such as de Gouges, to use Jacques Rancière's terms, "acted as subjects that did not have the rights that they had and had the rights that they had not."[110] They demonstrated the injustice of their exclusion from the instituted order of rights by enacting the rights that they were denied and bringing to view the possibility of instituting rights in a much more egalitarian fashion.

Arendt's proposal of a right to have rights gives rise to perplexities regarding the source and status of this right, as I highlighted before. But bearing in mind her account of revolutionary beginnings, perhaps we can take these perplexities as helpful starting points for coming to grips with the distinctive features and challenges of struggles that bring forth new rights or position new subjects as rights-bearers. As the brief discussion of de Gouges underscores, such struggles expose us to the abyss of freedom in ways similar to the revolutionary declarations of the eighteenth century. They introduce new rights claims that break with the instituted order, reinvent the meanings of equality and freedom, and disclose new political and normative worlds. A right to have rights, with the perplexities arising from its groundlessness, urges us to attend to how these claims reenact and augment the principle of equaliberty, as they introduce imaginative possibilities for reconfiguring the relationship between rights, citizenship, and humanity. In what follows, I draw on these Arendtian insights to understand the distinctive characteristics and challenges of the contemporary rights struggles waged by undocumented immigrants.

Political Practices of Founding Human Rights

As a result of the increasingly restrictive asylum and immigration policies adopted across the world, millions of immigrants have found themselves in an irregular status that confines them to a life of invisibility and uncertainty. Over the past two decades, however, undocumented immigrants have refused to be passive victims and have organized to contest their condition of rightlessness. Perhaps one of the most memorable mobilizations was that of *sans-papiers*, who occupied churches and various other public sites in 1996 to challenge the French government's anti-immigrant policies and to demand a right to regularization. *Sans-papiers'* actions garnered significant attention, especially among scholars interested in questions of human rights and citizenship. For many, *sans-papiers* demonstrated the democratic possibilities arising from an insurgent politics that can push human rights and citizenship beyond their institutional confines.[111] This conclusion is very much in line with the argument I make in this chapter: Human rights owe their origins, guarantees, and reinvention to political practices of declaring and enacting rights in ways that are not fully authorized by the prevailing institutional and normative frameworks. But there is also a need to complicate this story, if we do not want to turn *sans-papiers* into another success story heralding the eventual triumph of human rights and postnational citizenship.

By rethinking *sans-papiers* in light of the previous discussion of a right to have rights—especially the suggestion that new rights claims should be understood as political acts of founding that expose us to the abyss and perplexities of new beginnings—I hope to provide an account that focuses attention on the unique challenges faced by undocumented immigrants in making claims to rights. Particularly important in this regard are the challenges arising from their precarious legal, political, and human standing. As "impossible subjects," or persons "who cannot be," to use Mae Ngai's apt terms, their presence in the political community is "simultaneously a social reality and a legal impossibility."[112] Becoming visible in order to demand rights is quite risky under these conditions, as the exposure renders undocumented immigrants vulnerable to various forms of state violence, including deportation. In addition, since they are often seen as lawbreakers and not as legitimate rights-holders, it is very difficult for them to exercise even their existing rights. Finally, when they venture to claim rights that they are not entitled to within the scope of existing domestic and international laws, there is the demanding task of validating these claims.

Given these unique challenges, it is important to ask: What does it mean to claim rights as "impossible" subjects? How do such subjects try to authorize their rights claims? In what ways do these claims draw on, challenge, and reconfigure the existing human rights framework? In what follows, I turn to the mobilizations of *sans-papiers* in France to address these questions and to highlight why we need to understand human rights in terms of political practices of founding. Demonstrations of French *sans-papiers* have subsided over the years, but their story remains quite relevant, disclosing the challenges, risks, frustrations, and double binds faced by subjects who claim rights that they are not yet authorized to claim.[113]

The term *"sans-papiers"* is the self-ascribed name of what started as a relatively small movement of irregular immigrants who mobilized for regularization in France. Immigrants have been active in French politics since the 1970s, organizing especially for housing-related demands. However, particularly in the mid-1990s, in response to changing immigration laws that made it very difficult to acquire and maintain legal residence in France, they started to form informal organizations (*collectifs de sans-papiers*) to demand a right to legal residence.[114] Since the mid-1990s, the movement has inspired similar struggles waged by migrants with irregular status in different European countries.[115]

The *sans-papiers* movement in France consists mainly of individuals from former colonies of France in West and North Africa, and the group's public demonstrations emerged in response to a set of restrictive immigration policies and laws. Of particular concern were the Pasqua Laws of 1993. These laws made it increasingly difficult to receive and renew residence permits, excluded undocumented immigrants from claims to social benefits, gave extraordinary powers to police and local authorities for identity checks, and extended the detention period. Particularly because of the changes in residency permit requirements, several immigrants who were legally residing in the country became "illegals."[116]

Sans-papiers came to the forefront of French politics with their occupations of public spaces. The movement elicited significant attention with its occupation of St. Bernard Church on June 28, 1996, especially because of the violent police eviction that followed. In the early morning of August 23, 1996, more than 1,000 police officers broke down the doors of the church with axes, and forced everyone into buses by using tear gas and dragging bodies down the stairs of the church.[117] The movement gained further attention and support with the introduction of the Debré Laws, named after the minister of the interior in Alain Juppé's conservative government, near the end of 1996. These laws ended the automatic renewal of 10-year residence permits and required French nationals hosting non-EU citizens to inform the authorities of their arrival and departure. It was the clause criminalizing hospitality that ignited an immense public reaction. Prominent figures made statements denouncing these laws, especially by reminding the French public of the Vichy regime that sent Jewish refugees to camps.[118] A petition drafted by 66 French filmmakers and calling for acts of civil disobedience against these laws received around 120,000 signatures. On February 22, 1997, there was a demonstration of 100,000 protestors in Paris, and similar protests were organized in other cities. As a result of this public pressure, the Juppé government changed the clause criminalizing those hosting undocumented immigrants.[119] But the bill that passed on March 26, 1997, still put migrants in a precarious condition, as it introduced compulsory fingerprinting of those requesting residency, increased police search powers, and denied the right to appeal to those whose requests for residence permits were turned down.

The restrictive policies introduced in the mid-1990s were maintained and expanded by the successive French governments, regardless of their ideological positions.[120] The current socialist government is a case in point. Perhaps one of the most controversial immigration decisions under François Hollande's presidency was the deportation of Leonarda Dibrani, a Roma girl from Kosovo, with her family in October 2013; Dibrani was detained in front of her classmates during a school field trip. Within a hostile environment that criminalizes immigration and renders various categories of migrants "illegal," *sans-papiers* continue to demand regularization. One of their recent demonstrations took place during September and October, 2013, in response to the new residency criteria introduced by Minister of Interior Manuel Valls. These criteria required *sans-papiers* to show eight pay slips to be eligible for work permits, an obviously impossible demand given that they were not supposed to work in the first place due to their irregular status.[121]

The ongoing struggles of *sans-papiers* underscore the challenges that undocumented immigrants face as they make rights claims in a context defined by restrictive immigration policies, increasing xenophobia, and new forms of racism. In addition to these challenges, these immigrants also confront the daunting task of making claims to rights that they are not yet legally entitled to. *Sans-papiers* claim several rights, including the right to regularization and residence, which cannot be easily accommodated within the framework of human rights law. Even the United Nations Convention for the Protection of the Rights of All Migrant Workers and Members of Their Families, despite its explicit recognition of migrants in irregular status as subjects entitled to rights, does not impose on states an obligation to regularize undocumented immigrants.[122] More strikingly, it allows states to not only discriminate against undocumented immigrants with respect to several rights, including freedom of movement, participation in public affairs, and family unity, but also impose sanctions on those with irregular status in line with their immigration laws and policies.[123] The fact that international human rights law justifies these distinctions demonstrates that *sans-papiers* cannot derive the validity of many of their rights claims from that law. Accordingly, these claims expose us to the perplexities of new beginnings. *Sans-papiers* "have no authority to do what they have set out to achieve," to recall Arendt's description of eighteenth-century revolutionaries, as they demand rights that do not yet exist in international human rights law.[124]

Sans-papiers' claims challenge not only the existing legal framework of human rights but also the moral universalism underlying it. The denial of many rights to undocumented immigrants within this framework reveals the divisions and stratifications within the seemingly all-inclusive formula of "common humanity."[125] This conclusion seems surprising given that human rights rest on a normative framework that renders moral community, in the words of Seyla Benhabib, "coextensive with all beings capable of speech and action, and potentially with all of humanity."[126] But the struggles of *sans-papiers* highlight that membership in this community is by no means certain because inclusion in the human species does not guarantee recognition as a human being capable of speech and action. The challenges of recognition are at the heart of Arendt's analysis of statelessness, as discussed at length in chapter 4. Following Aristotle, Arendt reminds us, we have come to understand human beings as "political animals" capable of speech.[127] But statelessness demonstrates that it becomes very difficult to be recognized as a human being in these terms when one is deprived of a political community that can render one's action and speech meaningful. Stateless people become *aneu logou* (i.e., without speech), not because they can no longer speak but because they can no longer render their speech audible, intelligible, and relevant. To rephrase an argument made by Jacques Rancière, in struggles such as the one waged by *sans-papiers*, it is not known in advance whether "a sonorous emission" will be "understood as speech, capable of enunciating what is just," or simply as "a noise signaling pleasure or pain, consent or revolt."[128] In other words, since one's humanity does not exist prior to the struggle waged for these rights but instead can only be established in and through these struggles, a moral framework appealing to common humanity would not be sufficient to validate the new rights claims of *sans-papiers*.

Sans-papiers' actions can be best described as political practices of founding, as they bring forth new subjects, propose new rights, and push already existing rights beyond their instituted formulations. Given that such political practices of founding lack prior authorization, how can the *sans-papiers* validate their actions and rights claims? In what follows, I highlight the inventive political practices that *sans-papiers* engage in to create a public space where they can appear and represent their plight in a new light. These practices aim at persuading their interlocutors by "elicit[ing] criteria that speak to the particular case at hand and in relation to particular interlocutors."[129] Especially important in this regard are *sans-papiers'* frequent references to French revolutionary history and the Rights of Man. These references highlight how rights claims can strive to achieve an exemplary validity by putting the imagination in motion and courting universal assent.

Sans-papiers contest their invisibility and immobility by creating public spaces in which their actions and speech can be taken into account. As highlighted in the last chapter, one of the most fundamental forms of rightlessness experienced by various categories of migrants is deprivation from a public space in which they can appear before others. In the case of *sans-papiers*, this problem arises from their invisibility, as they are forced to inhabit a "space of non-existence," to use Susan Bibler Coutin's phrase. This does not mean that they are literally non-existent. In fact, as Coutin underlines, undocumented immigrants continue to work in public, ride on the bus, and send their children to schools. However, "like characters who experience a temporal lift in a Star Trek episode, they come in and out of existence."[130] Occupying this paradoxical space of existence and non-existence, they are forced to act as inconspicuously as possible, since even mundane activities such as driving can become illicit acts warranting deportation.[131] In addition to invisibility, another distinctive feature characterizing the contemporary predicament of undocumented immigrants is immobility; they cannot move in public freely without the perpetual fear of being exposed. What is at stake in this immobility is ultimately the loss of a right to act and speak, if we were to follow Arendt's peculiar understanding of freedom of movement in terms of both "the freedom to depart and begin something new and unheard-of" and "the freedom to interact in speech with many others and experience the diversity that the world always is in its totality."[132]

Occupying public spaces that they are not entitled to inhabit, *sans-papiers* contest the immobility and invisibility imposed by the lack of legal status. By engaging in unauthorized practices of "taking" public sites, they come out of the shadows and establish a stage where they can appear to others as subjects entitled to equal rights.[133] Madjiguène Cissé, one of the spokespersons for the *sans-papiers* movement, highlights the crucial importance of such practices for establishing political and human standing:

> In France up until now our fate as immigrants was: either take part in the Republic's process of integration, or be deported like cattle. At the heart of this approach was the notion that we are "underground," which has a very strong negative charge. . . . We have made ourselves visible to say that we are here, to say that we are not in hiding but we're just human beings.[134]

As Cissé's statement highlights, French citizenship and immigration policies force those who lack proper legal status to live in the shadows, as inconspicuously as possible and always with the fear of deportation. *Sans-papiers* dwell in a "zone of indistinction," to use Giorgio Agamben's phrase, situated between politics and nature, *bios* and *zoē*, human and non-human.[135] Refusing to hide in this zone where they are deprived of rights and constantly exposed to violence (i.e., always ready to be "deported like cattle"), *sans-papiers* become visible with their occupations of public spaces. This visibility carries a great risk, but it is also a necessary condition for *sans-papiers* to position themselves as subjects entitled to rights; this double bind highlights one of the distinctive challenges defining the struggles waged by undocumented immigrants who claim and enact the rights that they do not officially have.

In the face of this inescapable conundrum, *sans-papiers* try to create a public stage by occupying sites that can draw attention to their predicament and perhaps even provide some validity for their claims. The movement started with the occupation of churches, which have historically been sites of sanctuary. In particular, the images of police violence against non-violent demonstrators, including women and children, in the aftermath of the forceful eviction from St. Bernard Church brought attention to the movement and garnered support for their demands. In addition to churches, *sans-papiers* occupied a variety of public buildings, including the offices of the European Parliament and UNICEF in 2005 and the union hall of the General Confederation of Labor in 2008.[136] As subjects excluded from formal political mechanisms and institutions, their occupation of these sites is crucial for claiming an equal share in politics.

Struggles of *sans-papiers* also highlight that the creation of such spaces of appearance should be accompanied by practices that demonstrate one's equality and freedom. Perhaps the most challenging task for *sans-papiers* was to present themselves as political subjects capable of acting and speaking on their own. As we have seen in the last two chapters, one of the main predicaments of statelessness for Arendt is being dependent on the charity of others in the absence of any possibility of intervening in the processes and decisions that affect one's life. From that perspective, even well-intentioned humanitarian efforts can paradoxically reproduce rightlessness if they undermine the equality and freedom of the subjects that they aim to help. Given this problem, a right to have rights denotes, first and foremost, a right to action and speech that must be asserted, if necessary, even against those who are acting out of compassion. From the very beginning, *sans-papiers* were resolved not to let others act and speak on their behalf. Although they welcomed the solidarity of other actors and organizations, they were also aware that letting others speak for their plight would reproduce their rightlessness.[137] The initial tensions between *sans-papiers* and the non-governmental groups who spoke on their behalf in the past are highlighted by the main spokespersons of the movement. Ababacar Diop, for example, underscores that *sans-papiers'* efforts to "take responsibility for their own affairs" by appearing in public and speaking for themselves "surprised most of these associations," which "insisted on carrying out various actions on our behalf."[138] A similar point is made by Madjiguène Cissé, who draws attention to the challenges of establishing autonomy: "They would tell us, 'Right, we the organizations have made an appointment to explain this or that;' and we had to say, 'But we can explain it very well ourselves.' Their automatic response is not to get people to be autonomous, but to speak for them."[139]

Creation of a public stage on which undocumented immigrants can appear as subjects with the capacity to make rights claims goes hand in hand with imaginative political practices that challenge their official identities, render their speech audible and intelligible, and provide some kind of authorization for their claims. In the case of the French struggle, perhaps the most important of these practices was the invention of a name. Prior to public demonstrations, these immigrants were known as *"les clandestins."* Refusing this pejorative term that confined them to a life in the shadows and coining a new name that highlighted "the fragility and fallibility of documents," *sans-papiers* drew attention to how even those immigrants who might have entered France legally could end up in an irregular situation due to administrative measures.[140] They contested the idea that lacking proper documentation should amount to being deprived of "a right to a right," or being cast aside as "sans droit," as a subject "without right" and "virtually outside the law," as Jacques Derrida highlights in his public address on *sans-papiers*.[141]

The movement's adoption of *sans-papiers* as a name underscores the importance of representational practices in mobilizing political subjects around common demands. In addition, such practices can bring into the open otherwise invisible forms of injustice and create a space for the articulation of new rights claims. Especially important in this regard are the frequent references to French revolutionary history and the republican discourse of the Rights of Man. The term *"sans-papiers"* itself is evocative of the radical figures of the French Revolution, as can be seen in Ababacar Diop's depiction of *sans-papiers* as "the defenders of liberty . . . the contemporary *sans-culottes*."[142] *Sans-papiers* became political subjects at least in part by inventing a name for themselves. The parallels between *sans-culottes* and *sans-papiers* are striking in this regard: *Sans-culottes* appropriated a derogatory term originally used as a salon society joke and turned it into a "republican emblem" to take issue with the privileges of wealth.[143] Adoption of a distinctive name was crucial for creating a public space in which they could appear before others, articulate their demands, and mobilize other citizens. As Arendt reminds us in passing in *The Human Condition*, *sans-culottes* "made their first appearance on the historical scene" and "won a distinction of their own" as they "adopt[ed] a costume of their own" and "derived their name."[144] Similarly, *sans-papiers* used the lack or dispossession they are known for (i.e., lack of proper documentation) as the basis of their new name. In addition, both *sans-culottes* and *sans-papiers* gave a new meaning to the names they adopted. Prior to the French Revolution, the term *"sans culottes"* (without the hyphen) meant a writer without a patron. Only with the Parisian insurrections, the term started to be used with the hyphen and became a substantive noun referring to the working men in towns and cities.[145] Similarly, *"sans-papiers"* has become a substantive noun referring to a political movement only with the mobilizations of immigrants in France. In both cases, the hyphen arises out of, and stands for, inventive practices of becoming political subjects.

Such inventive practices are crucial not only for appearing in public but also for politically authorizing new rights claims. The actions of *sans-papiers* underscore that new rights claims cannot have the irrefutable validity of mathematical truths; these claims are in need of representative practices that strive to "woo" or "court" the assent of others.[146] Such claims can achieve an exemplary validity by way of representational practices, which involve "an imaginative element, the ability to see or to forge new connections," to use Linda Zerilli's terms.[147] *Sans-papiers* try to persuade their interlocutors and validate their rights claims by tying their new rights claims to French revolutionary history in innovative ways.

These connections become palpable in the public demonstrations of *sans-papiers*. For example, in May and June 2010, hundreds camped in front of the opera house at the Place de la Bastille in Paris. This opera house was opened on the eve of the 200th anniversary of the storming of the Bastille. By choosing this symbolic site, *sans-papiers* "claimed a place for themselves in the revolutionary and republican history in France"—a place that they were not officially entitled to claim as outsiders with no right to reside in France.[148] Another striking example of *sans-papiers'* efforts to authorize their new rights claims by invoking other revolutionary events in France can be found in their references to the Paris Commune. *Sans-papiers* started their demonstrations at the Church of St. Ambroise on March 18, 1996, and it is interesting to note that it was on March 18 of 1871 that the Paris Commune seized power in the city. As Vincenzo Ruggiero notes, one of the slogans that *sans-papiers* used at the time was "March 18, 1996, *on c'est lèvé* (we have risen)."[149]

Perhaps the most important element that *sans-papiers* has appropriated from this revolutionary history is the form of the declaration itself. More than anything else, the adoption of this political genre highlights that practices of claiming new rights, not unlike revolutionary beginnings, are characterized by perplexities arising from their groundlessness. On February 25, 1997, the French newspaper *Libération* published a *sans-papiers* manifesto that resembled the eighteenth-century revolutionary declarations:

> We the Sans-Papiers of France, in signing the appeal, have decided to come out of the shadows. From now on, in spite of the dangers, it is not only our faces but also our names which will be known. We declare . . .[150]

It is important to note how this prologue positions *sans-papiers* as subjects with the constituent power to declare rights. What follows this inaugural gesture is a series of propositions that strive to authorize this declaration, which cannot derive its validity from prevailing legal and normative orders. To do this, *sans-papiers* present an account of their rightlessness as migrants "arbitrarily thrown into illegality" and highlight the paradox of rightlessness in a country that trumpets its dedication to the

Rights of Man. In addition, to make a case for the right to regularization, the manifesto also draws attention to the specific contributions that *sans-papiers* make to French society: "We pay our taxes, our rent, our bills and our social security contributions—when we are allowed regular employment!" The reference to taxes is particularly striking, as it reminds the readers of the key eighteenth-century idea that taxation without representation is tyrannical. In fact, in his memoir of the struggle, Ababacar Diop invokes this idea to go beyond the demand for regularization and make a case for the right to vote in local elections.[151] The inventive connections that *sans-papiers* forge between such familiar ideas and their unorthodox demand for the right to regularization are crucial to their efforts to render their rights claims intelligible and valid in the eyes of others.

Toward the end of the manifesto, *sans-papiers* use the phrase "we demand" repetitively, and even assertively, to make a claim to a right that is not recognized in existing domestic or international laws:

> We demand papers so that we are no longer victims of arbitrary treatment by the authorities, employers and landlords. We demand papers so that we are no longer vulnerable to informants and black-mailers. We demand papers so that we no longer suffer the humiliation of controls based on our skin, detentions, deportations, the break-up of our families, the constant fear. . . . We demand that the European and international conventions, to which the French Republic has subscribed, are respected.[152]

It is important to note in this statement how *sans-papiers* try to garner support for their demands by appealing to the European and international conventions. They invoke these conventions in addition to the republican discourse of the Rights of Man to provide their demand for papers with an authorizing ground. But these conventions do not recognize the right to regularization as a legitimate demand. As mentioned earlier, even the Convention on Migrant Workers does not oblige the states to regularize undocumented immigrants. What is at stake in this manifesto, as well as in the other statements and public demonstrations of *sans-papiers*, is the declaration of a new right. This declaration leaves the *sans-papiers* with perplexities that are not unlike the ones confronted by the eighteenth-century revolutionaries who were not authorized to found a new body politic. The turn to international law in the *sans-papiers* manifesto is not unlike the eighteenth-century revolutionaries' search for a higher law to resolve the perplexities of founding.

Several scholars have proposed rethinking *sans-papiers*' political practices as a new form of citizenship: *Sans-papiers* do lack the legal status of citizenship, but as they engage in these public demonstrations, they act *as if* they were citizens.[153] In agreement with this point, what I would like to emphasize is the *lack of prior authorization* for these acts of citizenship. *Sans-papiers*' struggles reveal that human rights understood as a right to have rights ultimately depend on a type of citizenship enacted by those who do not have a legitimate standing and yet who thrust themselves into the public spaces from which they are excluded. More importantly, this paradoxical citizenship involves practices of claiming rights that one is not entitled to according to prevailing legal and normative frameworks.

From an Arendtian perspective, these practices reenact and augment the principle of equaliberty that becomes manifest in the eighteenth-century declarations, and they are indispensable to the continuous reinvention of human rights. *Sans-papiers*' words and deeds affirm this principle in many respects: They demonstrate that equality and freedom are to be understood not as inherent human attributes, but instead as political achievements that are in need of each other. In addition, *sans-papiers*' protests highlight that the subjects of rights are not passive beneficiaries but political actors capable of declaring and vindicating rights in struggles affirming their political and human standing. Their struggles also call attention to the impossibility of understanding politics of human rights solely in terms of putting normative constraints on an existing constitutional order, as they point to the possibility that rights can be turned against that order for the purpose of proposing a new one.

Understood in these terms, the validity of *sans-papiers*' rights claims cannot be detached from their political practices augmenting the principle of equaliberty. As mentioned earlier, *sans-papiers* try to anchor their demands in the revolutionary history of France and the republican discourse of the Rights of Man. These efforts, to quote from Arendt's reflections on augmentation, do involve "*religare*," or "binding themselves back to a beginning," but by engaging in them, *sans-papiers* are not "merely revolving back to an 'early period' in order to retrieve ancient rights and liberties."[154] In fact, their practices of augmentation bring to view new subjects and rights that the legal and normative framework of this earlier period could not accommodate. Because of this novelty, augmentation in the case of *sans-papiers* consists of "the extraordinary capacity to look upon yesterday with the eyes of centuries to come," and it is never simply conservation but also amendment.[155]

Practices of augmentation involve amendment also because they can bring to view violent exclusions of the political founding itself. To remember Arendt's discussion of civil disobedience, augmentation can alert the political community to these exclusions and has the potential to provoke a rethinking of the founding itself, especially its meaning for the present and the future.

When *sans-papiers* invoke French revolutionary symbols to justify their acts, they augment the principle of equaliberty not only by affirming the Rights of Man but also by drawing attention to the violent exclusions that went hand in hand with this universalist discourse. *Sans-papiers'* amendment of the revolutionary beginning can be seen in their public statements that directly tie the colonial past to the rights claims they make, as highlighted by the words of Madjiguène Cissé:

> [W]e are all from former French colonies, most of us from West-African countries, Mali, Senegal, Guinea and Mauritania. But there are also among us several Mahgreb people (Tunisians, Moroccans and Algerians); there is one man from Zaire and a couple who are Haitians. So it's not an accident that we all find ourselves in France: our countries have had a relationship with France for centuries.[156]

Ababacar Diop also refers to this colonial past to establish *sans-papiers'* entitlement to rights, as he reminds his audience of the military service of the colonial subjects fighting with the French:

> Whenever the motherland was threatened, France called on her colonies to save her. Millions of foreigners perished so that the French could live in liberty. This sacrifice, willingly undertaken by foreigners to defend the land of the "rights of man and of the citizen," must be remembered.[157]

In addition, *sans-papiers* call attention to ongoing forms of domination ("neo-colonialism") to establish the validity of their claims to a right to legally reside in France.[158] As their actions and statements manifest the principle of equaliberty and take it beyond its original context, they do not simply conserve it by appealing to what it meant in an earlier period. They instead change its meaning both by revealing the violent exclusions of French republicanism and proposing a new configuration of the relationship between rights, citizenship, and humanity.

Needless to say, there are risks in these efforts to mobilize the colonial past in the service of contemporary rights claims. In fact, such efforts can simply fail and give rise to a nationalistic backlash. Instead of validating the rights claims of undocumented immigrants, they could end up undermining them. This risk is particularly apparent in the argument that Diop makes; his effort to justify the right to regularization on the basis of the military sacrifices made by African soldiers risks reinforcing the anti-immigrant discourse insisting that "to be French, you have to earn it."[159] But such risks might also be among the defining characteristics of new rights claims. As the discussion above highlights, these claims do not logically extend from the existing legal and normative framework of human rights but instead creatively appropriate it and take it in new directions. Their validity depends on political practices that simultaneously affirm and challenge the values, norms, and institutions of the political community in question, as can be seen in sans-papiers' invocation of the colonial past. Political risks attending these practices are crucial to understanding the challenging tasks involved in struggles that contest the existing system of rights.

Arendt's call for a right to have rights provides significant insights into the distinctive features and challenges of the contemporary struggles waged by sans-papiers and other migrants who contest their precarious legal, political, and human standing. First, this phrase succinctly captures the most fundamental demand made by sans-papiers: a right to politics, especially action and speech. Second, a right to have rights alerts us to the abyss of freedom in new rights claims, which cannot be easily accommodated by existing conceptions of human rights. It urges us to understand these new claims as declarations, or as new beginnings pervaded by the perplexities of political founding. Third, Arendt's proposal highlights that the universality of human rights is inextricably tied to political practices of declaring, claiming, and vindicating them, which are indispensable to the ongoing augmentation and validation of the principle of equaliberty. Finally, as can be seen in sans-papiers' frequent references to the French revolutionary and colonial history, authorization of new rights claims requires representational practices that can set imagination in motion and elicit the assent of one's interlocutors. Practices such as coining names, oc-cupying symbolic spaces, and choosing historic dates are crucial to not only turning invisible subjects into authors of words and deeds but also rendering communicable what might otherwise seem unintelligible within the instituted order of rights and citizenship.

As I argue in this chapter, Arendt's call for a right to have rights moves us away from the quest for foundations that could provide a universal jus-tification for human rights and turns our attention instead to the chal-lenging question of finding a new guarantee for these rights. The forego-ing discussion suggests that such a guarantee is in need of political practices of declaring, enacting, and reinventing human rights. But aren't these practices too fragile, risky, and uncertain? Once the mobilization is over, one might ask, wouldn't the subjects who engaged in these practices be relegated back to the condition of rightlessness if the rights declared and enacted were not followed by the institutionalization of rights in rela-tively durable structures? Declaration of a right might inaugurate some-thing new, but does it signify anything more than a hollow promise with-out such institutional protections of equality and freedom? Why not outline a set of concrete institutional solutions that can enforce a right to have rights instead of finding some kind of vain solace in the fleeting mo-ments of political action?

The Arendtian response to these possible objections rests on a rejection of the false choice that they force us to make between founding and con-stitution, action and institution, radical novelty and relative permanence. Political founding, as exemplified in revolutionary beginnings such as the declarations of rights, brings together what we have now come to see as irreconcilable opposites: "the concern with stability and the spirit of the new."[160] Rethinking human rights in terms of political founding high-lights the crucial importance of establishing lasting institutions for these rights. From an Arendtian perspective, these institutions are vital not only for providing relatively stable, permanent guarantees for human rights but also for preserving the revolutionary spirit that inaugurated these rights in the first place.

But reconsidering Arendt's notion of a right to have rights in light of her reflections on the perplexities of revolutionary beginnings also brings out some tensions between human rights and the institutional orders es-tablished to protect them, adding new insights to the point first intro-duced in chapter 1. First, an exclusive focus on institutional solutions risks overlooking that even the institutional guarantees of human rights owe their origins as well as their ongoing preservation and amendment to political action. For Arendt, political institutions, unlike works of art, or products of making, which can have independent existence, "depend for continued existence upon acting men."[161] Institutional mechanisms established to protect human rights might end up petrifying these rights in a set of laws if they are severed from the political practices of founding and refounding that are indispensable to the ongoing augmentation of the principle of equaliberty.[162] As a result, these mechanisms can lose their responsiveness to new problems of rightlessness, and they can even become oblivious to their own role in the reproduction of conditions that give rise to these problems. Second, a solely institutionalist focus might also miss that human rights are not simply normative constraints on an established constitutional order. To the extent that human rights can also set in motion struggles challenging the various forms of injustice that can be inflicted by existing legal and normative frameworks, they are best understood as political inventions that remain between constituent and constituted power, revolution and instituted order, new beginnings and established norms.

Conclusion: The Struggle Remains Undecided

The whole struggle remains undecided, and K. dies a perfectly natural death; he gets exhausted. What he strove to achieve was beyond the strength of any one man. But though his purpose remained unaccomplished, his life was far from being a complete failure. The very fight he has put up to obtain the few basic things which society owes to men has opened the eyes of the villagers, or at least of some of them. His story, his behavior, has taught that both human rights are worth fighting for and that the rule of the castle is not divine law and, consequently, can be attacked.[1]

ARENDT'S DISCUSSION of Kafka in her essay "The Jew as Pariah" provides a very good starting point for reconsidering the main arguments that this book makes about her political thought and the contemporary human rights struggles of migrants. Her reflections on K., the main character of *The Castle,* are all the more pertinent given the tendency to describe the predicaments of today's migrants with references to Kafka: They are either trapped in Kafkaesque bureaucratic situations in which they cannot even prove who they are[2] or detained in a "Motel Kafka" operated by a private security company unconstrained by the rule of law.[3] In addition, K.'s struggle to obtain a legal title to remain in the village also brings him closer to contemporary migrants such as *sans-papiers* who are trying to establish a right to lawful residence. Arendt's affirmation of K.'s struggle adds a new meaning to the conventional understanding of "Kafkaesque," as it reveals the political agency of a pariah who refuses to accept the status of being an outcast dependent on favors or privileges and rebels against that condition in the name of rights. This meaning is very much in line with Arendt's salutation of stateless people as "modern pariahs" positioned to be "the forerunners" or "the avant-garde" of political struggles in a world increasingly characterized by rightlessness.[4] Taking my starting point from this double meaning of "Kafkaesque," I want to conclude by reiterating the importance of critically examining the perplexities of human rights for the purposes of understanding both the contemporary problems of rightlessness and the struggles that they give rise to.

Arendt takes K.'s struggle as representative of the challenges that Jews faced in establishing their equality in a social order demanding assimilation, but her comments on K. speak directly to the problems she addresses in her account of statelessness as well. It is quite puzzling that Arendt describes *The Castle* as "the one novel in which Kafka discusses the Jewish problem" or "the only one in which the hero is plainly a Jew," given that K. is not described as Jewish in the novel. What renders K. Jewish, according to Arendt, is not "any typically Jewish trait," but instead that "he is involved in situations and perplexities distinctive of Jewish life."[5] Along these lines, it could be argued that K. is a hero who is stateless not because he is literally deprived of citizenship but because his life is defined by "situations and perplexities" characteristic of statelessness. As a stranger neither fully recognized by the political authorities nor welcomed by society, K. lives "a non-official, unpredictable, troubled, and strange kind of life,"[6] one that resembles in many ways that arbitrary lawlessness afflicting stateless people whose lives become dependent on favors and privileges that can be withdrawn. Arendt also emphasizes that K. is a stranger "belong[ing] neither to the common people nor to its rulers."[7] She notes that his citizenship is "a paper one" and highlights his precarious legal, political, and human standing as someone who is "charged continuously with being superfluous."[8]

Arendt's examination of K.'s predicament in terms of the equivocalities of Jewish emancipation resonates with her efforts to understand the plight of the stateless in terms of the perplexities of human rights. In both cases, Arendt refuses to turn the problem into an unfortunate exception to an otherwise well-functioning system; instead she urges us to examine the organizing principles and underlying assumptions of the system itself. Nevertheless, the critique she offers does not forgo political emancipation and human rights but instead invites a radical rethinking of their terms.

For Arendt, K.'s plight reveals the paradoxical assumptions and effects of Jewish emancipation. Emancipation is supposed to provide legal and political guarantees of equality and freedom to enable the "admission of . Jews *as Jews* to the ranks of humanity, rather than a permit to ape the gentiles or an opportunity to play the parvenu."[9] But the possibility of instituting such guarantees is constantly undermined by the expectation of assimilation that demands relinquishing one's Jewish identity. K. tries to follow the assimilationist route at first and tries to become "indistinguishable" simply by asking for basic human rights such as "home, work, family, and citizenship."[10] But throughout his struggle he realizes that assimilation will not result in the recognition of his fundamental human rights. As a superfluous stranger, it is impossible for him to lead an ordinary life and become a member of society given that he is faced with conditions that have turned human rights into "exceptional" privileges to be granted from authorities.[11]

In the case of the stateless, Arendt engages in a similar examination, turning this time to the perplexities pervading the eighteenth-century idea of the Rights of Man. These were assumed to be natural, inalienable rights independent of political and social qualifications. But the very moment the stateless appeared in their naked humanity, they found it impossible to be recognized as subjects entitled to rights. In an international system organized around the principle of nationality, human rights came to stand for exceptional rights reserved for those "who had nothing better to fall back upon" and were dependent upon the generosity and charity of others.[12]

In each case, Arendt offers a critical inquiry that brings to view the challenges of equal recognition in the modern nation-state and questions the prevailing assumptions about political community, membership, equality, and rights. And in each case, she takes issue with modern humanism, which works with the assumption of an "abstract" humanity and fails to fully attend to its violent exclusions.[13] But Arendt's thorough critique of modern equality, humanism, and human rights does not lead to the conclusion that these are merely illusory ideals; instead, she engages in a rethinking of these concepts in light of the challenging problems she examines.

In the case of K., Arendt refuses the conclusion that his struggle for rights ultimately fails because it cannot achieve the goals it pursues. She highlights the political significance of K.'s struggle, which sets an example for other villagers by demonstrating to them "both that human rights are worth fighting for and that the rule of the castle is not divine law and, consequently, can be attacked."[14] Whereas the villagers unquestioningly accept that every element of their lives is dependent on the favors granted by the authorities at the Castle, K. insists on having a residence title and a permanent occupation as rights that should be recognized by these authorities. As one of the villagers, Pepi, tells him at one point, precisely the fact that "he was making claims . . . was provocative."[15] Arendt highlights this point in a different essay on Kafka where she argues that K.'s strangeness in the village resides in the fact that he refuses to accept gifts and demands instead human rights; it is this unsettling practice that renders K.'s actions "rather exceptional and therefore scandalous."[16] Precisely because K. insists on the scandalous practice of claiming rights in a society characterized by rightlessness, his struggle achieves an exemplarity and discloses a different world with new possibilities. There is no guarantee that struggles such as K.'s will lead to "the establishment upon earth of a commonly conditioned and commonly controlled humanity," to use Arendt's terms, but without them we cannot even begin to consider this possibility.[17]

Arendt's argument about the political significance of K.'s struggle for human rights resonates with the conclusions that she draws from her critical inquiry of human rights. Far from suggesting that human rights are simply illusory or hypocritical, she proposes rethinking them in terms of a right to have rights, or a right "to live in a framework where one is judged by one's actions and opinions" and "a right to belong to some kind of organized community."[18] Arendt leaves open the question of what kind of a "framework" or "community" this new right would entail, but she invokes "humanity" as its guarantee and emphasizes the importance of cultivating a shared sense of positive responsibility in response to the challenging problems of global politics. In line with her conclusion about K.'s fight, she adds cautiously: "It is by no means certain whether this is possible."[19]

Arendt's analyses of the Jewish emancipation and the twentieth-century crisis of statelessness interweave a radical critique of human rights with their radical rethinking. Her arguments about K. and the stateless gesture to a democratic politics of human rights, centered on the agency of pariahs who contest their condition of rightlessness and manifest, with their actions, the possibilities of a new political and normative order. This politics is characterized by uncertainty, and we can complicate Arendt's treatment of K. further in this regard: After all, the novel is unfinished, and although Arendt declares K. to be dead in the passage quoted above, he is still alive when the narrative breaks off in the middle of a sentence; even Kafka was not sure what to make of *The Castle*. Given the uncertainties, risks, and challenges of guaranteeing human rights, there is a need to engage in critical inquiries that explore the contemporary conditions that give rise to new forms of rightlessness as well as the struggles that contest these conditions.

This book proposed one such critical inquiry by rethinking and revising the key concepts of Arendt's political theory in light of the struggles of asylum seekers, refugees, and undocumented immigrants. This critical inquiry highlights that problems such as expansion of immigration detention, normalization of deportation, and long-term refugee encampment are neither accidental incidents nor simply failures arising from the weak implementation of human rights norms. They are systemic problems that reveal the perplexities in the existing human rights framework. We cannot understand the arbitrary detention of asylum seekers and undocumented immigrants, for example, without scrutinizing how contemporary human rights norms continue to uphold the principle of territorial sovereignty, to recall one of the arguments made in chapter 3. Similarly, it is not possible to understand why refugees are kept in camps for decades without examining how the principle of nationality continues to shape contemporary humanitarian policies that promote repatriation, as highlighted in chapter 4. But understanding these problems in terms of the perplexities of human rights does not entail the problematic conclusion that these rights necessarily produce rightlessness. Arendt's account of statelessness points to another possibility, as it highlights how these perplexities can be politically navigated and reworked to rethink human rights in response to challenging problems of rightlessness.

Undertaking this kind of a critical inquiry also demands a new reading of Arendt, one that does not refrain from revising some of her arguments and conclusions. In fact, just as Arendt's political thought proves to a be critical resource for understanding contemporary problems and struggles of migrants, these problems and struggles provide significant insights into the possibilities of rethinking Arendtian politics. We cannot grasp contemporary challenges of asylum and immigration by simply applying Arendt's ideas; those ideas need to be reinterpreted and modified by taking into account these challenges. The question can no longer be "What would Hannah say?," to borrow Jeremy Waldron's provocative question, but instead how can we "think things through here and now, as she thought about them there and then."[20]

One example of this rethinking can be seen in chapter 2, which centers on Arendt's political/social distinction. In many ways, this distinction risks excluding from politics various human rights issues related to workplace or family. But it turns out that Arendt uses this conceptual distinction in multiple, conflicting, and quite puzzling ways. If one reason why we cannot simply apply Arendt's analysis to contemporary context is the novelty of the problems we face, the other reason is that her political thought is far from a coherent and transparent discourse. Perhaps this observation is not surprising given that Arendt did not try to develop a "system" of thought; her corpus is rife with perplexities that are part and parcel of any theoretical effort to comprehend the distinctive features of historical and contemporary phenomena without resorting to given categories or frameworks. In this regard, what Arendt once said about Marx can be equally valid for her own work: "Such fundamental and flagrant contradictions rarely occur in second-rate writers; in the work of the great authors, they lead into the very center of their work."[21] Arendt's political theory is characterized by perplexities, and engaging with them is crucial for locating the possibilities of rethinking Arendtian politics beyond Arendt.

Such a rethinking can also unsettle the conventions that have come to shape our interpretations of Arendt, including the tendency to treat her as a theorist of freedom, fascinated by the capacity to initiate new beginnings and inattentive to questions of equality and justice. As Arendt's analyses of the Jewish emancipation and statelessness highlight, her political theory takes its bearings from challenging problems that underscore the inextricable connections between freedom, equality, and justice.[22] My effort to rethink rightlessness for the purposes of understanding the precarious legal, political, and human standing of asylum seekers, refugees, and undocumented immigrants gives support to this point: Arendt's political theory provides crucial resources illuminating the violent injustice of problems that might not be recognized as human rights violations. Particularly important in this regard is the critical phenomenology that chapter 4 traces in Arendt's account of *vita activa* in *The Human Condition*. What has often been read as an exclusionary schema glorifying the public action of free citizens while relegating laboring bodies to invisibility can be reinterpreted as a powerful critical framework alerting us to the conditions that make it very difficult for some subjects to live lives that can be recognized as "human." Breaking with the conventions that prevail in our readings of Arendt gives rise to a new understanding of the injustice of detention and encampment, for example, as practices undermining the possibilities of cultivating a trust in the reality and regularity of life, establishing a relatively durable dwelling place, and creating public spaces to appear and act in the company of fellow human beings.

Conditions that unmake the legal, political, and human standing of asylum seekers, refugees, and undocumented immigrants have been contested in various struggles, and this book maintains that a critical inquiry centered on the perplexities of human rights offers crucial insights into the distinctive features and challenges of the new rights claims articulated in these struggles as well. Contemporary struggles of migrants point to the challenging task of validating rights claims that cannot be easily accommodated by the existing legal and normative frameworks of human rights; this difficulty is perhaps most obvious in the case of the increasingly globalized demand for unconditional regularization. As I argued in chapter 5, these struggles urge us to shift the focus of the debates on human rights. In particular, the scholarly conversation in the fields of political theory and philosophy has centered primarily on the question of how to establish a normative foundation that could provide a universal justification for human rights. Although this is certainly an important question, there are many other puzzles posed to us by the contemporary struggles of migrants. Arendt's proposal of rethinking human rights in terms of a right to have rights can provide us with a helpful starting point for attending to these puzzles, and her account of revolutionary beginnings can reorient our gaze to the distinctive promises, challenges, and frustrations of struggles that bring forth rights claims that cannot be authorized by existing legal and normative frameworks. My Arendtian account highlights the need to turn our attention from foundation to founding, and it urges a close examination of political practices of founding and refounding human rights. For this purpose, I put special emphasis on declaration as an inaugural speech act that brings forth new rights or takes existing rights in unpredictable directions, exposes us to the abyss of freedom, and leaves us with perplexities regarding its source of origin and validity. Such declaratory practices are crucial for reinventing human rights in response to challenging problems of rightlessness, as highlighted in my discussion of the *sans-papiers* movement. The universal validity of human rights, according to this account, cannot be detached from these political practices that introduce us to new political subjects, transform our political and normative world, and inaugurate new understandings of equality and freedom.

The book offers an emphatically political understanding of human rights in response to these contemporary struggles of migrants, but what it means by "political" is quite different from how the term has come to be used in some of the recent debates on human rights. Several scholars, drawing on the political theory of John Rawls, especially his book *The Law of Peoples*, have taken issue with various metaphysical and post-metaphysical quests for foundations as well and proposed a "political" or "practical" understanding of human rights. These theorists refuse to use a philosophically derived conception of justice to assess the existing practice of human rights; they instead look at existing international institutions and practices to clarify what human rights are.[23] Although this attention to existing institutions and practices is a welcome move, the Rawlsian approach works with a somewhat narrow understanding of politics, especially when considered from an Arendtian perspective. Bound by the norms and institutions of the existing human rights system, the Rawlsian approach has no room for the rights claims that question the regulative norms and underlying assumptions of this system. Its vision of politics is even further narrowed because it understands the main function of human rights in terms of international intervention or action.[24] Such a "political" conception would offer limited help in understanding the pervasive problems migrants face or the new rights claims they make.

The Arendtian account of human rights differs from this position in several ways: First, it provides a different understanding of "politics," centered on the struggles of subjects whose rights are at stake, and not on the interventions of external actors. It highlights that the struggles of these subjects are crucial to reframing particular forms of injustice as problems of rightlesssness, challenging existing configurations of human rights, and validating new rights claims. Second, the Arendtian account provides a critical assessment of the existing human rights institutions, examining the extent to which they allow for or undermine such political possibilities. As I argued throughout this book, there is an ineluctable tension between human rights and the institutions established to guarantee them; this tension arises not only because institutions can turn against the very rights that they were supposed to uphold but also because human rights can be mobilized for the purpose of challenging existing institutional orders and proposing new ones. Third, the Arendtian account resists the foundationalist quest not because of its faithfulness to the existing system of human rights but because of its goal of understanding how new rights claims validate themselves in the absence of prior authorization. Its Montesquieuan reading of modern rights declarations as public statements manifesting the "principle" of equaliberty provides it with a critical edge. Resisting the foundationalist and anti-foundationalist positions, the Arendtian perspective draws attention to how this principle achieves a universal validity as it is reenacted time and again in different contexts.

The critical inquiry developed in this book gestures toward a democratic cosmopolitics—a political and normative vision arising from the practices of contesting rightlessness and reinventing human rights beyond the framework of territorial sovereignty.[25] This vision highlights the need to grapple with the perplexities of global politics, especially those arising from the proliferation of human rights mechanisms along with the ever-growing population of rightless subjects. The challenging task is to face up to the questions raised by global processes without yielding to either a "reckless optimism" that holds onto a "desperate hope" or "reckless despair" that succumbs to a "desperate fear," to appropriate Arendt's description of the two common attitudes adopted in response to the catastrophes of twentieth century.[26] A critical thinking that is attuned to perplexities is promising in this regard precisely because it questions an evolutionary understanding of human rights in terms of a linear narrative of progress, but it does so without subscribing to a totalizing critique that suggests that human rights inevitably lead to nothing other than suffering and violence because of their inextricable connection to sovereign power.

The analysis offered in this book can be taken in several new directions. First, the concepts of "statelessness" and "rightlessness" can be extended and revised for the purpose of thinking about the problems and struggles of an increasing number of citizens whose legal, political, and human standing has been significantly undermined. This problem faces us all the more forcefully, as various forms of globalization, which have been applauded for developing new forms of interconnectedness, also risk introducing a "deflation of citizenship."[27] Many decisions are now being made at the global level without the constraints of accountability, transparency, and the rule of law. Arendt's discussion of statelessness and her efforts to rethink the connection between human rights and citizenship in terms of a right to have rights could prove to be quite illuminating in efforts to examine novel forms of rightlessness created in the context of globalization.[28] Within this context, growing economic inequality is perhaps the most challenging problem that makes it difficult for an ever-expanding number of people to effectively exercise civil and political rights, and there is the risk that the failure to address this issue will turn social and economic rights into anachronisms of a bygone era. Homelessness is one of the manifestations of this contemporary problem that highlights the fragility of rights associated with citizenship.[29] Finally, there is also the resurgence of racial and ethnic stratifications, which has effectively turned an increasing number of people into second-class citizens. Concepts of "rightlessness" and "statelessness" can provide crucial insights, especially in understanding how racial minorities become a superfluous and precarious underclass as a result of policies such as ghettoization and incarceration.[30] Such studies can also contribute to the scholarship on Arendt's political thought by developing her concepts beyond the limits of her thinking about class and race.

These contemporary problems give rise to new struggles for rights, and the Arendtian critical inquiry offered in this book can also be extended and revised by examining the distinctive challenges and contributions of these struggles that introduce new understandings of citizenship, rights, and humanity. There are now struggles for migrant rights in many countries. In the United States, for instance, undocumented immigrants have been interweaving the language of human rights ("No Human Being is Illegal") with the civil disobedience tactics of the Civil Rights movement and "outing" practices of AIDS activism. One striking example of this creative bricolage can be seen in the bus tour of undocumented immigrants, known as "Undocubus." Going around the country with a bus that carries the slogan *"Sin Papeles, Sin Miedo"* ("No papers, no fear"), these immigrants have been declaring their undocumented status at public gatherings.[31] Their actions highlight the political significance of occupying public space and claiming rights that one is not yet entitled to claim. These political practices of founding and refounding are important not only for establishing the universal validity of human rights but also for reinventing and reaffirming citizenship in the face of global transformations that continue to dilute it. Such struggles do have a cosmopolitical dimension, as they represent new possibilities of enacting the right to politics across territorial borders. We need careful examinations of these struggles, attending to not only their achievements and promises but also their challenges and risks. After all, they are far from unequivocal success stories, and just like K.'s struggle for human rights, they remain undecided.

Notes

Introduction

1. Nina Bernstein, "Music Scholar Barred From U.S., But No One Will Tell Her Why," *The New York Times*, September 17, 2007.

2. "Mills Assistant Professor Nalini Ghuman Returns to Campus," Mills College, last modified February 12, 2008, accessed September 15, 2011, http://www.mills.edu/news/2008/newsarticle02112008ghuman_returns.php.

3. Bernstein, "Music Scholar Barred."

4. Arendt, *The Origins of Totalitarianism*, 279–280; 286.

5. Arendt, *The Origins of Totalitarianism*, 282.

6. Arendt, *The Origins of Totalitarianism*, 295–297.

7. Arendt, *The Origins of Totalitarianism*, 302.

8. Brysk and Shafir, "Globalization and the Citizenship Gap," 6.

9. This is the official figure for 2013, according to a report prepared by the Population Division of Department of Economic and Social Affairs at the United Nations. See *International Migration Report 2013* (United Nations, ST/ESA/SER.A/346), December 2013, accessed February 8, 2014, http://www.un.org/en/development/desa/population/publications/pdf/migration/migrationreport2013/Full_Document_final.pdf#zoom=100.

10. Differences in juridical status are of crucial significance in determining one's entitlement to rights, as I discuss especially in chapters 3 and 5, but it is important not to overlook the common problems that these different categories of migrants share. In fact, to address these, various international and non-governmental organizations have started to challenge the categorical distinctions drawn between refugees, asylum seekers, trafficked persons, stateless persons, foreign students, permanent residents, temporary visitors, and undocumented immigrants. See, for example, Office of the United Nations High Commissioner for Human Rights, "The Rights of Non-Citizens," 2006, accessed February 7, 2014, http://www.ohchr.org/Documents/Publications/noncitizensen.pdf. In addition,

these efforts draw attention to how these distinctions can be invoked in racially discriminatory ways. See Open Society Justice Initiative, "The Rights of Non-Citizens: A Discussion Among Global Advocates," February 2004, accessed February 7, 2014, http://www.justiceinitiative.org/db/resource2/fs/?file_id=13,880.

11. Seyla Benhabib, *The Rights of Others*, 154.

12. *Oxford English Dictionary* notes that one meaning of migration is "residence in a foreign country; banishment," but it adds that this meaning "is based on a misprint for *extermination*." The latter term denotes in one of its now obsolete senses "expulsion from the bounds or limits of a country, state, or community; banishment, excommunication." Even if the association of migration with expulsion originates in a misprint, it is worth recalling this meaning to emphasize that migration, in many cases, is not an unimpeded movement across borders.

13. As I discuss in chapter 1, these perplexities have been at the center of political and theoretical debates since the eighteenth-century declarations of the Rights of Man. For recent analyses of these perplexities, see, for example, Balfour and Cadava, "Claims of Human Rights"; Benhabib, "Reason-Giving and Rights-Bearing," 41–46; Hunt, *Inventing Human Rights*, 19–22; Slaughter, *Human Rights, Inc.*, 11–14, chap. 1; Wallach, "Constitutive Paradoxes."

14. Arendt, *The Origins of Totalitarianism*, 296–297.

15. Arendt, *The Human Condition*, 5.

16. Arendt, *The Origins of Totalitarianism*, 292.

17. Arendt, *The Origins of Totalitarianism*, 293.

18. Arendt, *The Origins of Totalitarianism*, 298.

19. Arendt, "Rights of Man," 37.

20. Arendt, "Rights of Man," 36.

21. There is an extensive literature tracing the institutionalization of international human rights after World War II. Among others, see Buergenthal, "Normative and Institutional Evolution"; Donnelly, *Universal Human Rights*. Although most studies take the immediate aftermath of World War II as a watershed moment, several identify early predecessors and trace the development of human rights to modern ideas and movements, including the eighteenth-century declarations of rights and anti-slavery campaigns. See, for example, Hunt, *Inventing Human Rights*; Ishay, *History of Human Rights*; Lauren, *Evolution of International Human Rights*. For a critical analysis of the assumptions underlying the historiography of human rights, see Moyn, *Last Utopia*.

22. See, for example, Henkin, *Age of Rights*, 23–24; Donnelly, *Universal Human Rights*, chap. 8.

23. See, among others, Keck and Sikkink, *Activists Beyond Borders*, chap. 3; Sikkink, "Principled Issue Networks," 418, 423. For the political impact of transnational advocacy networks, see also the several chapters in Risse-Kappen, Ropp, and Sikkink, *Power of Human Rights*. Samuel Moyn highlights that the 1970s constitute a crucial turning point in the history of human rights; he draws a connection between the dramatic growth in the number of non-governmental human rights organizations and the disillusionment with various radical utopian projects on the political left. See Moyn, *Last Utopia*, chap. 4.

24. Sikkink, "Power of Principled Ideas."

25. Beitz, *Idea of Human Rights*, 115.

26. The phrase is in the title of two books, one by Louis Henkin, and the other by Norberto Bobbio. For Bobbio, "the age of rights" goes further back and includes the

revolutionary declarations of the eighteenth century, but he also sees the aftermath of World War II as a turning point in terms of the "positivization, generalization and internationalization" of human rights. Bobbio, *Age of Rights*, 43; see also 32.

27. Ignatieff, "Human Rights as Idolatry," 53.

28. Donnelly, *Universal Human Rights*, 35–37; see also Vincent, *Politics of Human Rights*, chap. 6.

29. Henkin, *Age of Rights*, 14.

30. On the impact of human rights on changing conceptions of legitimate statehood, see, for example, Barkin, "Evolution of the Constitution of Sovereignty"; Cohen, *Globalization and Sovereignty*, chap. 3; Donnelly, "New Standard of Civilization?"; Henkin, *Age of Rights*, 14–16; Reus-Smit, "Social Construction of Sovereignty"; Sikkink, "Principled Issue-Networks."

31. Arendt, *The Origins of Totalitarianism*, 280.

32. Arendt, *The Origins of Totalitarianism*, 280–281.

33. See Article 2.1 of ICCPR.

34. See Grant, "Rights of Migrants"; Weissbrodt, *Human Rights of Non-Citizens*, chap. 3.

35. This preliminary overview offers a quick glance at some of the international legal and normative developments regarding the human rights of migrants since the completion of Arendt's analysis of statelessness. Chapter 3 provides a detailed critical engagement with the ramifications of these developments. For a comprehensive survey, see Weissbrodt, *Human Rights of Non-Citizens*.

36. See, for example, Cohen, "Changing Paradigms of Citizenship," 258–259; Jacobson, *Rights Across Borders*, 9–10; Sassen, *Guests and Aliens*, chap. 7; Soysal, *Limits of Citizenship*, chap. 8.

37. Brubaker, *Citizenship and Nationhood*, 31.

38. See, for example, Jacobson's commentary on *Plyler v. Doe*, a 1982 case in which the US Supreme Court recognized that the children of undocumented children have a right to public education; *Rights Across Borders*, 101–102. For a critical assessment of the Court's reasoning in *Plyler v. Doe*, see Bosniak, *The Citizen and the Alien*, 64–68.

39. For the "devaluation" argument, see Jacobson, *Rights Across Borders*, 9; for the "postnational" thesis, see Soysal, *Limits of Citizenship*. Jacobson's lament is rooted in a communitarian framework that takes the nation-state as a bounded political community resting on a pact between citizens and the state; within this framework, membership is posited as the prerequisite of having a share in the allocation of goods in a society. For other examples of this framework, see, among others, Walzer, *Spheres of Justice*, chap. 2; Schuck and Smith, *Citizenship without Consent*.

40. For denationalization, see, among others, Bosniak, "Citizenship Denationalized"; Sassen, "Repositioning of Citizenship." For disaggregation of citizenship, see Benhabib, *The Claims of Culture*, chap. 6; Benhabib, *The Rights of Others*, 145–146; Cohen, "Changing Paradigms of Citizenship," 258–259.

41. See, for example, Jorge Bustamante, "Report of the Special Rapporteur on the Human Rights of Migrants" (A/HRC/17/33), 2012, accessed February 11, 2014, http://www.ohchr.org/en/Issues/Migration/SRMigrants/Pages/AnnualReports.aspx. See also Office of the United Nations High Commissioner for Human Rights, *The Rights of Non-Citizens*, accessed July 18, 2012, http://www.ohchr.org/Documents/Publications/noncitizensen.pdf.

42. See, for example, Basok, "Post-National Citizenship"; Bhabha, "'Get Back'"; Bloch, "Right to Rights?"; Bosniak, "Citizenship Denationalized," 468–469; Castles and Davidson, *Citizenship and Migration*, 18–19, 95–96; Gibney, "Precarious Residents," 5–6; Maher, "Who Has a Right to Rights?"; Morris, "Britain's Asylum and Immigration Regime"; Nash, "Between Citizenship and Human Rights"; Schuster and Solomos, "Rights and Wrongs"; Stasiulis, "International Migration"; Stasiulis and Bakan, "Negotiating Citizenship."

43. Soysal, *Limits of Citizenship*, 134. For a recent clarification of her argument in response to critics, see Soysal, "Postnational Citizenship."

44. Benhabib, *The Rights of Others*, 163.

45. Arendt, *The Origins of Totalitarianism*, 267–268; emphasis mine.

46. Arendt, *The Origins of Totalitarianism*, 276.

47. For a collection bringing together these earlier criticisms along with commentary, see Waldron, *Nonsense upon Stilts*.

48. See, among others, Anderson, "Force and Consent"; Doty, *Imperial Encounters*; Douzinas, *Human Rights and Empire*; Guilhot, *Democracy Makers*; Mutua, *Human Rights*.

49. See in particular Agamben, *Homo Sacer*.

50. See, among others, Brown, "'The Most We Can Hope For'"; Kennedy, *Dark Sides of Virtue*, chap. 1.

51. See Rancière, "Who is the Subject?".

52. See, among others, Brown, *Manhood and Politics*, 23–31; Pitkin, "Justice"; Wolin, "Democracy and the Political." For criticisms that trace the problems in Arendt's critique of human rights back to her political/social distinction, see in particular Cohen, "Modern Form of the Social"; Rancière, "Who is the Subject?"; Schaap, "Enacting the Right."

53. This point draws on Hanna Pitkin's comprehensive analysis of the meaning of "social" in Arendt's works; see Pitkin, *The Attack of the Blob*.

54. Arendt, "Preface" to *Between Past and Future*, 14.

55. Arendt, *The Origins of Totalitarianism*, 281–282.

56. For a summary of the debates on the right to asylum during the drafting process, see Morsink, *Universal Declaration*, 75–79.

57. See, among others, Kateb, *Hannah Arendt*, 16–22; Pitkin, "Justice."

58. As I discuss at length in chapter 4, this formulation rests on not only Arendt's peculiar take on Aristotle's famous definition of man but also Jacques Rancière's strikingly similar reflections on that definition. See in particular Rancière, *Disagreement*, 21–23.

59. Arendt, *The Origins of Totalitarianism*, 296–298.

60. See Benhabib, *The Rights of Others*; Birmingham, *Hannah Arendt*; Serena Parekh, *Hannah Arendt*.

61. See Arendt, "What is Freedom?," 152–153.

62. Balibar, "(De)constructing the Human," 731.

63. Balibar, "What is a Politics of the Rights of Man?," 212.

64. Agamben, *Homo Sacer*, 54; *Means Without End*, 112; emphasis in the original.

Chapter 1

1. Arendt, *The Origins of Totalitarianism*, 298; "Rights of Man," 35.

2. Arendt, *The Origins of Totalitarianism*, 291.

3. Bentham, "Anarchical Fallacies," 497. For Bentham's attempts to get rid of confusion and equivocality in legal language, see in particular Waldron, *Nonsense upon Stilts*, 34–39.

4. Bentham, "Anarchical Fallacies," 501.

5. See, for example, Burke, *Reflections*, 163–166.

6. Burke, *Reflections*, 149, 119; emphasis in the original.

7. Marx, "On the Jewish Question."

8. The analysis below expands on, and at times revises, my argument in a previously published article; see Gündoğdu, "'Perplexities.'"

9. Arendt, "From Hegel to Marx," 74; emphasis in the original. Two points need to be emphasized to clarify the goals of this chapter: First, as I turn to Arendt's reflections on Socrates, I do not try to find a "method" that is at work in all of her works. For an analysis that aims at understanding Arendt's corpus in terms of a methodological consistency, see Buckler, *Hannah Arendt*. My analysis is instead directed at the more specific goal of understanding *how* Arendt's critical inquiry of human rights proceeds. Second, as indicated by this emphasis on "how," I also do not use "method" in its more technical sense as a systematic procedure of testing knowledge claims in an empirical inquiry. For an analysis that finds in Socrates resources for rethinking "method" in this more technical sense, see Meckstroth, "Socratic Method and Political Science."

10. Brunkhorst, "Are Human Rights Self-Contradictory?," 191–192.

11. Rancière, "Who Is the Subject?" It is not only Arendt's critics, however, who cast her analysis of statelessness as a total renunciation of the Rights of Man; some of her sympathetic readers also arrive at this conclusion. For example, Julia Kristeva argues that "Arendt denounces the secularization and universalism of the rights of man as the *hidden source* of . . . modern anti-Semitism." See Kristeva, *Hannah Arendt*, 119; emphasis added. In a statement that resonates with Rancière's argument, Susannah Young-ah Gottlieb suggests that Arendt's critique of human rights draws attention to "the *tautological* and therefore *empty* formulas that would make humanity into its own guarantor." Gottlieb, *Regions of Sorrow*, 35; emphasis added. What is missing from both of these conclusions is Arendt's attentiveness to the equivocal and contingent effects of the Rights of Man as a discourse pervaded by perplexities. In addition, it is important to note that Arendt herself endorses a fairly universalistic idea when she contends that "a right to have rights" is to be "guaranteed by humanity itself," as I discuss in chapter 5. See Arendt, *The Origins of Totalitarianism*, 298.

12. Arendt, *The Origins of Totalitarianism*, 290; *Elemente und Ursprünge*, 601. Arendt herself translated the work into German, and her choice of "die Aporien" for "the perplexities" deserves attention, as I hope to demonstrate in this chapter. For a brief history of *The Origins of Totalitarianism*, highlighting the interesting interaction between its English and German versions, see Ludz, "Hannah Arendt's Book." Christoph Menke also notes the use of the term "aporia" in the German version of *The Origins of Totalitarianism*; however, he does not examine the implications of this term for understanding *how* Arendt proceeds in her critical inquiry of human rights or *how* she approaches the "perplexities" under consideration. See Menke, "Aporias of Human Rights."

13. Arendt, *Thinking*, 4–5; "Thinking and Moral Considerations," 159–160. In her discussion of Eichmann, Arendt highlights his frequent use of stock phrases and clichés as a sign of his inability to think; see *Eichmann in Jerusalem*, 49, 86.

14. Arendt, *Thinking*, 4; see also "Thinking and Moral Considerations," 160.

15. For Arendt's critique of Heidegger, see in particular "What is Existential Philosophy?," 176–182; see also "Heidegger the Fox." For further discussion, see Biser, "Calibrating Our 'Inner Compass' "; Villa, *Arendt and Heidegger*, 230–240.

16. Arendt, *Thinking*, 174–175.

17. Arendt invokes the examples of Alcibiades and Critias, who drew from the Socratic examination the troubling conclusion that, "[i]f we cannot define what piety is, let us be impious." *Thinking*, 175–176; "Thinking and Moral Considerations," 177. For Arendt's concerns about nihilism, see also Fine, *Cosmopolitanism*, 119–120.

18. Arendt, *The Origins of Totalitarianism*, 281–282.

19. Arendt, *The Origins of Totalitarianism*, 275. In contrast to historical accounts that applaud the Minority Treaties as the precursors of human rights norms, Arendt's analysis underscores that these treaties set a dangerous precedent for the racial politics of the twentieth century. More specifically, it urges us to understand mass denationalizations and forced deportations as problems closely connected with the failure of the international community to address the question of minorities. For a positive account of the Minority Treaties, see, for example, Lauren, *Evolution of International Human Rights*, 115–117. For a critical analysis that links minority protection to the racial politics of the twentieth century, see Weitz, "From the Vienna to the Paris System."

20. Arendt, *The Origins of Totalitarianism*, 276.

21. Arendt, *The Origins of Totalitarianism*, 284.

22. Arendt, *The Origins of Totalitarianism*, 280.

23. Arendt, *The Origins of Totalitarianism*, 269.

24. Arendt, "Thinking and Moral Considerations," 168–169; *Thinking*, 168–169. Arendt works here with a Kantian understanding of "exemplar" as "a particular that in its very particularity reveals the generality that otherwise could not be defined." Arendt, *Lectures on Kant's Political Philosophy*, 77; see also "Some Questions of Moral Philosophy," 143–145. For Arendt's discussion of Socrates, see also Villa, *Socratic Citizenship*, 246–298.

25. Arendt, *Thinking*, 170.

26. Arendt, *Thinking*, 169–170.

27. Arendt, *Thinking*, 172. In this regard, Socrates, who always starts from his own perplexities or the ones arising from the assertions of his interlocutors, stands in contrast to Zeno, whose paradoxes are "unasserted counterfactuals." For this point, see Vlastos, "Socratic Elenchus," 2, 8.

28. Arendt, *Thinking*, 169–170. Arendt draws a contrast between earlier and later dialogues: The former have Socratic characteristics and "frequently conclude inconclusively, without a result"; see Arendt, "Socrates," 15. In the later dialogues, Socrates comes to articulate Platonic doctrines and ideas; see *Thinking*, 168. But the distinction is not watertight, as Arendt cites *Gorgias* as a relatively late dialogue that remains aporetic; see *Thinking*, 180. Although her distinction resembles that of Vlastos, her inclusion of *Gorgias* among the later dialogues departs from his suggestion to include it in early dialogues. For Vlastos's classification of Plato's dialogues, see "Chronological Order," 135.

29. For a compelling account that highlights the "Jewish" dimensions of Arendt's argument for an alternative form of thinking that resists dogmatism, refrains from codification, grapples with perplexities, and affirms the lack of final resolution, see Ring, *Political Consequences of Thinking*, chap. 9.

30. Arendt, "Socrates," 19.

31. Arendt, "Socrates," 14.

32. Arendt, "Socrates," 15. Arendt affirms the crucial importance of an aporetic and dialogic mode of thinking also in her following statement: "True understanding does not tire of interminable dialogue and 'vicious circles,' because it trusts that imagination eventually will catch at least a glimpse of the always frightening light of truth." Arendt, "Understanding and Politics," 322. Her idea that we can find out what might be truthful in our opinions only by engaging in a dialogue with others is also present in Karl Jaspers's account of Socrates in *The Great Philosophers*. Arendt edited a portion of this work that included the chapter on Socrates, and it is quite probable that Jaspers's portrait had an impact on her reflections on Socrates; see Jaspers, *Socrates, Buddha, Confucius, Jesus*, 5–21.

33. Mill, "On Liberty," 37. For a similar point, see Serena Parekh, "Resisting 'Dull and Torpid' Assent," 755. For Mill's turn to the Socratic example, see Urbinati, *Mill on Democracy*, chap. 4; Villa, *Socratic Citizenship*, chap. 2.

34. Arendt, "Introduction *into* Politics," 101, 152.

35. Arendt, *Thinking*, 172. For the "gadfly" metaphor, see Plato's *Apology* (30e).

36. Arendt, *Thinking*, 173. For the "midwifery" metaphor, see Plato, *Theatetus* (148e–151a).

37. Arendt, *Thinking*, 172.

38. Arendt, *Thinking*, 172. The "sting ray" metaphor appears in Plato's *Meno* (80a–d).

39. Arendt, *Thinking*, 173; emphasis in the original. At first look, these metaphors might suggest that thinking is a specialized craft that Socrates possesses and his interlocutors lack, and critics have painted a negative picture of Socrates along these lines; see, for example, Rancière, *Ignorant Schoolmaster*, 29. Arendt's reading, however, suggests that neither Socrates nor any of his interlocutors has a privileged access to truth; only the aporetic inquiry that they jointly undertake can reveal the truthfulness of the opinions that they examine. For another reading that challenges the idea that Socrates is in possession of a truth that he is withholding from his interlocutors, see Nehamas, "Voices of Silence," 180–182.

40. Beardsworth, *Derrida and the Political*, 32.

41. Arendt, "Truth and Politics," 242.

42. Sarah Kofman, "Beyond Aporia?," 10. For Arendt's use of "navigational" metaphors in relation to thinking, see Biser, "Calibrating Our 'Inner Compass.'"

43. Arendt, *Thinking*, 193.

44. Arendt, "On Hannah Arendt," 336. See also Arendt's description of Lessing as "promoting a new kind of thinking that needs no pillars and props, no standards and traditions to move freely without crutches over unfamiliar terrain." Arendt, "On Humanity in Dark Times," 10.

45. Arendt, *Thinking*, 192; see also Arendt, *Lectures on Kant's Political Philosophy*, 76, 83. For further discussion of Arendt's Kantian understanding of judgment, see, among others, Zerilli, *Feminism and the Abyss of Freedom*, 125–163.

46. Derrida, *Aporias*, 32. Richard J. Bernstein highlights that Derrida's reflections on aporia bear similarities with Arendt's argument about "thinking without banisters"; see Bernstein, "Derrida," 402–403. However, he also draws attention to the differences between the two thinkers, arguing that Derrida takes aporia as an existential experience of an abyss and mystifies decision as a groundless act severed from knowledge and judgment.

47. Arendt, " 'Rights of Man.' "

48. In an essay on the relationship between crisis and thinking in Arendt, Jakob Norberg suggests that "a question finally appears as a question" in a crisis that reveals the insufficiency of existing solutions. Norberg, "Arendt in Crisis," 134. Along similar lines, I suggest that human rights become a Socratic *ti esti* question for Arendt in the face of the crises of twentieth century, especially the plight of statelessness.

49. Arendt, "Rights of Man," 26.

50. Arendt, "Rights of Man," 34.

51. Rancière, "Who Is the Subject?," 302.

52. Rancière, "Who Is the Subject?," 306, 302.

53. Frank, "Political Theory of Classical Greece," 178.

54. Arendt, *On Revolution*, 159–161. For a more detailed discussion of Arendt's reflections on the abyss that confronts us in modern revolutions, see chapter 5.

55. Arendt, *On Revolution*, 45.

56. Arendt, *On Revolution*, 192, 161.

57. Arendt, *The Origins of Totalitarianism*, 296.

58. Arendt, *On Revolution*, 175; see also *The Origins of Totalitarianism*, 54. For a similar point, see Pitkin, *Attack of the Blob*, 73.

59. Arendt, *The Origins of Totalitarianism*, 300.

60. Arendt, *On Revolution*, 108.

61. Arendt, *The Origins of Totalitarianism*, 299.

62. For this point, see also Balibar, "(De)constructing the Human," 732.

63. Arendt, *The Origins of Totalitarianism*, 299.

64. Burke, *Reflections*, 288.

65. Arendt, *The Origins of Totalitarianism*, 299.

66. Arendt, *The Origins of Totalitarianism*, 301.

67. Arendt, *On Revolution*, 149.

68. Arendt, *On Revolution*, 109.

69. Arendt, *The Origins of Totalitarianism*, 291. For Arendt's invocation of the "savage" imagery in her discussion of statelessness, see chapter 4.

70. Rancière, "Who Is the Subject?," 298. For readings that highlight the affinities between Arendt and Burke on this score, see, among others, Brunkhorst, "Equality and Elitism," 189; Cohen, "Modern Form of the Social," 169, 183. Recognizing Arendt's ambivalence about Burke, Margaret Canovan nevertheless concludes that she is closer to his understanding of inherited rights; see Canovan, "Lasting Institutions," 146–147. For readings that emphasize the points of divergence between Arendt and Burke, see, among others, Birmingham, *Hannah Arendt*, 45–46; Isaac, "New Guarantee on Earth," 64–65.

71. Burke, *Reflections*, 120, 122.

72. Arendt, *The Origins of Totalitarianism*, 176.

73. For the problems of modeling political community on kinship, see Stevens, *Reproducing the State*.

74. Arendt, *The Origins of Totalitarianism*, 290.

75. Arendt, *The Origins of Totalitarianism*, 291. On the emergence of the Rights of Man within this modern context defined by the increase in state power and inequalities of capitalist society, see also Donnelly, *Universal Human Rights*, 58–59.

76. Arendt, *The Origins of Totalitarianism*, 299.

77. Agamben, *Homo Sacer*, 128. Precisely because of the problems and dangers of the Burkean position, Arendt does not argue for the restoration of "inherited" rights in the face of statelessness; instead, even in her early reflections on this problem, she highlights that the question is one of "somehow or other restoring to them [the stateless] the inalienable rights of man." Arendt, "Stateless People," 153.

78. See Balibar, "(De)constructing the Human," 733–734.

79. Balibar, "(De)constructing the Human," 733; emphasis in the original.

80. For an analysis of both of these possibilities in the works of Étienne Balibar and Claude Lefort, see Gündoğdu, "A Revolution in Rights."

81. This reading challenges more institutionalist portrayals of Arendt; see, for example, Waldron, "Arendt's Constitutional Politics." For a reading that reconsiders Arendt beyond the binary logic of institutionalism/anti-institutionalism, see Kalyvas, *Democracy and the Politics of the Extraordinary*, chap. 9.

82. Arendt, *The Origins of Totalitarianism*, 230. See also her review of J.-T. Delos's book, *La Nation*; Arendt, "The Nation," 139.

83. Arendt, *The Human Condition*, 245. For Arendt's critique of sovereignty, see, among others, Arato and Cohen, "Banishing the Sovereign?"

84. Arendt, "The Nation," 141. Arendt makes a similar point in her consideration of Karl Renner's and Otto Bauer's proposal for "a federation of peoples." See Arendt, "Concerning Minorities," 366–368; see also *The Origins of Totalitarianism*, 231–32n. Several scholars have argued that Arendt advocates a republican federation as the guarantor of equal rights; see, among others, Axtmann, "Globality, Plurality and Freedom," 107–111; Beiner, "Arendt and Nationalism," 55; Benhabib, "Philosophical Foundations of Cosmopolitan Norms," 15; Cohen, "Modern Form of the Social," 175.

85. Arendt, "Crisis of Zionism," 336. For Arendt's advocacy of a European federation or "commonwealth," see, for example, "The Minority Question," 130. For Arendt's emphasis on the need to integrate Jews and Arabs in Palestine in a Mediterranean or European federation, see "Can the Jewish-Arab Question Be Solved?," 197.

86. Arendt, *On Revolution*, 232–239.

87. For the exclusion of African Americans and Native Americans from the *consensus universalis* founding the American republic, see Arendt, "Civil Disobedience," 90–92. The next chapter addresses the failure of the American revolutionaries to address poverty as a political problem; for this failure, see Arendt, *On Revolution*, 68–69.

88. Arendt, *The Origins of Totalitarianism*, 298.

89. Arendt, "Karl Jaspers," 87, 81.

90. Arendt, "Karl Jaspers," 89.

91. Arendt, "Karl Jaspers," 84–85, 93–94. For extensive discussions of Arendt's arguments about federalism at the international level, see Axtmann, "Globality, Plurality and Freedom," 111ff; Klusmeyer, "Hannah Arendt's Case for Federalism."

92. Attending to these perplexities, Lars Rensmann attributes to Arendt a notion of "cosmopolitics from below," which is grounded in bottom-up practices that contest the exclusions of existing institutional configurations of rights. See Rensmann, "Grounding Cosmopolitics." My reading of Arendt's proposition of the right to have rights, discussed in chapter 5, centers on such political practices.

93. Rancière, "Who Is the Subject?," 302; emphasis added. Hauke Brunkhorst makes a similar criticism, arguing that Arendt's analysis casts the Rights of Man

among the origins of totalitarianism: "The totalitarian outcome is already en-shrined in the original concept of the human being to whom the Age of Enlighten-ment had ascribed universal rights. . . . Seen in this light, human rights are them-selves among the origins of totalitarianism." Brunkhorst, "Are Human Rights Self-Contradictory?," 191–192.

94. The emphasis on equivocality and contingency can especially be found in Arendt's historiographical reflections in response to Eric Voegelin's critique of *Origins*. According to Voegelin, Arendt's analysis of totalitarianism "is apt to endow historical causality with an aura of fatality." Voegelin, "Review," 73. For Arendt's response, see "Reply to Eric Voegelin." For a discussion of Arendt's historiographi-cal approach, see, among others, Benhabib, *Reluctant Modernism*, 63–69; Disch, *Hannah Arendt*, chap. 4; Luban, "Explaining Dark Times."

95. Arendt, "Understanding and Politics," 325. Here I draw on Lisa Disch, who suggests that Arendt borrows this distinctive understanding of "crystallization" from Kant; see Disch, *Hannah Arendt*, 147–148. In addition, Arendt uses the term "crystallization," along with her famous "pearl diver" metaphor, in describing Walter Benjamin's thinking about the past; see Arendt, "Walter Benjamin," 206. For the influence of Benjamin on Arendt's understanding of history in terms of "crystallization," "configuration," or "constellation," see Benhabib, *Reluctant Modernism*, 64; Herzog, "Illuminating Inheritance," 7; Holman, "Dialectics and Distinction," 347–348.

96. Arendt, "Understanding and Politics," 325.

97. Arendt, *On Revolution*, 34.

98. Arendt, *On Revolution*, 239.

99. Arendt, *On Revolution*, 53.

100. Arendt, *The Origins of Totalitarianism*, 91.

101. Arendt, *The Origins of Totalitarianism*, 117.

102. Arendt, *The Origins of Totalitarianism*, 106.

103. Arendt makes a similar point in the following comments about Clem-enceau: "The greatness of Clemenceau's approach lies in the fact that it was not directed against a particular miscarriage of justice, but was based upon such 'ab-stract' ideas as justice, liberty, and civic virtue. It was based, in short, on those very concepts which had formed the staple of old-time Jacobin patriotism and against which much mud and abuse had already been hurled." Arendt, *The Origins of Totalitarianism*, 110.

104. Arendt, *The Origins of Totalitarianism*, xviii; see also 157, 161, 221.

105. Arendt, *The Origins of Totalitarianism*, 206. For critical assessments of Arendt's analysis of imperialism, especially her "boomerang" thesis, see King and Stone, *Hannah Arendt*.

106. Arendt, *The Origins of Totalitarianism*, 278.

107. Balibar, " 'Rights of Man,' " 49–50.

108. Agamben, *Homo Sacer*, 131–133.

109. Agamben, *Homo Sacer*, 127–128.

110. Agamben, *Homo Sacer*, 127.

111. Agamben, *Homo Sacer*, 11.

112. Agamben, *Homo Sacer*, 10–11; see also *Means Without End*, 15–26. In many respects, Agamben's critique of human rights is at odds with his own theo-retical commitments to understanding history in terms of contingency. For this point, see Gündoğdu, "Potentialities of Human Rights."

113. Beardsworth, *Derrida and the Political*, 47. Beardsworth describes here Derrida's approach to aporia, but his description is equally apt for Arendt's approach.

114. Rancière, "Who Is the Subject?," 302.

115. Arendt, *The Origins of Totalitarianism*, 296–297.

116. Arendt, "'Rights of Man,'" 37; *The Origins of Totalitarianism*, 298.

Chapter 2

1. For an analysis underscoring the inextricable connections among human rights issues, see, for example, Ackerly, *Universal Human Rights*, 216–223

2. See, for example, Cohen, "Modern Form of the Social"; Rancière, "Who Is the Subject?"; Schaap, "Enacting the Right." These criticisms resonate with others that take issue with Arendt's controversial conception of "the social." See, among others, Bernstein, "Rethinking the Social"; Habermas, "Hannah Arendt's Communications Concept of Power," 219–220; Pitkin, "Justice"; Wolin, "Democracy and the Political." Arendt's most troubling invocation of the political/social distinction appears in her essay on school desegregation in the United States; she questions the policy of desegregation by arguing that discrimination in the social realm is legitimate as long as it does not affect the political realm. See Arendt, "Reflections on Little Rock," 206. For several critics of Arendt, this essay represents her tendency to disregard the perspectives of the marginalized and raises questions about the contemporary efforts to rethink human rights along Arendtian lines; see, for example, Simmons, *Human Rights Law*, chap. 1.

3. See, among others, Isaac, "New Guarantee on Earth"; James Ingram, "What is a 'Right to Have Rights'?"; Rensmann, "Grounding Cosmopolitics."

4. Arendt, "What is Freedom?," 151, 168.

5. Arendt, "Socrates," 17.

6. Arendt, *The Human Condition*, 32.

7. Arendt, *The Human Condition*, 30.

8. Arendt, *The Human Condition*, 31.

9. Arendt, *The Human Condition*, 37.

10. Arendt, *The Human Condition*, 28–29.

11. Arendt, *The Human Condition*, 35.

12. Arendt, *The Human Condition*, 45, 46.

13. See, among others, Brown, *Manhood and Politics*, 23–31; Wolin, "Democracy and the Political." Norma Claire Moruzzi provides an unorthodox reading of *The Human Condition*, as she argues that Arendt's prologue to the book brings to view an embodied understanding of the human condition and provides resources for questioning the exclusions that are justified in the rest of the book; see Moruzzi, *Speaking through the Mask*, chap. 1.

14. Reinhardt, *The Art of Being Free*, 148, 149.

15. Arendt, *The Human Condition*, 41.

16. Arendt, *The Human Condition*, 47.

17. Rancière, "Who Is the Subject?," 298–299. For an analysis that draws on and develops Rancière's critique of Arendt, see Schaap, "Enacting the Right."

18. Isaac, "New Guarantee on Earth"; Isaac, "Hannah Arendt on Human Rights"; James Ingram, "What Is a 'Right to Have Rights'?"

19. Serena Parekh, *Hannah Arendt*, chap. 4. For Arendt's discussion of the relationship between "public" and "private" rights, see Arendt, "Public Rights and Private Interests."

20. See Schaap, "Enacting the Right"; James Ingram, *Radical Cosmopolitics*, 195, 224. Elsewhere, Ingram identifies a closer affinity between Arendt and Rancière, suggesting that his approach to the politics of rights is "an emendation and extension of her framework," and not its total rejection. James Ingram, "What Is a 'Right to Have Rights'?," 412n; see also "Politics of Recognition," 237.

21. As the discussion below highlights, the Arendtian position on human rights might have more to share with critics of these rights than some readings would suggest. Here I have in mind the stark contrast that Jeffrey Isaac draws between Hannah Arendt and Noam Chomsky. As Isaac uses the resources of Arendt's political theory to counter Chomsky's critique NATO's "humanitarian" intervention in Kosovo, he risks losing the critical edge of her account of human rights. See Isaac, "Hannah Arendt on Human Rights." For a critique of Isaac's position from an Arendtian perspective, see Owens, *Between War and Politics*, chap. 6.

22. Benhabib, *Reluctant Modernism*, 23.

23. Pitkin, *The Attack of the Blob*, 17.

24. Bernstein, "Rethinking the Social," 115, 111. Perhaps these paradoxes are inevitable given that Arendt's goal is not to assign a fixed meaning to "the social" but instead to offer a "historical phenomenology," as Philip Walsh underscores: "Arendt takes it ['the social'] to name a historically variable set of meaningful human activities, which are bound up with other distinct kinds of relationships, the names for, and meanings of which are also more or less unstable." Walsh, "Arendt on the Social," 127.

25. Arendt, "Socrates," 19. Reflecting on the paradoxes in Marx's thinking about labor, Arendt argues that "[s]uch fundamental and flagrant contradictions rarely occur in second-rate writers; in the work of the great authors they lead into the very center of their work." Arendt, *The Human Condition*, 104–105. I propose to take this comment as an invitation to closely engage with the puzzles posed by Arendt's multiple, conflicting uses of "social," working with the assumption that the "fundamental and flagrant" contradictions that her readers identify in her treatment of this topic can take us to "the very center" of her work. My reading strategy also draws on Hanna Pitkin's suggestion that the paradoxes pervading Arendt's reflections on "the social" are best understood not as idiosyncratic inconsistencies but instead as challenging conundrums that we all confront in theorizing complex, multi-faceted issues that demand working at different scales. Pitkin, *The Attack of the Blob*, 241. Such paradoxes, Pitkin argues, are best approached by a "dialectical" mode of thinking, which aims at not resolving these tensions but finding a more promising "way of living with ambiguity and inconsistency." Allowing us to engage with multiple, conflicting ideas simultaneously, such dialectical thinking can "loosen the grip of existing assumptions on our thinking" and help us assess the limits and strengths of each perspective. Pitkin, *The Attack of the Blob*, 247–248. Pitkin's "dialectical thinking" is analogous to the aporetic inquiry discussed in the last chapter; I hope to engage in a similar critical exercise as I read Arendt against Arendt in this chapter.

26. Arendt, "On Hannah Arendt," 316; emphasis in the original.

27. Arendt, "On Hannah Arendt," 317. Philip Walsh notes that Arendt might have also been influenced by Karl Mannheim's distinction between "politics" and "administration" in *Ideology and Utopia*. Walsh, "Arendt on the Social," 136–137.

28. Arendt, "On Hannah Arendt," 318; emphasis in the original.

29. Arendt, "On Hannah Arendt," 318–319.

30. See, for example, Clarke, "Social Justice," 340; Myers, *Worldly Ethics*, 119–120; Schaap, "Politics of Need," 161.

31. UNHCR, *Handbook for Emergencies*, 221.

32. Fraser, *Unruly Practices*, 163; emphasis in the original.

33. Clarke, "Social Justice," 342. Bonnie Honig makes a similar argument in her revised account of "the social," when she suggests that "not everything is political in this (amended) account; it is simply the case that nothing *is* ontologically protected from politicization." Honig, "Toward an Agonistic Feminism," 147; emphasis in the original.

34. For a similar point, see Disch, *Hannah Arendt*, 65–66.

35. Arendt, *The Human Condition*, 40–46. My point builds on Kirstie McClure's argument; see McClure, "The Social Question, Again," 103–106. Understood in these terms, Arendt's account of "the rise of the social" anticipates some of the arguments in Michel Foucault's work on governmentality; see, for example, Foucault, *Security, Territory, Population*.

36. Pitkin, *The Attack of the Blob*, 252; see also 16. Seyla Benhabib also points to this meaning as "the most defensible way to salvage the Arendtian distinction"; see Benhabib, *Reluctant Modernism*, 140. For another account that revises Arendt's notion of "the social" along these lines, see Zerilli, *Feminism and the Abyss of Freedom*, 3–4.

37. Pitkin, *The Attack of the Blob*, 196.

38. Arendt, *On Revolution*, 61.

39. Arendt, *On Revolution*, 60; see also 110.

40. Arendt, *On Revolution*, 114.

41. See, for example, the following conclusion: "It [the French Revolution] was overwhelmed by the cares and worries which actually belonged in the sphere of the household and which, even if they were permitted to enter the public realm, could not be solved by political means, since they were matters of administration, to be put into the hands of experts, rather than issues which could be settled by the twofold process of decision and persuasion." Arendt, *On Revolution*, 91.

42. Hanna Pitkin, *The Attack of the Blob*, 219.

43. Bernstein, "Rethinking the Social," 117.

44. Arendt, *On Revolution*, 61.

45. Arendt, *On Revolution*, 62.

46. For the distinction between "need" and "necessity," see Pitkin, *The Attack of the Blob*, 190. For a critique of Arendt's tendency to conflate need with natural necessity, see Fraser, *Unruly Practices*, 160n; Schaap, "Politics of Need," 164. As Pitkin notes, however, Arendt does not always conflate these two; Arendt's second statement about Marx, quoted above, is a case in point.

47. Arendt, *On Revolution*, 62–63. Arendt locates this original contribution in Marx's early works, and dismisses the later works as reinscribing a form of historical determinism that ties violence to "the iron laws of historical necessity." *On Revolution*, 64. Whether such a break between early and late Marx can be posited

is a difficult question, but these positive remarks on Marx are worthy of attention because they draw attention to how social problems such as poverty can be approached politically in an Arendtian framework.

48. Arendt, *On Revolution*, 63.

49. Many scholars have taken issue with Arendt's history of the French Revolution. See, for example, Disch, "How Could Hannah Arendt?"; Hobsbawm, *Revolutionaries*, 201–208; Scheuerman, "Revolutions and Constitutions."

50. Arendt, *On Revolution*, 69.

51. Arendt, *On Revolution*, 69. In support of her point, Arendt quotes at length from John Adams's *Discourses on Davila*: "The poor man's conscience is clear; yet he is ashamed . . . He feels himself out of the sight of others, groping in the dark. Mankind takes no notice of him. He rambles and wanders unheeded. In the midst of a crowd, at church, in the market . . . he is in as much obscurity as he would be in a garret or a cellar. He is not disapproved, censured, or reproached; *he is only not seen* . . . To be wholly overlooked, and to know it, are intolerable. If Crusoe on his island had the library of Alexandria, and a certainty that he should never again see the face of man, would he ever open a volume?" Quoted in Arendt, *On Revolution*, 69. For an insightful analysis that takes issue with Arendt's political/social distinction but draws on her discussion of poverty to rethink a politics that is not oblivious to human needs, see Myers, *Worldly Ethics*, 113–122. In a problematic move, Arendt suggests that it was John Adams, freed from the urgent demands of necessity, who could understand the political dimensions of poverty, whereas the poor, captivated in the realm of necessity by their basic needs, could not comprehend their plight as one of political invisibility, let alone act upon and contest it. Arendt, *On Revolution*, 69. For a critique of Arendt's denial of this capacity to the poor, see Schaap, "Politics of Need," 165. Arendt's account of the labor movement, which I discuss below, complicates this conclusion, as it highlights that those who find themselves relegated to the realm of necessity can articulate their plight in political terms. This possibility is also recognized in Arendt's account of the "pariah" tradition, which embraces those "bold spirits" who become conscious of the position of Jews as outcasts, translate their plight into political terms, and rebel against conditions that deny them equal standing within the political community. See Arendt, "The Jew as Pariah," 275. For an illuminating analysis that shows how Arendt's account of the "pariah" tradition unsettles her political/social distinction, see Ring, "The Pariah as Hero."

52. The reading I provide below brackets off questions related to historical accuracy in Arendt's account of the French Revolution. This move is justified given that the main goal of my reading is to clarify Arendt's argument about what might hinder politicization of challenging issues such as poverty. Accordingly, I am interested in why Arendt takes issue with Robespierre's characterization of the poor, for example, and I do not assess whether she provides an accurate representation of his actions and motives.

53. I borrow the term from Didier Fassin, who draws on E. P. Thompson and James Scott and reinterprets the term "moral economy" to capture the production and circulation of a shared set of values and norms defining our moral world. Fassin, "Compassion and Repression," 365; *Humanitarian Reason*, 266n; see also Watters, "Refugees at Europe's Borders," 395–396.

54. Arendt, *On Revolution*, 75.

55. Arendt, *On Revolution*, 75.

56. Arendt, *On Revolution*, 74–75.

57. Abensour, "Saint-Just," 144.

58. Abensour, "Saint-Just," 144.

59. Arendt, *On Revolution*, 91–92.

60. Melville, "Billy Budd," 7; see Arendt, *On Revolution*, 87.

61. Arendt, *On Revolution*, 82.

62. Arendt, *On Revolution*, 83.

63. Arendt, *On Revolution*, 83, 84.

64. Melville, "Billy Budd," 69.

65. Arendt, *On Revolution*, 84, 86.

66. Arendt, *On Revolution*, 88–89. To understand the propensity of compassion to entail inequality between the sufferers and those identifying with their suffering, it is worth remembering the ambivalent etymology of the term: "From the fourteenth century to the beginning of the seventeenth, the word (deriving from Latin *com*, together, and *pati*, to suffer) was used to describe both *suffering together with one another*, or 'fellow feeling,' and an emotion felt *on behalf of another who suffers*. In the second sense, compassion was felt not between equals but from a distance—in effect, from high to low: 'shown towards a person in distress by one who is free from it, who is, in this respect, his superior.' When the first sense fell out of use, which it did fairly quickly, the remaining sense hovered between charity and condescension." Garber, "Compassion," 20. Arendt takes issue with both meanings of the term, but she expresses even a stronger disapproval of the second meaning, which brings compassion closer to pity.

67. Arendt, *On Revolution*, 86; *The Human Condition*, 182; "On Humanity in Dark Times," 31. For Arendt's critique of compassion as an unworldly passion, see also Moruzzi, *Speaking through the Mask*, 30–32.

68. Arendt, *On Revolution*, 81; for a similar point, see also "On Humanity in Dark Times," 12–17.

69. Arendt, *On Revolution*, 86.

70. Arendt, *On Revolution*, 87.

71. Arendt, *On Revolution*, 89.

72. Arendt, *On Revolution*, 90.

73. Arendt, *On Revolution*, 75.

74. Arendt, *On Revolution*, 93.

75. Arendt, *On Revolution*, 111; the French term means, among other things, destitute, wretched, miserable, unfortunate.

76. Arendt, *On Revolution*, 85; the French term can be translated as "weak men."

77. Arendt, *On Revolution*, 85; the French term can be translated as "always miserable" or "always wretched."

78. Arendt, *On Revolution*, 109.

79. Arendt, *On Revolution*, 111.

80. Rancière, "Who Is the Subject?," 302, 298.

81. Rancière, "Who Is the Subject?," 307.

82. Arendt, *The Origins of Totalitarianism*, 292.

83. Hunt, *Inventing Human Rights*.

84. We see this argument in Rousseau and Bentham, among others. Rousseau, for example, makes a strong case for including animals in natural law; "deprived of enlightenment and of freedom, they cannot recognize that Law," he argues, but as

living beings who "in some measure partake in our nature through the sentience with which they are endowed . . . they must also participate in natural right." Rousseau, "Discourse on the Origin," 127–128. Without using the language of natural right that he detested, Bentham also insists on the need for including animals in legislation by underscoring the capacity of suffering that they share with human beings: "[T]he question is not, Can they *reason*? nor, Can they *talk*? but, Can they *suffer*?" Bentham, *Introduction to the Principles of Morals*, 236n; emphasis in the original.

85. On the connections between these two different forms of advocacy, see Nyers, *Rethinking Refugees*, 85–88. For the early history of humanitarianism, see Barnett, *Empire of Humanity*, chap. 2.

86. Arendt, *The Origins of Totalitarianism*, 292. For the dependence of the stateless on the charity, generosity, or goodwill of others, see *The Origins of Totalitarianism*, 296; for the unreliability of compassion, see also "Guests from No-Man's-Land," 212.

87. Arendt, *The Origins of Totalitarianism*, 293.

88. This is Michael Ignatieff's "thin" definition of human rights. See Ignatieff, *Human Rights as Politics and Idolatry*, 56. For criticisms of Ignatieff on this score, see, for example, Brown, "'The Most We Can Hope For'"; Wallach, "Human Rights as an Ethics of Power," 120–126.

89. Malkki, "Speechless Emissaries," 388.

90. UNHCR, "Prominent Refugees." Accessed January 30, 2014. http://www.unhcr.org/pages/49c3646c74.html.

91. Arendt, *The Origins of Totalitarianism*, 287.

92. Verdirame and Harrell-Bond, *Rights in Exile*, 289.

93. This formulation draws on Butler's interpretation of Foucault's notion of governmentality: "Governmentality is broadly understood as a mode of power concerned with the maintenance and control of bodies and persons, the production and regulation of persons and populations, and the circulation of goods insofar as they maintain and restrict the life of the population." Butler, *Precarious Life*, 52.

94. Fassin, "Compassion and Repression," 372; see also Ticktin, "Where Ethics and Politics Meet."

95. Arendt, *The Human Condition*, 313.

96. Arendt, *On Revolution*, 85.

97. Leebaw, "Politics of Impartial Activism," 224; see also Calhoun, "Imperative to Reduce Suffering," 90.

98. Leebaw, "Politics of Impartial Activism," 227.

99. Although military humanitarian intervention is quite a novel practice, taking its current form particularly with the United Nations' "Responsibility to Protect" initiative established in 2005, similar ambitious projects mobilizing compassion for the purposes of more radical social transformation were not lacking in the history of humanitarianism. On this point, see Barnett, *Empire of Humanity*, 37–41; Calhoun, "Imperative to Reduce Suffering," 76–78.

100. For the drastic transformation of humanitarianism since the 1990s, see, among others, Barnett, *Empire of Humanity*, 184–185; Chandler, "Road to Military Humanitarianism"; Cohen, *Globalization and Sovereignty*, chap. 3; Douzinas, *Human Rights and Empire*; Kennedy, *Dark Sides of Virtue*, chap. 8; Leebaw, "Politics of Impartial Activism"; Orford, *Reading Humanitarian Intervention*, chap. 1.

101. Arendt, *On Revolution*, 86–87.

102. Leebaw, "Politics of Impartial Activism," 232.

103. Arendt, *On Revolution*, 89.

104. Arendt, *On Revolution*, 82; see also 86.

105. Rancière, "Who Is the Subject?," 309. For similar criticisms targeting the characterization of human beings as victims in the contemporary human rights discourse, see, for example, Badiou, *Ethics*, chap. 1; Žižek, "Against Human Rights."

106. Rancière, "Who Is the Subject?," 305, 307.

107. Rancière, "Who Is the Subject?," 307.

108. Jean Cohen also highlights this danger in her critical account of the humanitarian functions that human rights have come to assume since the 1990s: "The risk is that the link between the politics of human rights and democratic politics gets severed when it is foreign states, foreign activists, and global governance institutions who under the humanitarian impulse, assert and purport to enforce the human rights of victims." Cohen, *Globalization and Sovereignty*, 173.

109. Arendt, *On Revolution*, 89. I provide a detailed discussion of what Arendt means by "principle" in chapter 5.

110. Arendt, *On Revolution*, 89, 88.

111. Arendt, *The Human Condition*, 214.

112. Arendt, *The Human Condition*, 213.

113. Arendt, *The Human Condition*, 215.

114. Arendt, *The Human Condition*, 215.

115. Arendt, *The Human Condition*, 182.

116. See, for example, Christodoulidis and Schaap, "Arendt's Constitutional Question," 114–115.

117. Arendt, *The Human Condition*, 219.

118. Arendt, *The Human Condition*, 216.

119. Seyla Benhabib, for example, suggests that the novelty of the labor movement lies in their transformation of "the dictates of self-interest into a common public goal" by invoking "principles, interests, values that have a generalizable basis." Benhabib, *Reluctant Modernism*, 146, 145.

120. Arendt, *The Human Condition*, 216.

121. On this point, see in particular Dietz, *Turning Operations*, 108–109, 221n; Bonnie Honig, "Toward an Agonistic Feminism," 143.

122. Arendt, *The Human Condition*, 214n.

123. Arendt, *The Human Condition*, 215.

124. Arendt, *The Human Condition*, 217. Margaret Canovan suggests that Arendt "provides *a rather lame explanation* designed to show that such political activity by the workers is only a temporary phenomenon." See Canovan, "Contradictions of Hannah Arendt's Political Thought," 13; emphasis added. But once we attend to Arendt's point about the unpredictable effects of political emancipation, we realize that she provides a much more convincing explanation for the politicization of workers.

125. Arendt, *The Human Condition*, 217.

126. Arendt, *The Human Condition*, 217.

127. Arendt, *The Human Condition*, 217.

128. Arendt, *The Human Condition*, 218; emphasis in the original.

129. Arendt, *The Human Condition*, 218.
130. Arendt, *The Human Condition*, 218.
131. Arendt, *The Human Condition*, 218.
132. Arendt, *The Human Condition*, 218.
133. Rancière, *Disagreement*, 29.
134. Rancière, *The Nights of Labor*, 20.
135. Rancière, *Disagreement*, 36.
136. Rancière, *Disagreement*, 40–42.
137. Rancière, *Disagreement*, 52; see also 40; "Who Is the Subject?," 302–303.
138. Arendt, *The Human Condition*, 219.
139. Rancière, *Disagreement*, 38.
140. Lefort, "Politics and Human Rights," 258.
141. Ignatieff, *Human Rights as Politics and Idolatry.*
142. See, among others, Clark, *Diplomacy of Conscience*; Keck and Sikkink, *Activists Beyond Borders*; Risse, Ropp, and Sikkink, *Power of Human Rights*; Thomas, *The Helsinki Effect.*
143. See, for example, Finnemore and Sikkink, "International Norm Dynamics"; Risse, "Let's Argue!" For transnational activism, see, among others, Keck and Sikkink, *Activists Beyond Borders*; Risse, Ropp, and Sikkink, *Power of Human Rights.*
144. See Agamben, *Homo Sacer*; Brown, "'The Most We Can Hope For'"; Kennedy, "International Human Rights Movement."
145. See Mutua, *Human Rights*; see also Doty, *Imperial Encounters*; Guilhot, *Democracy Makers.*
146. See Guilhot, *Democracy Makers*; see also Anderson, "Force and Consent."
147. For these calls, see, for example, Agamben, *Means without End*, 22–23; Brown, "'The Most We Can Hope For,'" 460. Wendy Brown's critique of human rights builds on her earlier work on rights; see, for example, *States of Injury*, chap. 3. For critical engagements with Brown's position on rights, see, among others, Baynes, "Rights as Critique"; Chambers, "Giving up (on) Rights?"; Zivi, "Feminism and the Politics of Rights."
148. This formulation draws on Judith Butler's interpretation of Antigone's resistance to Creon. See, for example, her following statement: "[S]he absorbs the very language of the state against which she rebels, and hers becomes a politics not of oppositional purity but of the scandalously impure." Butler, *Antigone's Claim*, 5.
149. This point is aligned with Étienne Balibar's suggestion that Arendtian politics of human rights is "groundless" in a Machiavellian sense: "[T]here is no transcendental or normative guarantee that the use of human rights in politics will produce the anticipated results or realize the right (*justice*, if you like) designated in 'the rights.'" Balibar, "On the Politics of Human Rights," 20–21; emphasis in the original.

Chapter 3

1. Haitian Ctrs. Council v. Sale, 823 F. Supp. 1028 (US Dist. 1993).
2. Lizzy Ratner, "The Legacy of Guantánamo," *The Nation*, July 21, 2003.
3. For the detention of asylum seekers, undocumented migrants, and HIV-positive refugees on Guantánamo, see Dastyari, "Refugees on Guantanamo Bay"; Wilsher, *Immigration Detention*, 240–242. For the marginalization of HIV-positive

refugees on Guantánamo, see Shemak, *Asylum Speakers*, 66–69. The 1987 statute barring the HIV-positive foreigners as "inadmissible undesirables" from entering the United States was not repealed until 2010.

4. International Coalition of Sites of Conscience, "Guantánamo Public Memory Project," 14, September 2011, accessed April 13, 2012, http://hrcolumbia.org/guantanamo/blueprint.pdf. Guantánamo has long been used as a site for containing undesirables, as highlighted in this report: "The unique qualities of the site—its legal ambiguity, political isolation and geographic proximity, and architectures of confinement—have been used and reused to detain people who fall between the boundaries of legal protections and political imperatives" (3).

5. Arendt, *The Origins of Totalitarianism*, 295.

6. Dastyari, "Refugees on Guantanamo Bay," 7. For the legal challenges faced by asylum seekers in Guantánamo, see also Shemak, *Asylum Speakers*, 52–60.

7. See Brandt Goldstein, "Guantanamo: The Prequel," *The Wall Street Journal*, December 4, 2007. In 1997, however, the Inter-American Commission on Human Rights ruled that the US policy of interdicting and forcefully returning Haitian refugees violated several rights under the American Declaration of the Rights and Duties of Man; it listed violations of the right to life, right to liberty, right to security of person, right to equality before the law, right to resort to courts, and right to seek and receive asylum. See The Haitian Centre for Human Rights et al. v. United States, Case 10.675, Inter-American Commission on Human Rights (IACHR), 1997, accessed May 19, 2012, http://www.refworld.org/docid/3ae6b71b8.html.

8. On "the proliferation of 'little Guantánamos' near airports and other border-spaces," see Feldman, "Terminal Exceptions," 340.

9. On the so-called "Pacific Solution," see Hyndman and Mountz, "Another Brick in the Wall?"; Rajaram and Grundy-Warr, "The Irregular Migrant as Homo Sacer." It can be argued that Guantánamo served as an example for Australian policies; see Dastyari, "Refugees on Guantanamo Bay."

10. See, for example, Basaran, *Security, Law and Borders*, chap. 3; Makaremi, "Governing Borders in France"; Bigo, "Detention of Foreigners."

11. Andrijasevic, "From Exception to Excess"; Klepp, "A Contested Asylum System"; Human Rights Watch, *Pushed Back, Pushed Around*. For an Arendtian critique of some of these border control practices, see, for example, Hayden, "From Exclusion to Containment."

12. Arendt, *The Origins of Totalitarianism*, 296.

13. On the shift from citizenship status to legal personhood as the basis of rights within a human rights framework, see, among others, Benhabib, *The Rights of Others*; Cohen, "Changing Paradigms of Citizenship" and "Dilemmas of Arendtian Republicanism"; Jacobson, *Rights Across Borders*; Sassen, "Repositioning of Citizenship"; Soysal, *Limits of Citizenship*. There are notable differences among these scholars, as noted in the Introduction. For a detailed account of the crucial developments regarding migrants' human rights, see in particular Grant, "Rights of Migrants"; Weissbrodt, *Human Rights of Non-Citizens*.

14. See, for example, Agamben, *Homo Sacer*; Esposito, *Third Person*.

15. Bosniak, "Human Rights within One State," 205, 201.

16. Fassin, *Humanitarian Reason*, 4; see also 264–265n.

17. See Donnelly, *Universal Human Rights*, 8. For an understanding of rights in terms of "the recognizable capacity to assert claims," see also Waldron, *Dignity, Rank, and Rights*, 50.

18. See, for example, Bohman, "Citizens and Persons," 331.

19. See the use of the term "rightless" in *The Origins of Totalitarianism*, 267, 279, 288n, 290, 293, 294, 295, 300; for "rightlessness," see *The Origins of Totalitarianism*, 295, 296.

20. Arendt, *The Origins of Totalitarianism*, 296.

21. Arendt, *The Origins of Totalitarianism*, 295.

22. Arendt, *The Origins of Totalitarianism*, 293–294; see also 296–297.

23. Keck and Sikkink, *Activists Beyond Borders*, 27.

24. Keck and Sikkink, *Activists Beyond Borders*, 27.

25. Arendt, *The Origins of Totalitarianism*, 293–294, 297.

26. Arendt, *The Origins of Totalitarianism*, 295–296; see also "Guests from No-Man's-Land," 212; "Disenfranchised and Disgraced," 233.

27. Arendt, *The Origins of Totalitarianism*, 288. Arendt revisits her argument about the precarious legal personhood of the stateless in her discussion of Eichmann's capture in Argentina and prosecution in Israel: "[I]t was Eichmann's de facto statelessness, and nothing else, that enabled the Jerusalem court to sit in judgment on him. Eichmann, though no legal expert, should have been able to appreciate that, for he knew from his own career that one could do as one pleased only with stateless people; the Jews had to lose their nationality before they could be exterminated." Arendt, *Eichmann in Jerusalem*, 240.

28. Arendt, *The Origins of Totalitarianism*, 447.

29. Arendt, *The Origins of Totalitarianism*, 296.

30. Arendt, "Statelessness," 2; see also *The Origins of Totalitarianism*, 296.

31. Arendt, *The Origins of Totalitarianism*, 286.

32. Arendt, "Statelessness," 2; see also *The Origins of Totalitarianism*, 296.

33. Arendt, *The Origins of Totalitarianism*, 286–287; see also 295.

34. For this point, see, for example, Guenther, *Solitary Confinement*, xxiv.

35. Arendt, *The Origins of Totalitarianism*, 283, 286.

36. Hegel, *Philosophy of Right*, 71. For the Hegelian elements in Arendt's argument about personhood, see Tsao, "Arendt and the Modern State," 127–128.

37. On civil and social death, see Guenther, *Solitary Confinement*, xviii–xxvii. Arendt's distinction between the stateless and the criminal has achieved a new salience in the contemporary setting. In the so-called War on Terror, the US government detained many of the suspects by referring to violations of immigration law (e.g., overstaying a visa). As David Cole notes, the government's goal was "to avoid those constitutional rights and safeguards that accompany the criminal process but that do not apply in the immigration setting." Cole, *Enemy Aliens*, 34. See also Wilsher, *Immigration Detention*, chap. 5.

38. Feinberg, "Nature and Value of Rights," 252. See also Honneth, *Struggle for Recognition*, 119–121.

39. Feinberg, "Nature and Value of Rights," 252.

40. Arendt, "Guests from No-Man's-Land," 212.

41. Arendt, *The Origins of Totalitarianism*, 301; emphasis added.

42. Arendt, *On Revolution*, 106; see also "Prologue," 12; *Denktagebuch*, vol. 1, 8. For a detailed, illuminating analysis of Arendt's account of *persona* as mask, see Moruzzi, *Speaking through the Mask*, especially chap. 3. Moruzzi's analysis centers on questions of social identity and does not go into the topic of legal personhood.

43. Arendt, "Prologue," 12.

44. Arendt, *On Revolution*, 107; see also "Prologue," 12–13.

45. See, for example, Noonan, *Persons and the Masks of Law*, 22, 27; Naffine, *Law's Meaning of Life*, 29–30.

46. Arendt, "Prologue," 12.

47. Arendt, *On Revolution*, 106. This etymology of *persona* is quite contested; see, for example, Trendelenburg, *History of the Word Person*, 6–8. For the etymology of *persona*, see also Mauss, "Category of the Human Mind," 14–15. Arendt is quite aware of the problems with this etymology, which makes her insistence on using it even more worthy of attention: "Although the etymological root of *persona* seems to derive from *per-zonare*, from the Greek ξωνη, and hence to mean originally 'disguise,' one is tempted to believe that the word carried for Latin ears the significance of *per-sonare*, 'to sound through.'" Arendt, *On Revolution*, 293n.

48. Dewey, "Corporate Legal Personality," 661, 660.

49. See the discussion in Naffine, *Law's Meaning of Life*, 29–30; see also Naffine, "Who are Law's Persons?," 349–350.

50. Naffine, *Law's Meaning of Life*, chap. 7. James Griffin's work, deriving human rights from the dignity of human beings as normative agents, can serve as a contemporary example. It is important to note that one of the sources that Griffin draws on is the fifteenth-century Italian philosopher Giovanni Pico della Mirandola's *Oration on the Dignity of Man*, which rests on theological assumptions about human dignity, especially the idea that it is God who left man "free to determine his own nature." See Griffin, *On Human Rights*, 31; see also 152. Griffin's secular formulation of dignity as normative agency no longer makes reference to God but still holds on to the idea of an inherent human attribute to which rights are attached. For the theological background of human dignity, see Habermas, "Concept of Human Dignity," 474; McCrudden, "Human Dignity," 658–659.

51. Naffine, *Law's Meaning of Life*, 358. Even post-metaphysical understandings of human dignity have a tendency to derive human rights from some intrinsically and uniquely human qualities. This idea can be seen in George Kateb's existential understanding of human dignity, which is rooted in the idea that human beings are superior to other species because of their distinctive capacity to serve as the stewards of nature. Kateb, *Human Dignity*; see in particular chap. 3. For an alternative account that takes issue with the efforts to derive human dignity from inherent human attributes, see Waldron, *Dignity, Rank, and Rights*. Waldron underscores the origins of dignity in the idea of rank or status and proposes rethinking the modern notion of human dignity in terms of the universalization of a high-ranking status that was reserved for only the nobility in the past. To highlight the crucial role that law plays in this universalization, Waldron draws on Arendt's understanding of personhood as an artifice created by law. See Waldron, *Dignity, Rank, and Rights*, 20.

52. Trendelenburg, "History of the Word Person," 21. For the impact of Christian theology on the modern conception of personhood, see Esposito, *Third Person*, 70–75; Mauss, "A Category of the Human Mind," 19–20.

53. Arendt, *On Revolution*, 107.

54. Arendt, *The Origins of Totalitarianism*, 277, 301; see also "Guests From No-Man's-Land," 212.

55. Villa, *Politics, Philosophy, Terror*, 119.

56. Villa, *Politics, Philosophy, Terror*, 138; see also Dossa, *Public Realm*, 93.

57. Arendt, *On Revolution*, 108. For an analysis, see also Owens, *Between War and Politics*, 100–101.

58. Arendt, *The Origins of Totalitarianism*, 299.

59. Arendt, *The Origins of Totalitarianism*, 301.

60. In her critical analysis of Israeli citizenship, Leora Bilsky makes a similar point about Arendt's understanding of personhood as an artificial mask: "The mask equalizes by covering the face of the actor. This characteristic of the mask highlights Arendt's inversion of the modern understanding of equality as a natural condition of human beings." Bilsky, "Citizenship as Mask," 74.

61. Arendt, "Introduction *into* Politics," 94. For a similar interpretation of Arendt in this regard, see Balibar, "(De)constructing the Human," 733–734.

62. I rely on the following sources in my discussion of *capitis diminutio*: Long, *Notes on Roman Law*, 2–4; Berger, *Encyclopedic Dictionary of Roman Law*, 380–381; Esposito, *Third Person*, 79.

63. Arendt, "We Refugees," 264–265.

64. See the entry on *"deportatio"* in Berger, *Encyclopedic Dictionary of Roman Law*, 432.

65. See the entry on *"interdicere aqua et igni"* in Berger, *Encyclopedic Dictionary of Roman Law*, 507.

66. Arendt, *The Origins of Totalitarianism*, 297.

67. For the possibilities of unmaking and diminishing personhood, often through the use of categories and hierarchies established by law, see, for example, Dayan, *The Law is a White Dog*, 40; Guenther, *Solitary Confinement*, 46–47.

68. Naffine, *Law's Meaning of Life*, 12.

69. Bosniak, "Human Rights within One State," 207.

70. On the precarious personhood of migrants, see Bosniak, "Human Rights within One State"; Dal Lago, *Non-Persons*; Johnson, "'Aliens' and the U.S. Immigration Laws"; McKanders, "Sustaining Tiered Personhood."

71. Noonan, *Persons and the Masks of Law*, 19.

72. Noonan, *Persons and the Masks of Law*, 26, 27.

73. Agamben, *Homo Sacer*, 123–125.

74. Arendt, *On Revolution*, 187; "Introduction *into* Politics," 178–179. For the Roman elements in Arendt's understanding of law, see, among others, Breen, "Law Beyond Command?," 21–24; Taminiaux, "Athens and Rome," 176–177; Tsao, "Arendt against Athens," 109.

75. Arendt, *The Origins of Totalitarianism*, 301.

76. Ricoeur, "Approaching the Human Person," 45.

77. This sentence draws on Ricoeur's formulations of personhood; see "Approaching the Human Person." Axel Honneth offers a similar understanding of personhood, as he suggests that the denial of rights entails not simply "the forcible restriction of personal autonomy" but also the "loss of self-respect, of the ability to relate to oneself as a legally equal interaction partner with all fellow humans." Honneth, *Struggles for Recognition*, 133, 134.

78. Brubaker, *Citizenship and Nationhood*, 24. For an analysis demonstrating the problems of denying long-term residents the right not to be deported, see Carens, *Ethics of Immigration*, 100–106.

79. Walters, "Deportation, Expulsion," 277; see also Gibney, "Is Deportation a Form of Forced Migration?"

80. Arendt, *The Origins of Totalitarianism*, 278.

81. European Convention of Human Rights (ECHR) has an explicitly stated prohibition against collective expulsion of aliens (Protocol No. 4, Article 4). ICCPR does not have such an explicit prohibition, but collective expulsion has come to be interpreted as a measure in violation of Article 13, which entitles an alien lawfully present in the territory of a state to an expulsion decision reached in accordance with law. For further discussion, see Office of the High Commissioner for Human Rights (OHCHR), "Expulsions of Aliens in International Human Rights Law," September 2006, accessed May 21, 2012, www2.ohchr.org/english/issues/migration/taskforce/docs/Discussion-paper-expulsions.pdf.

82. OHCHR, "Expulsions of Aliens," 17–18.

83. See Article 33 of the 1951 Convention Relating to the Status of Refugees and its 1967 Protocol; hereafter, the Refugee Convention. Accessed June 13, 2012, http://www.unhcr.org/3b66c2aa10.html.

84. See Allain, "*Jus Cogens* Nature of *Non-Refoulement*," 535; Fabbricotti, "Inhuman or Degrading Treatment," 658–659.

85. See Article 33 (2) of the Refugee Convention.

86. Arendt, *The Origins of Totalitarianism*, 282.

87. On the securitization of asylum and immigration, see, for example, Bigo, "Security and Immigration"; Huysmans, *Politics of Insecurity*.

88. Normalization of deportation plays a role similar to the construction of walls in this regard. For an analysis of walls as symptoms of a waning sovereignty, see Brown, *Walled States*.

89. De Genova, "Migrant 'Illegality' and Deportability," 439.

90. *N. v. The United Kingdom*, Appl. No. 26565/05, Council of Europe: European Court of Human Rights, May 27, 2008, accessed May 12, 2012. http://hudoc.echr.coe.int/sites/eng/pages/search.aspx?i=001-86490.

91. Cover, "Foreword: *Nomos* and Narrative."

92. Seyla Benhabib, *Another Cosmopolitanism*, 70; see also 48–49.

93. Cover, "Violence and the Word," 1601.

94. See, for example, Bohmer and Shuman, *Rejecting Refugees*; Tuitt, *False Images*.

95. See Shuman and Bohmer, "Representing Trauma"; Bohmer and Shuman, "Producing Epistemologies of Ignorance."

96. Bohmer and Shuman, *Rejecting Refugees*, 11. For the challenges that asylum seekers face in authorizing their testimonies, see also Shemak, *Asylum Speakers*, chap. 1; Simmons, *Human Rights Law*, chap. 6; Tuitt, *False Images*, chap. 5.

97. Fassin, "Compassion and Repression," 372. See also Fassin, *Humanitarian Reason*; Ticktin, *Casualties of Care*; Ticktin, "Where Ethics and Politics Meet"; Watters, "Refugees at Europe's Borders."

98. For an analysis of this development, see, among others, Harvey, "Dissident Voices"; see also Fabbricotti, "Inhuman or Degrading Treatment."

99. N v. UK, §42.

100. N v. UK, §47–50.

101. N v. UK, §44.

102. N v. UK, §49.

103. Quoted in N v. UK, §17.

104. N v. UK, §47.

105. This statement is from the ruling of the Court of Appeal in the UK; quoted in N v. UK, §16.

106. Arendt, *The Origins of Totalitarianism*, 288.

107. Arendt, *The Origins of Totalitarianism*, 296.

108. Airey v. Ireland quoted in N v. UK, Joint Dissenting Opinion of Judges Tolkens, Bonello, and Spielmann, §6; hereafter Dissenting Opinion.

109. N v. UK, Dissenting Opinion, §8.

110. N v. UK, Dissenting Opinion, §26.

111. N v. UK, Dissenting Opinion, §9.

112. The dissenting judges ruled out this more promising possibility, as they stressed that they would not offer a different interpretation of the scope of Article 3; they argued that N.'s case concerned civil rights, not socioeconomic rights. See N v. UK, Dissenting Opinion, §6 and §24.

113. See, for example, Arendt, *The Origins of Totalitarianism*, 300–302.

114. In this sense, today's asylum seekers are similar to the refugees that Arendt wrote about: "No one really knows what to do with them once compassion asserted its just claim and reached its inevitable end." Arendt, "Guests from No-Man's-Land," 212.

115. Karara v. Finland (1998), S.C.C. v. Sweden (2000), Bensaid v. UK (2001), Arcila Henao v. The Netherlands (2003), Ndangoya v. Sweden (2004), Amegnigan v. the Netherlands (2004). See the discussion of these cases in N v. UK, §36–41.

116. Robert Cover, "Violence and the Word," 1628. For an analysis that shows how a humanitarian framework cannot help but sacrifice lives as a result of "either a sorting that emphasizes survival . . . or one that emphasizes severity of need," see Redfield, "Sacrifice, Triage, and Global Humanitarianism," 205.

117. See the references to this "high threshold" in N. v. UK, §38 and §43.

118. Agamben, *Homo Sacer*, 139; emphasis added.

119. See note 115 for the list of these cases. For Agamben's appropriation of this Latin term, see in particular *Homo Sacer*, 71, 82, 139.

120. Fassin, *Humanitarian Reason*, 119.

121. Bloch and Schuster, "At the Extremes of Exclusion"; Wilsher, *Immigration Detention*, chap. 6.

122. Migreurop, "Encampment Map," December 19, 2012, accessed July 7, 2014. http://www.migreurop.org/IMG/pdf/Carte_Atlas_Migreurop_8012013_Version_anglaise_version_web.pdf. For the difficulty of estimates, see also Gorski, Fernández, and Manavella, "Right-Based Approach," 3. For a critical analysis of the proliferation of "camps" in Europe, see, for example, Duvall, Gündoğdu, and Raj, "Borders, Power, and Resistance."

123. Global Detention Project, "France Detention Profile," last updated April 2009, accessed May 24, 2012. http://www.globaldetentionproject.org/countries/europe/france/introduction.html#c1938. Maximum length of detention was increased from 32 days to 45 days in June 2011. It is also important to note the evolution of time limits for immigration detention since the 1980s; in France, maximum length of immigration detention used to be 7 days in 1981. See Flemish Refugee Action, "Factsheet: The Detention of Migrants in France," January 2014, accessed July 7, 2014. http://pointofnoreturn.eu/wp-content/uploads/2013/12/PONR_Factsheet_FR_HR.pdf.

124. Arendt, *The Origins of Totalitarianism*, 279, 284.

125. Arendt, *The Origins of Totalitarianism*, 286.

126. For the use of solitary confinement in immigration detention in the United States, see Ian Urbina and Catherine Rentz, "Immigrants Held in Solitary Cells, Often for Weeks," *The New York Times*, March 23, 2012.

127. Jesuit Refugee Service-Europe, *Becoming Vulnerable in Detention*, 8, 43–45.

128. Nina Bernstein, "Companies Use Immigration Crackdown to Turn a Profit," *The New York Times*, September 28, 2011. See also American Civil Liberties Union of New Mexico, *Outsourcing Responsibility*.

129. UNHCR, "UNHCR's Guidelines," 3–5.

130. *Saadi v. the United Kingdom*, 13229/03, Council of Europe: European Court of Human Rights, January 29, 2008, accessed May 23, 2012. http://hudoc.echr.coe.int/sites/eng/pages/search.aspx?i=001-84709.

131. Saadi v. UK, §61. In a previous case, Chahal v. UK (1996), the Court had already established that detention for the purposes of deportation was a legitimate measure even if there was no risk of absconding, provided that it was not indefinite.

132. Sub-paragraph (f) of Article 5 (1) allows "the lawful arrest or detention of a person to prevent his effecting an unauthorized entry into the country or of a person against whom action is being taken with a view to deportation or extradition."

133. Saadi v. UK, §47.

134. Saadi v. UK, §51–53.

135. Linda Bosniak, "Human Rights within One State," 210.

136. Amuur v France quoted in Saadi v. UK, §64; for the discussion of what constitutes "unauthorized" entry, see Saadi v. UK, §65. On this point, see also Cornelisse, *Immigration Detention and Human Rights*, 310–312.

137. Saadi v. UK, §78; see also §76–77.

138. Saadi v. UK, §80.

139. The UK government justified detention of Saadi in these terms; see Saadi v. UK, §18; the majority of the judges agreed with this assessment (§77).

140. Saadi v. UK, §78. The attempt to give Oakington a humanitarian aura overlooks the fact that "*any* deprivation of liberty involves the state's monopoly on the use of violence, no matter how 'relaxed' (!) the regime at a particular detention centre may be." Cornelisse, *Immigration Detention and Human Rights*, 308; emphasis in the original.

141. Saadi v. UK, §25.

142. On the lack of generally recognized guidelines regarding the maximum duration of detention, see Amnesty International, *The Netherlands*, 23; on the lack of a global definition of what "arbitrary" detention means, see Saadi v. UK, §68.

143. "Directive 2008/115/EC of The European Parliament and of the Council of 16 December 2008 on Common Standards and Procedures in Member States for Returning Illegally Staying Third-Country Nationals." Accessed November 21, 2013. http://eur-lex.europa.eu/LexUriServ/LexUriServ.do?uri=OJ:L:2008:348:0098:0107:EN:PDF.

144. Saadi v. UK, §79.

145. Saadi v. UK, The Joint Partly Dissenting Opinion of Judges Rozakis, Tulkens, Kovler, Hajiyev, Spielmann, and Hirvelä, 33; hereafter Partly Dissenting Opinion.

146. Saadi v. UK, Partly Dissenting Opinion, 33.

147. Saadi v. UK, Partly Dissenting Opinion, 34; emphasis in the original.
148. Torpey, *Invention of the Passport*, 156.
149. Arendt, *The Origins of Totalitarianism*, 296.
150. Saadi v. UK, Partly Dissenting Opinion, 36.
151. Saadi v. UK, Partly Dissenting Opinion, 32; emphasis added.
152. Bhabha, "Internationalist Gatekeepers?," 161. It is also important to note that the distinctions that asylum advocates draw between "asylum seekers" and "undocumented immigrants" have come to be abused by states to undermine the credibility of asylum claims, as can be seen in the use of terms such as "bogus asylum seekers." For states' tendency to manipulate these distinctions, see, for example, Dummett, *On Immigration and Refugees*, 44–45.
153. Roberto Esposito, "The *Dispositif* of the Person," 24. For an analysis of the fissures that borders introduce to the notion of "humanity" within a human rights framework, see Kesby, *Right to Have Rights*, chap. 4.
154. Esposito, *Third Person*, 74.
155. Judith Butler, *Precarious Life*, 86.
156. For this view, see, for example, Esposito, "The *Dispositif* of the Person," 24. As an alternative to "the personhood-deciding machine," Esposito develops a theory of the "impersonal," drawing on figures such as Simone Weil, Emmanuel Levinas, Michel Foucault, and Gilles Deleuze. Esposito, *Third Person*, 13; see also chap. 3.

Chapter 4

1. John Hooper, "Italian Police Begin to Round Up Romanians," *The Guardian*, November 2, 2007. This decree was not turned into law, but the Italian government continued to handle the expulsion of foreigners by adopting a series of decrees to avoid the rule of law; see Codini, "Developments in Law," 72–73.
2. Butler, *Precarious Life*, 98.
3. Arendt, *The Origins of Totalitarianism*, 293.
4. Arendt, *The Origins of Totalitarianism*, 297.
5. As Lewis P. Hinchman and Sandra K. Hinchman highlight in their phenomenological reading of Arendt, her conceptual distinctions, including those between action, work, and labor, are to be understood not as "categories" but instead as "existentials" that "seek to illuminate what it means to be-in-the-world." See Hinchman and Hinchman, "In Heidegger's Shadow," 197.
6. Arendt, *The Human Condition*, 9.
7. See, among others, Kateb, *Hannah Arendt*, 16–22; Pitkin, "Justice." For a defense of Arendt's aesthetic understanding of action, see Villa, "Beyond Good and Evil."
8. Arendt, *The Human Condition*, 7.
9. Arendt, *The Human Condition*, 8.
10. Arendt, *The Human Condition*, 9.
11. Ricoeur, "Action, Story and History," 61.
12. Arendt, *The Human Condition*, 7.
13. Arendt, *The Human Condition*, 48, 98–100.
14. Arendt, *The Human Condition*, 152.
15. Arendt, *The Human Condition*, 137.
16. Arendt, *The Human Condition*, 9; see also 177–178, 247.
17. Arendt, *The Human Condition*, 23, 188.

18. Villa, *Arendt and Heidegger*, 28.

19. Kateb, *Hannah Arendt*, 6, 3; see also Bhikhu Parekh, *Hannah Arendt*, 121–123.

20. Villa, *Arendt and Heidegger*, 27; emphasis added.

21. Bhikhu Parekh, *Hannah Arendt*, 122; see also Bakan, "Hannah Arendt's Concepts of Labor and Work"; Voice, "Labour, Work and Action," 37–38.

22. Villa, *Arendt and Heidegger*, 26.

23. O'Sullivan, "Hannah Arendt," 229.

24. Ring, "On Needing Both Arendt and Marx," 435. Not all readers who locate in *The Human Condition* a hierarchical ranking of human activities would agree with this conclusion; see, for example, Bhikhu Parekh, who suggests that, although labor, work, and action "are not equally important" for Arendt, each is "indispensable" to the constitution of the human world. Bhikhu Parekh, "Hannah Arendt's Critique of Marx," 71, 70.

25. See, for example, Dana Villa, who suggests that Arendt embraces the Aristotelian idea of freedom: "Better that some should be free on the basis of the unfreedom of others than that all should be mired in the necessity of the household." Villa, *Arendt and Heidegger*, 28.

26. This phrase was coined by the feminist theorist Mary O'Brien; quoted in Dietz, *Turning Operations*, 125.

27. See, for example, Brown, *Manhood and Politics*, 25. This criticism has been articulated by several feminist theorists; for a critical review of the feminist reception of Arendt, see in particular Dietz, *Turning Operations*, 119–138. For a feminist defense of Arendt's account of labor, see Veltman, "Simone de Beauvoir."

28. Dietz, *Turning Operations*, 103. See also Honig, "Toward an Agonistic Feminism," 143; Pitkin, *The Attack of the Blob*, 179.

29. Benhabib, *Reluctant Modernism*, 133–136; Dietz, *Turning Operations*, chap. 8.

30. Arendt, *The Human Condition*, 9.

31. As Margaret Canovan highlights, Arendt provides us with a selective phenomenology in *The Human Condition*, centered on "the human activities that have most bearing upon politics." Canovan, *Hannah Arendt*, 101.

32. For this clarification, see especially Canovan, *Hannah Arendt*, 130–131.

33. Arendt, *The Human Condition*, 9, 22.

34. Arendt, *The Human Condition*, 14, 16.

35. Arendt, *The Human Condition*, 15–16.

36. Arendt, *The Human Condition*, 22.

37. Arendt, "Labor, Work, Action," 30; see also *The Human Condition*, 17.

38. This concern can be seen in Arendt's critique of Marx; taking issue with his characterization of man as a laboring being, she argues that he overlooks the distinctions between human activities and ends up attributing to labor some of the characteristics of work and action. See *The Human Condition*, 87, 101–102, 306. *The Human Condition* had its origins in a project on the "totalitarian elements" in Marxism; in an attempt to sketch out that project, Arendt notes in her "thinking diary" in July 1951 that one of these elements consists of Marx's "definition of man as a laboring being, identification of labor with work on the one hand, confusion of labor with action on the other." See *Denktagebuch*, vol. 1, 102–103. For Arendt, although these activities are interrelated, there is a need for distinctions to understand *vita activa* in its multifarious dimensions without reducing it to a single activity or principle.

39. Arendt, *The Human Condition*, 84.

40. Dietz, *Turning Operations*, 193; see also 193–194, 197.

41. For this point, see also Curtis, *Our Sense of the Real*, 44–45; Serena Parekh, *Hannah Arendt*, 50–54.

42. Arendt, *The Human Condition*, 106.

43. Arendt, *The Human Condition*, 107, 108.

44. Arendt, *The Human Condition*, 121.

45. Arendt, *The Human Condition*, 108.

46. Arendt, *The Human Condition*, 106.

47. Particularly interesting in this regard is Arendt's quite lengthy discussion of Swiss zoologist and biologist Adolf Portmann; see *Thinking*, 27–30. Arendt draws from Portmann's argument that the form in which an animal appears is not simply a matter of function (i.e., self-preservation) but more importantly a matter of self-representation developed "in relationship to a beholding eye." *Life of the Mind*, 28. She finds crucial resources in Portmann's work for questioning the metaphysical hierarchy that prioritizes being over appearance and for establishing "the urge to self-display" as a common characteristic of all living beings; see *Life of the Mind*, 29. There are also several references to Portmann's work in *Denktagebuch*; see vol. 2, 645, 647, 649, 684, 701. When Arendt taught a seminar on thinking at the New School in 1974, she included in the assigned readings, along with the works of Aristotle, Cicero, Descartes, Hegel, and Heidegger, two books by Portmann—*Animal Camouflage* (1959) and *Animal Forms and Patterns: A Study of the Appearance of Animals* (1967). See Arendt, "'Thinking,' Seminar—1974." In a very illuminating reading of Arendt, Robert W. Major suggests that Arendt's later turn to Portmann indicates a shift in her understanding of the human body—a shift from "a metabolic body whose home is nature," as articulated in *The Human Condition*, to "a lived body whose home is the world of appearances," as proposed in *Thinking*. Major, "Hannah Arendt's 'Unusual' Distinction," 149. My reinterpretation of labor suggests that even *The Human Condition* displays elements of a phenomenological understanding of the human body as an embodied living organism inhabiting, preserving, and changing its earthly environment and the world.

48. Arendt, *The Human Condition*, 120; emphasis mine. This statement is striking given the tendency to treat "labor" as a non-human activity among Arendt's readers; Dana Villa, for example, concludes that "[l]abor does not qualify as a specifically *human* activity." Villa, *Arendt and Heidegger*, 26; emphasis in the original. Similarly, Arendt's critics highlight her "unwillingness to affirm the possibility of a uniquely human form of labor"; see Holman, "Dialectics and Distinction," 339.

49. Arendt, "Labor, Work, Action," 34.

50. Arendt, *The Human Condition*, 107–108; "Labor, Work, Action," 34.

51. Arendt, *The Human Condition*, 108.

52. For world-alienation, see, for example, Curtis, *Our Sense of the Real*, 77–85; Kateb, *Hannah Arendt*, 158–160.

53. Arendt, *The Human Condition*, 2.

54. Arendt, *The Human Condition*, 3. For this point, see also Curtis, *Our Sense of the Real*, 45–46.

55. Arendt, *The Human Condition*, 121.

56. Arendt, *The Human Condition*, 120. This position can also be discerned in Arendt's critique of Marx, especially in her fundamental disagreement with the

idea that revolution will emancipate man from labor; see *The Human Condition*, 104–105. Arendt's interpretation of Marx has important problems, including her perhaps deliberate disregard of the fact that he is talking about the abolition of alienated labor, and not labor as such; for a detailed discussion of these problems, see, among others, Holman, "Dialectics and Distinction," 336–339; Bhikhu Parekh, "Hannah Arendt's Critique of Marx," 84–90; Suchting, "Marx and Hannah Arendt," 50–52. Leaving aside these interpretive problems, it is important to note that Arendt's critique of Marx proceeds from her claim that the elimination of labor would impoverish human life, ridding it of "its very liveliness and vitality"; what would be left as a result would be nothing other than "a lifeless life." Arendt, *The Human Condition*, 120.

57. Arendt, *The Human Condition*, 107; "Labor, Work, Action," 33–34.

58. Ricoeur, "Action, Story and History," 62; emphasis in the original.

59. For example, George Kateb argues that "Arendt's talents are best engaged by what is extraordinary, not by the normal." See Kateb, "Political Action," 135.

60. Hannah Arendt, "The Jew as Pariah," 295.

61. Arendt, "We Refugees," 264, 265.

62. Arendt, *The Human Condition*, 106.

63. Arendt, *The Human Condition*, 119. For this point, see also Tsao, "Arendt Against Athens," 117.

64. Arendt, *The Human Condition*, 119–120.

65. Arendt, *The Human Condition*, 120. Tsao also draws attention to this loss, but he does not explain why Arendt considers a life without labor a "vicarious" one. Tsao, "Arendt Against Athens," 117.

66. Arendt, *The Human Condition*, 83n; see also 107n.

67. Arendt, *The Human Condition*, 107n.

68. Batnitzky, *Idolatry and Representation*, 132.

69. Arendt, *The Human Condition*, 107n.

70. Arendt, *The Human Condition*, 100. For further discussion, see, among others, Canovan, *Hannah Arendt*, 124–125.

71. Villa, *Arendt and Heidegger*, 140. See also Seyla Benhabib, who argues that Arendt's "phenomenological essentialism" assigns a fixed place to each activity on the basis of transhistorical distinctions between action, work, and labor. Benhabib, *Reluctant Modernism*, 123–124.

72. Arendt, *The Human Condition*, 73.

73. Markell, "Arendt's Work," 26–27. Mary Dietz makes a similar point when she argues that labor, work, and action should not be treated as "things-in-themselves," as they are "externally bound to and connected by each other." Dietz, *Turning Operations*, 193.

74. Markell, "Arendt's Work," 37n. For the formulation of "distinctions and articulations," see Arendt, *The Human Condition*, 15, 17, 316; for "articulations," see also, 78, 85, 141, 228. Given Arendt's obsession with etymology, it is quite probable that her choice of the word "articulation," which simultaneously captures division into distinct parts and connection by joints, is not accidental. The word "Gliederung," which Arendt used in her German translation of *The Human Condition*, also has this equivocality: The term means division and classification, but it also denotes connection as a word linked to "Glied," which means limb and joint. See Arendt, *Vita activa*, 26, 27, 97, 103, 167, 290, 403.

75. Arendt, "On Violence," 145, 151.

76. The main textual evidence for the hierarchical reading of *vita activa* comes from a passage in which Arendt discusses Pericles's Funeral Oration. Arendt takes the speech as a testament to the Athenian citizens' faith in politics as a potentiality that arises out of acting and speaking together in public. She suggests that this Periclean faith "sufficed to elevate action to the highest rank in the hierarchy of the *vita activa*." *The Human Condition*, 205. As Roy Tsao puts it, this passage "draw[s] attention to beliefs of the Greeks that she cannot herself endorse." Tsao, "Arendt against Athens," 99. Whereas the Funeral Oration indicates that "men can enact *and* save their greatness at the same time," Arendt points out that "acting and speaking men need the help of *homo faber*" to endow their action with immortality. Arendt, *The Human Condition*, 205, 173; see also Tsao, "Arendt against Athens," 110–111.

77. Following his perceptive analysis attending to the distinctions and articulations within *vita activa*, Patchen Markell concludes that "work and not action is the most important concept in *The Human Condition*." See Markell, "Arendt's Work," 18. My reading draws a somewhat different conclusion, as it suggests that it is impossible to have a hierarchical ranking of these concepts precisely because each captures an activity that makes a distinctive, irreplaceable contribution to living a life that can be recognized as human.

78. Arendt, *The Human Condition*, 320.

79. Arendt, *The Human Condition*, 321.

80. Arendt, *The Human Condition*, 322.

81. See Agamben, *Homo Sacer*, 166–180. Several critics highlighted the problems in Agamben's account of camps, including his overgeneralization from Nazi extermination camps. See, for example, Agier, *Managing the Undesirables*, 183–184.

82. Arendt, *The Origins of Totalitarianism*, 445; see also 440.

83. Arendt, *The Origins of Totalitarianism*, 445.

84. Arendt, *The Origins of Totalitarianism*, 284. It is impossible to understand why and how camps became the solution to the refugee problem without attending to "[t]he coupling of state sovereignty and nationalism with border control" in the interstate system shaped by World War I. Sassen, *Guests and Aliens*, 78.

85. See, among others, Nyers, *Rethinking Refugees*; Soguk, *States and Strangers*.

86. Verdirame and Harrell-Bond, *Rights in Exile*, 288. Repatriation was initially adopted as a matter of political expediency in response to the Indochinese refugee crisis in the 1980s; within time, however, it has become an organizing principle of the international refugee protection regime, with the effect of creating protracted encampment as a pervasive problem. Adelman and Barkan, *No Return, No Refuge*, 18–19.

87. United Nations High Commissioner for Refugees (UNHCR), "Protracted Refugee Situations," 1.

88. Milner and Loescher, "Responding to Protracted Refugee Situations," 3.

89. In 2003, approximately 73 percent (4.5 million) of refugees in protracted situations were dependent on the UNHCR aid. See UNHCR, "Protracted Refugee Situations," 2.

90. See, for example, Verdirame and Harrell-Bond, *Rights in Exile*, chaps. 4 and 5; Smith, "Warehousing Refugees."

91. Stevens, "Prisons of the Stateless," 66; see also Wilde, "*Quis Custodiet Ipsos Custodes*?"

92. Most of the discussion in this chapter centers on refugee camps, though in the last section on Arendt's understanding of action and speech, I also discuss immigration detention, especially the problem of solitary confinement. Generally speaking, refugee camps can be characterized as spaces of bureaucratic administration and disciplinary control, and my goal is to understand how these spaces shape and constrain fundamental human activities such as labor, work, and action. One striking exception to this model of camp as a space of humanitarian governance is the collection of Sahrawi refugee camps located in Tindouf, Algeria. These camps have not been established by the UNHCR, and the Algerian government gave the refugees extensive autonomy in this territory; as a result, there is a unique situation of refugee settlement that allows a considerable degree of self-government and relatively stable forms of living. For a detailed account with photographs, see Herz, *From Camp to City*.

93. See, for example, Hyndman, *Managing Displacement*, 127.

94. Arendt, *The Human Condition*, 106.

95. According to the UNHCR standards, the minimum food ration for one person in a refugee camp consists of 2,100 calories; the ration includes 400 grams of rice, wheat or maize, 60 grams of beans, peas or lentils, 25 grams of oil, 100 grams of fortified blended food, 15 grams of sugar, and 5 grams of salt. Canadian Broadcasting Company, "Anatomy of a Refugee Camp," accessed June 26, 2014, http://www.cbc.ca/news2/background/refugeecamp/refugees/refugee.html.

96. UNHCR, *Handbook for Registration*, 140.

97. Verdirame and Harrell-Bond, *Rights in Exile*, 140.

98. UNHCR, *Registration*; see in particular sections 2.6, 2.8, 6.2, 6.3, 7.4, 8.1, 11.6.

99. Butler, *Precarious Life*, 98; Arendt, *The Human Condition*, 118. Understood in these terms, long-term encampment involves an "existential" harm, as it makes it very difficult for a refugee to be recognized as "a unique individual who is irreplaceable and not exchangeable for another" and not to be treated simply as "one more human being in a species." Kateb, *Human Dignity*, 10. See also Zygmunt Bauman's provocative analysis that highlights how refugees are stripped of their "differences, individualities, idiosyncrasies," reduced to a "faceless mass," and turned into "human waste" to be dumped in camps; *Liquid Times*, 40–41.

100. Verdirame and Harrell-Bond, *Rights in Exile*, 216–218; Agier, *Managing the Undesirables*, 138.

101. Quoted in Abdi, "In Limbo," 9.

102. Arendt, "We Refugees," 268–269.

103. Russell and Stage, "Leisure as Burden," 114. For the overwhelming sense of boredom in camps, see also Bousquet, "Living in a State of Limbo," 35, 40; Chan and Loveridge, "Refugees 'in Transit,'" 746.

104. Russell and Stage, "Leisure as Burden," 114.

105. Russell and Stage, "Leisure as Burden," 118.

106. Sultan and O'Sullivan, "Psychological Disturbances in Asylum-Seekers," 593. Although Sultan and O'Sullivan use this phrase to capture the experience in long-term detention, it adequately represents the situation in many refugee camps that hinder the normalization of life.

107. Agier, *Managing the Undesirables*, 72, 137.

108. Arendt, "We Refugees," 266–267. Suicide is the most extreme incident related to life-alienation in camps; other possible manifestations of this problem

244   NOTES TO PAGES 144–147

are restlessness, irritability, daydreaming, and absentmindedness. See Feyissa, "More Than One Way." Feyissa's first-hand account, based on her experience as an Ethiopian refugee living in camps for more than 15 years, highlights that day-dreaming and absentmindedness can be seen as symptoms of life-alienation: "Initially, this problem [absentmindedness] was a source of amusement. . . . However, it is of some concern to hear that some refugees do not remember which day it is, which month, or even which year it is. Some seem more affected by absentmindedness than they realize, talking to themselves and gesturing emotionally. Others are sleepwalkers. Many refugees absentmindedly leave their home at night and disappear." Feyissa, "More Than One Way," 18.

109. Quoted in Abdi, "In Limbo," 9.

110. Arendt, *The Human Condition*, 115.

111. Arendt, *The Human Condition*, 108. Arendt uses these terms to describe the experience of laboring under conditions of poverty.

112. Agier, *Managing the Undesirables*, 152. These initiatives challenge the well-established idea that refugees in camps suffer from a "dependency mentality," characterized by a lack of willingness to work to achieve self-sufficiency. As Gaim Kibreab highlights, refugees show this willingness whenever they find opportunities in favorable environments; dependence on humanitarian aid is instead a systematic condition created by the constraints in camp life. See Kibreab, "The Myth of Dependency." Especially important in this regard are factors such as the isolation of camps, host countries' restrictions on the movement and employment of refugees, political disempowerment, and humanitarian policies that make aid dependent on residence in camps. See Werker, "Refugee Camp Economies."

113. Dudley, "Feeling at Home," 751.

114. Verdirame and Harrell-Bond, *Rights in Exile*, 233.

115. Arendt, "We Refugees," 269. As this statement highlights, Arendt adopts a deeply ironic style in this essay; for a close analysis attending to the stylistic elements of "We Refugees," see Stonebridge, "Refugee Style."

116. Arendt, *The Human Condition*, 136. For the complexities in this deceptively simple formula, see Major, "Hannah Arendt's 'Unusual' Distinction," 143–147.

117. Arendt, *The Human Condition*, 137.

118. Arendt, *The Human Condition*, 139.

119. Arendt, *The Human Condition*, 140–141.

120. Arendt, *The Human Condition*, 157.

121. Arendt, *The Human Condition*, 173.

122. Scarry, *The Body in Pain*, 144.

123. Scarry, *The Body in Pain*, 291.

124. Arendt, *The Human Condition*, 173.

125. Arendt, *The Human Condition*, 152.

126. Markell, "Arendt's Work," 35.

127. Mihaly Csikszentmihalyi, "Why We Need Things," 23. Iris Marion Young makes a similar point in her reflections on "home" as a dwelling place inhabited by everyday artifacts that "carry sedimented personal meaning as retainers of personal narrative;" these artifacts provide human beings with physical anchors and establish "a continuity between past and present." See Young, "House and Home," 139–140.

128. Markell, "Arendt's Work," 31. For the web of relationships that artifacts establish, see also Csikszentmihalyi, "Why We Need Things," 27–28.

129. Arendt, *The Human Condition*, 173.

130. Arendt, *The Origins of Totalitarianism*, 293.

131. Arendt, *The Origins of Totalitarianism*, 300.

132. For an example of this reading, see Klausen, "Hannah Arendt's Primitivism." For my critique of this reading, see Gündoğdu, "Arendt on Culture and Imperialism."

133. Arendt, *The Human Condition*, 10.

134. Arendt, *The Origins of Totalitarianism*, 300–301.

135. For the crucial importance Arendt attaches to givenness, see in particular Birmingham, *Hannah Arendt*, chap. 3.

136. Arendt, *The Origins of Totalitarianism*, 302. See also Arendt's following remark about the stateless Jews: "[T]hey create the uncanny impression, in their complete dependence upon the compassion of others, in their naked mere-humanity, of something utterly inhuman." Arendt, "Guests from No-Man's-Land," 212.

137. Agier, *Managing the Undesirables*, 79. Drawing on Agier's work, Zygmunt Bauman provides an illuminating description of refugee camps as "artifices of temporary installation made permanent." See Bauman, *Liquid Times*, 45.

138. Agier, *Managing the Undesirables*, 151; Verdirame and Harrell-Bond, *Rights in Exile*, 238–239.

139. UNHCR, *Handbook for Emergencies*, 221.

140. See the photographs available on the website of "Recyclable Refugee Camp," accessed January 9, 2014, http://www.ivesmaes.com/r-r-c/Ives%20 Maes%20Recyclable%20Refugee%20Camp.swf.

141. Maes, *Recyclable Refugee Camp*, 103–104. Maes points out that the material is actually not biodegradable (112). His emphasis on recyclability is also linked to his effort to take issue with the contemporary obsession with socially responsible art.

142. Scarry, *The Body in Pain*, 291; emphasis in the original.

143. Scarry, *The Body in Pain*, 291.

144. Even in those rare instances when camps are built in ways that take into account the needs of refugees, living a life in limbo can hinder such transformation. Camps for Syrian refugees in Kilis, Turkey, highlight this problem. These container camps, with their playgrounds, grocery stores, power lines, and hot-water tanks strike observers as luxurious compared to many makeshift camps. But the refugees in these camps, despite their expressions of gratitude, protest the uncertainty, boredom, and unhappiness characteristic of camp life: "We hoped it was one month or two months. . . . We wake up, we sleep, we wake up, we sleep, we eat food, we always watch TV to see what's going on. We're all very bored. There is no purpose in a life like this. One day is like another." Quoted in Mac McClelland, "Container City," *The New York Times Magazine*, February 16, 2014.

145. Agier, *Managing the Undesirables*, 155–157, 186, 189.

146. Agier, *Managing the Undesirables*, 238n.

147. Verdirame and Harrell-Bond, *Rights in Exile*, 18.

148. Verdirame and Harrell-Bond, *Rights in Exile*, 240. The fact that the refugees in Ogujebe could be uprooted by force highlights that the camps they live in were not considered to be relatively stable dwelling places belonging to them. Encampment as well as uprooting of these refugees are signs of their dispossession from "property," to use the term in Arendt's sense: "Originally, property meant no more or less than to have one's location in a particular part of the world and therefore to belong to the body politic." Arendt, *The Human Condition*, 61. Arendt

distinguishes "property" from "wealth" and highlights the crucial importance of having "property" for being able to enjoy public and private life. The condition of uprooted refugees highlights that deprivation from "property" is accompanied by the loss of a part in public life as well as the loss of a private place of one's own.

149. Arendt, *Willing*, 217; see also *The Human Condition*, 177; "Introduction *into* Politics," 113.

150. Arendt, *The Human Condition*, 23, 188.

151. Arendt, *The Human Condition*, 26; see also 178–179. As Jerome Kohn puts it, for Arendt, action always "signifies deed and speech, either a deed and its account, a deed accounted for, or speech-as-deed." Kohn, "Freedom," 124.

152. Arendt, *The Human Condition*, 206.

153. See, for example, Villa, "Beyond Good and Evil."

154. See especially Kateb, *Hannah Arendt*, 16–22; Pitkin, "Justice."

155. Arendt, *The Human Condition*, 179.

156. Arendt, *The Human Condition*, 182.

157. Arendt, *The Human Condition*, 184.

158. Arendt, *The Origins of Totalitarianism*, 296–297.

159. Arendt, *The Origins of Totalitarianism*, 296.

160. Arendt, *The Human Condition*, 23.

161. Arendt, "What is Freedom?," 167; see also *Willing*, 199.

162. Arendt, "What is Freedom?," 149.

163. Arendt, "What is Freedom?," 169.

164. Arendt, "Introduction *into* Politics," 119.

165. See Beiner, "Arendt and Nationalism," 55; Canovan, "Lasting Institutions," 148.

166. Arendt, *The Origins of Totalitarianism*, 297.

167. Arendt, *The Human Condition*, 198.

168. For a discussion of "portable" polis, see Ring, "The Pariah as Hero"; Krause, "Undocumented Migrants," 342–343; see also Euben, *Platonic Noise*, 114.

169. Arendt, *The Origins of Totalitarianism*, 438.

170. This statement by a detained asylum seeker is quoted in Margaret Talbot, "The Lost Children: What Do Tougher Detention Policies Mean for Illegal Immigrant Families?" *New Yorker*, March 3, 2008.

171. Sultan and O'Sullivan, "Psychological Disturbances," 594. For the use of solitary detention in the US immigration system, see Ian Urbina and Catherine Rentz, "Immigrants Held in Solitary Cells, Often for Weeks," *The New York Times*, March 23, 2013.

172. See, for example, PICUM, "PICUM's Main Concerns," 36–37.

173. Arendt, *The Origins of Totalitarianism*, 451.

174. Arendt, *The Origins of Totalitarianism*, 452. Arendt's account of camps highlights the crucial importance of "the freedom to express one's sense of aliveness as a distinct being," as Anna Yeatman argues; one crucial dimension of this freedom consists in the memorialization of death, and contemporary practices of immigration detention risk obliterating freedom understood in this sense, as I argue below. See Yeatman, "Individuality and Politics," 80.

175. Arendt, *The Origins of Totalitarianism*, 452. In this work, Arendt refers to these spaces as "holes of oblivion," where people can be treated "as if they had never existed" and made to "disappear in the literal sense of the word." Arendt, *The Origins of Totalitarianism*, 434, 442. But as she notes later in *Eichmann in Jerusalem*, it is

after all humanly impossible to obliterate all the traces of those confined in these spaces: "The holes of oblivion do not exist. Nothing human is that perfect, and there are simply too many people in the world to make oblivion possible. One man will always be left alive to tell the story." Arendt, *Eichmann in Jerusalem*, 232–233. Even in the case of immigration detainees who die in solitary confinement, there is often (though not always) the possibility of reconstructing their stories with various forms of testimony, as illustrated by the several newspaper accounts and human rights reports that have appeared in the recent years. See, for example, Nina Bernstein, "Immigrant Detainee Dies, and a Life Is Buried, Too," *The New York Times*, April 2, 2009.

176. Athwal and Bourne, "Driven to Despair," 107.

177. Nina Bernstein, "Officials Say Detainee Fatalities Were Missed," *The New York Times*, August 17, 2009.

178. Nina Bernstein, "Few Details on Immigrants Who Died in Custody," *The New York Times*, May 5, 2008.

179. Arendt, *The Human Condition*, 198.

180. Arendt, *The Human Condition*, 184, 182.

181. Agier, *Managing the Undesirables*, 151, 152.

182. Arendt, *The Human Condition*, 7; emphasis in the original.

183. Arendt, *The Human Condition*, 175, 176.

184. Arendt, "Socrates," 16–17.

185. Arendt, "Socrates," 17.

186. Arendt, "Introduction *into* Politics," 118.

187. Arendt, "Introduction *into* Politics," 118. For *isēgoria*, see especially Wood, "Demos," 121–124.

188. Arendt, *The Origins of Totalitarianism*, 297.

189. Arendt, *The Origins of Totalitarianism*, 297.

190. Arendt, *The Human Condition*, 27.

191. Arendt, *The Human Condition*, 27.

192. Arendt, *The Human Condition*, 27; see also "Introduction *into* Politics," 118.

193. Rancière, *Disagreement*, 22–23; emphasis in the original. For an analysis, see also Nyers, *Rethinking Refugees*, 38, 75–77.

194. Balibar, "(De)constructing the Human," 733.

195. Malkki, "Speechless Emissaries," 387.

196. Arendt, *The Origins of Totalitarianism*, 297, 299; Malkki, "Speechless Emissaries," 388.

197. Malkki, "Speechless Emissaries," 393.

198. Belinda Goldsmith, "Asylum Seekers Sew Lips Together," *The Guardian*, January 18, 2002.

199. Becky Gaylord, "Afghans Write of Hunger Strike at Australian Detention Camp," *The New York Times*, January 22, 2002.

200. Edkins and Pin-Fat, "Through the Wire," 24. For a similar analysis, see Pugliese, "Penal Asylum." For a critical analysis that highlights the problems of approaching lip-sewing as a creative form of political agency, see Owens, "Re-claiming 'Bare Life?'"

201. Fassin, "Compassion and Repression," 372; see also Fassin, "Policing Borders," 221.

202. Gaylord, "Afghans Write of Hunger Strike."

203. Patrick Barkham, "No Waltzing in Woomera," *The Guardian*, May 24, 2002.

204. This formulation draws on a distinction introduced by Nicholas Xenos: "Homelands are places that are unchanging and to which one must return, no matter how hostile they may be to the returnee. Homes can be made and remade, if there is space for them." Xenos, "Refugees," 427.

205. Arendt, *The Origins of Totalitarianism*, 297.

206. Arendt, *The Origins of Totalitarianism*, 297.

207. Although the slaves were considered "socially dead," Patterson argues, they "remained nonetheless an element of society" and their "liminal incorporation" set them apart from not only enfranchised citizens but also aliens. Patterson, *Slavery and Social Death*, 45–46.

Chapter 5

1. Michelman, "Parsing 'a Right to Have Rights,'" 201.

2. Arendt, *The Origins of Totalitarianism*, 296–297.

3. Arendt, "'Rights of Man,'" 37; *The Origins of Totalitarianism*, 298.

4. Arendt, "'Rights of Man,'" 30; see also *The Origins of Totalitarianism*, 297.

5. Arendt, "'Rights of Man,'" 37.

6. Benhabib, *Reluctant Modernism*, 82; see also 193–196.

7. Birmingham, *Hannah Arendt*, 3. See also Serena Parekh, *Hannah Arendt*, chaps. 5–6.

8. As examples of this focus on the question of foundations, see, among others, Griffin, *On Human Rights*; Nickel, *Making Sense of Human Rights*.

9. Markell, "Review."

10. Arendt, *Willing*, 207.

11. Sofia Näsström makes a similar move in her discussion of "the right to have rights" and engages with Arendt's Montesquieuan understanding of "principle." See Näsström, "Right to Have Rights." Departing from Näsström, who contends that the principle animating this right is "responsibility," I make a case for "equaliberty" by taking into account Arendt's discussion of statelessness, her reflections on *isonomia*, and Balibar's argument about the Rights of Man.

12. Arendt, *The Origins of Totalitarianism*, 298; emphasis added.

13. For Arendt's emphasis on the need for a "new guarantee" for human dignity, see also *The Origins of Totalitarianism*, ix.

14. On the heuristic function of regulative ideas in Kant, see, among others, Guyer, *Kant*, 169.

15. Arendt, *The Origins of Totalitarianism*, 298. Elisabeth Young-Bruehl notes that Arendt follows Heinrich Blücher's declaration for a "League for the Rights of Peoples" in proposing that the right to have rights is to be guaranteed by humanity itself. Young-Bruehl, *Hannah Arendt*, 257; see also 248.

16. Arendt, "Karl Jaspers," 82.

17. Arendt, "Karl Jaspers," 83.

18. Arendt, "Karl Jaspers," 83. Arendt's emphasis on the importance of political responsibility and positive solidarity can also be seen in her essay on Lessing, which affirms the Roman understanding of *humanitas* as "a readiness to share the world with other men." Arendt, "On Humanity in Dark Times," 25.

19. Arendt, "Karl Jaspers," 83.

20. Michelman, "Parsing 'a Right to Have Rights,'" 207. My effort to rethink human rights beyond the question of foundations also draws on Étienne Balibar's

proposal to read Arendt in terms of "the idea of a *foundationless* [*grundlose*] politics of rights." See Balibar, "On the Politics of Human Rights," 18.

21. Michelman, "Parsing 'a Right to Have Rights,'" 202.

22. For an approach adopting this interpretation, see Benhabib, *The Rights of Others*, 56–58.

23. Michelman, "Parsing 'a Right to Have Rights,'" 204. Balibar makes a similar proposal when he suggests that a right to have rights should not be understood as "the equivalent of a *Grundnorm* from which all the concrete rights could be deduced or justified." Arendt's proposition, he argues, denotes instead the need to address the question of how to realize human rights as "an immanent practical problem." See Balibar, "On the Politics of Human Rights," 21.

24. Arendt, *On Revolution*, 206.

25. Arendt, *The Burden of Our Time*, 439; emphasis added.

26. Werner Hamacher moves in this direction when he suggests that "the right to have rights" is to be understood as "a *privi-legium* in the strictest sense, a prelegal premise, a protoright." See Hamacher, "Right to Have Rights," 353.

27. Arendt, *On Revolution*, 204–205.

28. Butler and Spivak, *Who Sings the Nation-State?*, 48. For a performative perspective on rights, drawing on Arendt and Butler, among others, see Zivi, *Making Rights Claims*.

29. Arendt, "What is Freedom?," 151.

30. For the distinction, see Hunt, *Inventing Human Rights*, 114–115.

31. Quoted in Baker, "Idea of a Declaration," 158; see also Gauchet, "Rights of Man."

32. See Forst, "Justification of Human Rights," 87.

33. Lefort, "Human Rights and Welfare State," 38.

34. Declaration is a political genre that inextricably interweaves rational argumentation and poetic world-disclosure. For the distinction between these two functions of language, see Habermas, *Philosophical Discourse of Modernity*, 199–210. For the impossibility of maintaining this distinction in demonstrations of equality (and we can include rights declarations and new rights claims among these demonstrations), see Rancière, *Disagreement*, 55–56.

35. Lefort, "Human Rights and Welfare State," 37; see also Lefort, "Politics and Human Rights," 257. For a discussion of Lefort's argument, see, for example, Cohen, *Globalization and Sovereignty*, 170–171.

36. For a reading that locates a disagreement between Arendt's and Lefort's views on this score, see Birmingham, *Hannah Arendt*, 11–12.

37. Arendt, *On Revolution*, 205.

38. Balibar, "What is a Politics of the Rights of Man?," 224. For Balibar's proposal to read Arendt's notion of a right to have rights for the purposes of understanding this "insurrectional" dimension of human rights, see "On the Politics of Human Rights," 22; *We, the People of Europe?*, 119.

39. Arendt, *Willing*, 198.

40. Arendt, *On Revolution*, 42.

41. Arendt, *On Revolution*, 28. For readings that contest this view and present Arendt as a theorist of relatively new beginnings, see Kalyvas, *Democracy and the Politics of the Extraordinary*, 223–224; Frank, *Constituent Moments*, 51.

42. Arendt, *On Revolution*, 210.

43. Arendt, *Willing*, 216.

44. Arendt, *Willing*, 212; see also *On Revolution*, 212.

45. Arendt, *On Revolution*, 212; *Willing*, 207.

46. Arendt, *On Revolution*, 183–184.

47. Arendt, *On Revolution*, 117; see also 39, 159–160; "What is Authority?," 135, 140. For a discussion of Arendt's reflections on this modern problem, see Moyn, "Hannah Arendt on the Secular."

48. Arendt, *On Revolution*, 161.

49. Arendt, *On Revolution*, 161; see also 182, 189.

50. Arendt, *On Revolution*, 206.

51. Arendt, *On Revolution*, 163, 184.

52. Arendt, *On Revolution*, 185. Jason Frank argues that Arendt overlooks "the dilemmas of collective self-authorization that pervade constituent moments" in her account of the American Revolution. Frank, *Constituent Moments*, 51. Yet Arendt's discussion of the American revolutionaries' appeals to absolutes highlights her attentiveness to some of these pressing dilemmas in the American context as well. For this point, see also Wilkinson, "Between Freedom and Law," 47–48.

53. Lyotard, *The Differend*, 142; see also 146.

54. Derrida, "Declarations of Independence," 9–10. For a comparison of Arendt and Derrida on this score, see Honig, "Declarations of Independence."

55. Derrida, "Force of Law," 14; see also Cornell, "Time, Deconstruction," 281.

56. Lyotard, *The Differend*, 142.

57. For an analysis of the differences between Arendt, Derrida, and Lyotard on this score, see Benhabib, "Democracy and Difference."

58. Arendt, *On Revolution*, 189, 188; "On Violence," 138.

59. Arendt, *On Revolution*, 189.

60. Arendt, *On Revolution*, 187; "Introduction *into* Politics," 179. For the Roman elements in Arendt's understanding of law, see, among others, Breen, "Law Beyond Command?," 21–24; Taminiaux, "Athens and Rome," 176–177; Tsao, "Arendt against Athens," 109.

61. Arendt, *On Revolution*, 188.

62. Arendt, *On Revolution*, 189, 188; see also "On Violence," 139–140.

63. Arendt, *On Revolution*, 193; emphasis in the original. On the paradox of declaring rights to be self-evident, see also Hunt, *Inventing Human Rights*, 19–20.

64. Douzinas, *The End of Human Rights*, 95.

65. Arendt, *On Revolution*, 192. For Arendt, "truth by its very nature is self-evident and therefore cannot be satisfactorily argued out and demonstrated." See "What is Authority?," 132.

66. Arendt, *On Revolution*, 193.

67. For a discussion of how Arendt's understanding of authority calls for the resistibility of laws, see Honig, "Declarations of Independence," 108–110.

68. As Arendt puts it, "men are equipped for the logically paradoxical task of making a new beginning because they themselves are new beginnings and hence beginners." Arendt, *On Revolution*, 211; see also *Willing*, 216–217.

69. Arendt, *On Revolution*, 212.

70. These conventional meanings have significantly shaped the interpretations of Arendt on this score. For example, her notion of principle comes too close to "a

rule of conduct" in George Kateb's argument that she has in mind a "depersonalized" mode of action "dominated by the effort to live up to the objective requirements of a single loyalty." See Kateb, *Hannah Arendt*, 12, 13. A similar conception of principle can be found in Lawrence J. Biskowski's suggestion that, for Arendt, "[o]ne's actions originate in the self and exemplify or manifest or embody one's principles." Biskowski, "Practical Foundations," 880. In Habermasian readings, Arendtian "principles" start resembling foundational propositions of a system; see, for example, David Ingram's characterization of these principles as "general presuppositions *of* reasoning" that are intrinsic to "dialogic deliberation." David Ingram, "Novus Ordo Seclorum," 237. For a critical analysis of the scholarship on Arendt's understanding of "principle," see Cane, "Principles of Political Action."

71. Montesquieu, *The Spirit of the Laws*, 21, 43.

72. Montesquieu, *The Spirit of the Laws*, 36, 44, 47.

73. Arendt, "Introduction *into* Politics," 195.

74. Arendt, "Montesquieu's Revision," 65. Arendt also follows Montesquieu when she singles out the principle of fear as "an antipolitical principle within the common world" and declares that "fear, properly speaking, is not a principle of action" (68). Unlike any other principle, fear undermines the possibility of constituting a common world, as it isolates human beings from each other and destroys human plurality (69). This point draws on Montesquieu, who argues that the principle of fear is "corrupt by its nature" and that despotism is likely to be destroyed because of this "internal vice" and can only be maintained by accidental circumstances such as climate. *The Spirit of the Laws*, 119.

75. Andreas Kalyvas arrives at a different conclusion in his reading that draws on Habermas to address the ambiguities in Arendt's notion of "principle." See, for example, his description of "the main task" of "general, clear, and stable principles" as "to counteract the intrinsic dangers of freedom and extraordinary deeds" or "to channel and *regulate* freedom." *Democracy and the Politics of the Extraordinary*, 242; emphasis added. This interpretation puts the emphasis on containing the risks of freedom (i.e., spontaneity, contingency, arbitrariness) and differs from Arendt's Montesquieuan understanding of the term.

76. Arendt, "What is Freedom?," 152.

77. Arendt, "What is Freedom?" 152; see also "Introduction *into* Politics," 193–194.

78. Similar to the reading offered here, Peg Birmingham also emphasizes the Montesquieuan and Augustinian elements in Arendt's notion of principle. Nonetheless, Birmingham's insightful interpretation leads to the conclusion that we can derive from Arendt's notion of natality "[t]he ontological foundation of the political" as well as the normative ground of human rights. See Birmingham, *Hannah Arendt and Human Rights*, 15; see also 12. My reading takes issue with the quest for foundations and instead examines the *political* principle that becomes manifest with modern revolutionary beginnings and that continues to animate new rights claims.

79. Arendt, "What is Freedom?," 153.

80. For the problems of the false choice between foundationalism and antifoundationalism, see Judith Butler, "Contingent Foundations," 39; Zerilli, *Feminism and the Abyss of Freedom*, 131.

81. Arendt, "Montesquieu's Revision of the Tradition," 65; see also Arendt, *Willing*, 201.

82. Arendt, *Lectures on Kant's Political Philosophy*, 83, 76. The literature on Arendt's Kantian understanding of "reflective judgment" is extensive; see, among others, Beiner, "Hannah Arendt on Judging"; Benhabib, "Judgment and the Moral Foundations"; Garsten, "Elusiveness of Arendtian Judgment"; Hayden, "Political Power of Judgement"; Passerin d'Entrèves, *Political Philosophy of Hannah Arendt*, chap. 3; Weidenfeld, "Visions of Judgment"; Wellmer, "Hannah Arendt on Judgment"; Zerilli, *Feminism and the Abyss of Freedom*, chap. 4.

83. Arendt, *Lectures on Kant's Political Philosophy*, 77.

84. Arendt, *Lectures on Kant's Political Philosophy*, 72.

85. Arendt, *Lectures on Kant's Political Philosophy*, 65. For "imagination," see also Zerilli, *Feminism and the Abyss of Freedom*, 144; Urbinati, *Representative Democracy*, 121–122.

86. Arendt, *Lectures on Kant's Political Philosophy*, 72.

87. Ferrara, "Two Notions of Humanity," 400–401; see also Ferrara, *The Force of the Example*, 77–78.

88. Arendt, *On Revolution*, 214.

89. Arendt, *On Revolution*, 201–202; see also Honig, *Political Theory*, 113–115.

90. See Jason Frank, *Constituent Moments*, 63, though Frank also locates a more promising understanding of democratic politics in Arendt's "Civil Disobedience." For a critique that suggests that Arendt overlooks "the potential for conflict and violence" in her account of political founding, see Keenan, "Promises, Promises," 318; see also Breen, "Violence and Power," 361–363.

91. Arendt, "Civil Disobedience," 53.

92. Arendt, "Civil Disobedience," 94.

93. Arendt, "Civil Disobedience," 83; emphasis in the original.

94. Arendt, "Civil Disobedience," 87–88. For Arendt's argument that consent cannot be understood as an unquestioning obedience of laws, see also "On Violence," 140.

95. Arendt, "Civil Disobedience," 90.

96. Balibar, "(De)constructing the Human," 731.

97. Arendt, "On Violence," 139–140. For Arendt's reflections on *isonomia*, see chapter 4.

98. Balibar, *Equaliberty*, 48–49; "Rights of Man," 48–49; "On the Politics of Human Rights," 23; "What is a Politics of the Rights of Man?," 212.

99. Balibar, "What is a Politics of the Rights of Man?," 212–213. See also Balibar, *Equaliberty*, 129; "New Reflections on Equaliberty," 312; *We, the People of Europe?*, 58–59.

100. Balibar, *Equaliberty*, 50; "Rights of Man," 49–50.

101. Arendt, *On Revolution*, 205. Different versions of this teleological history can be seen, for example, in Lauren, *Evolution of International Human Rights*; Ishay, *History of Human Rights*.

102. Lefort, "Human Rights and the Welfare State," 38.

103. Peg Birmingham criticizes Lefort for failing to recognize the validity of human rights beyond the specific contexts in which they were declared. See Birmingham, *Hannah Arendt and Human Rights*, 11. But as I highlight in this discussion, Lefort underscores how the principle introduced by the eighteenth-century declarations sets into motion political practices of demanding and reformulating human rights beyond that original context.

104. Dubois, *"La République Métissée,"* 22.

105. *Another Cosmopolitanism*, 47; see also *The Rights of Others*, 179. Benhabib's use of the term differs from that of Derrida in important ways; for these differences, see Honig, "Another Cosmopolitanism?," 125; Thomassen, "Politics of Iterability," 129–131.

106. Benhabib, *The Rights of Others*, 197.

107. Benhabib, *Another Cosmopolitanism*, 49; emphasis in the original.

108. See, for example, Benhabib, "Is There a Human Right to Democracy?," 197–199; "Reason-Giving and Rights-Bearing," 40–41.

109. Scott, *Only Paradoxes to Offer*, 36, 34.

110. Rancière, "Who Is the Subject?," 304. Though I draw on Rancière's eloquent articulation of this paradox, I am also using it in a way counter to his purpose in his critique of Arendt, as I highlighted in chapter 1. See also Judith Butler's analysis of such "performative contradictions" in *Excitable Speech*, 89–90.

111. See, for example, Krause, "Undocumented Migrants"; McNevin, *Contesting Citizenship*; Schaap, "Enacting the Right." My earlier treatment of this movement is very close to the account provided by these scholars; see Gündoğdu, "Potentialities of Human Rights."

112. Ngai, *Impossible Subjects*, 5, 4; see also 56, 75.

113. Miriam Ticktin notes that the *sans-papiers* movement has been "rendered redundant" despite its continuing protests; see *Casualties of Care*, 41. Ticktin's account, highlighting how *sans-papiers* demonstrations have lost their disruptive effects over the years and become "a tourist curiosity" (58), cautions against taking this movement as a success story. Nevertheless, given the ongoing struggles of the undocumented immigrants across the world, the movement achieves a new political relevance, as its story has been appropriated in different contexts and can shed light on the unique challenges of making rights claims when one has an irregular status.

114. Nicholls, "Cities and the Unevenness," 1663–1664.

115. See, for example, the mobilizations of *sin papeles* demanding *"papeles para todos"* (papers for everyone) in Spain; Varela, "Residency Documents for All!" For comparative analyses of undocumented migrants' mobilizations, see, among others, Chimienti, "Mobilization of Irregular Migrants"; Chimienti and Solomos, "Social Movements of Irregular Migrants"; Varela Huerta, "Migrant Struggles."

116. McNevin, "Political Belonging," 142–143. See also Christian E. O'Connell, "Plight of France's Sans-Papiers Gives a Face to Struggle over Immigration Reform," *Human Rights Brief* 4, no. 1 (Fall 1996), accessed March 18, 2013, http://www.wcl.american.edu/hrbrief/v4i1/pasqua41.htm.

117. For firsthand accounts of the occupation and eviction, see Cissé, *Parole de Sans-Papiers*, 113–116; Diop, *Dans La Peau d'un Sans-Papiers*, 169–173.

118. See, for example, Jacques Derrida's speech delivered at a public demonstration on December 21, 1996. Derrida, "Derelictions," 137.

119. For the public reaction against Debré Laws, see, among others, *Immigration and Insecurity*, 73–74; Rosello, *Postcolonial Hospitality*, 40–41; "The Sans Papiers Movement: A Climax in the History of French Immigration," *No Border Network*, accessed August 15, 2011, http://www.noborder.org/without/france.html.

120. For the convergence of French "left" and "right" governments on immigration, see Balibar, *We, the People of Europe?*, 34.

121. "In Paris, Undocumented Workers Intensify Their Protests," *France 24*, October 8, 2013, accessed December 24, 2013, http://www.france24.com/en/20131008-paris-african-undocumented-workers-intensify-protests-valls/. The French government's demand confirms Matthew Gibney's observation that undocumented migrants often find themselves in a "rights trap," as they "must bring themselves to the attention of state authorities" to be able to claim rights. See Gibney, "Precarious Residents," 31.

122. See Article 35 of the International Convention on the Protection of the Rights of All Migrant Workers and Members of their Families, accessed March 18, 2013, http://www.unhcr.org/refworld/pdfid/3ae6b3980.pdf.

123. For the distinctions between regular and irregular migrants in international human rights law, see Bosniak, "Human Rights, State Sovereignty"; Dauvergne, *Making People Illegal*, 21–28; Kesby, *Right to Have Rights*, 108–110; Noll, "Why Human Rights Fail." Even scholars who argue that the human rights framework, relying on the principle of non-discrimination, does not exclude irregular migrants, note these distinctions. See, for example, Grant, "Rights of Migrants," 38; Weissbrodt, *Human Rights of Non-Citizens*, 185–186.

124. Arendt, *On Revolution*, 184.

125. Kesby, *Right to Have Rights*, 110–111. For a historical overview of these divisions within humanity, see Douzinas, "Paradoxes of Human Rights," 52–55.

126. Benhabib, *Situating the Self*, 32.

127. Arendt, *The Origins of Totalitarianism*, 297.

128. Rancière, *Disagreement*, 23.

129. Zerilli, *Feminism and the Abyss of Freedom*, 144.

130. Coutin, "Illegality, Borderlands," 173; see also Coutin, *Legalizing Moves*, 40. Saskia Sassen argues that undocumented immigrants are "unauthorized yet recognized subjects," highlighting how their social practices can "earn them citizenship claims." Sassen, "Repositioning of Citizenship," 12. But such recognition becomes difficult to attain due to immobility and invisibility imposed by the ever-present threat of detention and deportation.

131. Coutin, "Illegality, Borderlands," 174; see also De Genova, "Migrant 'Illegality' and Deportability"; Nyers, "No One is Illegal," 132–133. As the *sans-papiers* example underscores, undocumented immigrants are not passive victims who meekly conform to the demands of invisibility and immobility. Even short of collective political mobilization, they develop inventive techniques, including strategies of concealment, to handle various difficult situations related to their condition of "illegality." For an illuminating analysis of these techniques, see Apostolidis, *Breaks in the Chain*, chap. 3.

132. Arendt, "Introduction *into* Politics," 129. As Leo Chavez points out, restrictions on movement instill in undocumented immigrants a sense of confinement, as can be seen in the metaphors they use to describe their lives: "chicken coop," "prison," "gilded cage." Chavez, *Shadowed Lives*, 157–158; see also Coutin, *Legalizing Moves*, 33.

133. For the importance of such unauthorized practices of "taking" for democratic politics, see Honig, *Democracy and the Foreigner*, 98–101. In her Arendtian analysis of the 2006 demonstrations for immigrant rights in the United States, Cristina Beltrán also emphasizes the importance of practices of "taking" for establishing

public presence and becoming visible. See Beltrán, "Going Public," 607–608. On the strategies of "outing" in the mobilizations of undocumented immigrants, see McNevin, *Contesting Citizenship*, 105, 131.

134. Cissé, "Sans-Papiers."

135. Agamben, *Homo Sacer*, 19–20.

136. For more information on the UNICEF occupation, see "Sans Papiers's Hunger-Strike Reaches 30th day at UNICEF," April 2005, accessed March 9, 2014, http://www.noborder.org/item.php?id=340.

137. The tensions between *sans-papiers* and advocacy groups became visible, for example, at the European Social Forum held in Paris in 2003. See Rodríguez, "We Need Your Support."

138. Diop, "Struggle of the 'Sans-papiers.'"

139. Cissé, "Sans-Papiers."

140. McNevin, "Political Belonging," 143; see also Diop, "Struggle of the 'Sans-Papiers.'" For a similar argument about the "non-status" migrants in Canada, see Nyers, "No One is Illegal," 135.

141. Derrida, "Derelictions," 135.

142. Diop, *Dans La Peau d'un Sans-Papiers*, 95. The resemblance between the two was not lost on the French public. In her account of the movement, Mireille Rosello draws attention to a cartoon published in the satirical newspaper *Le Canard enchaîné* on August 21, 1996. In this cartoon, Alain Juppé and Jean-Louis Debré, the then prime minister and the minister of the interior, respectively, look at the *sans-papiers* who are demonstrating in public and compare them to the revolutionary *sans-culottes*: Ça commence par les sans-papiers ça finit par les "sans-culotte" (It begins with *sans-papiers* and ends with *sans-culottes*). Rosello, "Representing Illegal Immigrants," 143.

143. Sonenscher, *Sans-Culottes*, chap. 2.

144. Arendt, *The Human Condition*, 218n, 218.

145. Sonenscher, *Sans-Culottes*, 58.

146. Arendt, *Lectures on Kant's Political Philosophy*, 72.

147. Zerilli, *Abyss of Freedom*, 162.

148. Karen Wirsig, "Workers without Status in France Emerge as a Social Force," *Socialist Project*, E-Bulletin, No. 421 (October 19, 2010), accessed August 11, 2011, http://www.unionbook.org/profiles/blogs/workers-without-papers-in.

149. Ruggiero, "Fight to Reappear," 53.

150. Quoted in Hayter, *Open Borders*, 143.

151. Diop, *Dans La Peau d'un Sans-Papiers*, 184.

152. Quoted in Hayter, *Open Borders*, 143.

153. For citizenship of *sans-papiers*, see Balibar, *We, the People of Europe?*, 46–50; Balibar, "What We Owe"; McNevin, *Contesting Citizenship*. For similar arguments about undocumented immigrants in different contexts, see, for example, Barbero, "Expanding Acts of Citizenship"; Nyers, "No One is Illegal." For an analysis that refuses to tie the protests of undocumented immigrants to frameworks of citizenship and rights, see De Genova, "Queer Politics of Migration." De Genova's analysis suggests that any politics centered on citizenship and rights is inevitably "trapped within the logic of sovereign state power" (117). This argument is similar to that of Giorgio Agamben in *Homo Sacer*, which, as I discussed in chapter 1, overlooks the multiple, equivocal, and contingent possibilities that one can locate in the histories and politics of rights, citizenship, and sovereignty.

154. Arendt, *On Revolution*, 198.

155. Arendt, *On Revolution*, 198.

156. Cissé, "Sans-Papiers."

157. Diop, "Struggle of the 'Sans-Papiers.'"

158. For a discussion of *sans-papiers*' references to French colonialism, see also McNevin "Political Belonging," 144–145; Ticktin, *Casualties of Care*, 46–48.

159. Mann, "Immigrants and Arguments," 380.

160. Arendt, *On Revolution*, 223. For an insightful analysis demonstrating the resistance of Arendtian action to these conventional oppositions, see Markell, "Rule of the People."

161. Arendt, "What is Freedom?," 153.

162. Arendt, "On Violence," 140. For a similar point about the dangers of petrifying human rights in a corpus of laws, see Lefort, "Politics and Human Rights," 260.

Conclusion

1. Arendt, "The Jew as Pariah," 295.

2. Bohmer and Shuman "Producing Epistemologies of Ignorance," 624–625.

3. Welch, *Detained*, 109–110.

4. Arendt, "The Minority Question," 128; "Active Patience," 141; see also "We Refugees," 274.

5. Arendt, "The Jew as Pariah," 290. For another reading that situates *The Castle* in the background of the Jewish question, see Boa, "*The Castle*," 63, 65.

6. Kafka, *The Castle*, 54.

7. Arendt, "The Jew as Pariah," 290.

8. Arendt, "The Jew as Pariah," 290–291. See, for example, the landlady's charge that K. is "a stranger, a superfluous person getting in everyone's way." Kafka, *The Castle*, 46.

9. Arendt, "The Jew as Pariah," 275; emphasis in the original. For the dilemmas and problems of the Jewish emancipation, see in particular Arendt, *Rahel Varnhagen*.

10. Arendt, "The Jew as Pariah," 291.

11. Arendt, "The Jew as Pariah," 293.

12. Arendt, *The Origins of Totalitarianism*, 293.

13. On the critique of humanism in Arendt's discussion of *The Castle*, Disch, *Hannah Arendt*, 182–183; see also Bernstein, *Hannah Arendt*, 42–44.

14. Arendt, "The Jew as Pariah," 295.

15. Kafka, *The Castle*, 259.

16. Arendt, "Franz Kafka, Appreciated Anew," 100.

17. Arendt, "The Jew as Pariah," 297.

18. Arendt, *The Origins of Totalitarianism*, 296–297.

19. Arendt, *The Origins of Totalitarianism*, 298.

20. Jeremy Waldron, "What Would Hannah Say?" *New York Review of Books*, March 15, 2007.

21. Arendt, *The Human Condition*, 104–105.

22. For the decisive role of "the Jewish question" in Arendt's entire corpus, see Bernstein, *Hannah Arendt*.

23. See, among others, Baynes, "Toward a Political Conception"; Beitz, *Idea of Human Rights*; Cohen, "Minimalism about Human Rights"; Joseph Raz, "Human Rights without Foundations." These scholars take as their starting point John Rawls's argument that the function of human rights is to "specify limits to a regime's internal autonomy." See Rawls, *The Law of Peoples*, 79.

24. For a similar point, see Cohen, *Globalization and Sovereignty*, 194–195.

25. I use the term "cosmopolitics," and not cosmopolitanism, precisely because of this emphasis on practices; for similar uses of the term, see, for example, Cheah and Robbins, *Cosmopolitics*; James Ingram, *Radical Cosmopolitics*.

26. Arendt, *The Origins of Totalitarianism*, vii.

27. See Brysk and Shafir, "Globalization and the Citizenship Gap," 6.

28. For an Arendtian critique of market globalization along these lines, see Somers, *Genealogies of Citizenship*. For the challenges posed by neoliberal globalization to a democratic understanding of human rights, see, among others, Goodhart, *Democracy as Human Rights*.

29. For an analysis of homelessness along Arendtian lines, see Feldman, *Citizens Without Shelter*.

30. On these problems, see, for example, Wacquant, *Urban Outcasts*.

31. See, for example, Eyder Peralta, "The Undocumented Bus: In Charlotte, a Different Kind of Coming Out," *NPR*, September 3, 2012, accessed March 24, 2013, http://www.npr.org/blogs/itsallpolitics/2012/09/03/160508224/the-undocumented-bus-in-charlotte-a-different-kind-of-coming-out.

Bibliography

Abdi, Awa M. "In Limbo: Dependency, Insecurity, and Identity amongst Somali Refugees in Dadaab Camps." *Refuge* 22, no. 2 (2005): 6–14.

Abensour, Miguel. "Saint-Just and the Problem of Heroism in the French Revolution," translated by Frank Philip. In *The French Revolution and the Birth of Modernity*, edited by Ferenc Fehér, 133–149. Berkeley: University of California Press, 1990.

Ackerly, Brooke A. *Universal Human Rights in a World of Difference.* Cambridge: Cambridge University Press, 2008.

Adelman, Howard, and Elazar Barkan. *No Return, No Refuge: Rites and Rights in Minority Repatriation.* New York: Columbia University Press, 2011.

Agamben, Giorgio. *Homo Sacer: Sovereign Power and Bare Life.* Translated by Daniel Heller-Roazen. Stanford, CA: University of Stanford Press, 1998.

Agamben, Giorgio. *Means without End: Notes on Politics*, translated by Vincenzo Binetti and Cesare Casarino. Minneapolis: University of Minnesota Press, 2000.

Allain, Jean. "The *Jus Cogens* Nature of *Non-Refoulement.*" *International Journal of Refugee Law* 13, no. 4 (October 2001): 533–558.

American Civil Liberties Union of New Mexico. *Outsourcing Responsibility: The Human Cost of Privatized Immigration.* January 2011. Accessed May 24, 2012. http://www.aclu-nm.org/wp-content/uploads/2011/01/OCPC-Report.pdf.

Amnesty International. *The Netherlands: The Detention of Irregular Migrants and Asylum-seekers.* June 2008. Accessed May 23, 2012. http://www.amnesty.org/en/library/info/EUR35/002/2008/en.

Anderson, Perry. "Force and Consent." *New Left Review* 17 (September-October 2002): 5–30.

Andrijasevic, Rutvica. "From Exception to Excess: Detention and Deportation across the Mediterranean Space." In *The Deportation Regime: Sovereignty, Space, and the Freedom of Movement*, edited by Nicholas De Genova and Nathalie Peutz, 147–165. Durham, NC: Duke University Press, 2010.

Apostolidis, Paul. *Breaks in the Chain: What Immigrant Workers Can Teach America about Democracy.* Minneapolis: University of Minnesota Press, 2010.

Arato, Andrew, and Jean Cohen. "Banishing the Sovereign? Internal and External Sovereignty in Arendt." *Constellations* 16, no. 2 (June 2009): 307–330.

Arendt, Hannah. "Active Patience." In *The Jewish Writings*, edited by Jerome Kohn and Ron H. Feldman, 139–142. New York: Schocken Books, 2007.

Arendt, Hannah. *The Burden of Our Time.* London: Secker & Warburg, 1951.

Arendt, Hannah. "Can the Jewish-Arab Question Be Solved?" In *The Jewish Writings*, edited by Jerome Kohn and Ron H. Feldman, 193–198. New York: Schocken Books, 2007.

Arendt, Hannah. "Civil Disobedience." In *Crises of the Republic*, 49–102. New York and London: Harcourt Brace Jovanovich, 1972.

Arendt, Hannah. "Concerning Minorities." *Contemporary Jewish Record* 7, no. 4 (August 1944): 353–368.

Arendt, Hannah. "The Crisis of Zionism." In *The Jewish Writings*, edited by Jerome Kohn and Ron H. Feldman, 329–337. New York: Schocken Books, 2007.

Arendt, Hannah. *Denktagebuch, 1950 bis 1973.* Edited by Ursula Ludz and Ingeborg Nordmann. München: Piper, 2003.

Arendt, Hannah. "Disenfranchised and Disgraced." In *The Jewish Writings*, edited by Jerome Kohn and Ron H. Feldman, 232–235. New York: Schocken Books, 2007.

Arendt, Hannah. *Eichmann in Jerusalem: A Report on the Banality of Evil.* New York: Penguin, [1963] 1977.

Arendt, Hannah. *Elemente und Ursprünge Totaler Herrschaft.* Münich und Zürich: Piper, [1955] 1986.

Arendt, Hannah. "Franz Kafka, Appreciated Anew." In *Reflections on Literature and Culture*, edited and with an introduction by Susannah Young-ah Gottlieb, 94–109. Stanford, CA: Stanford University Press, 2007.

Arendt, Hannah. "From Hegel to Marx." In *The Promise of Politics*, edited by Jerome Kohn, 70–80. New York: Schocken Books, 2005.

Arendt, Hannah. "Guests from No-Man's-Land." In *The Jewish Writings*, edited by Jerome Kohn and Ron H. Feldman, 211–213. New York: Schocken Books, 2007.

Arendt, Hannah. "Heidegger the Fox," In *Essays in Understanding 1930–1954: Formation, Exile, and Totalitarianism*, edited by Jerome Kohn, 361–362. New York: Schocken Books, 1994.

Arendt, Hannah. *The Human Condition*, 2nd ed. Chicago: University of Chicago Press, [1958] 1998.

Arendt, Hannah. "Introduction *into* Politics." In *The Promise of Politics*, edited by Jerome Kohn, 93–200. New York: Schocken Books, 2005.

Arendt, Hannah. "The Jew as Pariah: A Hidden Tradition." In *The Jewish Writings*, edited by Jerome Kohn and Ron H. Feldman, 275–297. New York: Schocken Books, 2007.

Arendt, Hannah. "Karl Jaspers: Citizen of the World?" In *Men in Dark Times*, 81–94. New York: Harcourt Brace & Company, 1968.

Arendt, Hannah. "Labor, Work, Action." In *Amor Mundi: Explorations in the Faith and Thought of Hannah Arendt*, edited by James W. Bernauer, 29–42. Boston, MA, and Dordrecht, Netherlands: M. Nijhoff, 1987.

Arendt, Hannah. *Lectures on Kant's Political Philosophy.* Edited with an interpretive essay by Ronald Beiner. Chicago: The University of Chicago Press, 1982.

Arendt, Hannah. "The Minority Question." In *The Jewish Writings*, edited by Jerome Kohn and Ron H. Feldman, 125–133. New York: Schocken Books, 2007.

Arendt, Hannah. "Montesquieu's Revision of the Tradition." In *The Promise of Politics*, edited by Jerome Kohn, 63–69. New York: Schocken Books, 2005.

Arendt, Hannah. "The Nation." *Review of Politics* 8, no. 1 (January 1946): 138–141.

Arendt, Hannah. "On Hannah Arendt." In *Hannah Arendt: The Recovery of the Public World*, edited by Melvyn A. Hill, 301–339. New York: St. Martin's Press, 1979.

Arendt, Hannah. "On Humanity in Dark Times: Thoughts about Lessing," translated by Clara and Richard Winston. In *Men in Dark Times*, 3–31. New York: Harcourt Brace & Company, 1968.

Arendt, Hannah. *On Revolution.* London and New York: Penguin, [1963] 1990.

Arendt, Hannah. "On Violence." In *Crises of the Republic*, 103–198. New York: Harcourt Brace Jovanovich, 1972.

Arendt, Hannah. *The Origins of Totalitarianism.* San Diego: Harcourt Brace Jovanovich, [1951] 1968.

Arendt, Hannah. "Preface: The Gap Between Past and Future." In *Between Past and Future*, 3–15. New York: Penguin, 1993.

Arendt, Hannah. "Prologue." In *Responsibility and Judgment*, edited by Jerome Kohn, 3–14. New York: Schocken Books, 2003.

Arendt, Hannah. "Public Rights and Private Interests." In *Small Comforts for Hard Times: Humanists on Public Policy*, edited by Michael Mooney and Florian Stuber, 103–108. New York: Columbia University Press, 1977.

Arendt, Hannah. *Rahel Varnhagen: The Life of a Jewess.* Edited by Liliane Weissberg. Translated by Richard and Clara Winston. Baltimore: Johns Hopkins University Press, 1997.

Arendt, Hannah. "Reflections on Little Rock." In *Responsibility and Judgment*, edited by Jerome Kohn, 193-213. New York: Schocken Books, [1959] 2003.

Arendt, Hannah. "A Reply to Eric Voegelin." In *Essays in Understanding 1930–1954: Formation, Exile, and Totalitarianism*, edited by Jerome Kohn, 401–408. New York: Schocken Books, 1994.

Arendt, Hannah. "'The Rights of Man'": What Are They?" *Modern Review* 3, no. 1 (1949): 25–37.

Arendt, Hannah. "Socrates." In *The Promise of Politics*, edited by Jerome Kohn, 5–39. New York: Schocken Books, 2005.

Arendt, Hannah. "Some Questions of Moral Philosophy." In *Responsibility and Judgment*, edited by Jerome Kohn, 49–146. New York: Schocken, 2003.

Arendt, Hannah. "Statelessness." Lecture given at Berkeley on April 22, 1955. Hannah Arendt Papers. Manuscript Division, Library of Congress, Washington, DC.

Arendt, Hannah. "The Stateless People." *Contemporary Jewish Record* 8, no. 2 (April 1945): 137–153.

Arendt, Hannah. *Thinking.* Vol. 1, *The Life of the Mind.* New York: Harcourt Brace Jovanovich, 1978.

Arendt, Hannah. "Thinking and Moral Considerations." In *Responsibility and Judgment*, edited by Jerome Kohn, 159–189. New York: Schocken, 2003.

Arendt, Hannah. "'Thinking,' Seminar—1974." Courses—New School for Social Research. Hannah Arendt Papers. Manuscript Division, Library of Congress, Washington, DC, n.d.

Arendt, Hannah. "Truth and Politics." In *Between Past and Future: Eight Exercises in Political Thought*, 227–264. New York: Penguin, 1993.

Arendt, Hannah. "Understanding and Politics (The Difficulties of Understanding)." In *Essays in Understanding 1930–1954: Formation, Exile, and Totalitarianism*, edited by Jerome Kohn, 307–327. New York: Schocken Books, 1994.

Arendt, Hannah. *Vita activa: oder vom tätigen Leben*. Munich and Zürich: Piper, 2002.

Arendt, Hannah. "Walter Benjamin," translated by Harry Zohn. In *Men in Dark Times*, 153–206. New York: Harcourt Brace & Company, 1968.

Arendt, Hannah. "We Refugees." In *The Jewish Writings*, edited by Jerome Kohn and Ron H. Feldman, 264–274. New York: Schocken Books, 2007.

Arendt, Hannah. "What Is Authority?" In *Between Past and Future*, 91–141. New York: Penguin, 1993.

Arendt, Hannah. "What Is Existential Philosophy?" In *Essays in Understanding 1930–1954: Formation, Exile, and Totalitarianism*, edited by Jerome Kohn, 163–187. New York: Schocken Books, 1994.

Arendt, Hannah. "What Is Freedom?" In *Between Past and Future*, 143–171. New York: Penguin, 1993.

Arendt, Hannah. *Willing*. Vol. 2, *The Life of the Mind*. New York: Harcourt Brace Jovanovich, 1978.

Athwal, Harmit, and Jenny Bourne. "Driven to Despair: Asylum Deaths in the UK." *Race & Class* 48, no. 4 (April 2007): 106–114.

Axtmann, Roland. "Globality, Plurality and Freedom: The Arendtian Perspective." *Review of International Studies* 32, no. 1 (January 2006): 93–117.

Badiou, Alain. *Ethics: An Essay on the Understanding of Evil*. Translated by Peter Hallward. London: Verso, 2012.

Bakan, Mildred. "Hannah Arendt's Concepts of Labor and Work." In *Hannah Arendt: The Recovery of the Public World*, edited by Melvyn A. Hill, 49–65. New York: St. Martin's Press, 1979.

Baker, Keith Michael. "The Idea of a Declaration of Rights." In *The French Idea of Freedom: The Old Regime and the Declaration of Rights of 1789*, edited by Dale Van Kley, 154–196. Stanford, CA: Stanford University Press, 1994.

Balfour, Ian, and Eduardo Cadava. "The Claims of Human Rights: An Introduction." *The South Atlantic Quarterly* 103, no. 2/3 (Spring/Summer 2004): 277–296.

Balibar, Étienne. "(De)constructing the Human as Human Institution: A Reflection on the Coherence of Hannah Arendt's Practical Philosophy." *Social Research* 74, no. 3 (Fall 2007): 727–738.

Balibar, Étienne. *Equaliberty: Political Essays*. Translated by James Ingram. Durham: Duke University Press, 2013.

Balibar, Étienne. "Is a Philosophy of Human Civic Rights Possible? New Reflections on Equaliberty." *South Atlantic Quarterly* 103, no. 2/3 (Spring/Summer 2004): 311–322.

Balibar, Étienne. "On the Politics of Human Rights." *Constellations* 20, no. 1 (March 2013): 18–26.

Balibar, Étienne. "'Rights of Man' and 'Rights of the Citizen': The Modern Dialectic of Equality and Freedom." In *Masses, Classes, Ideas: Studies on Politics and Philosophy Before and After Marx*, translated by James Swenson, 39–59. New York: Routledge, 1994.

Balibar, Étienne. *We, the People of Europe?: Reflections on Transnational Citizenship.* Translated by James Swenson. Princeton, NJ: Princeton University Press, 2004.

Balibar, Étienne. "What Is a Politics of the Rights of Man?" In *Masses, Classes, Ideas: Studies on Politics and Philosophy Before and After Marx*, translated by James Swenson, 205–225. New York: Routledge, 1994.

Balibar, Étienne. "What We Owe to the Sans-Papiers." In *Social Insecurity*, edited by Len Guenther and Cornelius Heesters, 42–43. Toronto: Anansi, 2000.

Barbero, Iker. "Expanding Acts of Citizenship: The Struggles of *Sinpapeles* Migrants." *Social & Legal Studies* 21, no. 4 (December 2012): 529–547.

Barkin, Samuel J. "The Evolution of the Constitution of Sovereignty and the Emergence of Human Rights Norms." *Millennium: Journal of International Studies* 27, no. 2 (June 1998): 229–252.

Barnett, Michael. *Empire of Humanity: A History of Humanitarianism.* Ithaca and London: Cornell University Press, 2011.

Basaran, Tugba. *Security, Law and Borders: At the Limits of Liberties.* London and New York: Routledge, 2011.

Basok, Tanya. "Post-national Citizenship, Social Exclusion and Migrants Rights: Mexican Seasonal Workers in Canada." *Citizenship Studies* 8, no. 1 (2004): 47–64.

Batnitzky, Leora. *Idolatry and Representation: The Philosophy of Franz Rosenzweig Reconsidered.* Princeton, NJ: Princeton University Press, 2000.

Bauman, Zygmunt. *Liquid Times: Living in an Age of Uncertainty.* Cambridge: Polity, 2007.

Baynes, Kenneth. "Rights as Critique and the Critique of Rights: Karl Marx, Wendy Brown, and the Social Function of Rights." *Political Theory* 28, no. 4 (August 2000): 451–468.

Baynes, Kenneth. "Toward a Political Conception of Human Rights." *Philosophy and Social Criticism* 35, no. 4 (2009): 371–390.

Beardsworth, Richard. *Derrida and the Political.* London: Routledge, 1996.

Beiner, Ronald. "Arendt and Nationalism." In *The Cambridge Companion to Hannah Arendt*, edited by Dana Villa, 44–62. Cambridge and New York: Cambridge University Press, 2000).

Beiner, Ronald. "Hannah Arendt on Judging." In *Lectures on Kant's Political Philosophy*, edited with an interpretive essay by Ronald Beiner, 89–156. Chicago: The University of Chicago Press, 1982.

Beitz, Charles R. *The Idea of Human Rights.* Oxford: Oxford University Press, 2009.

Beltrán, Cristina. "Going Public: Hannah Arendt, Immigrant Action, and the Space of Appearance." *Political Theory* 37, no. 5 (October 2009): 595–622.

Benhabib, Seyla. *Another Cosmopolitanism.* Edited by Robert Post. Oxford and New York: Oxford University Press, 2006.

Benhabib, Seyla. *The Claims of Culture: Equality and Diversity in the Global Era.* Princeton, NJ: Princeton University Press, 2002.

Benhabib, Seyla. "Democracy and Difference: Reflections on the Metapolitics of Lyotard and Derrida." *Journal of Political Philosophy* 2, no. 1 (March 1994): 1–23.

Benhabib, Seyla. "Is There a Human Right to Democracy? Beyond Interventionism and Indifference." In *Philosophical Dimensions of Human Rights: Some Contemporary Views*, edited by Claudio Corradetti, 191–213. Dordrecht: Springer, 2012.

Benhabib, Seyla. "Judgment and the Moral Foundations of Politics in Arendt's Thought." *Political Theory* 16, no. 1 (February 1988): 29–51.

Benhabib, Seyla. "Reason-Giving and Rights-Bearing: Constructing the Subject of Rights." *Constellations* 20, no. 1 (2013): 38–50.

Benhabib, Seyla. *The Reluctant Modernism of Hannah Arendt*. Lanham, MD, and Oxford: Rowman & Littlefield, [1996] 2003.

Benhabib, Seyla. *The Rights of Others: Aliens, Residents and Citizens*. Cambridge and New York: Cambridge University Press, 2004.

Benhabib, Seyla. *Situating the Self: Gender, Community, and Postmodernism in Contemporary Ethics*. New York: Routledge, 1992.

Bentham, Jeremy. "Anarchical Fallacies." In *The Works of Jeremy Bentham*, edited by John Bowring, vol. 2, 489–534. Edinburgh: W. Tait; London: Simpkin, Marshall, 1839.

Bentham, Jeremy. *An Introduction to the Principles of Morals and Legislation*. Vol. 2. London: W. Pickering, 1823.

Berger, Adolf. *Encyclopedic Dictionary of Roman Law*. Philadelphia, PA: American Philosophical Society, 1953.

Bernstein, Richard J. "Derrida: The Aporia of Forgiveness?" *Constellations* 13, no. 3 (September 2006): 394–406.

Bernstein, Richard J. *Hannah Arendt and the Jewish Question*. Cambridge, MA: MIT Press, 1996.

Bernstein, Richard J. "Rethinking the Social and the Political." *Graduate Faculty Philosophy Journal* 11, no. 1 (1986): 111–130.

Bhabha, Jacqueline. "'Get Back to Where You Once Belonged': Identity, Citizenship, and Exclusion in Europe." *Human Rights Quarterly* 20, no. 3 (August 1998): 592–627.

Bhabha, Jacqueline. "Internationalist Gatekeepers? The Tension Between Asylum Advocacy and Human Rights." *Harvard Human Rights Journal* 15 (Spring 2002): 155–181.

Bigo, Didier. "Detention of Foreigners, States of Exception, and the Social Practices of Control of the Banopticon." In *Borderscapes: Hidden Geographies and Politics at Territory's Edge*, edited by Prem Kumar Rajaram and Carl Grundy-Warr, 3–33. Minneapolis: University of Minnesota Press, 2007.

Bigo, Didier. "Security and Immigration: Toward a Critique of the Governmentality of Unease." *Alternatives* 27, no. 1 (February 2002 Supplement): 63–92.

Bilsky, Leora. "Citizenship as Mask: Between the Imposter and the Refugee." *Constellations* 15, no. 1 (March 2008): 72–97.

Birmingham, Peg. *Hannah Arendt and Human Rights: The Predicament of Common Responsibility*. Bloomington: Indiana University Press, 2006.

Biser, Ashley N. "Calibrating Our 'Inner Compass': Arendt on Thinking and the Dangers of Disorientation." *Political Theory* 42, no. 5 (October 2014): 519–542.

Biskowski, Lawrence J. "Practical Foundations for Political Judgment: Arendt on Action and World." *The Journal of Politics* 55, no. 4 (November 1993): 867–887.

Bloch, Alice. "The Right to Rights? Undocumented Migrants from Zimbabwe Living in South Africa." *Sociology* 44, no. 2 (April 2010): 233–250.

Bloch, Alice, and Liza Schuster. "At the Extremes of Exclusion: Deportation, Detention and Dispersal." *Ethnic and Racial Studies* 28, no. 3 (May 2005): 491–512.

Boa, Elizabeth. *"The Castle."* In *The Cambridge Companion to Kafka*, edited by Julian Preece, 61–79. Cambridge and New York: Cambridge University Press, 2002.

Bohman, James. "Citizens and Persons: Legal Status and Human Rights in Hannah Arendt." In *Hannah Arendt and the Law*, edited by Marco Goldoni and Christopher McCorkindale, 321–334. Oxford and Portland, OR: Hart, 2012.

Bohmer, Carol, and Amy Shuman. "Producing Epistemologies of Ignorance in the Political Asylum Application Process." *Identities: Global Studies in Culture and Power* 14, no. 5 (October 2007): 603–629.

Bohmer, Carol, and Amy Shuman. *Rejecting Refugees: Political Asylum in the 21st Century*. London and New York: Routledge, 2008.

Bosniak, Linda. *The Citizen and the Alien: Dilemmas of Contemporary Membership*. Princeton, NJ: Princeton University Press, 2006.

Bosniak, Linda. "Citizenship Denationalized." *Indiana Journal of Global Legal Studies* 7, no. 2 (Spring 2000): 447–508.

Bosniak, Linda. "Human Rights, State Sovereignty and the Protection of Undocumented Migrants under the International Migrant Workers' Convention." In *Irregular Migration and Human Rights: Theoretical, European, and International Perspectives*, edited by Barbara Bogusz, Ryszard Cholewinski, Adam Cygan, and Erika Szyszczak, 311–341. Leiden and Boston: Martinus Nijhoff Publishers, 2004.

Bosniak, Linda. "Human Rights within One State: Dilemmas of Personhood in Liberal Constitutional Thought." In *Are Human Rights for Migrants? Critical Reflections on the Status of Irregular Migrants in Europe and the US*, edited by Marie-Bénédicte Dembour and Tobias Kelly, 201–221. Abingdon: Routledge, 2011.

Bousquet, Gisele. "Living in a State of Limbo: A Case Study of Vietnamese Refugees in Hong Kong Camps." *Center for Migration Studies Special Issues* 5, no. 2 (March 1987): 34–53.

Breen, Keith. "Law Beyond Command? An Evaluation of Arendt's Understanding of Law." In *Hannah Arendt and the Law*, edited by Marco Goldoni and Christopher McCorkindale, 15–34. Oxford and Portland, OR: Hart, 2012.

Breen, Keith. "Violence and Power: A Critique of Hannah Arendt on the 'Political.'" *Philosophy & Social Criticism* 33, no. 3 (May 2007): 343–372.

Brown, Wendy. *Manhood and Politics: A Feminist Reading in Political Theory*. Totowa, NJ: Rowman & Littlefield, 1988.

Brown, Wendy. "'The Most We Can Hope For . . .': Human Rights and the Politics of Fatalism." *The South Atlantic Quarterly* 103, no. 2/3 (Spring/Summer 2004): 451–463.

Brown, Wendy. *States of Injury: Power and Freedom in Late Modernity*. Princeton, NJ: Princeton University Press, 1995.

Brown, Wendy. *Walled States: Waning Sovereignty*. New York: Zone Books, 2010.

Brubaker, Rogers. *Citizenship and Nationhood in France and Germany*. Cambridge, MA: Harvard University Press, 1992.

Brunkhorst, Hauke. "Are Human Rights Self-Contradictory? Critical Remarks on a Hypothesis by Hannah Arendt," *Constellations* 3, no. 2 (October 1996): 190–199.

Brunkhorst, Hauke. "Equality and Elitism in Arendt." In *The Cambridge Companion to Hannah Arendt*, edited by Dana Villa, 178–198. Cambridge and New York: Cambridge University Press, 2000.

Brysk, Alison, and Gershon Shafir. "Introduction: Globalization and the Citizenship Gap." In *People Out of Place: Globalization, Human Rights, and the Citizenship Gap*, edited by Alison Brysk and Gershon Shafir, 3–9. New York and London: Routledge, 2004.

Buckler, Steve. *Hannah Arendt and Political Theory: Challenging the Tradition*. Edinburgh: Edinburgh University Press, 2011.

Buergenthal, Thomas. "The Normative and Institutional Evolution of International Human Rights." *Human Rights Quarterly* 19, no. 4 (November 1997): 703–723.

Burke, Edmund. *Reflections on the Revolution in France*. Edited by Conor Cruise O'Brien. London: Penguin, 2004.

Butler, Judith. *Antigone's Claim: Kinship between Life and Death*. New York: Columbia University Press, 2000.

Butler, Judith. "Contingent Foundations." In *Feminist Contentions: A Philosophical Exchange*, introduced by Linda Nicholson, 35–57. New York: Routledge, 1995.

Butler, Judith. *Excitable Speech: A Politics of the Performative*. New York and London: Routledge, 1997.

Butler, Judith. *Precarious Life: The Powers of Mourning and Violence*. London and New York: Verso, 2004.

Butler, Judith, and Gayatri Chakravorty Spivak. *Who Sings the Nation-State?: Language, Politics, Belonging*. London and New York: Seagull Books, 2007.

Calhoun, Craig. "The Imperative to Reduce Suffering: Charity, Progress and Emergencies in the Field of Humanitarian Action." In *Humanitarianism in Question: Politics, Power, Ethics*, edited by Michael Nathan Barnett and Thomas George Weiss, 73–97. Ithaca, NY: Cornell University Press, 2008.

Cane, Lucy. "Hannah Arendt on the Principles of Political Action." *European Journal of Political Theory*. Published electronically February 24, 2014. doi: 10.1177/1474885114523939.

Canovan, Margaret. "The Contradictions of Hannah Arendt's Political Thought." *Political Theory* 6, no. 1 (February 1978): 5–26.

Canovan, Margaret. *Hannah Arendt: A Reinterpretation of Her Political Thought*. Cambridge: Cambridge University Press, 1992.

Canovan, Margaret. "Lasting Institutions: Arendtian Thoughts on Nations and Republics." *Graduate Faculty Philosophy Journal* 21, no. 2 (1999): 133–151.

Carens, Joseph H. *The Ethics of Immigration*. Oxford and New York: Oxford University Press, 2013.

Castles, Stephen, and Alastair Davidson, *Citizenship and Migration: Globalization and the Politics of Belonging*. New York: Routledge, 2000.

Chambers, Samuel A. "Giving up (on) Rights? The Future of Rights and the Project of Radical Democracy." *American Journal of Political Science* 48, no. 2 (April 2004): 185–200.

Chan, Kwok B., and David Loveridge. "Refugees 'in Transit': Vietnamese in a Refugee Camp in Hong Kong." *International Migration Review* 21, No. 3 (Autumn 1987): 745–759.

Chandler, David G. "The Road to Military Humanitarianism: How the Human Rights NGOs Shaped A New Humanitarian Agenda." *Human Rights Quarterly* 23, no. 3 (August 2001): 678–700.

Chavez, Leo R. *Shadowed Lives: Undocumented Immigrants in American Society.* Fort Worth, TX: Harcourt Brace Jovanovich College Publishers, 1992.

Cheah, Pheng, and Bruce Robbins, eds. *Cosmopolitics: Thinking and Feeling Beyond the Nation.* Minneapolis, MN: University of Minnesota Press, 1998.

Chimienti, Milena. "Mobilization of Irregular Migrants in Europe: A Comparative Analysis." *Ethnic and Racial Studies* 34, no. 8 (August 2011): 1338–1356.

Chimienti, Milena, and John Solomos. "Social Movements of Irregular Migrants, Recognition, and Citizenship." *Globalizations* 8, no. 3 (June 2011): 343–360.

Christodoulidis, Emilios, and Andrew Schaap. "Arendt's Constitutional Question." In *Hannah Arendt and the Law*, edited by Marco Goldoni and Christopher McCorkindale, 101–116. Oxford and Portland, Oregon: Hart Publishing, 2012.

Cissé, Madjiguène. *Parole de Sans-Papiers.* Paris: La Dispute, 1999.

Cissé, Madjiguène. "The Sans-Papiers—A Woman Draws the First Lessons." June 1997. Accessed March 18, 2013. http://www.bok.net/pajol/madjiguene2.en.html.

Clark, Ann Marie. *Diplomacy of Conscience: Amnesty International and Changing Human Rights Norms.* Princeton, NJ: Princeton University Press, 2001.

Clarke, James P. "Social Justice and Political Freedom: Revisiting Hannah Arendt's Conception of Need." *Philosophy & Social Criticism* 19, no. 3–4 (July 1993): 333–347.

Codini, Ennio. "Developments in Law and Regulations." In *The Fourteenth Italian Report on Migrations 2008*, edited by Vincenzo Cesareo, 65–77. Milan: Polimetrica, 2009.

Cohen, Jean L. "Changing Paradigms of Citizenship and the Exclusiveness of the Demos." *International Sociology* 14, no. 3 (September 1999): 245–268.

Cohen, Jean L. *Globalization and Sovereignty: Rethinking Legality, Legitimacy, and Constitutionalism.* Cambridge: Cambridge University Press, 2012.

Cohen, Jean L. "Rights, Citizenship, and the Modern Form of the Social: Dilemmas of Arendtian Republicanism." *Constellations* 3, no. 2 (October 1996): 164–189.

Cohen, Joshua. "Minimalism about Human Rights: The Most We Can Hope For?" *The Journal of Political Philosophy* 12, no. 2 (2004): 190–213.

Cole, David. *Enemy Aliens: Double Standards and Constitutional Freedoms in the War on Terrorism.* New York and London: The New Press, 2003.

Cornelisse, Galina. *Immigration Detention and Human Rights: Rethinking Territorial Sovereignty.* The Hague/Boston: Martinus Nijhoff, 2010.

Cornell, Drucilla. "Time, Deconstruction, and the Challenge to Legal Positivism: The Call for Judicial Responsibility." *Yale Journal of Law and the Humanities* 2, no. 1 (Winter 1990): 267–298.

Coutin, Susan Bibler. "Illegality, Borderlands, and the Space of Nonexistence." In *Globalization Under Construction: Governmentality, Law, and Identity*, edited by Richard Warren Perry and Bill Maurer, 171–202. Minneapolis and London: University of Minnesota Press, 2003.

Coutin, Susan Bibler. *Legalizing Moves: Salvadoran Immigrants' Struggle for U.S. Residency.* Ann Arbor: University of Michigan Press, 2000.

Cover, Robert. "Foreword: *Nomos* and Narrative," *Harvard Law Review* 4 (1983–1984): 4–68.

Cover, Robert. "Violence and the Word." *The Yale Law Journal* 95 (1985–1986): 1601–1629.

Csikszentmihalyi, Mihaly. "Why We Need Things." In *History from Things: Essays in Material Culture*, edited by Steven Lubar and W. David Kingery, 20–29. Washington and London: Smithsonian Institution Press, 1993.

Curtis, Kimberley. *Our Sense of the Real: Aesthetic Experience and Arendtian Politics*. Ithaca, NY: Cornell University Press, 1999.

Dal Lago, Alessandro. *Non-Persons: The Exclusion of Migrants in a Global Society*. Translated by Marie Orton. Milan, Italy: IPOC di Pietro Condemi, 2009.

Dastyari, Azadeh. "Refugees on Guantanamo Bay: A Blue Print for Australia's 'Pacific Solution'?" *AQ: Australian Quarterly* 79, No. 1 (January-February 2007): 4–8, 40.

Dauvergne, Catherine. *Making People Illegal: What Globalization Means for Migration and the Law*. Cambridge and New York: Cambridge University Press, 2008.

Dayan, Colin. *The Law Is a White Dog: How Legal Rituals Make and Unmake Personhood*. Princeton, NJ: Princeton University Press, 2011.

De Genova, Nicholas. "Migrant 'Illegality' and Deportability in Everyday Life." *Annual Review of Anthropology* 31(2002): 419–447.

De Genova, Nicholas. "The Queer Politics of Migration: Reflections on 'Illegality' and Incorrigibility." *Studies in Social Justice* 4, no. 2 (2010): 101–126.

Derrida, Jacques. *Aporias: Dying—Awaiting (One Another at) the Limits of Truth*. Translated by Thomas Dutoit. Stanford, CA: Stanford University Press, 1993.

Derrida, Jacques. "Declarations of Independence." *New Political Science* 15 (Summer 1986): 7–15.

Derrida, Jacques. "Derelictions of the Right to Justice (But What Are the 'Sans-Papiers' Lacking?)." In *Negotiations*, edited by Elizabeth Rottenberg, 133–144. Stanford, CA: Stanford University Press, 2002.

Derrida, Jacques. "Force of Law: The 'Mystical Foundation of Authority.'" In *Deconstruction and the Possibility of Justice*, edited by Drucilla Cornell, Michel Rosenfeld, and David Gray Carlson, 3–67. New York and London: Routledge, 1992.

Dewey, John. "The Historic Background of Corporate Legal Personality." *The Yale Law Journal* 35, no. 6 (April 1926): 655–673.

Dietz, Mary. *Turning Operations: Feminism, Arendt, and Politics*. New York: Routledge, 2002.

Diop, Ababacar. *Dans La Peau d'un Sans-Papiers*. Paris: Seuil, 1997.

Diop, Ababacar. "The Struggle of the 'Sans-papiers': Realities and Perspectives." Translated by Iain Nappier. April 4, 1997. Accessed February 25, 2013. http://www.bok.net/pajol/sanspap/sptextes/ababacar2.en.html.

Disch, Lisa. "How Could Hannah Arendt Glorify the American Revolution and Revile the French? Placing *On Revolution* in the Historiography of the French and American Revolutions." *European Journal of Political Theory* 10, no. 3 (July 2011): 350–371.

Disch, Lisa Jane. *Hannah Arendt and the Limits of Philosophy*. Ithaca, NY, and London: Cornell University Press, 1994.

Donnelly, Jack. "Human Rights: A New Standard of Civilization?" *International Affairs* 74, no. 1 (January 1998): 1–23.

Donnelly, Jack. *Universal Human Rights in Theory and Practice.* 2nd ed. Ithaca, NY: Cornell University Press, 2003.

Dossa, Shiraz. *The Public Realm and the Public Self: The Political Theory of Hannah Arendt.* Waterloo, Ontario: Wilfrid Laurier University Press, 1989.

Doty, Roxanne Lynn. *Imperial Encounters: The Politics of Representation in North-South Relations.* Minneapolis: University of Minnesota Press, 1996.

Douzinas, Costas. *The End of Human Rights: Critical Legal Thought at the End of the Century.* Oxford and Portland, OR: Hart Publishing, 2000.

Douzinas, Costas. *Human Rights and Empire: The Political Philosophy of Cosmopolitanism.* Abingdon, Oxford, and New York: Routledge-Cavendish, 2007.

Douzinas, Costas. "The Paradoxes of Human Rights." *Constellations* 20, no. 1 (March 2013): 51–67.

Dubois, Laurent. "*La République Métissée*: Citizenship, Colonialism, and the Borders of French History." *Cultural Studies* 14, no. 1 (Winter 2000): 15–34.

Dudley, Sandra. "Feeling at Home: Producing and Consuming Things in Karenni Refugee Camps on the Thai-Burma Border." *Population, Space and Place* 17, no. 6 (November/December 2011): 742–755.

Dummett, Michael. *On Immigration and Refugees.* London: Routledge, 2001.

Duvall, Raymond, Ayten Gündoğdu, and Kartik Raj. "Borders, Power, and Resistance: Bounding and Challenging Europe." In *Europe and Its Boundaries: Words and Worlds, Within and Beyond,* edited by Andrew Davison and Himadeep Muppidi, 225–241. Lanham: Lexington Books, 2009.

Edkins, Jenny, and Véronique Pin-Fat. "Through the Wire: Relations of Power and Relations of Violence." *Millennium—Journal of International Studies* 34, no. 1 (August 2005): 1–24.

Esposito, Roberto. "The *Dispositif* of the Person." *Law, Culture and the Humanities* 8, no. 1 (February 2012): 17–30.

Esposito, Roberto. *Third Person: Politics of Life and Philosophy of the Impersonal.* Translated by Zakiya Hanafi. Cambridge: Polity, 2012.

Euben, Peter J. *Platonic Noise.* Princeton, NJ: Princeton University Press, 2003.

Fabbricotti, Alberta. "The Concept of Inhuman or Degrading Treatment in International Law and Its Application in Asylum Cases." *International Journal of Refugee Law* 10, no. 4 (October 1998): 637–661.

Fassin, Didier. "Compassion and Repression: The Moral Economy of Immigration Policies in France." *Cultural Anthropology* 20, no. 3 (August 2005): 362–387.

Fassin, Didier. *Humanitarian Reason: A Moral History of the Present.* Berkeley and Los Angeles: University of California Press, 2012.

Fassin, Didier. "Policing Borders, Producing Boundaries: The Governmentality of Immigration in Dark Times." *Annual Review of Anthropology* 40 (October 2011): 213–226.

Feinberg, Joel. "The Nature and Value of Rights." *The Journal of Value Inquiry* 4, no. 4 (1970): 243–257.

Feldman, Leonard C. *Citizens without Shelter: Homelessness, Democracy and Political Exclusion.* Ithaca, NY: Cornell University Press, 2004.

Feldman, Leonard C. "Terminal Exceptions: Law and Sovereignty at the Airport Threshold." *Law, Culture and the Humanities* 3, no. 2 (June 2007): 320–344.

Ferrara, Alessandro. *The Force of the Example: Explorations in the Paradigm of Judgment*. New York: Columbia University Press, 2008.

Ferrara, Alessandro. "Two Notions of Humanity." *Political Theory* 31, no. 3 (June 2003): 392–420.

Feyissa, Abebe. "There Is More Than One Way of Dying: An Ethiopian Perspective on the Effects of Long-Term Stays in Refugee Camps." With Rebecca Horn. In *Refugee Rights: Ethics, Advocacy, and Africa*, edited by David Hollenbach, 13–26. Washington, DC: Georgetown University Press, 2008.

Fine, Robert. *Cosmopolitanism*. London and New York: Routledge, 2007.

Finnemore, Martha, and Kathryn Sikkink. "International Norm Dynamics and Political Change." *International Organization* 52, no. 4 (1998): 887–917.

Forst, Rainer. "The Justification of Human Rights and the Basic Right to Justification: A Reflexive Approach." In *Philosophical Dimensions of Human Rights: Some Contemporary Views*, edited by Claudio Corradetti, 81–106. Dordrecht: Springer, 2012.

Foucault, Michel. *Security, Territory, Population: Lectures at the Collège de France, 1977–1978*. Edited by Arnold I. Davidson. Translated by Graham Burchell. New York: Picador, 2007.

Frank, Jason A. *Constituent Moments: Enacting the People in Postrevolutionary America*. Durham, NC: Duke University Press, 2010.

Frank, Jill. "The Political Theory of Classical Greece." In *Oxford Handbook of Political Theory*, edited by John S. Dryzek, Bonnie Honig, and Anne Phillips, 175–192. Oxford and New York: Oxford University Press, 2006.

Fraser, Nancy. *Unruly Practices: Power, Discourse and Gender in Contemporary Social Theory*. Minneapolis: University of Minnesota Press, 1989.

Freedman, Jane. *Immigration and Insecurity in France*. Aldershot: Ashgate, 2004.

Garber, Marjorie. "Compassion." In *Compassion: The Culture and Politics of an Emotion*, edited by Lauren Berlant, 15–27. New York and London: Routledge, 2004.

Garsten, Bryan. "The Elusiveness of Arendtian Judgment." *Social Research* 74, no. 4 (Winter 2007): 1071–1108.

Gauchet, Marcel. "Rights of Man." In *A Critical Dictionary of the French Revolution*, edited by François Furet and Mona Ozouf; translated by Arthur Goldhammer, 820–821. Cambridge, MA: Belknap Press of Harvard University Press, 1989.

Gibney, Matthew. "Is Deportation a Form of Forced Migration?" *Refugee Survey Quarterly* 32, no. 2 (June 2013): 116–129.

Gibney, Matthew. "Precarious Residents: Migration Control, Membership and the Rights of Non-citizens." United Nations Development Programme Human Development Reports, April 2009. Accessed July 9, 2014. http://hdr.undp.org/sites/default/files/hdrp_2009_10.pdf.

Goodhart, Michael. *Democracy as Human Rights: Freedom and Equality in the Age of Globalization*. New York and London: Routledge, 2005.

Gorski, Héctor C. Silveira, Cristina Fernández, and Alejandra Manavella. "A Right-Based Approach to Migration Policies in a Context of Emergencies: 'Expelling States' and Semi-Persons in the European Union." University of Barcelona, 2008. Accessed April 12, 2012. http://www.libertysecurity.org/IMG/pdf_deliverable_dic_2008.pdf.

Gottlieb, Susannah Young-ah. *Regions of Sorrow: Anxiety and Messianism in Hannah Arendt and W.H. Auden*. Stanford, CA: Stanford University Press, 2003.

Grant, Stefanie. "The Recognition of the Rights of Migrants within the UN Human Rights System: The First 60 Years." In *Are Human Rights for Migrants? Critical Reflections on the Status of Irregular Migrants in Europe and the US*, edited by Marie-Bénédicte Dembour and Tobias Kelly, 25–47. Abingdon, Oxon, and New York: Routledge, 2011.

Griffin, James. *On Human Rights*. Oxford and New York: Oxford University Press, 2008.

Guenther, Lisa. *Solitary Confinement: Social Death and Its Afterlives*. Minneapolis: University of Minnesota Press, 2013.

Guilhot, Nicholas. *The Democracy Makers: Human Rights and International Order*. New York: Columbia University Press, 2005.

Gündoğdu, Ayten. "Arendt on Culture and Imperialism: Response to Klausen." *Political Theory* 39, no. 5 (October 2011): 661–667.

Gündoğdu, Ayten. "'Perplexities of the Rights of Man': Arendt on the Aporias of Human Rights." *European Journal of Political Theory* 11, no. 1 (January 2012): 4–24.

Gündoğdu, Ayten. "Potentialities of Human Rights: Agamben and the Narrative of Fated Necessity." *Contemporary Political Theory* 11, no. 1 (February 2012): 2–22.

Gündoğdu, Ayten. "A Revolution in Rights: Reflections on the Democratic Invention of the Rights of Man." *Law, Culture and the Humanities* 10, no. 3 (October 2014): 367–379.

Guyer, Paul. *Kant*. London: Routledge, 2006.

Habermas, Jürgen. "The Concept of Human Dignity and the Realistic Utopia of Human Rights." *Metaphilosophy* 41, no. 4 (July 2010): 464–480.

Habermas, Jürgen. "Hannah Arendt's Communications Concept of Power." In *Hannah Arendt: Critical Essays*, edited by Lewis P. Hinchman and Sandra K. Hinchman, 211–229. Albany: State University of New York Press, 1994.

Habermas, Jürgen. *The Philosophical Discourse of Modernity: Twelve Lectures*. Cambridge, MA: MIT Press, 1987.

Hamacher, Werner. "The Right to Have Rights (Four-and-a-Half Remarks)." *The South Atlantic Quarterly* 103, no. 2/3 (Spring/Summer 2004): 343–356.

Harvey, Colin. "Dissident Voices: Refugees, Human Rights and Asylum in Europe." *Social & Legal Studies* 9, no. 3 (September 2000): 367–396.

Hayden, Patrick. "Arendt and the Political Power of Judgement." In *Hannah Arendt: Key Concepts*, edited by Patrick Hayden, 167–184. Durham: Acumen, 2014.

Hayden, Patrick. "From Exclusion to Containment: Arendt, Sovereign Power, and Statelessness." *Societies Without Borders* 3, no. 2 (June 2008): 248–269.

Hayter, Teresa. *Open Borders: The Case Against Immigration Controls*. London: Pluto Press, 2000.

Hegel, Georg Wilhelm Friedrich. *Philosophy of Right*. Translated by T. M. Knox. Oxford and New York: Oxford University Press, 1967.

Henkin, Louis. *The Age of Rights*. New York: Columbia University Press, 1990.

Herz, Manuel, ed. *From Camp to City: Refugee Camps of the Western Sahara*. Basel: Lars Müller, 2012.

Herzog, Annabel. "Illuminating Inheritance: Benjamin's Influence on Arendt's Political Storytelling." *Philosophy and Social Criticism* 26, no. 5 (September 2000): 1–27.

Hinchman, Lewis P., and Sandra K. Hinchman. "In Heidegger's Shadow: Hannah Arendt's Phenomenological Humanism." *The Review of Politics* 46, no. 2 (April 1984): 183–211.

Hobsbawm, E. J. *Revolutionaries: Contemporary Essays.* London: Weidenfeld and Nicolson, 1973.

Holman, Christopher. "Dialectics and Distinction: Reconsidering Hannah Arendt's Critique of Marx." *Contemporary Political Theory* 10, no. 3 (August 2011): 332–353.

Honig, Bonnie. "Another Cosmopolitanism? Law and Politics in the New Europe." In *Another Cosmopolitanism*, edited by Robert Post, 102–127. Oxford and New York: Oxford University Press, 2006.

Honig, Bonnie. "Declarations of Independence: Arendt and Derrida on the Problem of Founding a Republic." *American Political Science Review* 85, no. 1 (March 1991): 97–113.

Honig, Bonnie. *Democracy and the Foreigner.* Princeton, NJ: Princeton University Press, 2001.

Honig, Bonnie. *Political Theory and the Displacement of Politics.* Ithaca, NY: Cornell University Press, 1993.

Honig, Bonnie. "Toward an Agonistic Feminism: Hannah Arendt and the Politics of Identity." In *Feminist Interpretations of Hannah Arendt*, edited by Bonnie Honig, 135–166. University Park, PA: Pennsylvania State University Press, 1995.

Honneth, Axel. *The Struggle for Recognition: The Moral Grammar of Social Conflicts.* Translated by Joel Anderson. Cambridge, MA: MIT Press, 1995.

Human Rights Watch. *Pushed Back, Pushed Around: Italy's Forced Return of Boat Migrants and Asylum Seekers, Libya's Mistreatment of Migrants and Asylum Seekers.* September 2009. Accessed April 1, 2012. http://www.hrw.org/sites/default/files/reports/italy0909web_0.pdf.

Hunt, Lynn. *Inventing Human Rights: A History.* New York: W.W. Norton & Co., 2007.

Huysmans, Jef. *The Politics of Insecurity: Fear, Migration and Asylum in the EU.* London and New York: Routledge, 2006.

Hyndman, Jennifer. *Managing Displacement: Refugees and the Politics of Humanitarianism.* Minneapolis: University of Minnesota Press, 2000.

Hyndman, Jennifer, and Alison Mountz. "Another Brick in the Wall? Neo-*Refoulement* and the Externalization of Asylum by Australia and Europe." *Government and Opposition* 43, no. 2 (Spring 2008): 249–269.

Ignatieff, Michael. *Human Rights as Politics and Idolatry*, edited by Amy Gutmann. Princeton, NJ: Princeton University Press, 2001.

Ingram, David. "Novus Ordo Seclorum: The Trial of (Post)Modernity or the Tale of Two Revolutions." In *Hannah Arendt: Twenty Years Later*, edited by Larry May and Jerome Kohn, 221–250. Cambridge, MA: MIT Press, 1996.

Ingram, James D. *Radical Cosmopolitics: The Ethics and Politics of Democratic Universalism.* New York: Columbia University Press, 2013.

Ingram, James D. "The Subject of the Politics of Recognition: Hannah Arendt and Jacques Rancière." In *Socialité et reconnaissance: Grammaires de l'humain*, edited by Georg W. Bertram, Robin Celikates, Christophe Laudou, David Lauer, 229–245. Paris: L'Harmattan, 2007.

Ingram, James D. "What Is a 'Right to Have Rights'? Three Images of the Politics of Human Rights." *American Political Science Review* 102, no. 4 (2008): 401–416.

Isaac, Jeffrey C. "Hannah Arendt on Human Rights and the Limits of Exposure, or Why Noam Chomsky Is Wrong about the Meaning of Kosovo." *Social Research* 69, no. 2 (2002): 505–537.

Isaac, Jeffrey C. "A New Guarantee on Earth: Hannah Arendt on Human Dignity and the Politics of Human Rights." *American Political Science Review* 90, no. 1 (March 1996): 61–73.

Ishay, Micheline R. *The History of Human Rights: From Ancient Times to the Globalization Era*. Berkeley: University of California Press, 2004.

Jacobson, David. *Rights Across Borders: Immigration and the Decline of Citizenship*. Baltimore: Johns Hopkins University Press, 1996.

Jaspers, Karl. *Socrates, Buddha, Confucius, Jesus: The Paradigmatic Individuals*. Edited by Hannah Arendt. Translated by Ralph Manheim. New York: Harcourt Brace Jovanovich, 1962.

Jesuit Refugee Service-Europe. *Becoming Vulnerable in Detention*. Civil Society Report on the Detention of Vulnerable Asylum Seekers and Irregular Migrants in the European Union (The DEVAS Project). Belgium, June 2010. Accessed April 12, 2012. http://www.detention-in-europe.org.

Johnson, Kevin R. "'Aliens' and the U.S. Immigration Laws: The Social and Legal Construction of Nonpersons." *The University of Miami Inter-American Law Review* 28, no. 2 (Winter 1996/1997): 263–292.

Kafka, Franz. *The Castle*. Translated by Anthea Bell. With an Introduction and Notes by Ritchie Robertson. Oxford and New York: Oxford University Press, 2009.

Kalyvas, Andreas. *Democracy and the Politics of the Extraordinary: Max Weber, Carl Schmitt, and Hannah Arendt*. Cambridge: Cambridge University Press, 2009.

Kateb, George. *Hannah Arendt: Politics, Conscience, Evil*. Totowa, NJ: Rowman & Allanheld, 1983.

Kateb, George. *Human Dignity*. Cambridge, MA: Belknap Press of Harvard University Press, 2011.

Kateb, George. "Political Action: Its Nature and Advantages." In *Cambridge Companion to Hannah Arendt*, edited by Dana Villa, 130–148. New York: Cambridge University Press, 2000.

Keck, Margaret E., and Kathryn Sikkink. *Activists Beyond Borders: Advocacy Networks in International Politics*. Ithaca, NY: Cornell University Press, 1998.

Keenan, Alan. "Promises, Promises: The Abyss of Freedom and the Loss of the Political in the Work of Hannah Arendt." *Political Theory* 22, no. 2 (May 1994): 297–322.

Kennedy, David. *Dark Sides of Virtue: Reassessing International Humanitarianism*. Princeton, NJ, and Oxford: Princeton University Press, 2004.

Kennedy, David. "The International Human Rights Movement: Part of the Problem?" *Harvard Human Rights Journal* 15 (Spring 2002): 101–125.

Kesby, Alison. *The Right to Have Rights: Citizenship, Humanity, and International Law*. Oxford and New York: Oxford University Press, 2012.

Kibreab, Gaim. "The Myth of Dependency among Camp Refugees in Somalia 1979–1989." *Journal of Refugee Studies* 6, no. 4 (1993): 321–349.

King, Richard H., and Dan Stone, eds. *Hannah Arendt and the Uses of History: Imperialism, Nation, Race, and Genocide.* New York: Berghahn Books, 2007.

Klausen, Jimmy Casas. "Hannah Arendt's Primitivism." *Political Theory* 38, no. 3 (June 2010): 394–423.

Klepp, Silja. "A Contested Asylum System: The European Union between Refugee Protection and Border Control in the Mediterranean Sea." *European Journal of Migration and Law* 12, no. 1 (2010): 1–21

Klusmeyer, Douglas. "Hannah Arendt's Case for Federalism." *Publius* 40, no. 1 (Winter 2010): 31–58.

Kofman, Sarah. "Beyond Aporia?," translated by David Macey. In *Post-Structuralist Classics*, edited by Andrew Benjamin, 7–44. London and New York: Routledge, 1988.

Kohn, Jerome. "Freedom: The Priority of the Political." In *The Cambridge Companion to Hannah Arendt*, edited by Dana Villa, 113–129. Cambridge University Press, 2000.

Krause, Monika. "Undocumented Migrants: An Arendtian Perspective," *European Journal of Political Theory* 7, no. 3 (July 2008): 331–348.

Kristeva, Julia. *Hannah Arendt.* Translated by Ross Guberman. New York: Columbia University Press, 2001.

Lauren, Paul Gordon. *The Evolution of International Human Rights: Visions Seen.* Philadelphia: University of Pennsylvania Press, 1998.

Leebaw, Bronwyn. "The Politics of Impartial Activism: Humanitarianism and Human Rights." *Perspectives on Politics* 5, no. 2 (June 2007): 223–239.

Lefort, Claude. "Human Rights and Welfare State." In *Democracy and Political Theory*, translated by David Macey, 21–44. Cambridge, UK: Polity Press, 1988.

Lefort, Claude. "Politics and Human Rights." In *The Political Forms of Modern Society: Bureaucracy, Democracy, Totalitarianism*, edited by John B. Thompson, 239–272. Cambridge, MA: MIT Press, 1986.

Long, Joseph Ragland. *Notes on Roman Law: Law of Persons, Law of Contracts.* Charlottesville, VA: The Michie Company, 1912.

Luban, David. "Explaining Dark Times: Hannah Arendt's Theory of Theory." *Social Research* 50, no. 1 (Spring 1983): 215–248.

Ludz, Ursula. "Hannah Arendt's Book on Totalitarianism: A Short Documentation of Its History." *Hannah Arendt Newsletter*, no. 5 (November 2001): 56–57.

Lyotard, Jean-François. *The Differend: Phrases in Dispute.* Translated by Georges Van Den Abbeele. Minneapolis: University of Minnesota Press, 1988.

Maes, Ives. *Recyclable Refugee Camp.* Ghent, Belgium: MER. Paper Kunsthalle, 2008.

Maher, Kristen Hill. "Who Has a Right to Rights? Citizenship's Exclusions in an Age of Migration." In *Globalization and Human Rights*, edited by Alison Brysk, 19–43. Berkeley and Los Angeles: University of California Press, 2002.

Major, Robert W. "A Reading of Hannah Arendt's 'Unusual' Distinction between Labor and Work." In *Hannah Arendt: The Recovery of the Public World*, edited by Melvyn A. Hill, 131–155. New York: St. Martin's Press, 1979.

Makaremi, Chowra. "Governing Borders in France: From Extraterritorial to Humanitarian Confinement." *Canadian Journal of Law and Society* 24, no. 3 (2009): 411–432.

Malkki, Liisa H. "Speechless Emissaries: Refugees, Humanitarianism, and Dehistoricization." *Cultural Anthropology* 11, no. 3 (August 1996): 377–404.

Mann, Gregory. "Immigrants and Arguments in France and West Africa." *Comparative Studies in Society and History* 45, no. 2 (April 2003): 362–385.

Markell, Patchen. "Arendt's Work: On the Architecture of *The Human Condition*." *College Literature* 38, no. 1 (Winter 2011): 15–44.

Markell, Patchen. "Review of *Hannah Arendt and Human Rights* by Peg Birmingham and *Hannah Arendt and the Challenge of Modernity* by Serena Parekh." *Notre Dame Philosophical Reviews*. December 1, 2008. Accessed March 13, 2013. http://ndpr.nd.edu/review.cfm?id=14788.

Markell, Patchen. "The Rule of the People: Arendt, *Archê*, and Democracy." *American Political Science Review* 100, no. 1 (February 2006): 1–14.

Marx, Karl. "On the Jewish Question." In *Marx: Early Political Writings*, edited by Joseph O'Malley, 28–56. Cambridge: Cambridge University Press, 1994.

Mauss, Marcel. "A Category of the Human Mind: The Notion of Person; The Notion of Self." In *The Category of the Person: Anthropology, Philosophy, History*, edited by Michael Carrithers, Steven Collins, and Steven Lukes, 1–25. Cambridge: Cambridge University Press, 1985.

McClure, Kirstie M. "The Social Question, Again." *Graduate Faculty Philosophy Journal* 28, no. 1 (2007): 85–113.

McCrudden, Christopher. "Human Dignity and Judicial Interpretation of Human Rights." *The European Journal of International Law* 19, no. 4 (September 2008): 655–724.

McKanders, Karla Mari. "Sustaining Tiered Personhood: Jim Crow and Anti-Immigrant Laws." *Harvard Journal on Racial and Ethnic Justice* 26 (2010): 163–210.

McNevin, Anne. *Contesting Citizenship: Irregular Migrants and New Frontiers of the Political.* New York: Columbia University Press, 2011.

McNevin, Anne. "Political Belonging in a Neoliberal Era: The Struggle of the Sans-Papiers." *Citizenship Studies* 10, no. 2 (May 2006): 135–151.

Meckstroth, Christopher. "Socratic Method and Political Science." *American Political Science Review* 106, no. 3 (August 2012): 644–660.

Melville, Herman. "Billy Budd." In *Billy Budd and Other Tales*, 7–88. New York and London: Signet Classics, 1979.

Menke, Christoph. "The 'Aporias of Human Rights' and the 'One Human Right': Regarding the Coherence of Hannah Arendt's Argument." *Social Research* 74, no. 3 (Fall 2007): 739–762.

Michelman, Frank. "Parsing 'a Right to Have Rights.'" *Constellations* 3, no. 2 (October 1996): 200–209.

Mill, John Stuart. "On Liberty." In *On Liberty and Other Writings*, edited by Stefan Collini, 1–115. Cambridge and New York: Cambridge University Press, 1989.

Milner, James, and Gil Loescher. "Responding to Protracted Refugee Situations: Lessons from a Decade of Discussion." *Forced Migration Policy Briefing* 6. Refugee Studies Centre, University of Oxford. January 2011. Accessed August

28, 2012. http://www.rsc.ox.ac.uk/publications/policy-briefings/RSCPB6-Res pondingToProtractedRefugeeSituations.pdf.

Montesquieu, Charles de. *The Spirit of the Laws*. Edited and translated by Anne M. Cohlar, Basia C. Miller, and Harold S. Stone. Cambridge: Cambridge University Press, 1989.

Morris, Lydia. "Britain's Asylum and Immigration Regime: The Shifting Contours of Rights." *Journal of Ethnic and Migration Studies* 28, no. 3 (July 2002): 409–425.

Morsink, Johannes. *The Universal Declaration of Human Rights: Origins, Drafting, and Intent*. Philadelphia: University of Pennsylvania Press, 1999.

Moruzzi, Norma Claire. *Speaking Through the Mask: Hannah Arendt and the Politics of Social Identity*. Ithaca, NY: Cornell University Press, 2000.

Moyn, Samuel. "Hannah Arendt on the Secular." *New German Critique* 35, no. 3 (Fall 2008): 71–96.

Moyn, Samuel. *The Last Utopia: Human Rights in History*. Cambridge, MA: Belknap Press of Harvard University Press, 2010.

Mutua, Makau. *Human Rights: A Political and Cultural Critique*. Philadelphia: University of Pennsylvania Press, 2002.

Myers, Ella. *Worldly Ethics: Democratic Politics and Care for the World*. Durham, NC: Duke University Press, 2013.

Naffine, Ngaire. *Law's Meaning of Life: Philosophy, Darwin and the Legal Person*. Oxford and Portland, OR: Hart, 2009.

Naffine, Ngaire. "Who Are Law's Persons? From Cheshire Cats to Responsible Subjects." *The Modern Law Review* 66, no. 3 (May 2003): 346–367.

Nash, Kate. "Between Citizenship and Human Rights." *Sociology* 43, no. 6 (December 2009): 1067–1083.

Näsström, Sofia. "The Right to Have Rights: Democratic, Not Political." *Political Theory* 42, no. 5 (October 2014): 543–568.

Nehamas, Alexandar. "Voices of Silence: On Gregory Vlastos' Socrates." *Arion: A Journal of Humanities and the Classics* 2, no. 1 (Winter 1992): 157–186.

Ngai, Mae. *Impossible Subjects: Illegal Aliens and the Making of Modern America*. Princeton, NJ: Princeton University Press, 2004.

Nicholls, Walter. "Cities and the Unevenness of Social Movement Space: The Case of France's Immigrant Rights Movement." *Environment and Planning A* 43, no. 7 (2011): 1655–1673.

Nickel, James. *Making Sense of Human Rights*. 2nd ed. Malden, MA: Blackwell Publishing, 2007.

Noll, Gregor. "Why Human Rights Fail to Protect Undocumented Migrants." *European Journal of Migration and Law* 12, no. 2 (2010): 241–272.

Noonan, John Thomas. *Persons and the Masks of Law: Cardozo, Holmes, Jefferson, and Wythe as Makers of the Masks*. Berkeley and Los Angeles: University of California Press, [1976] 2002.

Norberg, Jakob. "Àrendt in Crisis: Political Thought in between Past and Future." *College Literature* 38, no. 1 (Winter 2011): 131–149.

Nyers, Peter. "No One Is Illegal between City and Nation." *Studies in Social Justice* 4, no. 2 (2010): 127–143.

Nyers, Peter. *Rethinking Refugees: Beyond States of Emergency*. New York: Routledge, 2006.

Orford, Anne. *Reading Humanitarian Intervention: Human Rights and the Use of Force in International Law*. Cambridge and New York: Cambridge University Press, 2003.

O'Sullivan, Noel. "Hannah Arendt: Hellenic Nostalgia and Industrial Society." In *Contemporary Political Philosophers*, edited by Anthony de Crespigny and Kenneth Minogue, 228–251. London: Methuen and Co., 1976.

Owens, Patricia. *Between War and Politics: International Relations and the Thought of Hannah Arendt*. Oxford: Oxford University Press, 2007.

Owens, Patricia. "Reclaiming 'Bare Life'?: Against Agamben on Refugees." *International Relations* 23, no. 4 (December 2009): 567–582.

Parekh, Bhikhu. *Hannah Arendt and the Search for a New Political Philosophy*. London and Basingstoke: The Macmillan Press, 1981.

Parekh, Bhikhu. "Hannah Arendt's Critique of Marx." In *Hannah Arendt: The Recovery of the Public World*, edited by Melvyn A. Hill, 67–100. New York: St. Martin's Press, 1979.

Parekh, Serena. *Hannah Arendt and the Challenge of Modernity*. New York and London: Routledge, 2008.

Parekh, Serena. "Resisting 'Dull and Torpid' Assent: Returning to the Debate on the Foundations of Human Rights." *Human Rights Quarterly* 29, no. 3 (August 2007): 754–778.

Passerin d'Entrèves, Maurizio. *The Political Philosophy of Hannah Arendt*. London: Routledge, 1994.

Patterson, Orlando. *Slavery and Social Death*. Cambridge, MA: Harvard University Press, 1982.

Pitkin, Hanna Fenichel. *The Attack of the Blob: Hannah Arendt's Concept of the Social*. Chicago: The University of Chicago Press, 1998.

Pitkin, Hanna Fenichel. "Justice: On Relating Private and Public." *Political Theory* 9, no. 3 (August 1981): 327–352.

Platform for International Cooperation on Undocumented Migrants (PICUM). "PICUM's Main Concerns About the Fundamental Rights of Undocumented Immigrants in Europe." October 2009. Accessed May 23, 2012. http://picum.org/picum.org/uploads/publication/Annual%20Concerns%202010%20EN.pdf

Plato. "Apology." In *Five Dialogues*, translated by G. M. A. Grube, 2nd ed., 21–44. Indianapolis, IN: Hackett, 2002.

Plato. "Meno." In *Five Dialogues*, translated by G. M. A. Grube, 2nd ed., 58–92. Indianapolis, IN: Hackett, 2002.

Plato. *Theatetus*. Translated by Robin H. Waterfield. London: Penguin, 1987.

Pugliese, Joseph. "Penal Asylum: Refugees, Ethics, Hospitality." *borderlands* (e-journal) 1, no. 1 (May 2002). http://www.borderlands.net.au/vol1no1_2002/pugliese.html.

Rajaram, Prem Kumar, and Carl Grundy-Warr. "The Irregular Migrant as Homo Sacer: Migration and Detention in Australia, Malaysia, and Thailand." *International Migration* 42, no. 1 (March 2004): 33–64.

Rancière, Jacques. *Disagreement: Politics and Philosophy*. Translated by Julie Rose. Minneapolis: University of Minnesota Press, 1999.

Rancière, Jacques. *The Ignorant Schoolmaster: Five Lessons in Intellectual Emancipation*. Translated by Kristin Ross. Stanford, CA: Stanford University Press, 1991.

Rancière, Jacques. *The Nights of Labor: The Workers' Dream in Nineteenth-Century France*. Translated by John Drury. Philadelphia: Temple University Press, 1989.

Rancière, Jacques. "Who Is the Subject of the Rights of Man?" *The South Atlantic Quarterly* 103, no. 2/3 (Spring/Summer 2004): 297–310.

Rawls, John. *The Law of Peoples.* Cambridge: Harvard University Press, 1999.

Raz, Joseph. "Human Rights without Foundations." In *The Philosophy of International Law,* edited by Samantha Besson and John Tasioulas, 321–337. Oxford: Oxford University Press, 2010.

Redfield, Peter. "Sacrifice, Triage, and Global Humanitarianism." In *Humanitarianism in Question: Politics, Power, Ethics,* edited by Michael Barnett and Thomas G. Weiss, 196–214. Ithaca, NY: Cornell University Press, 2008.

Reinhardt, Mark. *The Art of Being Free: Taking Liberties with Tocqueville, Marx, and Arendt.* Ithaca, NY: Cornell University Press, 1997.

Rensmann, Lars. "Grounding Cosmopolitics: Rethinking Crimes against Humanity and Global Political Theory with Arendt and Adorno." In *Arendt and Adorno: Political and Philosophical Investigations,* edited by Lars Rensmann and Samir Gandesha, 129–153. Stanford, CA: Stanford University Press, 2012.

Reus-Smit, Christian. "Human Rights and the Social Construction of Sovereignty." *Review of International Studies* 27, no. 4 (Oct 2001): 519–538.

Ricoeur, Paul. "Action, Story and History: On Re-Reading *The Human Condition.*" *Salmagundi,* no. 60 (Spring-Summer 1983): 60–72.

Ricoeur, Paul. "Approaching the Human Person." Translated by Dale Kidd. *Ethical Perspectives* 6, no. 1 (April 1999): 45–54.

Ring, Jennifer. "On Needing Both Arendt and Marx: Alienation and the Flight From Inwardness." *Political Theory* 17, no. 3 (August 1989): 432–448.

Ring, Jennifer. "The Pariah as Hero: Hannah Arendt's Political Actor." *Political Theory* 19, no. 3 (August 1991): 433–452

Ring, Jennifer. *The Political Consequences of Thinking: Gender and Judaism in the Work of Hannah Arendt.* Albany, NY: State University of New York Press, 1997.

Risse, Thomas. "Let's Argue!: Communicative Action in World Politics." *International Organization* 54, no. 1 (Winter 2000): 1–39.

Risse-Kappen, Thomas, Stephen C. Ropp, and Kathryn Sikkink, eds. *The Power of Human Rights: International Norms and Domestic Change.* Cambridge and New York: Cambridge University Press, 1999.

Rodríguez, Encarnación Gutiérrez. "'We Need Your Support, but the Struggle Is Primarily Ours': On Representation, Migration and the Sans Papiers Movement, ESF Paris, 12th–15th November 2003." *Feminist Review,* No. 77 (2004): 152–156.

Rosello, Mireille. *Postcolonial Hospitality: The Immigrant as Guest.* Stanford, CA: Stanford University Press, 2001.

Rosello, Mireille. "Representing Illegal Immigrants in France: From *Clandestins* to *L'affaire Des Sans-Papiers de Saint-Bernard.*" *Journal of European Studies* 28, no. 1 (January 1998): 137–151.

Rousseau, Jean-Jacques. "Discourse on the Origin and Foundation of Inequality among Men *or* Second Discourse." In *The Discourses and Other Early Political Writings,* edited and translated by Victor Gourevitch, 111–222. Cambridge and New York: Cambridge University Press: 1997.

Ruggiero, Vincenzo. "The Fight to Reappear." *Social Justice* 27, no. 2 (Summer 2000): 45–60.

Russell, Ruth V., and Frances K. Stage. "Leisure as Burden: Sudanese Refugee Women." *Journal of Leisure Research* 28, no. 2 (1996): 108–121.

Sassen, Saskia. *Guests and Aliens*. New York: The New Press, 1999.

Sassen, Saskia. "The Repositioning of Citizenship: Emergent Subjects and Spaces for Politics." *Berkeley Journal of Sociology* 46 (2002): 4–26.

Scarry, Elaine. *The Body in Pain: The Making and Unmaking of the World*. Oxford and New York: Oxford University Press, 1985.

Schaap, Andrew. "Enacting the Right to Have Rights: Jacques Rancière's Critique of Hannah Arendt." *European Journal of Political Theory* 10, no. 1 (January 2011): 22–45.

Schaap, Andrew. "The Politics of Need." In *Power, Judgment and Political Evil: In Conversation with Hannah Arendt*, edited by Andrew Schaap, Danielle Celermajer, and Vrasides Karales, 157–169. Farnham, England: Ashgate, 2010.

Scheuerman, William E. "Revolutions and Constitutions: Hannah Arendt's Challenge to Carl Schmitt." In *Law as Politics: Carl Schmitt's Critique of Liberalism*, edited by David Dyzenhaus, 252–280. Durham, NC: Duke University Press, 1998.

Schuck, Peter H., and Rogers M. Smith. *Citizenship without Consent: Illegal Aliens in the American Polity*. New Haven, CT: Yale University Press, 1985.

Schuster, Liza, and John Solomos. "Rights and Wrongs across European Borders: Migrants, Minorities and Citizenship." *Citizenship Studies* 6, no. 1 (March 2002): 37–54.

Scott, Joan Wallach. *Only Paradoxes to Offer: French Feminists and the Rights Of Man*. Cambridge, MA: Harvard University Press, 1996.

Shemak, April. *Asylum Speakers: Caribbean Refugees and Testimonial Discourse*. New York: Fordham University Press, 2011.

Shuman, Amy, and Carol Bohmer. "Representing Trauma: Political Asylum Narrative." *Journal of American Folklore* 117, no. 466 (Autumn 2004): 394–414.

Sikkink, Kathryn. "Human Rights, Principled Issue-Networks, and Sovereignty in Latin America," *International Organization* 47, no. 3 (Summer 1993): 411–441.

Sikkink, Kathryn. "The Power of Principled Ideas: Human Rights Policies in the United States and Western Europe," 139–170. In *Ideas and Foreign Policy: Beliefs, Institutions, and Political Change*, edited by Judith Goldstein and Robert O. Keohane. Ithaca, NY: Cornell University Press, 1993.

Simmons, William Paul. *Human Rights Law and the Marginalized Other*. Cambridge: Cambridge University Press, 2011.

Smith, Merrill, ed. "Warehousing Refugees: A Denial of Rights, a Waste of Humanity." In *World Refugee Survey 2004*, 38–56. U.S. Committee for Refugees and Immigrants. Accessed September 5, 2012, http://www.uscrirefugees.org/2010Website/5_Resources/5_5_Refugee_Warehousing/5_5_1_Refugee_Warehousing_FAQ/Warehousing_Refugees_A_Denial%20_of_Rights.pdf.

Soguk, Nevzat. *States and Strangers: Refugees and Displacements of Statecraft*. Minneapolis: University of Minnesota Press, 1999.

Somers, Margaret R. *Genealogies of Citizenship: Markets, Statelessness, and the Right to Have Rights*. Cambridge and New York: Cambridge University Press, 2008.

Sonenscher, Michael. *Sans-Culottes: An Eighteenth-Century Emblem in the French Revolution*. Princeton, NJ: Princeton University Press, 2008.

Soysal, Yasemin Nuhoğlu. *Limits of Citizenship: Migrants and Postnational Membership in Europe*. Chicago: University of Chicago, 1994.

Soysal, Yasemin Nuhoğlu. "Postnational Citizenship: Reconfiguring the Familiar Terrain." In *The Blackwell Companion to Political Sociology*, edited by Kate Nash and Alan Scott, 333–341. Oxford: Blackwell Publishers, 2001.

Stasiulis, Daiva K. "International Migration, Rights, and the Decline of 'Actually Existing Liberal Democracy.'" *New Community* 23, no. 2 (April 1997): 197–214.

Stasiulis, Daiva, and Abigail B. Bakan, "Negotiating Citizenship: The Case of Foreign Domestic Workers in Canada," *Feminist Review* 57 (Autumn 1997): 112–139.

Stevens, Jacob. "Prisons of the Stateless: The Derelictions of UNHCR." *New Left Review* 42 (November-December 2006): 53–67.

Stevens, Jacqueline. *Reproducing the State*. Princeton, NJ: Princeton University Press, 1999.

Stonebridge, Lyndsey. "Refugee Style: Hannah Arendt and the Perplexities of Rights." *Textual Practice* 25, no. 1 (2011): 71–85.

Suchting, W. A. "Marx and Hannah Arendt's *The Human Condition*." *Ethics* 73, no. 1 (October 1962): 47–55.

Sultan, Aamer, and Kevin O'Sullivan. "Psychological Disturbances in Asylum-Seekers Held in Long Term Detention: A Participant-Observer Account." *The Medical Journal of Australia* 175, no. 11–12 (December 2001): 593–596.

Taminiaux, Jacques. "Athens and Rome." In *The Cambridge Companion to Hannah Arendt*, edited by Dana Villa, 165–177. Cambridge University Press, 2000.

Thomas, Daniel C. *The Helsinki Effect: International Norms, Human Rights, and the Demise of Communism*. Princeton, NJ: Princeton University Press, 2001.

Thomassen, Lasse. "The Politics of Iterability: Benhabib, the Hijab, and Democratic Iterations." *Polity* 43, no. 1 (January 2011): 128–149.

Ticktin, Miriam, *Casualties of Care: Immigration and the Politics of Humanitarianism in France*. Berkeley: University of California Press, 2011.

Ticktin, Miriam. "Where Ethics and Politics Meet: The Violence of Humanitarianism in France." *American Ethnologist* 33, no. 1 (February 2006): 33–49.

Torpey, John C. *The Invention of the Passport: Surveillance, Citizenship, and the State*. Cambridge and New York: Cambridge University Press, 2000.

Trendelenburg, Adolf. *A Contribution to the History of the Word Person*. Translated by Carl H. Haessler. Chicago: The Open Court Publishing, 1910.

Tsao, Roy T. "Arendt against Athens." *Political Theory* 30, no. 1 (February 2002): 97–123.

Tsao, Roy T. "Arendt and the Modern State: Variations on Hegel in *The Origins of Totalitarianism*." *Review of Politics* 66, no. 1 (Winter 2004): 105–138.

Tuitt, Patricia. *False Images: Law's Construction of the Refugee*. East Haven, CT: Pluto Press, 1996.

UNHCR. *Handbook for Emergencies*. 3rd ed. 2007. Accessed January 9, 2014. http://www.unhcr.org/472af2972.html.

UNHCR. *Handbook for Registration: Procedures and Standards for Registration, Population Data Management and Documentation*. September 2003. Accessed September 6, 2012, www.unhcr.org/refworld/pdfid/3f967dc14.pdf.

UNHCR. "Protracted Refugee Situations." Executive Committee of the High Commissioner's Programme, Standing Committee, 30th Meeting. EC/54/SC/

CRP.14. June 10, 2004. Accessed August 28, 2012. http://www.unhcr.org/
40ed5b384.html.

UNHCR. *Registration: A Practical Guide for Field Staff*. 1994. Accessed September 6, 2012. http://biblioteca.hegoa.ehu.es/system/ebooks/9771/original/
Registration._A_practical_guide_for_field_staff.pdf.

UNHCR. "UNHCR's Guidelines on Applicable Criteria and Standards Relating to
the Detention of Asylum-Seekers." February 1999. Accessed May 28, 2012.
http://www.unhcr.org/refworld/pdfid/3c2b3f844.pdf.

Urbinati, Nadia. *Mill on Democracy: From the Athenian Polis to Representative
Government*. Chicago: The University of Chicago Press, 2002.

Urbinati, Nadia. *Representative Democracy: Principles and Genealogy*. Chicago:
Chicago University Press, 2006.

Varela, Amarela. "Residency Documents for All! Notes to Understand the Movement of Migrants in Barcelona." *Refuge* 26, no. 2 (2009): 121–132.

Varela Huerta, Amarela. "Migrant Struggles for the Right to Have Rights: Three
Examples of Social Movements Powered by Migrants in New York, Paris and
Barcelona." *Transfer: European Review of Labour and Research* 14, no. 4
(Winter 2008): 677–694.

Veltman, Andrea. "Simone de Beauvoir and Hannah Arendt on Labor." *Hypatia*
25, no. 1 (Winter 2010): 55–78.

Verdirame, Guglielmo, and Barbara Harrell-Bond. *Rights in Exile: Janus-faced
Humanitarianism*. New York and Oxford: Berghahn Books, 2005.

Villa, Dana R. *Arendt and Heidegger: The Fate of the Political*. Princeton, NJ:
Princeton University Press, 1996.

Villa, Dana R. "Beyond Good and Evil: Arendt, Nietzsche, and the Aestheticization of Political Action." *Political Theory* 20, no. 2 (May 1992): 274–308.

Villa, Dana R. *Politics, Philosophy, Terror: Essays on the Thought of Hannah
Arendt*. Princeton, NJ: Princeton University Press, 1999.

Villa, Dana R. *Socratic Citizenship*. Princeton, NJ: Princeton University Press,
2001.

Vincent, Andrew. *The Politics of Human Rights*. Oxford: Oxford University Press,
2010.

Vlastos, Gregory, "The Chronological Order of the Dialogues." In *Socratic Studies*, edited by Myles Burnyeat, 135. Cambridge and New York: Cambridge University Press, 1994.

Vlastos, Gregory. "The Socratic Elenchus." In *Socratic Studies*, edited by Myles
Burnyeat, 1–38. Cambridge and New York: Cambridge University Press, 1994.

Voegelin, Eric. "Review of the Origins of Totalitarianism." *The Review of Politics*
15, no. 1 (January 1953): 68–76.

Voice, Paul. "Labour, Work and Action." In *Hannah Arendt: Key Concepts*, edited
by Patrick Hayden, 36–51. Durham: Acumen, 2014.

Wacquant, Loïc. *Urban Outcasts: A Comparative Sociology of Advanced Margin-
ality*. Cambridge and Malden, MA: Polity, 2008.

Waldron, Jeremy. "Arendt's Constitutional Politics." In *The Cambridge Companion to Hannah Arendt*, edited by Dana Villa, 201–219. Cambridge and New
York: Cambridge University Press, 2000.

Waldron, Jeremy. *Dignity, Rank, and Rights*. Edited and introduced by Meir Dan-
Cohen. New York: Oxford University Press, 2012.

Waldron, Jeremy. *Nonsense upon Stilts: Bentham, Burke and Marx on the Rights of Man*. London and New York: Methuen, 1987.

Wallach, John R. "Constitutive Paradoxes of Human Rights: An Interpretation in History and Political Theory." *Studies in Law, Politics, and Society* 56 (2011): 37–65.

Wallach, John R. "Human Rights as an Ethics of Power." In *Human Rights in the "War on Terror,"* edited by Richard Ashby Wilson, 108–136. Cambridge and New York: Cambridge University Press, 2005.

Walsh, Philip. "Hannah Arendt on the Social." In *Hannah Arendt: Key Concepts*, edited by Patrick Hayden, 124–137. Durham: Acumen, 2014.

Walters, William. "Deportation, Expulsion, and the International Police of Aliens." *Citizenship Studies* 6, no. 3 (2002): 265–292.

Walzer, Michael. *Spheres of Justice: A Defense of Pluralism and Equality*. New York: Basic Books, 1983.

Watters, Charles. "Refugees at Europe's Borders: The Moral Economy of Care." *Transcultural Psychiatry* 44, no. 3 (September 2007): 394–417.

Weidenfeld, Matthew C. "Visions of Judgment: Arendt, Kant, and the Misreading of Judgment." *Political Research Quarterly* 66, no. 2 (June 2013): 254–266.

Weissbrodt, David. *The Human Rights of Non-citizens*. Oxford and New York: Oxford University Press, 2008.

Weitz, Eric D. "From the Vienna to the Paris System: International Politics and the Entangled Histories of Human Rights, Forced Deportations, and Civilizing Missions." *American Historical Review* 113, no. 5 (December 2008): 1313–1343.

Welch, Michael. *Detained: Immigration Laws and the Expanding I.N.S. Jail Complex*. Philadelphia: Temple University Press, 2002.

Wellmer, Albert. "Hannah Arendt on Judgment: The Unwritten Doctrine of Reason." In *Hannah Arendt: Twenty Years Later*, edited by Larry May and Jerome Kohn, 33–52. Cambridge, MA: MIT Press, 1996.

Werker, Eric. "Refugee Camp Economies." *Journal of Refugee Studies* 20, no. 3 (September 2007): 461–480.

Wilde, Ralph. "*Quis Custodiet Ipsos Custodes?*: Why and How UNHCR Governance of 'Development' Refugee Camps Should be Subject to International Human Rights Law." *Yale Human Rights and Development Law Journal* 1 (1998): 107–128.

Wilkinson, Michael A. "Between Freedom and Law: Hannah Arendt and the Promise of Modern Revolution and the Burden of 'the Tradition.'" In *Hannah Arendt and the Law*, edited by Marco Goldoni and Christopher McCorkindale, 35–61. Oxford and Portland, Oregon: Hart Publishing, 2012.

Wilsher, Daniel. *Immigration Detention: Law, History, Politics*. Cambridge and New York: Cambridge University Press, 2012.

Wolin, Sheldon. "Democracy and the Political." *Salmagundi*, no. 60 (Spring-Summer 1983): 3–19.

Wood, Ellen Meiksins. "Demos versus 'We, the People': Freedom and Democracy Ancient and Modern." In *Demokratia: A Conversation on Democracies, Ancient and Modern*, edited by Josiah Ober and Charles Hedrick, 121–137. Princeton, NJ: Princeton University Press, 1996.

Xenos, Nicholas. "Refugees: The Modern Political Condition." *Alternatives* 18, no. 4 (Fall 1993): 419–430.

Yeatman, Anna. "Individuality and Politics: Thinking With and Beyond Hannah Arendt." In *Action and Appearance: Ethics and the Politics of Writing in Hannah Arendt*, edited by Anna Yeatman, Phillip Hansen, Magdalena Zolkos, and Charles Barbour, 69–86. New York: Continuum, 2011.

Young, Iris Marion. "House and Home." In *On Female Body Experience: "Throwing Like a Girl" and Other Essays*, 123–154. New York: Oxford University Press, 2005.

Young-Bruehl, Elisabeth. *Hannah Arendt: For Love of the World*, 2nd ed. New Haven and London: Yale University Press, 2004.

Zerilli, Linda. *Feminism and the Abyss of Freedom*. Chicago: The University of Chicago Press, 2005.

Zivi, Karen. "Feminism and the Politics of Rights: A Qualified Defense of Identity-Based Rights Claiming." *Politics & Gender* 1, no. 3 (September 2005): 377–397.

Zivi, Karen. *Making Rights Claims: A Practice of Democratic Citizenship*. Oxford and New York: Oxford University Press, 2012.

Žižek, Slavoj. "Against Human Rights." *New Left Review* 34 (July-August 2005): 115–131.

Index

Note: Locators followed by the letter 'n' and 'nn' refer to notes.

protracted stays in, 96, 140, 149–50, 155–7, 207, 242*n*86, 243*n*99, 245*n*137
rightlessness and action in, 141, 153, 156–7
rightlessness and labor in, 141–5, 243*nn*92, 95, 99, 106, 108, 244*nn*112, 115
rightlessness and work in, 141, 149–52, 245*nn*141, 144, 148
suicide in, 143, 243*n*108
See also "Recyclable Refugee Camp" project (Maes); United Nations High Commissioner for Refugees
refugees
Arendt on, 135, 142, 143
dehumanization of, 141–2
Geneva Convention regarding, 9, 108, 118, 123, 236*nn*112, 114
on Guantánamo Bay, 90–1
humanitarian representation of, 77, 159
humanitarian response to, 77–8
nationality norm and, 140
See also refugee camps; repatriation; United Nations High Commissioner for Refugees
Rensmann, Lars, 221*n*92
repatriation
Arendt on, 31
refugees and, 140, 207, 242*n*86
revolution
Arendt on the "abyss of freedom" in, 38, 166, 173–4
in the modern era, 174–5
and the right to have rights, 166, 173–81
See also American Revolution; French Revolution
Ricoeur, Paul, 105, 130, 135, 234*n*77
rightlessness
action and, 152–62
Arendt on statelessness and the condition of, 2–3, 17, 25–6, 91–8, 232*nn*27, 37
deportation and, 107–16, 235*nn*81, 88, 236*nn*112, 114
detention and, 116–24
labor and, 139–45
overview, 2–6, 17–21, 126–9, 162–3, 208, 211–12
persisting in an age of rights, 11, 17, 92–4
precarious personhood and, 93–4, 107–25
reconsidered with *The Human Condition*, 129–39

speechlessness and, 21, 116, 158–61, 191
work and, 145–52
See also human rights; humanitarianism; human rights as politics and anti-politics; personhood; refugee camps
Rights of Man and Citizen. *See* Declaration of the Rights of Man and Citizen (1789)
right to have rights
Arendt on, 46, 53, 165, 168–70, 206
as a right to action and speech, 76, 194, 200
as a right to citizenship and humanity, 13, 27, 39, 53
equaliberty principle and, 23, 181–7, 199–201
groundlessness of, 165–6, 169–70
humanity as the guarantee of, 168–9, 217*n*11, 248*n*15
overview, 21–4, 164–8, 200–2
perplexities of, 168–73
revolution, or political founding, and, 173–81
sans-papiers, 23–4, 167–8, 187–200
right to work, 15, 55, 96, 144, 190, 205
Ring, Jennifer, 130
Robespierre, Maximilien de, 70–1, 73, 175, 226*n*52
Romans
Arendt on political founding and, 174–5, 181
Arendt's understanding of law and, 23, 99–100, 105, 147, 177, 178
legislation as a political activity, 147
personhood and, 99, 100, 102–3, 105
Roma people, 126–7, 152, 190
Rosenzweig, Franz, 136–7
Rousseau, Jean-Jacques, 101, 227*n*84
Ruggiero, Vincenzo, 196
rule of law
camps and the, 141
Castle, The and the, 203
detention and the, 117
globalization and the, 211
imperialism and the, 50
in Italy, 238*n*1
migrants and the, 11, 108
Russell, Ruth, 143

Saadi, Shayan Baram, 119
Saadi v. UK (2008), 18, 119–24, 125, 237*nn*130–1, 139
Saint-Just, Louis Antoine de, 70–1

Printed in the USA/Agawam, MA
April 7, 2015

512088.056